The Апсуаа
Abkhazians

The Аҧсуаа
Abkhazians
a handbook

edited by
George Hewitt

ST. MARTIN'S PRESS

ST. MARTIN'S PRESS

THE ABKHAZIANS: A HANDBOOK

© 1998 by The Contributors

St. Martin's Press, Scholarly and Reference Division,
175 Fifth Avenue, New York, N.Y. 10010

First published in the United States of America in 1998

Typeset and designed by Nicholas Awde/Desert♥Hearts
Scans by Emanuela Losi
Covers by Nick Awde
Photographs by Nikolai Rakhmanov, taken from *Abkhazija*,
edited by Shota Shakaya (Planeta, Moscow, 1979)
Additional maps by Nick Awde & Kieran Meeke
Printed in Great Britain

ISBN 0-312-21975-X

Library of Congress Cataloging-in-Publication Data

The Abkhazians : a handbook = [Aphsuaa] / edited by George Hewitt.
    p.   cm. — (Peoples of the Caucasus handbooks)
Includes bibliographical references (p.   ) and index.
ISBN 0-312-21975-X (cloth : alk. paper)
    1. Abkhazians.   2. Abkhaziía (Georgia)—History.   2. Abkhaziía
(Georgia)—History—Autonomy and independence movements.
I. Hewitt, George B.   II. Series.
DK679.A25A225   1998
947.58—dc21   98-39209
                                                                    CIP

This volume is dedicated to

TATIANA KHIBA

Embodiment of *Apswara*

'Abkhazian virtue'

"What is to be the future of this Earthly Paradise? Its ancient and primaeval inhabitants are gone. They have been exiled for a quarter of a century; their dwellings and their tombs are alike lost in the glorious vegetation that feeds nothing but bears and mosquitoes and fevers. A people that had lived the same life in the same place since the beginning of history has been dispersed and destroyed. The Abkhasians have vanished, leaving behind them no records, and hardly sufficient material for the ethnologist who desires to ascertain to what branch of the world's 'families' they belonged."

— *DOUGLAS FRESHFIELD on The Solitude of Abkhasia*
('The Exploration of the Caucasus', 2nd edn, London, 1902, p211)

"Of the early history of the Abkhasian race little is known, and little was probably to be known. More than two thousand years since we find them, in Greek records, inhabiting the narrow strip between the mountains and the sea, along the central eastern coast of the Euxine, precisely where later records and the maps of our own day place them . . . The remnant of the old Abkhasian nation . . . have at last, in time of full peace and quiet, been driven from the mountains and coast where Greek, Roman, Persian, and Turkish domination had left them unmolested for more than two thousand years . . . and nothing remains but the fast crumbling memorials of a sad history of national folly rewarded by oppression, oppression by violence, violence by desolation."

— *WILLIAM GIFFORD PALGRAVE*
('Essays on Eastern Questions', London, 1872, pp 256 & 270)

"Were the land properly cultivated, Abasia (as this part of Circassia is called) would be a paradise. The soil is so fertile, and the climate so temperate, that nearly every description of grain, fruit, and vegetable might be grown with very little trouble . . . Loving their wild country with passionate devotion, no reverses dishearten them. War is both their duty and their happiness . . . A soft breeze just filled the sails, and with really sad hearts we watched landmark after landmark disappear, until, on rounding the headland of the bay, the last light of the little town was shut out, and we said farewell, probably for ever, to the loveliest spot we have ever seen."

— *MRS HARVEY*
('Turkish Harems & Circassian Homes', London, 1871, pp 220, 251 & 270)

Аԥсадгьыл зцәызыз зегьы ицәызит.
apsadgʲyl ztɕʷydzyz zagʲy jyɕʷydzyjt'
He who has lost his homeland has lost everything.
— *Abkhazian proverb*

Contents

The Abkhazians' famed longetivity and horsemanship are combined in
this elder, dressed in traditional costume ('cherkesska'), so suitable for
travelling on horseback

Preface

With two exceptions, the articles in this volume were written specifically to appear here. Shamba's contribution was handed to me in Sukhum in 1995 when an entirely different collection of essays was envisaged, whilst Popkov's eyewitness account of the sad events of July 1989 formed part of a book he intended to publish on the general question of Soviet nationalities. As far as I am aware, that work has never appeared in print, but from the copy of the whole manuscript he personally gave me in late summer 1989 the section on Abkhazia was translated that autumn and is here published for the first time.

It is impossible fully to understand the determination finally to control their own destiny with which the Abkhazians under the leadership of Vladislav Ardzinba have been pursuing their goals since 1989 to the present day without a proper appreciation of what happened (and why) in the republic that July, especially as Georgian propaganda depicts the crisis as one carefully planned and plotted by the Abkhazians in connivance with Moscow. Therefore, I have included Popkov's abbreviated but still lengthy account as a necessary corrective. When the fighting began, Popkov was participating in a dig in southern Abkhazia.

Lak'oba's historical article on the period 18th century to 1917 contains an entirely new interpretation of Abkhazia's union with Russia.

The articles by the Abkhazian contributors (Anchabadze, Avidzba, Bargandzhia, Bgazhba, Dbar, Lak'oba and Shamba) were submitted in Russian and were translated by me, as were Appendices 1-3 in the Further Reading section. I am grateful to Professor Donald Rayfield (Queen Mary Westfield, London) for reading and commenting on the translation of Avidzba's paper, to Dr Tanya Bowyer-Bower (SOAS) for doing the same with Dbar's contribution, and to Dr Vjacheslav ('Slava') Chirikba for numerous helpful comments but especially for the many valuable observations stemming from his reading through the draft of the entire book. Any errors are my own responsibility. The remaining articles were written in English by their authors. The map in the Introduction was redrawn on computer by Claire Ivison (SOAS) from an original by Miss Amra Hewitt, that for Abkhazia Today by Nick Awde from an original by Miss Gunda Hewitt, and the text of the Abkhazian Constitution of 1917 was made available by Miss Charlotte Hille (Leiden).

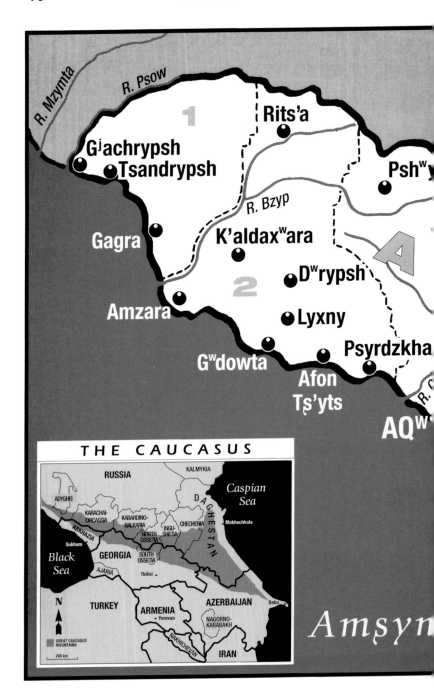

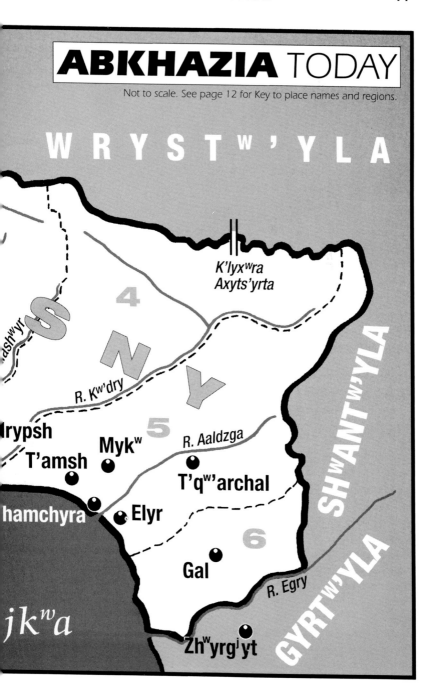

ABKHAZIA TODAY

Not to scale. See page 12 for Key to place names and regions.

WRYST^w'YLA

K'lyx^wra
Axyts'yrta

SNY

4

...sh^wyr

R. K^w'dry

SH^wANT^w'YLA

Irypsh

Myk^w

5

R. Aaldzga

T'amsh

T'q^w'archal

hamchyra

Elyr

6

Gal

GYRT^w'YLA

R. Egry

...jk^wa

Zh^wyrg^jyt

There is an inconsistency in transcribing certain proper names. Where a consonant is glottalised in Caucasian pronunciation, I normally indicate this, as with our contributor, Stanislav Lak'oba (in Abkhaz Lakʷ'aba). However, when reference is to a Russian publication, since Cyrillic does not indicate glottalisation, simple transcription of the Cyrillic produces the form 'Lakoba'. Where discrepancy between transcription from Cyrillic and the actual form in Abkhaz is greater, the Abkhaz version is usually placed in brackets (e.g. Bgazhba [Bghaʒʷba]). In most cases 'kh' is used for the back voiceless fricative, whereas in transcribing actual Abkhaz 'x' is employed. Similarly, both 'y' and 'ə' are used to represent the neutral vowel.

All illustrations were selected and placed by me.

GEORGE HEWITT, FBA
Professor of Caucasian Languages
School of Oriental & African Studies,
London, 1997

K E Y
to map on previous page

1. Gagra Borough
2. Gudauta District
3. Sukhum District
4. Gulripsh District
5. Ochamchira District
6. Gal District

ABKHAZ NAME	OTHERWISE KNOWN AS:	ABKHAZ NAME	OTHERWISE KNOWN AS:
Apsny	Abkhazia	Dʷrypsh	Durypsh, Duripsh
Wyrystw'yla	Russia	Pshʷy	Pskhu
Shʷantw'yla	Svaneti(a)	Psyrdzxa	Psyrtskha
Gyrtw'yla	Mingrelia	Aqʷ'a	Sukhum
Amşyn Ejkʷa	Black Sea	Gʷmsta	Gumista
Gjachrypsh	Gechrypsh,	KJ'alashʷyr	K'elasur
	Gechripsh, Leselidze	Gʷlrypsh	Gulrypsh, Gulripsh
Tsandrypsh	Tsandripsh, Gantiadi	Kw'dry	K'odor
Amzara	Pitsunda	Ochamchyra	Ochamchira
Mysra	Mjussera	Mykʷ	Mokvi
Gʷdowta	Gudauta	Aaldzga	Ghalidzga
Lyxny	Lykhny	Elyr	Ilori
Afon Tş'yts	New Athos	Egry	Ingur
	(Russian Novyj	K'lyxʷra Axyts'yrta	K'lukhor Pass
	Afon)	Zhʷyrgjyt	Zugdidi

Introduction
George Hewitt

The Land and its People

The Abkhazians call themselves 'Apswa'.[1] The country name is 'Apsny'.[2] The capital is most widely known as Sukhum,[3] though the native term is 'Aqʷa'.[4] Three other important towns are Gudauta, T'q'varchal (T'qʷarchal), a mining-industrial centre, and, one of the most popular coastal resorts, Gagra in the north, often referred to as the 'Pearl' of the Black Sea.[5]

The Language

The Abkhaz (Abkhaz-Abaza)[6] language belongs to the small, geographically defined North West Caucasian language-family, whose other two members are Circassian and Ubykh. No serious commentator doubts that these languages underwent a long development in, and were spoken from prehistoric times across, a compact area which will have roughly coincided with the range of territory occupied by their speakers at the time of the Russian conquest of the North Caucasus in 1864 (see the map below). This extended from the Abkhaz-Mingrelian border northwards along the coast to the River Kuban and inland to the Ossetian and Chechen territories in the North Central Caucasus.

It has been suggested that the range of North West Caucasian speakers must once have been wider, reaching at least the River Don in the north and southwards into regions that are today inhabited by Kartvelian speakers (Mingrelians and Georgians — see below, also Chapters 2 and 3); for other possible linguistic affiliations (in ancient Anatolia or the modern North Caucasus) see Chapter 2. However, it is certain that there is no genetic link with the Kartvelian (or South Caucasian) languages (Georgian, Mingrelian, Laz, Svan) — indeed, no relationship for Kartvelian has been proved with any other language still spoken or extinct.

Colchis and Graeco-Roman chroniclers

The ancient world referred in general to the Black Sea's (or Pontic Euxine's) eastern coast, of which Abkhazia is a part, as Colchis. It is extremely difficult to try to identify with any confidence the ethnicity of

the carriers of most of the tribal names used by classical authors writing
before the time of Christ in reference to the denizens of contemporary
Abkhazia and their neighbours, though the possibilities for speculation
are virtually limitless.

However, we are on safer ground from early in the modern era when
we find reference in Latin to the *gens Absilae* (Pliny Secundus Major, first
century), which ethnic group obviously corresponds to the *Apsîlai* in the
Greek of Arrian a century later. To the north of this group, Arrian
locates a tribe he called *Abasgoí*.

Attempting to argue that anything other than the Abkhazians' own
ethnonym could have provided the source for the Graeco-Roman
'Apsilians' smacks of sophistry, whilst the Greek term for the 'Abazgians'
must surely derive from the ethnonym 'Abaza', the self-designation of
today's Abazinians (see Hewitt, 1993a) — the ancestors of the
Abazinians, who speak the Abaza dialect, still had over 1,000 years of
residence in Abkhazia before migrating to their present dwelling in the
North Caucasus. There is no reason to believe that the local distribution
of Abkhazian and Kartvelian tribes will have substantially altered since
the start of historical records right up to the movement of populations
that began in the wake of the North (West) Caucasian migrations in and
after 1864.

In 1404 an insightful European traveller, Johannes de
Galonifontibus, wrote in his significant but little-known diary:

> Beyond these [Circassians] is Abkhazia (*Apcasia*), a small hilly
> country . . . They have their own language . . . To the east of
> them, in the direction of Georgia (*Ioriania*), lies the country
> called Mingrelia (*Mengrelia*) . . . They have their own language
> . . . Georgia is to the east of this country. Georgia is not an
> integral whole . . . They have their own language. (Tardy, 1978)

Thus, in the high mountains to the east of the upper reaches of the
K'odor valley the Abkhazians' eastern neighbours will always have been
the Svans, whilst in the lowland regions there will have been contact
with the (Laz-)Mingrelians — the linguistic evidence of language-
contact is testimony to a long period of symbiosis (cf. Hewitt, 1988 &
1989a; 1991; 1992a; 1992b).

North West Caucasian tribes and their distribution

North West Caucasian speakers were distributed across their ancestral
homeland at the end of the Caucasian war as shown below:

Distribution of North West Caucasian tribes (Circassians, Ubykhs, Abkhaz-Abazinians) with the main Circassian dialectal divisions prior to the mass emigration of 1864

The first wave of Abazinians crossed the K'lukhor Pass from Abkhazia in the 14th century (as acknowledged in the *Georgian Encyclopaedia*, vol. I, in 1975) to form eventually the speakers of the T'ap'anta sub-dialect of Abaza, whilst the ancestors of the second sub-dialect, Ashkharywa, a bridge between Abaza and more standard forms of Abkhaz, followed some time around the 17th century.

In the 1640s the (half-Abkhazian) Turkish traveller Evliya Çelebi visited the Caucasus. From the book he wrote of his travels it is clear that he regarded the land along the coast from Mingrelia as Abaza territory (even today in Turkey 'Abaza' is the general term applied to Abkhazians and Abazinians), noting of his so-called Chach tribe (cf. the main princely Chachba family) that they *also* spoke Mingrelian (many southern Abkhazians even today — at least before the war — tending to grow up with Mingrelian as their second language).

The examples Çelebi quotes of the "extraordinary and surprising Abaza language" clearly represent a form of Abkhaz-Abaza (probably

Sadz), while the examples he gives of what he styles "Sadz Abaza" are the earliest attestation we possess of Ubykh.

Sadz was in fact the dialect of Abkhaz spoken immediately to the south of Ubykh — is it possible that the Abkhaz plural-form *A'sadzkʷa* (Асаӡҟуа) was the source of Arrian's '*San(n)ig(ian)s*'. Following Chirikba (1996), who regards Sadz as a separate 'south-western' dialect within the Abkhaz-Abaza group, we can name the three remaining 'south-eastern' dialects as: Ahchypsy, Bzyp, and Abzhywa (= 'middle one') — the sub-

Idealised view of the New Athos Monastery of Simon the Canaanite, reputed to have brought Christianity to Abkhazia in the first century

dialect of Ts'abal (Upper K'odor valley) presumably derived from the speech of the tribe of the Missimians (*Misimianoi*), placed in this locale by Agathias (sixth century). When Russia finally took control of the North Caucasus after defeating the last remnants of resistance amongst the North West Caucasians, the entire Ubykh nation, together with most of the Circassians, all the Sadz, Ahchypsy and Ts'abal Abkhazians, and many other North Caucasians chose to migrate to Ottoman lands — a flavour of the misery of their hasty departure is conveyed by 'Papers respecting the settlement of Circassian emigrants in Turkey (presented to the House of Commons, June 6th 1864)'.

Descendants of those migrants form today a substantial diaspora spread over a number of formerly Ottoman territories, though most are concentrated in Turkey, where there are certainly many more North West Caucasians than in the Caucasus, the Abkhazian population perhaps exceeding half a million. Apart from in the two Circassian villages found in Israel, the native Caucasian languages have not been taught amongst the exiles, and younger speakers today often command (at most) a passive knowledge of their ancestral tongue(s).

Ubykh became extinct in the autumn of 1992 with the death of Tevfik Esenç — for a summary of the history of the Ubykhs in Turkey see Dumézil (1965), whilst the Abkhazian author Bagrat Shinkuba (Bagrat' Shink^{w}ba) wrote a novel based on their history entitled, in its English translation, *Last of the departed* (Raduga, 1986). This means that in Abkhazia today one finds only the two dialects of Bzyp (north of Sukhum) and Abzhywa, the literary base. In the last Soviet census (1989) there was an all-union Abkhazian population of 102,938 (a 13.2 per cent increase on the figure for 1979), 93.3 per cent regarding Abkhaz as their first language. Of these 95,853 lived in Georgia, representing 1.8 per cent of this republic's population, whilst of these 93,267 lived in Abkhazia itself. The all-union total for Abazinians was 33,801 (a 14.6 per cent increase on 1979), 93.4 per cent giving Abaza as their first tongue.

Abkhazian relations with Georgia

Georgian propaganda persistently blames Kremlin intrigue for the enmity between Abkhazians and Kartvelians. Even if one were to concur in the ascription of (much of) the blame to the Kremlin, one should recall that it was a Georgian, Ioseb Jughashvili (a.k.a. Stalin), who largely determined that policy.[7] But if one takes the trouble to examine the history of regional relations since the 19th century migrations, one soon appreciates that there is no need to look beyond Georgia's frontiers to find the explanation of this ethnic antagonism. And perhaps the basest aspect of the long-running confrontation is the way that some academics in Tbilisi have been prepared over the years to prostitute their disciplines in the service of local chauvinist politics.[8]

The first to suggest that the Abkhazians were relative newcomers to the territory which we have qualified as autochthonously theirs seems to have been the Georgian historian Davit Bakradze. Writing in 1889 (pp 271-73), he argued that the Abkhazians came over the mountains, driving out the Mingrelians and eventually forcing them over the River Ingur, so that in his day only the area between the rivers Ingur and Tskhenists'q'ali was Mingrelian-speaking; without giving a precise date to this hypothesised southern push, he seems to suggest that it must have occurred after the 11th and before the 17th century. It is interesting to note that, when the Georgian educationalist Iak'ob Gogebashvili was publishing articles about Abkhazia and Mingrelia in the 1870s, he described the inhabitants of Abkhazia's southernmost province (now called Gal but then known as Samurzaq'an[o]) as "a branch of the Abkhazian race." And yet, when he later included reference to these people in his famous children's book *Nature's door*, he switched their ethnicity, saying: "The Mingrelians and the Samurzaq'anoans are one people" (p512 of the 1912 edition)[9] — note, however, that according to even Bakradze's testimony Mingrelian was not spoken on the Samurzaq'anoan/Gal side of the Ingur when he was penning his monograph!

However, it is the self-taught literary critic, P'avle Ingoroq'va, who is generally regarded as the progenitor of this tendentious 'theory', which he originally propounded in the Georgian journal *Mnatobi* ('Luminary') in 1949, repeating the material as the fourth chapter of his monumental *Giorgi Merchule* (1954). In short he tried to argue, largely on the basis of specious Kartvelian etymologies of toponyms in Abkhazia, that the 'Abkhazians' referred to in medieval Georgian sources had been a Kartvelian tribe with no genetic affiliation to today's North West Caucasian Abkhazians.

These last, he claimed, migrated from the North Caucasus only in the 17th century, displacing the Kartvelians resident there and adopting the ethnonym of the dislodged population. In partial support of this extraordinary historical fabrication he adduced the testimony of Evliya Çelebi to the effect that the Abkhazians of his day were speakers of Mingrelian — we saw above that the text actually says that they "also speak Mingrelian." Ingoroq'va does not refer to Bakradze, and it is unclear whether he knew of that earlier work, but, since it is known that preparations were underway in the late forties to deport the entire Abkhazian population either to Kazakhstan or Siberia, it is likely that Ingoroq'va was writing to order, providing an academic 'justification' for their removal from 'Kartvelian' land. Knowing what was expected of them, most of Tbilisi's academic elite wrote favourable reviews of Ingoroq'va's 1954 opus,[10] But with the deaths of Stalin and Beria and the subsequent reversal of anti-Abkhazian measures, Ingoroq'va spent the rest of his long life a deserved academic pariah. That was until the heady days of resurgent nationalism as Soviet Communism headed for collapse . . .

In the weekly organ of the Georgian Writers' Union *Lit'erat'uruli Sakartvelo* ('Literary Georgia' — April 21st 1989) critic Rost'om Chkheidze published a lavish praise of Ingoroq'va, urging his academic re-habilitation for his "contribution to the study of the history of Western Georgia."[11] Zviad Gamsakhurdia himself, then one of a band of unofficial oppositionist leaders, in the Russian pamphlet *Letopis' 4* ('Chronicle 4' — 1989), which he designed to instruct his fellow-Mingrelians how to conduct anti-Abkhazian agitation, urged them to read Ingoroq'va to learn why the true inheritors of the territory of Abkhazia were Mingrelians. Again in the Georgian paper *Kartuli pilmi* ('Georgian film' — September 6th 1989) Gamsakhurdia sought to lecture the late Andrej Sakharov on how the Abkhazians had come to Abkhazia only "two to three centuries ago"!

After the first Kartvelian-Abkhazian skirmishes in July 1989, a predictable consequence of the hysteria whipped up against the Abkhazians by a barrage of propaganda issuing from Tbilisi, a two-part article published over the New Year 1989-90 in another Georgian paper *Sakhalkho ganatleba* ('Popular education') the Svan linguist, Aleksandre Oniani, strove through linguistic argumentation to buttress the Ingoroq'va hypothesis, even though his date for the Abkhazians' arrival on "Georgian" soil was "400-500 years ago," presumably because he knew that Çelebi's text when correctly translated does not support a 17th century influx.[12] This resurrection of the Ingoroq'va fantasy was not accidental — it was in complete harmony with, and underpinned, an anti-Abkhazian campaign, which, since the media was still under typical Soviet central control, must have been officially supported by the Georgian government.

When fighting broke out on July 15-16th 1989, the quick introduction of Soviet Interior Ministry forces restored calm and kept the warring parties at bay. But if Georgia broke free of the Soviet Union (as it then existed or in a revised form such as envisaged by Gorbachev), no such help would be forthcoming (as indeed it was not after Georgia's August 14th 1992 invasion of Abkhazia), and so the only protection would be if Abkhazia were to distance itself from Georgian control, which is what Abkhazians set out to achieve by peaceful and wholly political means.

Future prospects

The Caucasus should and could be one of the great cultural and tourist centres of Europe with its stupendous mountain-scenery and lovely coastal resorts, with its huge diversity of exotic languages (many endangered), and with a unique treasury of folk-traditions in various fields. Abkhazia with its sub-tropical climate was long the USSR's riviera. But there can be no capitalising on these potential riches by any of the prospective beneficiaries until peace allows for proper development of necessary infrastructure. For all the money that Western institutions are pouring into Georgia, a glance at the map reveals that there remains only one direct rail-link to the North Caucasus and beyond, and this passes through Abkhazia. It has been closed to through-traffic since 1992, and until a viable settlement is achieved, Georgia will never be able to safeguard passage of goods or people between it and its main neighbour to the north. It is, therefore, in the interests of both Georgia and its trading-partners to help promote that settlement. The world, however, in its wisdom seems determined to force upon Abkhazia a return to something like the *status quo ante bellum*. Sadly, the evidence below suggests that the Kartvelians have failed to learn any lessons from their errors of the past, and so there is a very real danger that they could be repeated, unless appropriate restraint is applied.

Tamaz Nadareishvili, leader of the Kartvelian group in the Abkhazian parliament since 1992 (after the Abkhazian victory in September 1993 it went into exile, styling itself the 'Supreme Council of the Abkhazian Autonomous Republic') and a deputy premier of Georgia since that exile, had no compunction about writing in 1996 that "already in 1913 Academician Ivane Dzhavakhishvili wrote: 'The population of Colchis belonged to three Georgian branches: Laz-Mingrelians, Apshil-Abkhazians, and Svans' " (1996, p5). Two pages later the reader is "informed" that "up to the 17th century (to be precise, up to 1621) the population of

The state symbol of Abkhazia: set against a green-white background, the golden horseman Sasrəqʷ'a (one of the mythical Narts), on his golden steed Bzow, is shooting at a star — an episode from the Nart epic

Abkhazia was purely Georgian; one met not a single representative with a North Caucasian surname . . . Historically, Abkhazia was the rear-part of Mingrelia."

Johannes de Galonifontibus' early 15th century observations would seem to have eluded Nadareishvili's notice. Even though no reference is given for the quote from Dzhavakhishvili, Georgia's most distinguished historian, it does in fact come from Appendix 2a to volume 1 of his *Kartveli eris ist'oria* ('History of the Georgian people', p427 of the 1960 edition). As early as 1853, long before a proper linguistic comparison had been made between the North West and the South Caucasian languages, Dimit'ri Q'ipiani had asserted that ". . . but to this tribe [Kartvelians] also belong the Mingrelians, Abkhazians, Svans . . . ," a claim that is explained thus by Uturashvili (1989, p254): "Q'ipiani's assignment of the Abkhazians to the Kartvel ethnos can, it appears, be explained by the long and intimate Kartvelo-Abkhazian cultural-historical relationship, by their multi-faceted common historical fate, which united both people . . . The Georgian thinker judged the Abkhazians ethno-culturally to be so close a tribe that he placed them among the Kartvel tribes." Such unrefined attitudes to ethnic categorisation in the late 19th century might well have occasioned what could still have been a genuine, if naive, belief that the Abkhazians did indeed constitute part of the Kartvelian group. Perhaps in this atmosphere it was only natural to seek linguistic support for the notion, and the start of Dzhavakhishvili's Appendix [referred to above] reveals what led him to assert that the Apsilians ('Apshilians' in a Georgian variant), and thus the Abkhazians, were a "Georgian" (more accurately, Kartvelian) tribe: it was a characteristically wild etymological speculation on the part of the eccentric Georgian-Scot, Nik'o (Nikolaj) Marr, that detected an entirely spurious root+extension *bas-kh- in the ancient name *Abaskoí* (variant of *Abasgoí*), which he then connected with a sequence *mas-kh-, postulated as a variant for the name of the south Georgian Meskhian tribe.[13]

State-flag of Abkhazia: the green and white stripes represent harmony between Islam and Christianity. The white hand of friendship represented Abkhazia on 13th century Genoese maps, while the seven white stars on the red background are the seven historical divisions of Abkhazia.

Innocently (let us assume) believing that the Apsilian-Abkhazians represented a Kartvelian branch, Dzhavakhishvili was quite happy to argue (p436) that they must once have occupied territory further south in today's Georgia, pointing to a possible parallelism of formation between the toponyms T'uapse (on the Circassian Black Sea coast) and Dvabzu (in the Georgian province of Guria).[14]

On the other hand, Nadareishvili has a quite different agenda. Today it is impossible to maintain that North West Caucasian Abkhazians are an offshoot of the Kartvelian tribes — if, therefore, Abkhazians have dwelt for millennia on the same territory, this territory can only be argued to be 'Kartvelian' by planting there a purely fictitious race of 'Kartvelian Abkhazians', which is precisely the inventing of history that we have delineated above. Thus, when Nadareishvili re-disseminates this quite deliberate slander against the Abkhazians and their history, his ulterior purpose is to be provocative and keep alive the implication that has underlain various anti-Abkhazian manifestations in Georgian politics since the 1940s, namely that the Abkhazians, unentitled to full rights in Abkhazia if relatively recent newcomers on 'Georgian' soil,[15] will always be faced with the threat of expulsion (or worse), should Tbilisi ever reestablish control.[16] That Nadareishvili's views are not those of just an eccentric maverick is proved by the fact that another member of his group, Gia Gvazava, interviewed in Georgian on Radio Liberty in April 1994, also stated that the Abkhazians were not indigenous to Abkhazia and that he, a Mingrelian, was a true "Abkhazian"!

On April 5th 1996 Zurab Erkvania, the so-called chairman of the 'Council of Ministers of the Abkhazian Autonomous Republic' (sc. in exile), described Abkhazia as the "oldest territory of Georgia," and ten days later President Eduard Shevardnadze contributed a typical apparatchik's reinterpretation of history with the following hyperbole: "Today's Abkhazia . . . is racism in force, racism in practice. There was never this amount of cruel, widescale persecution, such exiling of hundreds of thousands of people from their native places, even in the times of Stalin, Beria and Lenin" (English corrected from Georgia's Internet site).[17]

Every right-thinking person would advise that mutual co-operation between the patchwork of peoples living in the relatively small expanse of territory that constitutes the Caucasus was in all their interests. But this ideal will only be achieved when the integrity and rights of each of the peoples concerned are acknowledged and fully respected by their neighbours and international players alike. Such elementary courtesy must itself be predicated on knowledge of the region and its inhabitants.

With the publication of this volume the relevant facts about Abkhazia have finally become accessible to the English-speaking world, which should thus be better placed to understand the philosophy behind Abkhazian aspirations. A convenient summary of the book, perhaps already familiar to some readers, is contained in an eloquently moving passage composed over 200 years ago:

> When in the Course of human events, it becomes necessary for one people to dissolve the political bands which have connected them with another, and to assume, among the powers of the earth, the separate and equal station to which the Laws of Nature and Nature's God entitle them, a decent respect to the opinions of mankind requires that they should declare the causes . . .
>
> *Preamble to the American Declaration of Independence*

1
Geography & the environment

Roman Dbar

The Republic of Abkhazia lies in the north-west Transcaucasus. The north-western and northern border of the Republic of Abkhazia first runs along the River Psou and then along the crest of the main watershed-ridge of the Greater Caucasus. In this sector it borders the Krasnodar and Stavropol regions of the Russian Federation. In the east the border passes along the Abkhaz-Svanetian (Sakʲ'an) ridge, the southern spur of the K'odor (Panajʷ) ridge, and the lower course of the River Ingur. Here the Republic of Abkhazia borders the Republic of Georgia, specifically its ethnographic provinces of Svanetia and Mingrelia. In the south the territory of the Republic of Abkhazia is washed by the waters of the Black Sea.

The average length of the territory of Abkhazia from north-west to south-east is 170km, and from south to north 66km. It lies between the northern latitudes of 43°35' and 42°27' and the eastern longitudes of 40° and 42°08'. The general area of the country is 8,700km².

Geomorphology

Abkhazia is a typical mountainous country. Almost the whole of its territory is covered with high, sharply dissected mountain-chains. If from the height of the main ridge of the Greater Caucasus one casts a glance over the mountain chains in Abkhazia, they make one think of gigantic waves of stone, congealed in their passage and gradually descending to the shore of the Black Sea. The incline of the territory of Abkhazia runs in a general direction from the south-west to the north-east.

The mountainous area is girded by hilly approaches which turn into the low-lying coastal plain in the east of the country or come to an abrupt end at the seashore in the west. The main ridge of the Greater Caucasus enters the frontiers of Abkhazia near the sources of the River Awadhara (Wadhara). Here on the north-western border the mountains

Lake Rits'a, nestling amidst high peaks 950m above sea-level in Northern
Abkhazia, is one of Abkhazia's main natural attractions; 2,490m long, its
maximum depth is 116m

rise to 2,500m above sea-level. Towards the south-eastern ridge there is an increase in height, and on the eastern border the Abkhazian mountain-chains already heave up to between 3,500 and 4,000m.

Passes across the main ridge within the confines of Abkhazia lie at heights of between 2,300 and 3,000m above sea-level. It is because of this that the majority of them are difficult to reach and for most of the year are closed for passage. The most manageable for passage is the K'lukhor Pass on the Abkhazian (Sukhum) Military Highway. The last century saw the growth of a great deal of traffic across the Marukh Pass as well. These passes are paths which are suitable for travel either by people on foot or by packhorse.

By the foothills of the southern slope of the Greater Caucasus lie deep longitudinal valleys along which rivers flow. The most significant of these are the Awadhara, Bavju, Baul (tributaries of the River Bzyp) and Chkhalta, as well as the upper course of the K'odor and the lower course of the Sak'en (Sakⁱ'an).

Valleys in the upper reaches carry traces of the movement of ancient glaciers, whilst in the lower reaches the rivers flowing along them cut into morainal deposits, forming terraces. In the extreme east of Abkhazia a belt of longitudinal valleys is sealed off by the Abkhaz-Svanetian (Sakⁱ'an) ridge — this is a high eroded spur of the Greater Caucasus which forms a watershed between the river basins of the K'odor and Ingur. The highest point of the ridge is the summit of Mount Khʷarikhra (3,710m).

In the east of Abkhazia from the summit of Khodzhal (3,309m) as far as the River K'odor, parallel to the main ridge, there rises the powerful latitudinal swell of the K'odor ridge, compacted with dense tufa-porphyritic rocks. Its blade-shaped crests and rocky peaks vie with the main chain itself of the Greater Caucasus for steepness and height.

In the north-east of the country, parallel with the main ridge, runs the Chkhalta ridge, which extends in the west to the Chedym ridge (the peak of Mount Khⁱymsa rises to 3,150m). The saw-shaped crests of these ridges, jagged with deep sand-filled holes eroded by ancient ice-formations, are bearers of small modern glaciers.

The relief to the south of this arc of ridges, weakly concaved in the north, is characterised by alternating meridional eroded, denuded ridges or deep river-bearing ravines.

A large portion of the territory in the north-west is taken up by two vast limestone massifs — that of Gagra (Arabika peak is 2,660m) and that of Bzyp (Nap'ra peak is 2,684m). These massifs are compounded with powerfully thick deposits of limestone, attenuated into gently sloping pleats and distinguished by active karsting processes. Here it is that one finds one of the largest caves on the planet — that of New Athos (= Afon Tṣ'yts; its internal volume is 1.5 million m^3), as well as one of the deepest — the Snowy Cave, with a charted depth of 1,300m.

In the eastern part of Abkhazia the zone of limestone development is quite narrow, and all the limestone ridges are separated by a distinct ledge from the belt of hilly mountain-approaches, which sink in the south to the sea-coast. The foothills descend and turn into a flat coastal plain. In the north-west this occurs only as separate strips in river-estuaries, whilst to the east of Sukhum it widens out into a broad continuous zone, reaching the Samurzaq'an(o) depression up to a width of 30m.

One can therefore divide Abkhazia geomorphologically into four longitudinal zones:

1. the zone of the main ridge of the Greater Caucasus
2. a zone of rolling, rocky ridges with deep longitudinal and transversal riverbeds
3. a zone of hilly mountain-approaches
4. a zone of coastal alluvial depression, consisting of separate sections — those of Tsandrypsh, Bzyp, Gudauta, Sukhum, Abzhywa and Samurzaq'an(o).

Climate

Abkhazia is characterised by a sharply pronounced vertical differentiation of climatic zones and an exceptional variety of climatic conditions. In the course of the 50km from the shore of the Black Sea up to the main ridge of the Greater Caucasus it is possible to experience all the climatic zones from humid subtropical to an arctic waste of eternal snows and glaciers.

Such a variety of climatic states is conditioned by the intricate composition of the complex of physical-geographical peculiarities — radiation from the sun and circulatory phenomena in the atmosphere, peculiarities of orography and the very important climatic factor that is the moderating activity of the Black Sea.

The territory of Abkhazia lies at the intersection of two of the terrestrial globe's climatic zones — the subtropical and the temperate. As regards the amount of direct radiation from the sun at warm times of the year, Abkhazia is akin to the Japanese subtropics, and at cold times of the year to the subtropics of the Mediterranean countries of Europe.

Winter in Abkhazia is the warmest in the entire territory of the former USSR. Average temperatures in January in the Gagra region are +7°C and in the environs of New Athos even higher at +7.1°C.

The capital of Abkhazia, the town of Sukhum (Aqᵂ'a), lies 80km south of Gagra, and here the average temperatures in January are +6°C. Further to the south the average temperatures fall, ignoring, as it were, the geographical latitude. In the towns of Ochamchira and Gal they are equivalent to +4.1°C. This phenomenon is conditioned by the lower protection afforded by the mountain ridges of the southern coastal depressions against encroachment by cold masses of air.

As the location rises, the average temperatures fall. Drop in temperature per 100m in height, starting from a height of 250m above sea-level, is around 0.6°C. This explains why the average temperatures for January on the main Caucasian ridge can reach as low as -20°C.

Because of the influence of the Black Sea, the period for the approach of maximum temperatures is one month late (occurring in August) in comparison with localities in conditions of a continental climate. The mean temperatures in August on the coast are equal to +23°C. The highest mean temperatures in the hottest month are found at the resort of Gagra, standing at +24.5°C.

The yearly amount of precipitation and its distribution across the territory of Abkhazia is dependent upon the closeness of the sea, the direction of the prevailing air-masses, and the character of the terrain. The mean annual amount of precipitation is 1,400mm.

The amount of precipitation along the coast increases from north to south, but especially pronounced is the rise in precipitation as altitude increases. Thus, for example, Sukhum (35m above sea-level) receives 1,390mm of precipitation, whereas Ts'ebelda (Ts'abal — 426m above sea-level) gets 1,788mm. Higher still in the upper reaches of the River K'odor the amount of precipitation exceeds 2,000mm per year, whilst in separate high-mountainous regions, it is true, this magnitude may reach 4,000mm per year.

The average relative humidity in Sukhum is equal to 72 per cent. The number of hours of sunshine in the capital of the republic consists of 2,238 hours per year. The maximum occurs in summer (812 hours), and the minimum in winter (317 hours).

Hydrography

The coasts of Abkhazia extend a distance of 240km on the eastern littoral of the Black Sea. The most picturesque section of coast is in the region of Gagra, where for a distance of about 20km spurs of the Gagra limestone massif descend right up to the seashore, dropping down to it from a height of almost 2,000m in steep slopes, which form the grandiose Gagra cornice.

To the south of Gagra the ridges gradually draw back from the shore, giving way to hilly mountain-approaches. The latter in their turn become the flat Bzyp depression with the Pitsunda promontory. To the east of the promontory of Pitsunda lie the conglomerative Mysra hills (Mjussera), which attain a height of 200m. This is one of the most picturesque spots of Abkhazia's Black Sea coast. Here a colossal conglomerative block is cut off by the sea and forms a sheer rocky shore with narrow sandy beaches. To the south of Sukhum the shoreline of Abkhazia is low-lying and to a significant degree straight-lined.

On the bottom of the Black Sea three zones are quite distinct: the continental shelf, extending to a depth of 200m; the continental slope, stretching between 200m and 2,000m; and the bottom of the hollow, occupying the depths from 2,000m to 2,243m.

The massive cave complex at New Athos was discovered in 1961. There are nine galleries of stalactites and stalagmites, open to the public in a 'son et lumière' presentation

Close to the shores of Abkhazia, the width of the continental shelf varies sharply. At the Gagra cornice it does not exceed one kilometre, but opposite Gudauta it reaches 35km. The average transparency of the water around Sukhum is around five metres. The greatest transparency of the Black Sea waters around the shores of Abkhazia occurs at the time of the autumn calms and attains 27m. The average annual temperatures of the water at Sukhum are +17°C. At the hottest time of year, in August, the temperature of the surface of the water along the coastline can reach +27°C or +28°C. The salinity of the surface of the water fluctuates from 17.5 per cent (in winter) to 18.2 per cent (in summer). It increases the greater the depth, and in ground-layers it stands at 22.5 per cent.

In terms of its hydrophysical and hydrochemical properties, the Black Sea stands out sharply among all other sea-reservoirs on the planet, for the fundamental feature which sets it apart from all others is the sharp difference in water-density between the surface-layer in the range 100-150m, the oxygen layer, and the water-mass lying deeper down, the hydrogen-sulphide layer.

These two strata are sharply distinguished in terms of temperature, salinity, dissolved gases, content of biogenic substances, and distribution of life-forms. As a result of the heavy presence of hydrogen-sulphides the water layer of the Black Sea at depths below 150-200m is devoid of life, with the exception of anerobic bacteria. As explained by Ascheron (1995, p4), the inrush of organic matter from the five major rivers that feed it (Kuban, Don, Dnieper, Dniester and Danube) is too much for the sea water, which would normally be expected to decompose it.

One of the strange shapes taken by some of the New Athos rock formations. Temperatures range between 12.6°C and 14.4°C in the caves.

Internal waters

The territory of Abkhazia with its abundance of precipitation possesses a very dense surface hydrographical network, represented by mountain-glaciers, rivers, lakes, springs and bogs.[1] The general glacial area in Abkhazia's mountains is equal to about 77km[2], which represents four per cent of the whole Greater Caucasus. The glaciers encountered in the mountains of Abkhazia are basically of the pendant, valleyed and peaked varieties. As regards their size, the glaciers are not large, and only some exceed a length of two kilometres. In all there are 131 glaciers in Abkhazia, where in the main they feed the system of two rivers: the K'odor and the Bzyp.

Abkhazia's rivers typically display a bewitching charm and wild indomitability. Their crystal-clear waters rush headlong down from high mountain-ledges, scatter in the white froth of waterfalls, cut through deep narrow gorges and, breaking loose in the foothill-zone, suddenly decelerate their flow as though preparing themselves to vanish gently in the embraces of a wave of the Black Sea.

The largest river in Abkhazia is the Bzyp, which finds its start on the southern slope of the main ridge at a height of 2,300m and has a course of 112km from source to estuary. At the sources of the river lie ten glaciers; the beds of the river and its tributaries possess hollows in the shape of inverted circus domes — the traces of recent glaciers. In mid-course the Bzyp buries itself in a deep and narrow tufa-porphyritic defile. The gorges in places are as narrow as three to four metres. Here the river acquires a large number of underground tributaries, raising the water over mounds and forming deep pits and shallows. The Bzyp cuts through to the coastal depression by penetrating between the rocky spurs of the Bzyp and Mamdzyshkha ridges and falls to the sea following lengthwise the area of the Mysra hills. The average annual flow of the Bzyp constitutes 96m^3 per second.

The second largest river in Abkhazia is the K'odor, which takes shape from the merger of the rivers Sak'en (Sak^j'an) and Gvandra (G^{w}andra). The length of the river is 105km (taken together with the Sak'en) and finds its start at a height of 3,200m, gathering its water from the glaciers and snows of the main ridge of the Greater Caucasus and the Abkhaz-Svanetian (Sak'en) ridge. In mid-course, in the region of the village of Lata, the K'odor flows along massive crystalline deposits of limestone, and the river-valley narrows to such an extent that the tops of trees on opposite banks become intertwined with their branches. The banks rise over the river in the sheer Bogada rocks to a height of 600-700m above sea-level. In its basin-area the K'odor excels all the rivers of Abkhazia, constituting 2,051m^2, whilst mean annual flow runs to around 144m^3 per second.

Between the basins of the rivers Bzyp and K'odor lie the basins of the large rivers K'elasur (K^j'ala$\int^w$yr), Gumista (G^{w}msta), Aapsta and Khypsta. To the east, on the K'odor ridge, yet another large river of Abkhazia, the Ghalidzga (Aaldzga), finds its start.

The total annual flow of all the rivers of Abkhazia amounts to around 13km^3, and practically the entire flow is made up of ecologically pure water. Over 300 springs with varying degrees of mineral water have been registered in Abkhazia. The most famous among them are the hydro-carbonated springs in the Awadhara river valley, the sulphate-bearing and chlorous springs of Zhvandrypsh (Zh^{w}adrypsh), the sulphurous springs in the valley of the River Basla, and the sulphurous springs of T'q^w'archal.

Gigantic underground-springs (gushers) occupy a special place. The source of the Mch'yshta is a typical powerful gusher. Here a water jet of immense proportions forms a transparent, swift-flowing river with its voluminous quantity of water. From the precipice of the Gagra cornice a gusher bursts forth which gives its start to the shortest river in Abkhazia, the Reproa — from source to its fall into the sea its length is less than 20m. A most beautiful powerful gusher is the Blue Lake in the Bzyp valley.

Throughout the mountainous terrain of Abkhazia there are many lakes — over 130 in number. In the high-mountain sector the most widespread lakes are peaked and moraino-sub-pondal. In the zone of compacted, tectonic breaches one finds deep lakes — fault-troughs and lakes formed by monumental mountain landslips that dam up the mountain-rivers. In the belt of limestone-diffusion there are karstal lakes with the characteristic roundish or funnel-shaped form. In the coastal zone of the Black Sea one meets small lakes or dried riverbeds formed by the flooding of beds of rivers propped up by shoreline dunes.

The largest and most picturesque lake in Abkhazia is Lake Rits'a. It lies at a height of 950m. above sea-level in the valley of the River Lashpsa in a deep mountain-hollow. From the north it is bordered by the high rocky ridge of Atsyt^{w}ak^w with the peaks of Atsyt^{w}ak^w (2,542m) and Agyapsta (Ag^{j}aptsa; 3,263m), from the east and south by spurs of the ridge of Rykh^{w}a, and in the south-west by the grandiose precipice of Mount Pṣah^{w}ishkha (2,222m). At its longest point Rits'a extends to 2,490m, and its maximum depth is 116m.

Soil and vegetation

Abkhazia is distinctive for its unusual richness and diversity of vegetative groups and for its extraordinary variety and tesselation of soils. In low- and mid-mountain regions the processes of erosion are advanced, but in places they are restrained to a significant extent by woodland-vegetation, for the woodland-cover of the territory of Abkhazia exceeds 60 per cent. The erosion of top-soil by run-off does not exceed 400-600 tons per square kilometre per year. Lowland plains are liable to bog-formation. On drained foothill-regions the Pleiocene-age processes of feralitisation have been in progress in surface-layers. As a result of this, secondary clay minerals (oxides of iron and aluminium) have been formed. In base and middle layers red soils have developed, and yellow soils in less rich, acidic layers. Acidic unsaturated podsol (yellow-earthed soil low in humus) forms in soft, friable deposits, whilst on remoistened terraces one finds podsol (yellow-earthed gleyey soil). The character of soil-formation makes these landscapes akin to the typical humid ones of the subtropics, but the comparatively cold winters, particularly in the foothill-zone, do not allow humid evergreen forests to grow here.

The flora of Abkhazia includes more than 2,000 species of plants, of which 149 are represented by arboreal and shrub forms, whilst the rest are herbaceous. Around 400 species are endemic to the Caucasus, but over 100 are found on the planet only in Abkhazia. Some of the endemic species occupy so restricted an environment that their habitat measures only a few hundred square metres, as, for instance, for the bell-flower (*Campanula paradoxa*) in the Bzyp river valley.

There are five vertical zones that can be distinguished for the soil-vegetative covering in Abkhazia. The first zone is the low-lying belt, limited to heights between zero and 30m above sea-level. In the narrow coastal layer the turfless sands are covered by the grassy vegetation of such species as spurge (*Euphorbia paralias*), holly (*Eryngium maritimum*), sarsaparilla (*Calistegia soldanella*), mustard (*Sinapis maritima*), lily (*Pancratium maritimum*), etc. On sandy ridges one meets thickets of the relic bamboo cereal (*Arundo donax*). On ancient dunes beyond the reach of the waves of the sea form weak-podsol and podsol soils, with alluvial soils in the river-estuaries — on the latter one finds shrubby growths of berry (*Rubus anatolicus*), thorns (*Paliurus spina*), *Ruscus pontica* and barberry (*Berberis orientalis*). Shrubby growths change into leaf-bearing coastal forests of hornbeam (*Carpinus orientalis*), elm (*Ulmus foliacea*) and hop-hornbeam (*Ostrya carpinofolia*) with such creepers as convolvulus (*Smilax excelsa*), clematis (*Clematis vitalba*) and bindweed (*Periploca graeca*) densely wound around them.

On the alluvial deposits, rich in lime, of the Pitsunda promontory and Mysra hills are preserved sectors of Mediterranean vegetation, which are represented by bright-coniferous forests of pine (*Pinus pithyusa*). In the undergrowth of this latter Mediterranean xerophyte species predominate. Common here are thorn (*Ruscus pontica*) and helianthemum or frostwort (*Cistus tauricus*), while on the grassy covering grow prairie turnip (*Psoralea bituminosa*) and the rarer plant *Cytinus rubra* (known to the Russians as *podladannik*), which is parasitic on the roots of *Cistus tauricus* (known to the Russians as *ladannik*). Pitsunda's pine-grove is a unique monument of nature, which forms part of the Pitsunda-Mysra nature reserve.

The vegetative cover of the coastal lowlands is represented by alder forests of *Alnus barbata* with infusions on drained river-beds of wing-nut (*Pterocarya pterocarpa*) and fig (*Ficus carica*). On high, well-drained places alder-forests are replaced by forests of broad-leafed oak and hornbeam or hornbeam and beech. The sub-forest of these trees is formed from dense, evergreen growths of rhododendron (*Rhododendron ponticum*) and azalea (*Rhododendrum uteum*). As the terrain drops, especially to the south-east, there are complexes of water-bog vegetation with growths of the relic aquatic walnut (*Trapa colchica*) and the endemic hibiscus (*Hibiscus ponticus*) plus *Rhamphicarpa medwedewi*, as at Lake Bebesyr.

The second zone is the zone of lowland and foothill forests at heights varying from 30 to 650m above sea-level. This belt is extremely rich in species and variegated in terms of vegetative groups. The soils here are represented by a combination of yellow and red earths with podsol and humus-carbonated soils. In southern Abkhazia combinations of red earths with podsol soils are more widely represented, whilst in the central and northern regions we have combinations of yellow earths with podsol and humus-carbonated soils.

The fundamental components of the forests of this zone are oak (*Quercus iberica*), chestnut (*Castanea sativa*), hornbeam (*Carpinus caucasica*), beech (*Fagus orientalis*) with a mixture of different maples and lime (*Tilia caucasica*). In the broad-leafed forests one finds a relic coniferous yew-tree (*Taxus baccata*), and on the hills of Mysra another relic, the red strawberry wood (*Arbutus andrachne*). Common in the sub-forest are the evergreen relics of tertiary flora: rhododendron (*Rhododendron ponticum*), heather (*Erica arborea*), cherry-laurel (*Laurocerasus officinalis*), holly (*Ilex aquifolium*) and butcher's broom (*Ruscus hypophyllum*). Mosses and lichens have also developed in abundance. This belt is most suited to economic activity and is thus subject to strong human pressure.

The third zone is the zone of forests that ranges between the heights of 650-2,200m above sea-level. This zone is characterised by the great contrast in the strongly differentiated terrain — deep ravines are replaced by high mountain-ridges with slopes of varying steepness and erosion, covered with dense forest, often giving way to grandiose rocky precipices and screes. In the cooler and damper climate of this belt two basic components of the vegetation complex dominate, namely the eastern beech (*Fagus orientalis*) and the Caucasian fir (*Abies nordmanniana*). It should be noted that the beech and fir in Abkhazia attain the maximum measurements known over the whole area of their distribution for the species *Fagus* and *Abies* — for example, at the spot Mramba in a gorge of the River K'odor the height of one Nordmannian fir equal to 85m has been registered, while for the eastern beech a trunk diameter of two metres at chest height is not uncommon. On the limestone deposits of the Gagra ridge are concentrated the nucleus of Abkhazia's relic flora. Unusual for its beauty among these is the bell-flower (*Campanula mirabilis*), and there are also aster (*Aster abchasicus*), potentilla (*Potentilla camillae*) and yam (*Dioscorea caucasica*).

The fourth zone is the zone of sub-alpine curved forests, shrubs and tall grasses, lying at heights of between 2,200 and 2,400m above sea-level. This transitional zone occupies a relatively narrow strip. Here soils of dark-coloured turf and turfy-podsol have developed. The arboreal vegetation is weighed down with deep coverings of snow at winter-time — the thickness of the snow-covering can reach 8-20m. The basic species forming Abkhazia's associative curved forests are the beech (*Fagus orientalis*) with cherry-laurel (*Laurocerasus officinalis*) and rhododendron (*Rhododendron caucasicum*), while there are also associations of birch (*Betula litvinovi*) and maple (*Acer trautvetteri*). Curved forests of Pontic oak (*Quercus pontica*) are rarely found. Characteristic for the sub-alpine tall grassy region in Abkhazia are a family of tall grasses that can reach a height of 2.5m, rough caulescence and broad leaves (20-60cm in diameter), absence of cereals forming turf, durability and colourfulness of flowering. Belonging to the most characteristic representatives for this belt are cow-parsnips (*Heracleum villosum, Heracleum pubescens, Heracleum ponticum*), angelica (*Angelica tatjanae*), cephalaria (*Cephalaria gigantea*), ploughman's spikenard (*Inula magnifica*), bell-flower (*Campanula lactiflora*), valerian (*Valeriana colchica*) and others.

The fifth zone is the zone of alpine meadows that stretches from 2,200-2,800m above sea-level. The mountain-meadow soils of this belt are poor and strongly skeletalised, thanks to permanent leaching by precipitations. The dominant position in Abkhazia's alpine meadows is occupied by vegetative associations with oats (*Festuca supina, Festuca ruprechtii*), cobresia (*Cobresia macrolepis*), gentian (*Gentiana pyrenaica*), woodruff (*Asperula abchasica*) and others.

Above 2,700m the vegetation cover manifests a predominance of vegetation-complexes typical of regions of rocky shards and scree, including saxifrage (*Saxifraga colchica*), milk-vetch (*Astragalus lewieri*), violet (*Viola biflora*), buttercup (*Ranunculus abchasicus*), larkspur (*Delphinium caucasicum*) and, nestling in the ground, juniper (*Juniperus pygmaea* and *Juniperus depressa*).

The animal world

The fauna of the Black Sea is basically similar to that of the Mediterranean but significantly poorer in species. Thus, the general number of animal species in the Black Sea stands at about 1,500 as against the 6,000 in the Mediterranean. About 160 varieties of fish live here. The poverty of the fauna in the Black Sea is conditioned by the low sunshine and the presence of hydrogen sulphide in its depths and also by the severe winter chills.

The most characteristic species of the Black Sea's ichthyofauna along the shores of Abkhazia are the beluga (*Huso huso*), the sturgeon of the Black and Azov Sea (*Acipenser guldenstadti*), the sevruga sturgeon (*Acipenser stellatus*), the Black Sea salmon (*Salmo trutta labrax*), anchovy (*Engraulis engracicholus ponticus*), the Black Sea herring (*Alosa kessleri pontica*), plaice (*Platichtys flesus luscus*), shark (*Squalus acantias*), five species of grey mullet (*Mugil*), skate (*Raia batis*, known in Abkhaz as *amsyn bga* 'sea-wolf')and others (including *Mullus barbatus* and *Trachurus mediterraneus ponticus*). It should be noted that a significant proportion of the Black Sea salmon stock spawns in the rivers of Abkhazia, thanks to their purity. Also extremely common here are three kinds of dolphin: *Delphinus delphinus ponticus*, *Phocaena phocaena* and *Tursiops tursio*.

Against a background of general richness and variety of animal-life in the Caucasus as a whole, the manifest poverty in species of land-creatures and the ichthyofauna of the internal reservoirs of the entire western Transcaucasus, including Abkhazia, demands attention. Although there are endemic species here, there is not a vertebrate which would not also be represented in Mediterranean countries. We often find here the self-same species or their sub-species. This latter circumstance most eloquently testifies to the genetic commonality of the fauna of these territories.

The alpine zone of Abkhazia is most obviously characterised by endemic fauna. A fundamental proportion of the endemic species of the Caucasus are concentrated here: the Caucasian aurochs (*Capra caucasica*), the Caucasian snowy field-vole (*Microtus nivalis*), the Promethean mouse (*Prometheomys schaposchnikowi*), the Caucasian black grouse (*Lyrurus mlocosiewieczi*) and the snowy partridge (*Tetragallus caucasicus*). One of the most important migratory routes for birds on the Eurasian continent passes across the territory of Abkhazia. There have been registered here 268 bird species, among which are rare and endangered varieties such as the eagle, golden eagle, lammergeyer, black vulture, falcon, hawk, rose-pelican, swan and large white heron.

Predators are represented by the Caucasian brown bear, the wolf, jackal, fox, lynx, feral cat, the forest- and rock-marten, badger, otter, Caucasian sub-species of the European mink and the weasel. The large number of caves in Abkhazia serve as refuges for a significant number of bats. At least 16 species of such cheiroptera live here. Ungulates are represented by, in addition to the Caucasian aurochs, the European noble deer, the roe-deer and chamois. Wild boar are very common.

From the representative reptiles and amphibians one can single out the Caucasian viper (*Viper kaznakowi*), endemic to the Caucasus, the Aesculapian grass-snake (*Elaphe longissima*), the Mediterranean tortoise (*Testudo graeca*), the grey toad (*Bufo bufo verrucosissima*). This last represents a sub-species of the grey toad, the largest of the species over the whole area of its habitat.

In the mountain rivers of Abkhazia the most widespread fish is the river-trout (*Salmo trutta*), which is a freshwater variety of the Black Sea salmon. In the marshy lakes on the coastal depressions the most common is the sazan and the crucian (carp), whilst in the rivers of the eastern part of Abkhazia one finds the sheat-fish.

From the comparatively variegated insect fauna one can mention two relic species of large predatory beetle, *Carabus caucasicus* and *Bramea ledereri*, which inhabit the coastal forests of Abkhazia's south-eastern region.

The protected nature-reserves of Abkhazia are represented by two reserves and one national park — the Pitsunda-Mysra and the Pskhu-Gumista (Psh^wy-G^wmsta) reserves and the Rits'a relic national park. The general area of all the protected lands consists of 82,000 hectares or about ten per cent of the territory of the country.

The war of 1992-93 led to the laying of a large number of mines, especially in the south-east of the republic, which remain to the present day (early 1998). Sukhum's renowned Institute of Experimental Pathology and Therapy, based on the Ape Nursery, a great tourist attraction, was destroyed and the apes let loose. Many trees were cut down for fuel, and, with a severe blockade imposed by Russia from early 1996 in response to requests for pressure on Abkhazia from Georgia, this destruction can be expected to continue. A community so reduced to fighting for its very survival has little time and resources to preserving its environment.

2
The origin of the Abkhazian people
Vjacheslav Chirikba

The ethnogenesis of any people is a complex problem, which may be tackled by marshalling evidence from a variety of such disciplines as linguistics, archaeology, anthropology, etc. Below I shall deal, somewhat briefly, with the first two of these, the linguistic and archaeological record proving crucial in the search for the origin of the Abkhazian people.

Proto-West Caucasian

The common ancestor of the modern Abkhazo-Adyghean languages, Proto-West Caucasian, can be dated approximately to the third millennium BC. At the final stage of its development it split into at least three dialects: Proto-Circassian, Proto-Abkhaz, and Proto-Ubykh. Though Ubykh linguistically occupies an intermediate position between Abkhaz and Circassian, some features indicate that originally it was closer to Abkhaz, only later undergoing substantial Circassian influence. One may, therefore, suppose that initially Proto-West Caucasian was divided into Proto-Circassian and Proto-Abkhaz-Ubykh dialects, later splitting into Proto-Abkhaz and Proto-Ubykh:

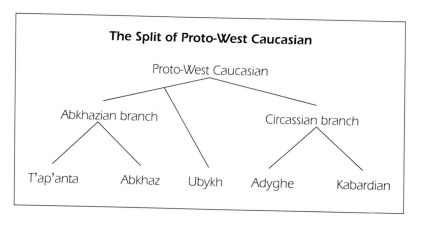

The Split of Proto-West Caucasian

Proto-West Caucasian

Abkhazian branch

Circassian branch

T'ap'anta   Abkhaz   Ubykh   Adyghe   Kabardian

An analysis of the common Abkhazo-Adyghean lexicon allows one to speculate on the economic activities of the distant Abkhazo-Adyghean ancestors: they grew different plants (apples, pears, plums, figs, nuts) and cereals (including different sorts of millet), bred cattle, sheep, goats, swine, horses, donkeys, and were hunting and fishing; they developed crafts such as weaving, spinning, metal-working (in copper, lead, silver, gold); they had a rich religious cult, worshipping *inter alios* gods of the smithy (*Shaˢʷy* = Circassian *λapˢy*) and thunder and lightning (*Afy* = Circassian *ˢy(-)ble*) (Chirikba, 1986, pp 397-401).

External connections of the West Caucasian languages

1. East Caucasian   On the basis of research by such scholars as Trubetzkoy (1922; 1930), Dumézil (1932; 1933), Balkarov (1964; 1966), Shagirov (1977), Abdokov (1976; 1981; 1983), and Nikolaev & Starostin (1994; cf. also Starostin 1985), I am personally convinced that the West Caucasian languages cannot be separated genetically from the East Caucasian languages. Abdokov and Nikolaev with Starostin have proposed patterns of regular sound-correspondences between the East and West Caucasian languages, publishing etymological dictionaries of the North Caucasian linguistic family. Their works provide to my satisfaction the final proof for the existence of a compact North Caucasian linguistic family with two branches: Western (or Abkhazo-Adyghean) and Eastern (or Nakh-Daghestanian, containing the Nakh group, consisting of Chechen, Ingush and Bats, plus the Daghestanian group, with some 26 languages such as Avar, Lezgi, Lak, Dargwa, Tabasaran, etc). The term 'North Caucasian languages' is to some extent relative, as several members of this family are spoken in Transcaucasia (e.g. Abkhaz, Bats, Udi). The term 'Ibero-Caucasian languages', traditional in Soviet Caucasology, which presupposed a genetic relationship between both branches of North Caucasian, on the one hand, and Kartvelian, on the other, can no longer be sustained.

2. Hattic   Besides the modern West Caucasian languages, other languages belonging to the same group might have existed in the past. Over recent decades a hypothesis has been gaining ground according to which a genetic relationship existed between Abkhazo-Adyghean languages and Hattic, the most ancient known language of Asia Minor (modern Turkey), spoken some four to five thousand years ago. Texts in this language, written by Hittite scribes in cuneiform script, were found during the excavations in Hattusas, capital of the Hittite Empire (east of modern Ankara). Hattians, who had created quite a high civilisation of their own and who are regarded as the inventors of the metallurgy of iron, had made a substantial impact on the social organisation and religious system of the kingdom of the Indo-European speaking Hittites.

The very first investigator of Hattic, E. Forrer (1919, pp 1033-34), established its non-Indo-European character and suggested its relationship with Abkhazo-Adyghean languages. The same view was proposed at roughly the same time by Bleichsteiner (1923). The main reasons were striking structural similarities (particularly, extensive use of prefixation) between this ancient language of Asia Minor, extinct since the early second millennium BC, and the languages of the West Caucasian group. These structural affinities were later discussed by Dunaevskaja (1960), Diakonov (1967) and Ardzinba (1979). These latter two also noted some material correspondences (in affixes) between Hattic and West Caucasian. Ivanov (1985) proposed many Hattic-West Caucasian material parallels, both in radical and affixal morphemes. Though not all these comparisons are equally convincing (largely because of the poor preservation of Hattic), Ivanov did in general manage to demonstrate the existence of this relationship. Hattic-West Caucasian similiarities in lexicon and grammar have been further investigated by Braun (1994), Taracha (1995) and Chirikba (1996, pp 406-32).

It has been suggested that Hattic was related to the language of the Kaskians, the warlike tribes inhabiting the vast mountainous territories to the north of the Hattians in the Anatolian Black Sea coastal area. The union of the Kaskian tribes was a rather formidable power which caused much strife for the neighbouring Hittite kingdom, whose rulers had tenaciously to fight the turbulent mountaineers until the very end of the Hittite state. At the upper reaches of the River Halys (modern-day Kızıl-Irmak in northern Turkey) Kaskians founded the powerful state of Kasku.

Analysis of Kaskian personal names and toponyms allowed Giorgadze (1961, pp 209-10) to postulate their linguistic relationship to Hattic (cf. also Melikishvili 1960, p9; Diakonov 1968, p12). One of the tribes known to be in the Kaskian tribal union were the Abeshla, whose name in some contemporary sources (e.g. Assyrian texts of the 12th century BC) was given as a synonym for Kaskians (cf. Inal-Ipa 1976, p129). It has been suggested that the name Kashka (Hittite *Kashkash*, Assyrian *Kashka*, Egyptian *Kshksh*) could be connected with the later designation of the Circassians (cf. tenth century Arabic *kashak*, Old Georgian *kashag-i*, Old Armenian *gashk*, Old Russian *kasogi*, Ossetic *kæsæg*, Byzantine Greek κασαχία 'Circassia', etc). At the same time the name Abeshla resembles the later designations for the Abkhazians (Old Georgian variants *apsil-/apshil-*, Old Armenian plural form *apshel-k*,

Greek *apsîlai*, Latin *[gens] Absilae*). These facts formed the basis for the hypothesis according to which Kashka represent the ancient ancestors of the Circassians, and Abeshla the ancestors of the Abkhazians. This would mean that already at that period Kaskians (later Circassians) and Abeshla (later Abkhazians) were separate, though closely related tribes (Melikishvili, 1960, p9; Diakonov 1968, p12; Inal-Ipa 1976, pp 122-135).

On the other hand, it is probable that the Nakh-Daghestanian languages can be linked with the ancient (extinct) Hurrian and Urartian languages, whose speakers lived some five to three thousand years ago on the territory of the Armenian plateau and adjacent areas, creating the high civilisations of Hurri and Urartu (Diakonov & Starostin, 1986).

The origin of the Abkhazo-Adyghean peoples

There exist several hypotheses explaining the formation of the Abkhazo-Adyghean peoples (Anchabadze, 1976, pp 8-25; Inal-Ipa, 1976; Markovin, 1978, pp 283-325; Fedorov, 1983, pp 27-31, 39-41, 56, 80-84; Klimov, 1986, p52). According to one such hypothesis, these peoples were formed approximately within the territory of their modern habitat (i.e. the West Caucasus), which can be confirmed by the existence of a shared lexicon reflecting the characteristic features of the geography of the Caucasian Black Sea coast: sea, beach, big fish, (bushy) mountain, ice, snow, cold/frost, wood, fir-tree, beech, oak, cornel, chestnut, wolf, bear, etc (cf. Klimov, 1986, p52). Important support for this hypothesis is the series of West Caucasian toponyms and hydronyms interpretable only in terms of Abkhazo-Adyghean languages. On the other hand, popular native tradition indicates a more southern origin for the Abkhazo-Adygheans.

In discussing the origin of the Abkhazo-Adyghean peoples, one can address at least three important questions linked to this problem: the ethnic identity of the people belonging to the Maikop culture; the appearance in the West Caucasus of the dolmen-culture; the probable genetic link of the West Caucasian languages with Anatolian Hattic and probably also Kaskian.

The early period of the famous Maikop culture is dated to the middle of the third millennium BC. It originated on the territory of the North-Western Caucasus (around the valley of the River Kuban and its tributaries) and then spread east, up to modern Chechenia, Ingushetia and the borders of Daghestan, where it approached the area of another major Caucasian civilisation, the Kuro-Arax culture. The famous tumuli found near the Adyghe city of Maikop (which gave the culture its name) contained large quantities of gold and silver ornaments and vessels, which resemble similar finds from Asia Minor (e.g. Alaca Hüyük in north-central Anatolia, on territory most probably populated by Hattians) and in the Middle East (Ur, southern Mesopotamia). The Maikop culture can be explained by local development, while providing evidence of intensive contacts with the ancient southern civilisations. It is noticeable that the territory of Abkhazia remained mostly outside the sphere of this culture.

The monuments of the mysterious dolmen-culture appeared about the same time as the Maikop culture developed (i.e. mid-third millennium BC). The area of this culture covers the whole Western Caucasus (Abkhazia included), but dolmens (burial stone 'houses') are unknown in Georgia, or indeed in other parts of the Caucasus, existing only in the area populated (or historically populated) by Abkhazo-Adygheans. The Russian investigator of the West Caucasian dolmens, V. Markovin, who undertook a comparative analysis of the dolmens of Eurasia, found that the earliest West Caucasian dolmens closely resemble similar monuments found in Thrace (modern European Turkey), Spain, Portugal, southern France, Sardinia, Syria, Jordan, and North Africa. According to the rather plausible conclusion of Markovin (1978, p285), the dolmen culture does not have its genetic roots in the cultures of the Kuban region and Caucasian Black Sea coast but can be regarded as an import from the south-west of Europe. As Markovin suggests, a large group of Mediterranean builders of dolmens might have migrated by sea to the Western Caucasus and settled here. Their first contacts with the local people of the Maikop culture will have been peaceful, so that both co-existed, but later, according to Markovin, the dolmen-builders may have pushed the people of Maikop eastwards, which could explain the eastward spread of this culture. Subsequently, the dolmen-people might have fallen under the cultural influence of the tribes of the Maikop and the later North Caucasian cultures, becoming assimilated by the indigenous population and adopting their language.

As to Abkhazia, the Mediterraneans were perhaps rather quickly assimilated by the proto-Abkhazians. Markovin even noticed local differences in the architectural features of the stone 'houses', which makes it possible to distinguish between the two dolmen-culture areas: north-western, which coincides with the Circassian-speaking domain, and south-eastern, now occupied by the Abkhazians. By the second millennium BC the Mediterranean dolmen-builders would have completely merged with the local Abkhazo-Adyghean tribes, for thereafter no visible population-changes are perceptible in the Western Caucasus. This allows Markovin (1978, pp 321-23) to conclude that the group of people who brought the idea of dolmens to the Western Caucasus would have been one of the major components in the formation of the Abkhazo-Adyghean ethnos.

Other authors, however, deny the imported character of dolmens and attribute their construction exclusively to the ancestors of the Abkhazo-Adygheans. Fedorov (1983, p29) thought that Maikopians were proto-Circassians, while the dolmen-builders were ancestors of the Abkhazians. But dolmens are found in much greater numbers in the North Caucasus than in Abkhazia, and it is difficult to suppose a major Abkhazian expansion to the North Caucasus prior to the periods of the Abkhazian Kingdom and the later northward migration of the ancestors of the Abazinians (Abaza). On the other hand, the identification of the people of the Maikop culture with the ancestors of the Circassians seems quite plausible.

According to Lavrov (1960), the idea of building dolmens was brought to the Caucasus not by a group of newcomers but by West Caucasians who themselves had travelled to the Mediterranean countries, bringing home from there the idea of dolmens. Inal-Ipa (1976, pp 79-100), who is also sceptical about the notion that dolmens were built by foreigners, argued that both archaeological and ethnographic evidence undeniably points to the local population, ancestors of the Abkhazo-Adygheans, as the builders of the dolmens in Western Caucasia. The question, however, remains as to exactly how the idea of building dolmens reached the Caucasus, as it is impossible to separate the West Caucasian dolmens from contemporary parallels found in the Mediterranean.

It is noteworthy that, despite differences in opinion as to the origin of the West Caucasian dolmen-culture, most authors (Lavrov, Inal-Ipa, Markovin, Fedorov) agree that their builders must have been one of the major components in the formation of the Abkhazo-Adygheans. Note that in Northern Anatolia dolmens are unknown, which means that the idea of building them could not have been brought from there to the Caucasus.

Let us now turn to the third of the afore-mentioned themes concerned with the ethnogenesis of the Abkhazo-Adygheans — the problem of Hattic. With Hattic and probably also Kaskian being likely to represent the most ancient specimens of Abkhazo-Adyghean, two important questions arise: firstly, must Hattic be regarded as the oldest attested West Caucasian dialect, or should we rather speak in terms of a Hattic-West Caucasian unity, much as some linguists place Hittite in relation to the rest of the Indo-European languages? Secondly, was the appearance of Hattic (and Kaskian) in central and north-eastern Asia Minor due to migration from the Caucasus, or, on the contrary, did the ancestors of Abkhazo-Adyghean speakers come to inhabit West Caucasia as a result of migration from their ancient Anatolian homeland? The third possibility is that the whole area, including north-eastern Anatolia and West Caucasia, was occupied by ethnically and linguistically related

Abkhazo-Adyghean tribes, who became extinct in Anatolia but who managed to preserve themselves in the mountains of the Western Caucasus.

This last hypothesis finds some justification in the toponyms of both ancient Anatolia and western and south-western Georgia, which might contain traces of an Abkhazo-Adyghean presence. Thus, the typical West Caucasian toponymic element *-psy 'water, river' is probably attested in such ancient Anatolian toponyms as *Aripsa* (city and fortress in northern Anatolia — cf. Diakonov 1968, p84); cf. also the oldest name of the River Ch'orokh in Ajaria (south-west Georgia) and north-eastern Turkey, namely *Apsara*, earlier called *Akampsis*, and the name of the city *Apsaroûs* in Byzantine Lazica (somewhere on the border between modern Ajaria and Turkey). Furthermore, the element -psa is also attested in such West Georgian hydronyms as *Supsa* and *Lagumpsa*.

The fact that Abkhazo-Adyghean toponyms (more specifically, hydronyms) are found not only in the Western Caucasus but also in the south (in West and South Georgia and in north-eastern Anatolia) could support the notion that at the turn of the third and second millennia BC nearly all the coastal area, approximately from modern Sinope in Turkey to Abkhazia and further to the north-west, was populated by proto-Abkhazo-Adyghean tribes (Diakonov, 1968, p13; Gordeziani, 1975, pp 8, 10; Inal-Ipa, 1976, pp 111, 117). It is quite feasible that some of these tribes might have been migrating within this vast expanse, leaving traces in the popular ethnogenetic traditions of these peoples. Thus, the fact that in the eighth century BC Kaskians were still mentioned in Assyrian sources among the peoples inhabiting Anatolia might indicate that only a part of these tribes had moved to the Caucasus, whilst the rest remained in Asia Minor, where they were subsequently assimilated by their neighbours.

Archaeological data also point to the southern connections of ancient West Caucasians, the most impressive of which are the monuments of the Maikop culture. Links with the ancient Middle Eastern civilisations are also attested by the so-called Maikop Tablet (found near Maikop), containing an undeciphered text, the writing-system of which finds some analogues in the system used in Byblos in Phoenicia (13th century BC) and in the signs of Hittite hieroglyphs or even Sumerian pictography.

The formation of the Abkhazian people

According to the data provided by archaeology, from as early as the dolmen-culture one can trace a cultural continuity in Abkhazia up to the times when indisputably Abkhazian tribes become known to history thanks to the reports of Greek and Roman authors. This means that since the second millennium BC the Western Caucasus had not witnessed any significant population-changes.

In the later part of the first millennium BC and the beginning of our era the population of the Caucasian Black Sea coast was characterised by a substantial tribal diversity, as noted by contemporary Greek and Roman writers, who mention here such tribes as Heniokhs, Achaeans, Kerkets, Koraksians, San(n)igs, Missimians, and so on. It is possible that most of them represented linguistically and culturally related tribes. Though Romans and Greeks, sadly, did not record specimens of the speech of the Caucasian tribes with whom they were directly or indirectly familiar, some of the names assigned to them from the start of the modern era can certainly be identified as references to the ancient Abkhazians.

The first known mention of one of these tribes, namely the *(gens) Absilae* (or *Apsilae*), occurs in the *Naturalis historia* of Gaius Secundus Pliny Major (first century AD). The modern continuation of this ethnonym is the Abkhazians' self-designation Apswa (= *'Aps(y)-wa*). In the second century Arrian has Greek *Apsîlai*, whilst seventh century Georgian attests *apshil-eb-i* = Armenian *apsheł-k* 'Abkhazians'. A slightly different rendition is the Old Georgian form *apsar-*, inserted into the Mariam and Machabeli manuscripts of the chronicle known as 'History and Eulogy of the Monarchs' by a scribe presumably demonstrating his erudition and knowledge of neighbouring languages. The text informs us that Queen Tamar of Georgia (1184-1213) gave her son Giorgi the second name Lasha — "which is translated," the chronicler explains, "as 'illuminator of the world' in the language of the Apsars" (in Abkhaz *'a-laṣa* means 'light').

Etymologically Proto-Abkhaz **apçə-wa* (reflecting the alveolo-palatal fricative still used in the Bzyp dialect) is probably derived from the root **pçə* 'die' (**a-* being a deictic prefix, **-wa* the usual ethnic suffix) and originally meant 'mortal one/one destined to die', serving as a general designation for a human being. The designation of humans as 'mortals', common in many traditions, had in ancient times its own ideological significance: all the world was, to the archaic mentality, divided into the realms of immortal gods and mortal humans. The semantic evolution from 'mortal' to the ethnonym 'Abkhazian' can be imagined thus: 'mortal' > 'people' > 'Abkhazian people' (Chirikba 1991).

The name of the other ancient Abkhazian tribe, *Abasgoí/Abaskoí*, first attested in Arrian, is preserved in the form *Abaza*, which is the modern self-designation of the Abazinians (cf. also Turkish *abaza* 'Abkhazian(-Abazinian)', Old Armenian *avaz* and Old Russian *obézǔ* 'Abkhazian').

Conceivably the Greek plural *Abasgoí* has its source in Circassian *abaze-khe*, plural of *abaze*, which today signifies in Circassian only 'Abazinian(s)'.

The modern name by which the Abkhazians are known in Russian and other European languages came via Georgian, where *apkhaz-i* 'Abkhazian' appears relatively late, in the Middle Ages; its original form was most probably **abazkh-i* (cf. Greek *Abasgoí*). The transformation of **abazkh-i* into *apkhaz-i* could have occurred in Mingrelian (as was suggested at the start of the 20th century by Marr), where metathesis

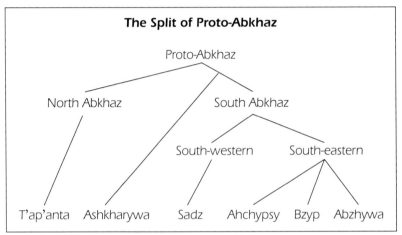

The Split of Proto-Abkhaz

Proto-Abkhaz

North Abkhaz   South Abkhaz

South-western   South-eastern

T'ap'anta   Ashkharywa   Sadz   Ahchypsy   Bzyp   Abzhywa

(transposition of sounds) is a regular phenomenon in consonant-complexes. This Mingrelianised form (with additional devoicing of **b* to *p* by assimilation) will have been borrowed by Georgians, who then passed it on to the Armenians (*apkhaz*), Persians (*ab/fkha:z*) and Russians (*abkhaz*), whence also English acquired *Abkhaz(ian)*. It is most probable, however, that Mingrelians borrowed this term not directly from Circassian *abaze-khe* but from Greek. One can conjecture that the Mingrelian form with *p* (from **b*) was borrowed before Greek beta, originally pronounced [b], was spirantised to [v], whilst the presence of a back fricative indicates that at the time in question Greek gamma, originally [g], had already been spirantised to [ɣ]. But even if the borrowing occurred after the Greek shift of [b] to [v], the cluster in the supposed Mingrelian form **awkhaz-i* (from **awazkh-i*, cf. Georgian *awazgia* 'Abkhazia' in the Georgian chronicle of Juansher) could have given *apkhaz-i*.

Another name known from ancient sources which also refers to an old Abkhazian tribe is the Greek *Misimianoí* 'Missimians' (sixth century Agathias). The most convincing explanation for this ethnonym, referring

Stamp on a shard carrying the name of Bishop Constantine,
first Christian pastor of Apsilia (Ts'ibilium — sixth century)

Fragment of a flag-stone mentioning one of the rulers of Abazgia
(from Tsandripsh — sixth century)

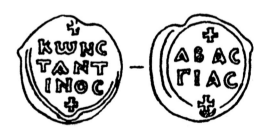

Pendant seal of Constantine the Abazgian
(from Pitsunda — end of seventh-start of eighth century)

to a tribe inhabiting the mountains of ancient Abkhazia in the upper reaches of the River K'odor, derives it from the name of the dominant Abkhazian aristocratic family in that region (around modern Ts'abal/Ts'ebelda) who in later times are known as *Mar'ʃan-aa* 'the Marshans' (Inal-Ipa 1976, pp 233-34).

It is remarkable that the modern Abkhazian name for their country, *Apsny*, seems to be attested as early as the seventh century Armenian Geography in the form *Psinun* (Butba 1990, pp 12-13). The ancient Abkhazian tribes clearly became consolidated into a single nation during the period of the Abkhazian Kingdom (eighth-tenth centuries). Between the 14th and 15th centuries a part of the Abkhazians moved from their historical Transcaucasian homeland to the North Caucasus, into regions formerly occupied by Iranian-speaking Alans, who had been defeated by the Mongol army and had fled the area. These Abkhazian newcomers settled along tributaries of the River Kuban (Great and Little Zelenchuk rivers) and River Kuma. The move was not a single act: various Abkhazian groups at different times were crossing the Great Caucasus range and settling on its northern slopes, rich in land and pastures.

The descendants of these migrants are the present-day T'ap'antas, or Abazinians. Though in specialist literature (mainly historical) one reads that T'ap'anta Abazinians came to the North Caucasus from the territory of north-western Abkhazia and adjoining areas, there are indications (folklore, toponymical, historical and archaeological) pointing at southern Abkhazia as the starting place for at least some (if not all) of the T'ap'anta groups (Lakoba 1991, pp 120-21). Analysis of the Kartvelian (specifically, Mingrelian) loans in T'ap'anta speaks in favour of this view (Dzhonua 1992). Later, probably at the beginning of the 17th century, another group of Abkhazians migrated to the North Caucasus from Abkhazia's mountain-regions — whence their name 'Ashkharywa' (in Abkhaz *a-ʃxa-'ry-wa* means 'mountaineer'). Some Ashkharywa speakers still call themselves *apsawa* 'Abkhazian'. To the present day the Ashkharywa dialect is much closer to Abkhaz proper than to T'ap'anta, though some features of it may be regarded as transitional between the two. Intensive contacts between T'ap'anta and Ashkharywa stimulated the process of their convergence, with overwhelming and ever growing influence of T'ap'anta, on which standard Abaza is based. Note that it was mainly Ashkharywas who migrated in the 19th century to Turkey. The mutual similarity is also strengthened by a considerable Kabardian influence on both of these North Caucasian dialects.

3
On the track of Abkhazia's antiquity
Giorgij Shamba

In origin the Abkhazian people are one of the most ancient inhabitants of the Caucasian Black Sea Littoral and linguistically (along with the Abazinians, Cherkess, Adyghes, Kabardians and Ubykhs) form the Abkhazo-Adyghe language-family in the Western Caucasus.

We Abkhazians have the proverb: *A₃ʷa axy wymhʷakʷ'a ats'yxʷa wyzhʷom* — 'Without saying the start of a word you can't say its end' — and this start says that man has been living in our region since prehistoric times (over half a million years), as attested by a whole series of sites occupied by primitive man of the Lower Palaeolithic epoch known as the 'Acheulian' period. These have been uncovered along the entire territory between the rivers Psou and Ingur — coincident (entirely by chance) with the current administrative borders. Today over 100 locations of ancient stone implements are known here. The best studied are Jashtkhʷa, Ankhʷa, Eshera (Jashyra), Lykhny, Algyta, Gal, the Psou-Khashpsa Delta and many others.

Early inhabitation

The first Stone Age sites were excavated by the Soviet-Russian archaeologists S. Zamjatnin and Lev Solov'ev, work subsequently conducted by their pupils and followers.[1] Drawing a map of palaeolithic monuments shows that their circle hardly extends beyond the frontiers of Abkhazia proper. This circumstance is interpreted by scholars as being dependent upon the favourable climatic conditions of the region, which have remained essentially unaltered to the present day. It is not accidental that gerontologists are inclined to link another phenomenon of our region, Abkhazian longevity, with the unique local natural conditions.

Indeed it is difficult today to name any stage of historical development in Abkhazia without it being represented among its archaeological monuments. To avoid being drawn into the labyrinth of deep antiquity, however, I shall start with a period of history relatively closer to us — namely the beginning of man's intense activity connected primarily with working the soil, which took place about seven to eight thousand years ago. Along the Caucasian Black Sea littoral and in some neighbouring areas the people of the time learned how to fashion implements from wood and stone, with the help of which they started to work the ground for sowing. At the same time it was already known how to bake earthenware dishes, polish weapons to enhance their external appearance, and so on. Naturally these and other innovations cannot have failed to lead to a sharp change in the life of society.

Man's principal achievement from all this was the final shift from gathering ready produce to production itself. This segment of time has been called the Neolithic or New Stone Age, to differentiate it from the Palaeolithic. To the number of best known archaeological monuments of this period belongs the Kistrik settlement, located within the precincts of the town of Gudauta and which was discovered and studied by the local regional specialist A. Lukin; his work has been continued by such experts as V. Bzhania, A. Gabelia and P. Khandzia.[2]

Up to today the circle of these settlements stretches from the district of Greater Sochi to the north-west and to the south-east into the central regions of the Eastern Black Sea littoral. In view of the similarity of tool-shapes, these sites have been united into an area of West-Transcaucasian 'Early Landworking' culture. Specialists such as Zurab Anchabadze, Solov'ev and Otar Dzhaparidze consider that this culture was created by the distant ancestors of the Abkhazo-Adyghe tribes. We observe a continuation of this Early Landworking culture also in the domestic monuments of subsequent periods chronologically linked to the start of the invention of the first metal (copper, copper-bronze) artefacts. Related to this are the settlements of Ochamchira, Mach'ara, G^{w}adikh^{w}y, G^{w}andra, Pichora. According to radio-carbon dating of the precise age of one of these monuments, the Mach'ara settlement has been established to have existed for 5,800 years on the eastern outskirts of Sukhum. Even then stone tools for working the land were widely used; amongst specialists these have come to be known as 'small hoes of the Sochi-Adler' or 'Sukhum' varieties (the terms derive from the places they were first discovered). Similar earth-working tools often appear along the valley of the River Rion (ancient Phasis) in such Mingrelian towns as Samt'redia, Doblagomi, and Natsikhvari.

Most scholars (such as B. Kurgin, Dzhaparidze, Rauf Munchaev, Shalva Inal-Ipa) consider that this West-Transcaucasian Early Landworking culture came in contact with the other contemporary culture of Central Transcaucasia, known as 'Kuro-Araxian', which was brought to an end by the distant ancestors of today's Transcaucasian peoples.

Further development of land cultivation and of the standard of building techniques led to the start of the erection from the end of the third millennium BC on the territory of West Caucasia from Abkhazia up to and including Adyghea of buildings constructed from large stone blocks and styled 'dolmens'. Judging by the excavated materials, these multi-ton structures, in parallel with the Egyptian pyramids, served as tombs. At the same time dolmens had their own local designations — among the Adyghes they are known as: *spywyn*, whilst the Abkhazian term is *ahat'gʷyn*.

Dolmens and cromlechs

Roughly contemporaneous with dolmens, other types of stone-graves were also constructed out of several concentric rings (e.g. those of Eshera [= Jashyra], which were discovered in 1969, had four circles each with a width of 11 metres). In the literature such structures have received the designation 'cromlech' (stone circle). It has been suggested that, given their complex configuration, cromlechs could not have been built without the application of a compass. This therefore leads us to conclude that over 3,000 years ago local builders knew the precise means of tracing a circumference and of measuring different segments of geometric figures as well as how to compose designs and subsequently transfer them onto a building site on an enlarged scale, etc.

Nor does this alone define the significance of cromlechs — the opinion has long taken root that cromlechs, the funeral cult aside, served as a place of observation for keeping watch over the movement of heavenly bodies, the course of the seasons, the change in the weather and other natural phenomena, on which the hard life of primitive man wholly depended. At any rate, the form, dimensions and choice of location of the Esheran cromlechs, from which the movement of the sun, moon and other heavenly bodies can be well observed from dawn to sunset, do not speak against this view.

There can be no doubt that the materials unearthed in dolmens and cromlechs (earthenware pots, tools, adornments) together with the funeral rite linked with them, so-called secondary burial (*apsej'tagara*), were the product of local religious beliefs. All these indicators are characteristic of the material and spiritual culture of the Abkhazo-Adyghean ethnic domain that lasted thousands of years. Ancient Greek, Latin, Arabic, and European literary sources, traditional ethnography and the oral folk-art of the Abkhazians and Adygheans serve as indirect confirmation of this.

It is true that it is not yet firmly established where Caucasian dolmens first developed — on the Black Sea Littoral or in the North West Caucasus — and this is a matter for future research. The important point for us is that dolmens and cromlechs are the oldest surface architectural structures in the Caucasus and in the whole of southern Russia. The period when the dolmen culture flourished extended even into the second millennium. It may be relevant that there occurred in one of the dolmen-culture periods (about 3,800 years ago) an invasion from the Caucasus of the Kaskian tribe into the Hittite Empire, of which cuneiform inscriptions speak with alarm. It has now been plausibly

A typical dolmen, rebuilt outside the State Museum (Sukhum) to illustrate the most ancient burial method attested in Abkhazia

argued that the Kaskians were the ancient forebears of the Adyghe (Circassian/Cherkess) tribes. Another tribe, the contemporary Abeshlas, is known from the sources to have resided in the same area of north-east Asia Minor — reference to the *Kashka* in one Assyrian document from the time of Tiglath-pileser I (1114-1076 BC) is replaced by another to the *Abeshla* in a variant reading, suggesting that the terms were either synonymous or referred to closely related peoples.

Some scholars have hypothesised that the Abeshlas were the distant ancestors of the ancient Abkhazian Apsilian tribes. To speak in the language of archaeology, the period that interests us roughly coincides with the start of the flourishing of Bronze Age culture (12th-ninth centuries BC) and the beginning of the widescale adoption of the iron-industry (ninth-seventh centures BC). This epoch, with reference to the Eastern Black Sea littoral, is provisionally styled the 'Colchian culture',[3] an archaeological term introduced to scholarship relatively recently, in the thirties of the 20th century. It was linked to the remarkable discovery of Bronze Age sites in Abkhazia (Eshera, Primorskoe [Arsaul], Bambora, Mg^{w}ydzyrkh^{w}a), and later during the extension of digs their boundaries of diffusion widened.

Cromlechs from the village of Eshera (2nd millennium BC)

Eastwards this culture reached the Likhi (Surami) Ridge [the divide between west and central Georgia — *editor*], south-eastwards to the town of Ordu (the northern frontiers of Asia Minor), north-westwards abutting the so-called Pri-Kuban culture, attributed to the proto-Adyghean Maeotian tribes. To the north and north-eastwards it abutted the Central Caucasian or so-called Koban culture, created by the distant ancestors of the Ossetes (the Alans). As for the finds of Abkhazia, they form their own local variant of the Bronze and Early Iron cultures. Primarily these are engraved bronze axes with handles, 'foot-rings', conical adornments crowned with figures of birds and animals, laurel-leaved lance-tips and so-called jug burials (an extension of dolmen burial practice). At that time prototypes for Colchian culture in general are represented in the form of bronze artefacts all along the Eastern Black Sea littoral (Ch'orokhi, Ureki, Kobuleti, Gal, Pichori, Gudava, Tageloni, Otobaja, Ochamchira, Myk^w,

T'amsh, Sukhum, Sukhum Hill, Lechkop, Eshera, Lykhny, Pitsunda, Khashpsa, Pilenkovo, Psou).

Worthy of mention is the fact that, over the whole time during which this Colchian culture was developing, no drastic change or substantive alteration in the typology of tools and weapons may be ascribed to the Bronze and Early Iron Periods. Moreover, the iron artefacts of significance (axes, long-bladed axes, spears) repeat with absolute exactness the forms of existing bronze artefacts. This implies that master ironworkers were to a certain extent descendants of local bronze-smelters, but this was a long process that took place over the second half of the second and the start of the first millennium BC. There are some finds where identical bronze and iron artefacts co-exist — e.g. the Eshera find or the Bambora complex — being finds of the transitional eighth-seventh centuries BC period.

At about the same time along the coast of the Eastern Black Sea littoral, again from the Psou to the Ch'orokhi, there developed 'dune-hills' which have received the provisional designation of settlements with 'textile ceramics', discovered by Solov'ev. Comparing the excavated objects (trough-shaped vessels with fabric imprints, little earthenware posts with horn-like tops, etc.) with traditional Abkhazian and Adyghe ethnographic data, Solov'ev concluded that this range of artefacts were fashioned by people occupied in the main with the weaving-trade and salt-working (here it is appropriate to recall the words of the father of history in the fifth century BC, Herodotus, concerning the inhabitants of the Eastern Black Sea littoral, the Colchians, sending the best woven wares to the world markets).

Black Sea expansion

In Urartian cuneiform inscriptions of the eighth century BC, particularly of the Kings Argishti and Sardur II, one finds references to a great union of the Igani or Iganiekhi tribes. Some researchers are inclined to see in these the name of the tribes *Heniokhs*, who figure quite often in ancient authors, and by whom they were considered to be the indigenous occupants of the lands, including Phasis (the lower reaches of the River Rioni) and Dioscurias (Sukhum).

Independently of all this, beginning from the sixth century BC the Caucasian Black Sea littoral became the arena of massive Greek colonisation. As a result, the local population, especially in the guise of its leadership, adapted to a degree to Greek culture, but the basic mass of people, as was only to be expected, continued living by their centuries old customs, which found reflection in the works of Graeco-Roman

Roman tower built atop the citadel of Anakopia, overlooking today's settlement of New Athos

authors, particularly when a description concerned geographic or ethnic taxonomy. Here, for understandable reasons, the record of the ancient authors has been distorted in being wholly adjusted to the language of the writer.

Thus, in conformity with the ancient settlement of Abkhazia the fixed tribal names are: *Corakes* ('ravens'), *Heniokhoi* ('drivers, charioteers'), *Macropōgōnes* ('longbeards', connected with the *Macrocephaloi* 'big-heads'), *Phtheirophagoi* ('lice-eaters'), and other hellenized sobriquets.

Nonetheless, thanks to these literary sources, we have acquired quite early testimony to the location of settlement of the Caucasian Black Sea littoral, including towns and inhabited spots. Thus, Pseudo-Scylaks of Caryanda, a writer of the fourth century BC whose source goes back to the sixth century, knew Dioscurias (Sukhum), Gyenos (Ochamchira), Phasis (Poti) and other settled locations. He also knew the river Apsar-Apsirt (modern Ch'orokhi).

Another author, Pliny Secundus Major (first century AD) in the same region mentions the river Acampseon-Acampsis. As is well known, hydronyms with the element -*ps*-/-*bz*- (which as a nominal root means 'water' in Circassian and Ubykh respectively; cf. Abkhaz *a-'psydz* 'fish') are found the whole length of the Eastern Black Sea littoral (Supsa, Duabza, Lagumpsa, Aapsta, Khipsta, Lashpsa, Bzyp, Nikopsia, Psakhias, Topsida, Isikups, Sheps and many others). There is also a group of toponyms containing the element -q^w*a*, which has been linked to Adyghe q^w*a* 'river-valley' (but cf. Abkhaz *a*-q^w*a'ra* 'stony river-bank'). They are found in central Colchis (modern Western Georgia): Chaq^w'a, Achidaq^w'a, Maltaq^w'a, Boq^w'a, Achq^w'a; in Abkhazia itself: Aq^w'a (Sukhum), Abzhaq^w'a, Tasraq^w'a, Sechq^w'a, and so on.

Starting from these linguistic data, many researchers (including the Georgian Ivane Dzhavakhishvili, the Mingrelian Simon Dzhanashia, plus the Abkhazians Zurab Anchabadze and Shalva Inal-Ipa) have postulated that in early times Abkhazo-Adyghean tribes must have resided in the central and south-eastern parts of Colchis.

This is not contradicted by the statement of Heracleides, a Greek writer of the fourth century BC, that before the coming of the Greeks (i.e. up to the sixth century BC) Heniokhs lived in Phasis. The Roman author of the first century, Pomponius Mela, remarked that Dioscurias (Sukhum) was in Heniokh territory. In the words of the pre-eminent geographer of antiquity, Strabo, at the start of our era, the Heniokhs constituted a great union of tribes, incorporating *inter alia* four kingdoms. In the words of Pliny Secundus, they razed Pitiunt (Pitsunda) to the ground.

The notable specialist on Colchian archaeology, Professor V. Kuftin, has contended that the Heniokhs were the oldest inhabitants of Colchis. Many other specialists in the history and culture of the West Caucasus consider that the Heniokhs of the ancient writers were a collective term for the separate tribes of the Caucasian Black Sea Littoral from whom subsequently the Abkhazo-Adyghe tribes took their origin.

In reality it is impossible to ignore the fact that from the start of our era, when contemporary writers began to become ever more interested in concrete data about local tribes, the provisional term *Heniokh* falls almost into oblivion, whilst in its stead there often came to be utilised the ethnonyms *Apsil, Abazg, Sanig* together with their own political associations and kings. Furthermore, archaeological discoveries during recent decades in Abkhazia and neighbouring localities, in harmony with written sources, have succeeded in attesting cultural artefacts of the Apsilians within the domains of three regions of Abkhazia (those of Gulrypsh, Sukhum and Ochamchira) with a proposed centre at Ts'ebelda (Ts'abal, ancient Tibeleos). Speaking of the area of extent of Apsilian culture during the first century of our era, some archaeologists trace them further to the east, all the way up to Chkhorots'q'u (in Mingrelia).

Individual monuments of Abazgian culture are attested in several places of the Gudauta and Gagra districts. Of great interest in this regard is the Pitsunda archaeological complex of the first centuries AD, located on Abazgian territory. One of the investigators of the Pitsunda burial-ground, Guram Lordkipanidze, has succeeded in tracing the presence of individual burials, so-called secondary interments, in the fifth-sixth centuries, i.e. echoes of dolmen-culture burials characteristic of the Bronze Age. It is noteworthy that this pagan rite was performed beside a Christian church built at the start of the fourth century, where

Golden bowl with biblical relief from the Bedia church. Usually on permanent display in Tbilisi, it was part of an exhibition in 1997 at New York's Metropolitan Museum.

in 325 Stratophil, Bishop of Pitsunda and famed throughout the Christian world, began his ministry. Such a combination of pagan and world (Christian) religions causes us no surprise because, in the words of the sixth century Byzantine historian, Procopius of Caesarea, the Abazgians still in his time ". . . revered groves and trees, deeming them to be gods." In the aforementioned groves and trees of Procopius, one assumes, it is not difficult to see the renowned Pitsunda pine-grove of the tertiary period. In this regard it is not without interest to note that on the eastern fringe of the Pitsunda promontory was located one of the seven holy places of Abkhazia, Sacred Ldzaa, revered by the Abkhazians from prehistoric times.

Ancient inscriptions can also serve in their way as a record for the placing of the Abazgians in these areas. Thus, in 1955 a lead seal of one of the leaders of the Abazgians (circa 700 AD) with the name 'Constantine the Abazgian' was found in Pitsunda (see illustration on p46). Very recently excavations of a church in Tsandrypsh (beside the River Psou) succeeded in unearthing a marble slab with the inscription *'Abazgias'* (see p46), dateable to no later than the sixth century.

Archaeologists have at their disposal several materials left behind by one more of the ancient Abkhazian tribes, the Sanigs.

As for the fourth Abkhazian tribe, the Missimians, in the words of Agathias (sixth century), they lived above the Apsilians in the heights overlooking the River K'odor. The material culture of the Missimians, thanks to their closeness to the Apsilians,[4] hardly differs from that of the latter. Later, at the start of the eighth century, a merging of all the ancient Abkhazian tribes took place into a unified Abkhazian princedom under Leon I with its capital at Anakopia (modern New Athos to the north of Sukhum). This is also the time when Abkhazian nationality began to take shape.

4
History:
first-18th centuries
Oleg Bgazhba

The ancient Abkhazian tribes of Apsilians, Abazgians, Sanigians are known to have dwelt on the territory of Abkhazia from the first centuries of our era. They had split off from the one-time but disintegrated ethno-cultural community of the Heniokhs, who also resided here. Politically speaking, they represented early-class states that were an organic, albeit peripheral, part of the Roman-Byzantine cultural world. For this reason the coastal fortifications of late-classical Abkhazia were part of the outer so-called 'Limes Ponticus' or Pontic Frontier, which was marked by castles at Pitsunda, Sebastopolis, and Ziganis, where the 'Theodosian', 'Claudian' and 'Valentian' cohorts were billeted. In Egypt there served a standing cohort bearing the title of 'First Cohort of the Abazgians'.

During the reign of the Emperor Justinian (527-565), because of the strained relations with Persia, an inner 'Limes Caucasicus' or Caucasian Frontier was also created, which encompassed the fortresses of the Abazgians, Apsilians and the Missimians, one of the Apsilian tribes — Trakhea, Tsibil, Tsakhar, etc. These and a range of other strongholds (Latin cl(a)usura) together with the local garrisons for payment defended the ancient roads along which three branches of the Great Silk Route (roads through Abazgia, Apsilia and Missimiania) began to run, as a result of Persian-Byzantine wars, over the territory of Abkhazia to the North Caucasus. It is not excluded that it was along just these paths that Byzantine monks brought over by way of contraband in their staffs the silkworm from China to Europe.

Control over the ancient Abkhazian early class states of the empire was effected via neighbouring Lazica, with which Apsilia had a border in the sixth century roughly along the basin of the River Ingur. But the relations of the ancient Abkhazian tribes with Byzantium were not unclouded. Proof of this are the battles by the walls of Trakhea (550) or Tsakhar (556) as well as the confrontation at the fortress of Tsibilium. It is entirely natural that the whole male population was mobilised, having as weapons swords of wrought damask (the earliest attestation of damask-steel on the territory of the former USSR), axes for hurling — 'Frenchies', with huge tips and leaden stabilisers against Persian elephants, catapults, and many others.

From the second to the seventh century on the territory of Abkhazia there existed the original 'Ts'ebelda/Ts'abal culture', defined by settlements, burials, town-sites, fortresses, churches, and so on.

It is widely believed that the first preaching of Christianity on the territory of Abkhazia was carried out by Andrew the First-Called and Simon the Canaanite — the latter according to ecclesiastical legend was buried in New Athos (north of Sukhum). The first reliable evidence, however, on the Christians of Abkhazia belongs to the end of the third and start of the fourth century, when Pitiunt (Pitsunda) was turned into a place of banishment for Christians, and so that is where their first community was formed in the Caucasus. Stratophil, Bishop of Pitiunt, represented this community at the first ecumenical church council at Nicaea in 325. Officially the local population of Abkhazia adopted Christianity in the thirties-forties of the sixth century during the reign of the Emperor Justinian the Great. It was at this time that the local population started to wear crosses beneath their clothing. The first pastor amongst the Apsilians was a Bishop Constantine (see illustration on p46). At the Imperial Court in Constantinople a school was founded where Abkhazian children were given special tuition, and at his own expense a church was constructed in Abkhazia itself by Justinian.

The split from the Greeks

In the seventh-eighth centuries power passed by right of inheritance in Abkhazia — a list of these rulers survives under the title of the 'Divan of Abkhazian Kings'. It is worth pointing out that the Abkhazian king Constantine II (he is the one to whom the pendant seal carrying the inscription 'Constantine the Abazgian' belongs — see illustration on p46) was married to the daughter of a Khazar king, whose sister was wife of the Byzantine emperor Constantine V. In 708-711, on his way back from Alania[1] to Byzantium, Lev the Isaurian visited here; he was the future emperor of Byzantium and progenitor of the Isaurian dynasty.

In 737 the Arab army of Murwan II ibn Muhammed invaded the Transcaucasus. It suffered a shattering defeat by the walls of Anakopia, the chief fortress of the Abkhazian princedom and subsequently the original capital of the Abkhazian Kingdom. This victory, as well as the support of the Byzantine Emperor Lev the Isaurian, and a dynastic marriage with Gurandukht', youngest daughter of Mir, king of Kartli, all helped Leon I the Abasgian to become ruler of a vast territory encompassing Abazgia, Apsilia, Missimiania and the Laz Kingdom — in practice almost the whole of Western Transcaucasia — which led through the passage of time to the formation of the early feudal state known as the Abkhazian Kingdom. The anonymous author of a Georgian chronicle of the 11th century describes this important event thus:

> "When the (Byzantine) Greeks grew weak, the ruler of the Abkhazians split off from them; by name he was Leon, nephew (being son of his brother) to the ruler Leon, upon whom possession of Abkhazia had been bestowed by right of inheritance. This second Leon was son of the daughter of the Khazar king and, availing himself of their (sc. Khazarian) might, divorced himself from the Greeks, seized control of Abkhazia and Egrisi as far as the Likhi (mountains)[2] and took upon himself the name of King of the Abkhazians."
>
> (See p251 of Q'aukhchishvili's 1955 edition of the Georgian chronicles = *Kartlis Tskhovreba* I, or pp 56-57 of Amichba [Amch'ba] 1988, where a Russian translation is appended).

This event is usually dated to between 788 and 797 (or the very end of the eighth century). From this time the Abkhazian Kingdom, one of the most powerful early-feudal states in the Caucasus, emerged into the political arena, and its capital was transferred from Anakopia to Kutaisi (in today's west Georgian province of Imereti). All of this hastened the process of consolidation between the Abkhazian tribes, the result of which became the shaping by the ninth century of an Abkhazian feudal nationality, the common ancestor of both the Abkhazians proper and also the Abazinians, which latter were later to resettle in the North Caucasus, where they live to the present day. This crossing via the K'lukhor Pass occurred in the 14th century in the wake of changes consequent upon the Mongol incursions into the Caucasus.

The Abkhazian Kingdom, with the Leonid dynasty at its head, lasted for some two centuries and was at its height by the time it came to an end. The Abkhazian kings conducted an active eastern policy in Transcaucasia in the struggle with Armenia for Kartli. Thus, the Abkhazian king Constantine III made an inscription on the Samts'evrisi church near Khashuri (the very centre of Georgia) where one reads of the construction here of a canal in the twentieth year of his reign. Another inscription concerns Hereti (an old eastern province of Georgia incorporating Saingilo in today's Azerbaijan) — this inscription on the

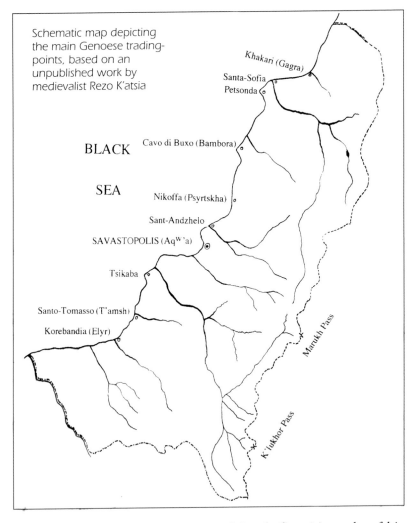

Schematic map depicting the main Genoese trading-points, based on an unpublished work by medievalist Rezo K'atsia

Khakari (Gagra)

Santa-Sofia
Petsonda

BLACK

Cavo di Buxo (Bambora)

SEA

Nikoffa (Psyrtskha)

Sant-Andzhelo

SAVASTOPOLIS (Aq^W'a)

Tsikaba

Santo-Tomasso (T'amsh)

Korebandia (Elyr)

Marukh Pass

K'lukhor Pass

Eredvi church (in today's province of South Ossetia) speaks of his campaign in this region. The cathedral at Ch'q'ondidi (later Mart'vili and known in Soviet times as Gegech'k'ori) in Mingrelia in particular was built by Constantine's successor, Giorgi II, who founded there an episcopate and adorned the cathedral with relics of the holy martyrs.

With the help of this king Byzantium effected the conversion of Alania in the North Caucasus. In the time of another Abkhazian king, Leon III, a cathedral was raised at Myk^w (near Ochamchira), where an episcopal seat was established. Then in 964 he had a constructional inscription done on the K'umurdo church (east of modern Vardzia, which is just north of the Georgian-Turkish border). This allows us to conclude that the south-eastern frontier of the Abkhazian Kingdom extended at this period to around the modern, largely Armenian-populated town of Akhalkalaki in southern Georgia.

Towards the end of the tenth century (975-978) the eastern policy of the Abkhazian Kingdom, which was leading objectively to the unification of a significant part of Western and Central Transcaucasia, found completion in the formation of a new state — the 'Kingdom of the Abkhazians and the Kartvelians' — which later became famous as the united Georgian Kingdom. Bagrat' III, whose father was Georgian (Gurgen IV of the west Georgian province of K'larjeti, in today's Turkey; his adoptive father was Davit III of T'ao, also now in Turkey) but whose mother, Gurandukht', belonged to the royal family of the Leonids, became in 978 the first king of this kingdom.

Arrival of the Genoans

It was also during the tenth century that the language of the church in Abkhazia shifted from Greek to Georgian (Inal-Ipa, 1965, p570). Up to the beginning of the 12th century Kutaisi remained the capital of the kingdom 'of the Abkhazians and Kartvelians' (Tbilisi became the capital only from 1122, after the expulsion from there of the Arab emirate that had been established in the seventh century), but the title of the Georgian Bagrat'ids preserved up to the middle of the 13th century in first place the name of the Abkhazians as a tribute to the memory of their leading role in the unification of the country. One can read about this not only in the Georgian chronicles but also on the coins of Bagrat' IV and Giorgi II found in the Abkhazian village of Lykhny — 'King of the Abkhazians and Kartvelians and the Most Noble' (*nobilissimus*). And at the royal Georgian court itself at the end of the 12th century the language of the ancestors of the contemporary Abkhazians (in the Georgian rendering 'Apsar' from the native Abkhazian ethnonym *Apswa*) was still well-known and respected. Thus, Queen Tamar (1184-1213) gave her son Giorgi the second name Lasha, which, as the chronicler noted, "is translated from the language of the Apsars[3] as enlightener of the universe" — in Abkhaz *'a-laşa* means 'clear, bright' and *'a-laşa-ra* 'brightness; enlightenment'.

Subsequently the development of feudal relations and the incursion of the Mongols helped to bring about the disintegration of the kingdom of the Abkhazians and Kartvelians (starting from the second half of the 13th century), which led in the final analysis to the formation of a host of kingdoms and princedoms, including that of Abkhazia.

At the head of the Abkhazian princedom (the Tskhum province) stood representatives of the Chachba family.[4] This surname is possibly first mentioned in the middle of the 11th century in connection with the siege of Anakopia.

The struggle between the Abkhazian Chachba and the Mingrelian Dadiani princes for Tskhum province lasted throughout the 14th century, as a result of which a section of the province became part of a new political entity, the Mingrelian princedom of Sabediano.

At the same time Genoese trading posts appeared in the territory of Abkhazia. The largest was called Sevastopolis/Savastopolis, which flourished as an important commercial and industrial centre and figures on European maps over the following 200 years (see the map on p62). The city's quarters, as before, spread over the left bank of the River Basla. On the red banner of the town was depicted a human palm, features retained as part of the modern flag of the post-Soviet Republic of Abkhazia (see p21).

Apart from Sevastopolis, other trading-posts were set up by the Genoese: Kakari (Gagra), Santa-Sofia (Alahadzy), Petsonda (Pitsunda), Cavo-di-Buxo (Bambora/Gudauta), Nikofia (Anakopia) and Tamansa/Tomasso (T'amsh). Administratively speaking, all these colonies were subject to the town of Kaffe (modern Feodosia in the Crimea).

In 1330 there already existed in Sevastopolis a large Catholic community with its own bishopric and cemetery, testifying to the settled nature of the Italian community. By the 15th century Sevastopolis had become the main port of the whole Eastern Black Sea Littoral; the Genoese even had a consul based here, as attested as early as 1354. The town also had Mingrelians, Armenians, Jews and Muslims living there. This was a time when differences were emerging between the Genoese and local princes, but which were successfully settled with the usual mixture of diplomacy and gifts.

It is impossible to underestimate the significance of the Genoese colonisation of Abkhazia in the 14th-15th centuries, for at this period, disregarding the slave trade, there was a flourishing of the local material culture, seen in the monuments which have been discovered by archaeologists during recent decades (fortresses, churches with graveyards and so on). At the same time a transit route for trade began to operate in the Middle Ages across Abkhazia to the North Caucasus (Genoa-Golden Horde).

Throughout the 15th-16th centuries the Mingrelian Dadiani princes sought to gain control of the remaining part of Abkhazia as far as Dzhigeti (i.e. the coastal area incorporating Sadz, Ubykh and neighbouring Circassian territory, known in Georgian as Dzhiketi), which was ruled by the native Abkhazian Chachba princes. As a result of this, the political boundaries of the Abkhazian and Mingrelian princedoms were constantly changing depending upon the situation, war or peace.

In the 17th century there occurred between the Abkhazian and Mingrelian feudals an internecine 'Thirty Year War', which was notable for its extraordinary cruelty. A most active part in this war was taken by representatives of the North-West Caucasian peoples — Sadz Abkhazian, Ubykh and West Circassian 'Dzhigets', Abazinians, East Circassian Kabardians — whom the Abkhazians urged to come to their help. As a result, its former territories of the Tskhum and, in part, the Bedian provinces were returned to the Abkhazian princedom. This facilitated the presence in these territories of significant communities of Abkhazian-speaking peasants. In this way the ethnic frontier between Abkhazians and Kartvelians, which until the start of the second millennium of our era had extended as far as the River Ingur, was not only restored but acquired simultaneously a state-political status, which has now been preserved for 300 years.

A Turkish fleet first appeared off the walls of Sevastopolis a year after the capture of Constantinople by Ottoman Turks, and in 1475, with the fall of Kaffe, the Genoese colonial system in the Black Sea was over. In 1578 the Turks settled in a very short time over the shores of the bay of Sukhum and in the first half of the 17th century, unable to gain control of the coast by land, blockaded it with their fleet from the sea. In 1723 they erected the fortress of Anaklia at the mouth of the Ingur and a year later built another fortress with four bastions on the ruins of ancient Sevastopolis. In the 1730s from 70 to 112 Turkish soldiers served in Sukhum-Kale (as Sevastopolis began to be called), with more than 70 in Anaklia.

Strengthening of political, economic and cultural contacts with the Ottoman Empire over the course of the 16th to 18th centuries led to the gradual spread of Sunni Islam amongst part of the Abkhazian population — starting with the feudals and their circle. During the time of Turkish domination the slave trade also flourished in Abkhazia, the source, no doubt, of the Abkhaz-speaking African community that could still be found around the village of Adzjʷybzha until well into the 20th century.

Conclusion

We have demonstrated that Abkhazia together with its autochthonous population enjoyed a history quite independent of any Kartvelian entity up to the time when, by right of dynastic succession, the united kingdom of the Abkhazians and Kartvelians came to subsume the 200-year-old Abkhazian Kingdom in 978. Following the disintegration of the united feudal Georgian state, which had gained control over much of the

Caucasus, in the wake of the Mongol invasions Abkhazia again became quite separate from the various Kartvelian kingdoms or principalities.

It had been intended to include in this volume a number of maps of the region dating from the 13th century to 1808 and thus coinciding with part of the period covered in this chapter, but their quality was not good enough for reproduction. The schematic map on p62, however, based on a work completed in 1986 (though yet to appear) by medievalist Rezo K'atsia, indicates the main trading points typically found on Italian maps of 13th-14th centuries, different spellings being attested on different maps. The earliest such chart of the Black Sea (of Venetian origin) that was to appear here hails from the 13th century, and immediately beneath the country name 'Abcazia' marks 'Chakari', followed by such toponyms as 'Peronda', 'Cauo de Bux', 'Sauastopoli', 'Tamusi' and 'Corbendina'. Given the Abkhazian etymology of Gagra ('Kakari' and variants) explained in the Introduction, we can give the lie at once to the following claim by Nadareishvili (1996, p7): "There exist about 15 historical maps of Abkhazia from the first to the 17th centuries . . . All historical names entered on them are Georgian, Kartvelian." T. Menke's map of the Black Sea coast from 1311 to 1390 includes under the country name 'Abasgia' the toponyms 'Cacari', 'Pezonda', 'Savastopoli', 'Tomasso' and 'Corbondia'. A Genoese chart dating from 1373-1399, though rather difficult to decipher, styles the country 'Anogazia'. The chart of Gulielmus Soleri (1385) places the open right hand of friendship symbol against the capital 'Savastopolli' and clearly includes 'Cacari' among some (again difficult to read) place names.

S. J. Shaw's *History of the Ottoman Empire and Modern Turkey* (vol. 1, Cambridge, 1976) includes a map entitled 'Decline of the Ottoman Empire and Rise of the Turkish Republic 1683-1975' which marks Abhazia (sic.), Mingrelia and Georgia as separate losses to the Ottoman Empire in the years 1775-1812. And finally C. M. Reinecke's map of 1808 for Asia Minor contains the name 'Absne' against the region, plainly an attempt to render the native designation 'Apsny'.

Direct relations with such non-adjacent states as Rome, Byzantium, Italy and Turkey were thus if great significance for Abkhazia for most of the first 18 centuries of the modern era.

5
History:
18th century-1917
Stanislav Lak'oba

In the eighties of the 18th century the Abkhazian Keleshbey Chachba (Shervashidze, according to the Georgian variant of the family's surname) suddenly found himself in power as Abkhazia's sovereign prince. Over three decades he conducted an independent state-policy, successfully manoeuvring between the interests of Turkey and Russia. The prince was distinguished for his intelligence, cunning and resolution, and his name was widely known beyond the frontiers of the Caucasus. Of tall stature, with a sharply lined face and flaming hair, he easily stood out from those around him and arrested the attention of his contemporaries — military men, diplomats and travellers.

Keleshbey speedily subordinated to himself the feudal aristocracy of Abkhazia, relying on the minor nobility and 'pure' peasants (Abkhaz *anxa'jᵂy-tskja*), each of which was armed with rifle, sabre and pistol. This permanent guard consisted of 500 warriors. Whenever war threatened, Keleshbey in no time at all would put out a 25,000-strong army, well armed with artillery, cavalry and even a naval flotilla. Up to 600 military galleys belonging to the ruler permanently cruised the length of the Black Sea coast from Batumi to Anapa — the fortresses at Poti (in Mingrelia) and Batumi (in Georgia) were under the command of his nephews and kinsmen.

During the first stage of his activities Keleshbey enjoyed the military and political backing of Turkey, under whose protectorate Abkhazia found itself. At the period when these relations were flourishing, the ruler built a 70-cannon ship in Sukhum and presented it to the Sultan.

However, Keleshbey, like his ruler-father Mancha (Manuchar) Chachba, who had been banished by the Sultan in the middle of the 18th century to Turkey along with his brothers Shirvan and Zurab, nurtured the secret dream of a fully free and independent Abkhazian state. Mancha and his brothers had been banished after his relative Khut'unia had fought against the Turks in 1757, killing 16 Turks before being killed himself. The Turks, in revenge, inspired a revolt against Mancha, ruler of the Bzyp lands, and finally banished him.

Keleshbey remembered how the Turkish authorities had dealt with his family. Only his uncle Zurab had succeeded in returning to Abkhazia and become ruler. During the time the Chachba princes were in exile, the Esheran princes, surnamed Dzjapsh-Ipa, had strengthened their position in Abkhazia, occupying the environs of Sukhum. Being unable to fight with such a family, Zurab attempted to preserve friendly relations with it and even married his nephew Keleshbey to a Dzjapsh-Ipa princess. Enlisting the support of this influential family, Zurab in 1771 raised a popular uprising against the Turks and expelled them from Sukhum. However, as a result of the treachery of one of the Chachbas, the Turks soon retook Sukhum fortress and then, eliminating Zurab, recognised Keleshbey as ruler of Abkhazia.

Keleshbey kept an attentive eye on the consolidation Russia was achieving in Eastern Georgia, where in 1801 the combined kingdom of Kartli and Kakheti had been abolished. The ruler hoped that the tsarist military presence in the Transcaucasus was a temporary phenomenon. Because of this, in 1803 he took the first purely formal step towards rapprochement with Russia, intending with its assistance to rid himself of Turkey's protectorate, which indeed happened after the unsuccessful assault of the Turkish fleet (three military vessels and eight rowing-boats) upon the shores of Abkhazia on July 25th 1806. Keleshbey had time to prepare and paraded an Abkhazian-Adyghean army of many thousands around the Sukhum fortress. The fleet swung about and departed.

The ruler of Abkhazia more than once launched raids into the territory of Mingrelia and Imereti; his armies reached as far as Kutaisi. On the left bank of the River Ingur he secured for himself the fortress of Anaklia. In 1802 Keleshbey sent a 20-thousand strong army with three cannon against the ruler of Mingrelia, Grigori Dadiani, and took hostage his son and heir, Levan. The desperate straits of Grigori Dadiani, powerless to restrain the onslaught of the king of Imereti, Solomon II, from one side and the Abkhazian ruler Keleshbey from the other forced him to become the first in Western Georgia to have recourse to the military assistance of Russia and to enter under its protection in 1803.

Russia tightens its grip

From this moment Mingrelia found itself at the spearhead of Russian politics in the region. However, weak-willed Grigori Dadiani was not suited to this role; it was his energetic and power-loving wife, Nina, who captured the ever greater attention of the tsarist authorities and the military command.

On October 24th 1804 Grigori Dadiani died unexpectedly. According to the testimony of the Catholic priest Nikolaj, the ruler of Mingrelia was poisoned by roast chicken, seasoned with venom, and, when he felt unwell, he was brought pills filled with opium. Father Nikolai informs us that all this was perpetrated by Princess Nina.

Relations between Russia and Abkhazia sharply deteriorated then and there, since the son of the poisoned ruler of Mingrelia was in the hands of Keleshbey. The Russian authorities demanded that Levan Dadiani be handed over at once. Keleshbey's impudent refusal was answered with military action: in March 1805 the Russian General Rykgof recaptured the fortress of Anaklia. As a result of hard negotiations, the Abkhazian ruler on April 2nd 1805 returned the hostage Levan, who had become the formal Mingrelian ruler, though at the time the effective ruler of Mingrelia right until Levan's coming of age remained his mother, Nina Dadiani. In response the Abkhazian ruler again seized the fortress of Anaklia in the Ingur estuary. At just this period Keleshbey was seeking to repair foreign relations with Napoleon's France and was even conducting a correspondence with its celebrated minister of foreign affairs, Talleyrand.

With the outbreak of the Russo-Turkish war (1806-1812), Russia sought to make use of Keleshbey in its own interests, the more so as the Russians had doubted the sincerity of Keleshbey ever since he made overtures to Russia. One of the influential officials in St Petersburg wrote in June 1806: "It is necessary to ascertain how frank is the devotion to Russia of Keleshbey."

In 1807 the Russian authorities directly suggested to the 60-year-old ruler of Abkhazia that he recapture the Turkish fortress at Poti, but he avoided any kind of military action. Count Gudovich, the commander of the armies of Russia in the Caucasus, was actively incited against Keleshbey by General Rykgof, who had become the Abkhazian ruler's sworn enemy. Thus, in a report of June 8th 1807 Rykgof notes: "Keleshbek (sic) only outwardly shows his friendship to Russia." In answer Count Gudovich addresses himself in a letter to Keleshbey with these harsh charges: "You did not take action to help our armies against the Turks; moreover, there is a growing suspicion regarding you that you are rendering help to the Turks' (July 14th 1807)."

With these important documents all mention of Keleshbey ceases for about a year. In all probability, the Russian forces in the Caucasus, spurred on by the ruler of Mingrelia, Nina Dadiani, decided to eliminate the obstinate Keleshbey and, utilising a truce with Turkey, to establish at the head of the Abkhazian princedom the ruler's illegitimate son, Seferbey, who enjoyed no right of succession but was the brother-in-law of Nina Dadiani.

The main pretender to the Abkhazian throne was Keleshbey's oldest son (by his first wife, a Dzjapsh-Ipa), by name Aslanbey, whom they determined to discredit. To achieve these aims Seferbey, with the support of Nina Dadiani and the active collaboration of the Russian military administration in the person of General Rykgof, organised a plot against Keleshbey, as a result of which he perished in the Sukhum fortress on May 2nd 1808.

Immediately after this killing the tone of the representative of the Russian administration changed in relation to the activity of Keleshbey. If about a year earlier Count Gudovich had accused the ruler of having a pro-Turkish orientation, already on May 20th 1808 he was informing Russia's Minister of Foreign Affairs, Count Rumiantsev, of "the death of Russia's devoted servant, the Abkhazian ruler Kelesh-bey . . ." It is from this time that the myth was created of the alleged devotion of Keleshbey Chachba to the Russian throne, and this myth exists to the present day.

The entire blame in official Russian documents of that time for the killing of Keleshbey is shifted onto Aslanbey, who is styled a "parricide." It was from none other than Seferbey and Rykgof that Count Gudovich received the very first accounts containing a description of this incident. At the same time the attempts of Aslanbey himself to clarify the situation were paid no attention by the Russian command. Thus, General Rykgof in a report to Count Gudovich says of Aslanbey: "In this evil deed he refuses to acknowledge his guilt under any pretext, referring to a plot against Keleshbey by outsiders. I have not so far responded to these letters of his . . ."

Such a strange reaction on the part of the general can only betoken that he and Gudovich were well aware of the true state of affairs. It would seem that their plan was to get rid of the independent-minded Keleshbey and set Seferbey on the throne. However, this scheme was only half realised. To the immense surprise of the organisers of the plot, it transpired that Seferbey did not command any authority among the Abkhazian community, whilst the people's entire sympathies were on the side of the "parricide" Aslanbey, now ruler of Abkhazia. Such a turn of events did not at all suit the tsarist authorities, and especially Nina Dadiani. Thus, on June 8th 1808 she informed the Russian emperor, Alexander I, that with her in Zugdidi was "our brother-in-law Sefer-bey" (he was married to Tamar Dadiani, sister of Grigori), who had given in her home an oath of fidelity to Russia and requested the help and assistance of the Russian forces in the struggle with the new ruler,

Aslanbey. The ruler of Mingrelia wrote that, in the event of Seferbey being recognised and Abkhazia being accepted as a subject of Russia, the border of the empire will be extended to the Crimea, for "the Abkhazians are not few in number." In reality Nina Dadiani was striving not so much for Russia but rather to pursue her own goals, understanding well the strategic and commercial importance of Abkhazia.

At the beginning of August 1808 Rykgof moved the combined forces of the ruler of Mingrelia and her two brothers-in-law, Manuchar (from Samurzaq'an[o]) and Seferbey Chachba, to Sukhum by order of Count Gudovich. But there succeeded in coming to the aid of Aslanbey in Sukhum his first cousin, the commandant of the Poti fortress, Kuchukbey Chachba (nephew of Keleshbey) with an army on three ships; by land about 300 Circassians arrived. The military operation, prepared by Rykgof, was not crowned with success. The fortress of Sukhum was not only not captured, but Seferbey returned back to Mingrelia.

As a result, the authority of Aslanbey rose even more. He enjoyed the strong support of the people, the upper strata of Abkhazian society, whilst his standing was high among the numerous offspring of Keleshbey (for example, his brother Hassanbey), which, given the mentality of the Abkhazians, could just not have been the case, had Aslanbey in fact killed his own father. Moreover, Aslanbey, who was married to the Sadzian (Dzhigetian) princess Gech (G'achba), enjoyed great respect in the West Abkhazian community of Sadzen and also among the Ubykhs and Adyghes.

In this way the official point of view of the Russian authorities, seeking to defame Aslanbey by charging him with parricide, remained only on paper and failed to turn the people away from the legitimate ruler.

It is necessary to note especially that over the course of almost the last 200 years, local historiography has been dominated by this theme of parricide, which was in truth a fabrication of the Russian military and administrators in the years 1808-10 for specifically political purposes.

At the same time Nina Dadiani, who had in reality poisoned her own husband, was given every conceivable support by the tsarist authorities, who defended her solely because she served the interests of Russia. Moreover, it was with Nina's help that they actively spread the rumours about Aslanbey being the alleged murderer of his father.

But the policy of discreditation had no success. Aslanbey enjoyed unconditional authority in the land also for the reason that Seferbey, who spent most of his time in Mingrelia under the defence of Russian bayonets, continually "kept asking to be given military forces to take the fortress of Sukhum, since he was left almost completely enfeebled and even in banishment." The Russian military requested that the Black Sea flotilla be despatched "to occupy Sukhum, where the parricide Arslan (sic) is gaining strength."

Assault on Sukhum

In an atmosphere of powerlessness, the well-known 'pleading points' of Seferbey (baptised Giorgi) also appear on August 12th 1808 in an appeal to Alexander in connection with the adoption of Abkhazia as a subject of Russia; they were composed in the Georgian language in Mingrelia under the dictation of Nina Dadiani and her confessor, the arch-priest Ioseliani. With rash frankness Seferbey informed the Tsar that all the appeals concerning the amalgamation of Abkhazia with Russia were written by "Ioann Ioseliani, who with a sincere heart advised me to deliver myself for protection to the Imperial throne."

It was on the basis of these illegal pleading points that Alexander on February 17th 1810 recognised Giorgi (Seferbey) in his charter "as the hereditary prince of the Abkhazian domains under the supreme protection, power and defence of the Russian Empire."[1] However, the moment this charter appeared — and for a significant time thereafter — Seferbey lived without interruption in the Russian province of Mingrelia and had no influence at all over Abkhazian affairs, which already for about two years had been governed by its legitimate ruler, Aslanbey. Seferbey himself, via Ioseliani the Mingrelian cleric, several times appealed to St Petersburg as he impatiently awaited both "royal charters and a landing-force from the Crimea for the subjugation of Sukhum-Kale."

But the unexpected happened. When, in June 1810, a Colonel Simonovich notified Seferbey in Kutaisi in the presence of the Mingrelian ruler Nina of the despatch of the charter and other royal decorations and requested that "he immediately set out for Abkhazia to receive them with necessary ceremonial," Seferbey refused point-blank. He explained to Simonovich that "it was exceedingly dangerous for him to receive them at the present time when his brother and rival commands Sukhum and thus virtually the whole of Abkhazia and that he (Aslanbey), hearing of his confirmation as ruler, when having been himself confirmed by the Porte, would assuredly attack him with Turkish forces, destroy and expel them all from Abkhazia."

Powerless, Seferbey asked for an adjournment of the ceremony "until such a time as Russian forces would reach Sukhum, and then with its subjugation under the power of his people he might be able to accept the marks of the All-gracious benevolence towards him."

General Tormasov, commander-in-chief in Georgia and on the Caucasian Line, 1808-11, "never expected" such a turn of events and was simply furious. He did not imagine that the new "legitimate ruler of all Abkhazia would be so impotent in the territory now assigned to his governance or that he would even fear to receive the royal charter of confirmation and the other signs of distinction and be unable to journey to his own home in Abkhazia through dread of his own brother . . ."

Furthermore, Seferbey actually appealed in person by letter to General Tormasov, requesting the help of Russian troops "without whom he could not even travel out of Mingrelia to his own domain." The Russian military administration found itself in a difficult position, but it was by now unable to refuse protection to Seferbey, since the charter of Alexander had been signed. Tormasov in his own instruction to Simonovich of June 15th 1810 noted that "there now remained no alternative for maintaining him other than to subjugate the fortress of Sukhum through force of arms and that by this means they should carry Sefer-Ali-bey into power over Abkhazia."

In this very epistle he shows interest in the details of the situation obtaining in Abkhazia and in the influence of Aslanbey. "Also give the ruler of Mingrelia, Princess Nina Georgievna, to understand," wrote Tormasov, "that the protections and grace shown by the Sovereign to Sefer-Ali-bey were consequent upon respect for her family-ties with him and thanks to her representation, and therefore she should with all possible means back him and confirm him as ruler of Abkhazia."

Thus had the fate of Aslanbey and the fortress of Sukhum-Kale been predetermined. According to the Russian war plan, it was envisaged that Sukhum would be stormed by a naval landing and a thrust by land from Mingrelia under the command of Major-General Orbeliani. By this time Russia had already recaptured the Turkish fortress at Poti. It remained to take Sukhum in order to secure control over the east coast of the Black Sea.

In March 1810 Admiral Marquis de Traverse, who was in charge of the ministry of naval military forces, issued an order on the cruising of Russian boats between Anapa and Sukhum, whilst on June 10th Vice-Admiral Jakovlev instructed Rear-Admiral Sarychev to despatch from Sevastopol to Sukhum a squadron composed of the 60-gun ship Varaxiil, the two frigates Voin and Nazaret, one advice-boat Konstantin, and two gunboats, with a battalion of four naval regiments of 640 men under the command of Lieutenant-Captain Dodt.

At four o'clock on the afternoon of July 8th 1810, this military squadron launched its raid on Sukhum; fire was opened on it from the fortress with cannon and guns. The following day the squadron drew closer, and at three in the afternoon it unleashed a storm of fire on the fortress from its own artillery. By evening almost the whole of the fortress artillery had been smashed and the town buildings demolished.

The seven Turkish boats anchored in the bay were sunk. On the morning of June 10th, Dodt disbarked a battalion of naval infantry with two cannon under the command of Major Konradin. However, it transpired that the landing-party had no siege-ladders.

Nevertheless, as a result of a two-hour bombardment by land and from sea the gates collapsed, and the Russian troops occupied the fortress. From the direction of the River K'odor a company of the Belevian regiment entered the town with two guns, headed by General Orbeliani, who had replaced the deceased Rykgof in the spring of 1809, and Russia's henchman, Seferbey.

Aslanbey was forced to secrete himself amongst his relatives in the Abkhazian community of Sadzen. In the fortress, according to Dodt's testimony, 300 Abkhazians and Turks were killed and 75 persons taken prisoner. The Russian landing-party lost 109 officers and men either dead or wounded. Dodt captured 62 cannons, 1,080 puds of gunpowder and much shot.

That same year up to 5,000 Abkhazians were resettled to Turkey. This was the first wave of Abkhazian emigration in the 19th century.

Peace with Turkey

As we have seen, it is impossible to describe these events as the "voluntary unification of Abkhazia with Russia" — a view which has remained the official point of view to the present day. As the documents show, the circumstances of those years are not so simple and merit detailed investigation, including study of not only the Russian texts but also of Turkish sources.

The military capture of Sukhum-Kale was but the first step of the aggressive policy of tsarist Russia in Abkhazia. To achieve a position of strength here Russia required a further half century of war against the Abkhazian people. The struggle between Seferbey and Aslanbey was principally a struggle between two influences: Russian and Turkish, whilst the taking of Sukhum-Kale was the victory not of Seferbey over Aslanbey but of Russia over Turkey in the battle for Abkhazia.

Seferbey, supported by Russian bayonets, still enjoyed no respect among the people, even though he moved to live in the Sukhum fortress, the only place in Abkhazia where he could feel safe. It was here by order of Tormasov in the autumn of 1810 under the guard of more than 100 Russian soldiers and officers that were conveyed, by a Colonel Merlin, the charter of Alexander I and the other signs of distinction that had been kept in the Poti fortress. Seferbey received them in Sukhum "at an assembly" and gave "publicly before the people an oath of eternal fidelity" to the Emperor of Russia, confirming it "with his own signature and seal."

However, the military authorities of Russia had an excellent understanding of the weakness of Seferbey and that "his party is still not terribly strong against his rival" Aslanbey, whose people in December 1810 still controlled even the outskirts of Sukhum despite the presence of 1,000 Russian soldiers. In March 1811 one reads in a document that Seferbey had "the smallest party," while the ruler Nina Dadiani feared an attack on Mingrelia from "the Abkhazians and mountaineers, who for the most part are followers of Arslanbey."

After the seizure of Sukhum real power lay in the hands of the Russian military commander of the fortress, Captain Agarkov, who controlled the actions of Seferbey. In his report to the authorities in January 1811 he speaks unflatteringly of the new ruler, noting that "the affairs of Abkhazia are in poor order." Seferbey was in a state of alarm and could not move against Aslanbey's people. As for the Abkhazians, continues Captain Agarkov, they have reached "such a pitch of boldness that they come up to the fortress with their weapons, sit around in groups and shoot at the soldiers, with the result that it is dangerous to move 100 paces outside it."

The whole of Abkhazia was in the grip of the strong emotions of the people. In extreme irritation General Tormasov, the commander of the Russian army in the Caucasus, wrote on March 15th 1811 to Seferbey that he was not taking "active measures against the party of the parricide . . . Arslan-bey, which is gradually growing and might gain superiority over us." Tormasov urged the ruler: "Strongly affirm your power over the Abkhazian people." The general reminded Seferbey: "You are confirmed the legitimate ruler by force of the arms and protection (of the emperor), have been restored to all your rights and enjoy the backing of the victorious Russian army . . ."

By the end of the war the Turks had lost all their bases on the Black Sea littoral of the Caucasus (Anapa, Sudzhuk-Kale, Sukhum-Kale, Anaklia, Poti). The international situation dictated the necessity of speedily concluding peace with Turkey. Preparing for the invasion of Russia, Napoleon's half-million strong army was massing on the Visla (Vistula).

In May 1812 the Peace of Bucharest was concluded between Russia and the Ottoman Empire. According to this treaty, Russia acquired the entire coast of Abkhazia and Mingrelia. In reality the unification with

Russia of Western Georgia (Mingrelia, Imereti, Guria) and Abkhazia was firmly guaranteed, and the security of the Crimea was enhanced. Ending the war with Turkey allowed the hastening of the conclusion of the war with Persia (1802-1813). Russia decided also on a grand strategic plan: having secured peace on all its southern borders, it deprived Napoleon of a collaborator in Turkey.

At the moment of Russia's confirmation in Sukhum-Kale Abkhazia occupied an intermediate position between the democratic, liberal societies of the mountaineers of the North West Caucasus and the feudal system of Georgia. However, in the spirit of its social organisation it was tightly linked with the Ubykh-Circassian world. Eye-witnesses particularly noted that in Abkhazia and its historical region of Samurzaq'an (joined to Russia in 1805) there did not exist feudal property in land and that free commoners (*anxa'jʷy*) made up almost all (three-quarters) of the population of the country. Serfdom here, as such, was unknown. On the other hand, in neighbouring Mingrelia, for example, serfdom was found in its most extreme forms, whilst in central Georgia its formation had already been completed in the 12th-14th centuries. In Abkhazia all categories of peasants were proprietors of land. Such right to land placed the lowest estates beyond dependence on the privileged.

The elements of family-tribal organisation were closely adapted to the system of Abkhazia's 'mountain feudalism'. Demonstrative in this regard is the character of the village-community (Abkhaz *a'kyta*), which was the 'fundamental basis' of Abkhazia's social structure: it united all strata of the population — the highest and lowest estates were steeped in the practice of the so-called 'milk-kinship' (in Russian *atalychestvo*) of the feudals with the peasants. The children of princes and the nobility, given out to peasant-families for their upbringing, became, as did their parents, close relatives of the latter. In fact, even conflict between the estates was reduced. With respect to this, the historian K'onst'ant'ine Mach'avariani, a Kartvelian, observed in 1913: "Between the highest and lowest estates in Abkhazia there was not the same antagonism and alienation that existed in Guria, Imereti and Georgia."[2]

Intimately bound up with the concept of the freedom of the individual were the right to change one's place of residence — 'freedom of resettlement', 'freedom of movement' — and the particular aspect of the institution of hospitality (*asasd'k'ylara*, where in Abkhaz *'asas* = 'guest', *ad'k'ylara* = 'receive'). Both peasants and feudals could be guests. If, for example, difficulties arose in a peasant's relations with a community (blood-feud, injustice in the people's court, discord with a feudal, etc), he could without hindrance transfer to another under the protection of a new patron and even keep for himself his land in the community he had abandoned.

In the conditions of land-ownership by farmstead (the *khutor*-system), arable tracts were not the property of the community as a whole but were the family- or homestead-property of the Abkhazians. Only pastures and woods were common to all and open for joint-utilisation. Mutual economic assistance and support facilitated an atmosphere of prosperity and provided the necessary income. Amongst the Abkhazians there was not a single beggar, which speaks of the relative justice of their social system.

True, in Abkhazia there existed an insignificant stratum of domestic slaves, taken, as a rule, as prisoners-of-war in the North Caucasus and in Western Georgia as the result of military raids. However, after two to three years the slave was permitted to marry, and his owner, whether feudal or peasant, apportioned him both land and utensils, enabling him to pass into the conditionally dependent lowest category of peasants ($ax^{w'}j^{w}y$ or *'agyrwa*).[3]

Great interest attaches to the *azats* or emancipated slaves, who had been liberated from varying peasant-estates and in general with no obligations to fulfil. In Abkhazian society they occupied the position of a sub-estate, since in the view of the Abkhazians each and every section of the people should possess maximal freedom. The emancipated slaves would become priests or teachers of the children of feudals and administered religious cults. In 1869 they numbered 2,200 .

Busying themselves with their rural economy, the Abkhazians took from the land just as much as was essential for life. They lived in perfect harmony with nature. The traditional religion of the Abkhazians, paganism, in no small degree facilitated such a natural relationship.

However, the most honourable occupations were military activity and hunting. A community was reminiscent of a military camp, and it lived in a distinctive 'military readiness.' The main reason for the close unity of all the members of a community was the threat from outside (such as raids of neighbouring peoples, the selling of prisoners-of-war, hostile relations between communities and privileged families, cattle-rustling), which bonded yet more strongly the highest estates with the lowest within the union of society.

The peasants vigilantly defended popular custom from any encroachments on the part of the highest estates and constituted the fundamental moral pivot of the Abkhazian community. The peasant was the very symbol of a free man. There are well known cases when some of these had renounced aristocratic titles and boasted of their "pure" peasant origin.

Alsanbey's struggle for power

As for the economy of the Abkhazians at this period, it had the character of natural consumption. Abkhazians occupied themselves with the working of metals, skins, wood, pottery and saddle-making, weaving and the preparation of gunpowder. However, this production of home-industry and rural domestic trade was not sold but bartered. Abkhazians felt hostility towards any kind of manifestation of commercial-financial relations. Trade in Sukhum and the coastal points of Gudauta, Ochamchira, K'elasur, and Gudava was in the hands of Turks, Armenians and Mingrelians, who paid a certain fee for this privilege to the ruler of Abkhazia and other feudals.

During the rule of Seferbey Chachba (1810-21) central rule was weakened completely. Civil dissensions blazed up with their former fury. Endowed with all the rights of a governing authority, Seferbey may have been the formal ruler but could not in any significant way influence the political situation within the country. The free communities of the Abkhazian mountain-regions (such as Pshʷy, Ajbga, Dal, Ts'abal) remained independent as before, "denying that they were subordinate" to Russia and its ruler.

As before the people deemed Aslanbey to be the real ruler of Abkhazia. From time to time he appeared here and raised rebellions. Thus, in July 1813 he was in Abkhazia but was immediately subjected to an attack from a Russian battalion with two guns supported by the militia of the ruler of Mingrelia, Levan Dadiani. Only by such means did Seferbey hang on to power. Guarded by Russian soldiers, he lived either in the Sukhum fortress or in Mingrelia, whose rulers backed him in the struggle with Aslanbey. After the death on February 7th 1821 of the ruler Seferbey there broke out in Abkhazia 'disturbances and uprisings'. Many Abkhazian princes wished to see as ruler Aslanbey or his brother Hassanbey — by his father he was brother to Seferbey. But Lieutenant-General Veljaminov, who was replacement as supreme commander in the Caucasus at this time for General Ermolov (absent in St Petersburg), on the advice of the ruler of Mingrelia, Levan Dadiani, declared "as ruler of Abkhazia" the widow of Seferbey, Princess Tamar Dadiani (aunt of Levan). To secure Tamar, Veljaminov issued a decree for the arrest of Hassanbey Chachba and his deportation to Siberia. The Abkhazians refused to accept Tamar as ruler of Abkhazia.

In the summer of 1821 Aslanbey returned to his homeland. With the support of his Sadz, Ubykh and Pshʷy kinsmen, he raised a rebellion, "seized the whole of Abkhazia" and lay siege to the Sukhum fortress. However, Prince Gorchakov, sent secretly with an army, crushed the rebels. He brought in a new ruler, Dimitrij (Omarbey), the son of Seferbey, and personally took charge of the punitive expedition. On his orders the villages around Sukhum were laid waste and torched. Having lived in Petersburg since childhood as a hostage, Dimitrij had forgotten his native language and customs and enjoyed even less authority than his father, Seferbey.

To guard Dimitrij, Gorchakov left in Lykhny two companies of the Mingrelian regiment under the command of Major Rakotsi. In fear of Aslanbey's followers, Dimitrij lived in Lykhny for about a year as a prisoner-of-war. However, on October 16th 1822, according to the version of his mother, Tamar Dadiani, he was poisoned by one of Aslanbey's men.

Shortly after Dimitrij's death the Emperor on February 14th 1823 bestowed on his brother Mikhail (Khamudbey) the title of ruler of Abkhazia — he ruled until 1864. The power of the still under-age Mikhail was very weak. In 1824 under the supervision of Aslanbey there again broke out an uprising, which embraced the whole of Abkhazia. More than 12,000 Abkhazians blockaded the Russian garrisons in the Sukhum fortress and the stronghold at Lykhny. Gorchakov issued an order to the commandant of Sukhum, Lieutenant-General Mikhin, to restore order.

With a detachment of 225 bayonet-bearers in May 1824 he carried out a night-attack on one of the Abkhazian villages and burned it down. Outraged at such savagery, the Abkhazian peasants destroyed the detachment and killed Mikhin. The rebellion flared up with renewed vigour. Aslanbey again returned by Turkish ship from Anapa. For one and a half months Russian soldiers defended the Lykhny stronghold, in which the ruler Mikhail was holding up. The situation greatly worried Ermolov. In July 1824 large military forces advanced into Abkhazia — 2,000 Russian soldiers and 1,300 cavalry from the Mingrelian militia. They were supported from the sea by the frigate Speshnyj with its own artillery. The punitive expedition was commanded by Gorchakov, who suppressed the outburst in August. Aslanbey was again forced to migrate to Turkey.

With the strengthening of the Russian military presence the power of the ruler Mikhail was strengthened too. From 1830 coastal military strongholds were erected — Gagra, Pitsunda, Bambora, Mramba (around Ts'ebelda = Ts'abal), Sukhum — as well as the military posts at Dranda, Kʷ't'ol, and Elyr (Ilor). From the 1830s to the 1860s several punitive expeditions were carried out against the disobedient Abkhazians living in the mountains of Ts'ebelda, Dal, Pshʷy, and Ajbga, who were taking an active part in the Russian-Caucasian war and supported the anti-Russian movement of Shamil in Daghestan.

Attention was firmly fixed on Abkhazia after the Crimean War

(1853-1856) and the subjugation of the Eastern Caucasus, which was completed in August 1859 with the submission of Shamil in the Daghestanian *aul* (village) of Gunib.[4] Shamil's end caused a severe complication of the position of the mountaineers of the North West Caucasus. They found themselves squeezed by Russian armies from both the Black Sea coast and the mountains.

Despite being surrounded, the Adyghes, Ubykhs and the West Abkhazian Sadz communities continued the unequal struggle with tsarism for a further five years. The mountaineers were banking on the active military and political support of England, France, and Turkey. However, the governments of these countries had already decided to pin no hope on the Caucasus.

In June 1861, on the initiative of the Ubykhs, a *mezhlis* or parliament was constituted not far from Sochi. It was known as the "Great and Free Assembly." The Ubykhs, the Circassian Shapsughs and Abadzekhs/Abzakhs, and the Abkhazian tribes of Ahchypsy, Ajbga as well as the coastal Sadzians strove to unite the mountain tribes into "one huge barrage." A special deputation from the *mezhlis*, headed by Izmail Barakaj-Ipa Dzjapsh, visited a range of European states.

Active participation in the liberation struggle in the West Caucasus was taken by Polish revolutionaries who intended to raise simultaneously an Abkhaz-Circassian and Polish revolt against the Russian Empire. Obsessed with this idea was Colonel Teofil Lapinskij (1827-86). At the end of 1862 he visited London at the head of an Abkhaz-Adyghean deputation. The deputation was received by the prime minister of England, Lord Palmerston.

Lapinski delivered this short speech in the prime minister's presence: "At the present moment the Abkhazians are the sole tribe who are continuing to mount powerful resistance to Russia in the Caucasus. But even they have become exhausted under the weight of the unequal battle and can be expected to hold out in such conditions for at most another three years. Then they will inevitably follow in the tracks of the other Caucasian tribes: they will move to Turkey. Europe ought, with a view to weakening the northern colossus and keeping its army somehow occupied in the south, when a serious blow is also struck from the opposing side, to support the valiant Abkhazians, forestall their banishment from their native soil and thus save perhaps all the mountain-peoples of the area. To whom if not England, the principal naval power in the world, should this noble and strategic initiative belong in this case?"

Palmerston refused any kind of assistance: "You are quite correct, Colonel, in your assessment of the Caucasus: tribe after tribe there is succumbing to the energetic pressure of Russia. All our ambassadors and consuls in the East have been informing me of this for some 40 years. Where is the wisdom in the Abkhazians now doing the very same?"

The deputation set sail from the shores of England with nothing.

Lapinski foresaw the speedy abolition of the Abkhazian princedom. Those in Mingrelia and Svanetia had already been abolished by this time, as had at an even earlier stage the Imeretian kingdom and the Gurian princedom. In May 1864 Russia brought the Caucasian War to an end with a victory parade of its forces in Krasnaja Poljana ('Red Glade' = Abkhaz $G^wbaa\ D^wy$ 'Field of the Gubaas') in the upper reaches of the River M(d)zymta. The final opposition to the Russian army in the Caucasus turned out to be the West Abkhazian social grouping of the mountain Sadzians and the unsubjugated communities of Psh^{w}y (upper reaches of the River Bzyp) and Ajbga (between the River Psou and the River Bzyp, beyond the upper reaches of the River Hashpsy). Georgian militias too participated in the defeat of the last centres of opposition in the Caucasus and celebrated the triumph along with the Russian army at Krasnaja Poljana on May 21st 1864.

One month after the ending of the war, in June 1864, Russia abolished the autonomous Abkhazian princedom. Abkhazia was reorganised into the Sukhum Military Sector (the Sukhum District from 1883) of the Russian Empire. The viceroy in the Caucasus, Mikhail Romanov, presented a plan for the colonisation of the eastern coast of the Black Sea. Alexander II approved the proposed plan to settle the territory from the mouth of the Kuban to the Ingur with Cossacks.

The Ubykhs and the Abkhazian mountain communities found themselves in a most grievous position. The tsarist authorities demanded of them that they abandon their native areas. The Ubykhs resettled to Turkey in virtually their entirety (45,000), as did the Sadzians (20,000). In 1864 up to 5,000 persons abandoned the community of Psh^{w}y alone.

That the autonomous Abkhazian princedom lasted for so long is explained by the fact that the ruler Mikhail possessed in latter years a great influence over the mountaineers of the North West Caucasus. Thus, he encouraged in every way the struggle of the Ubykhs with the tsarist forces and introduced a food tax to help the Ubykhs, which was obligatory for everyone in Abkhazia. At the start of his rule he was inclined to be pro-Russian, but from the 1850s on he began to cleave towards Turkey.

The people in revolt

We read in numerous documents of the "autonomy of Abkhazia" and the "autonomous government of the ruler" for the years 1810 to 1864. The last ruler of Abkhazia, Mikhail, was arrested in November 1864 and resettled by the Russian forces to Voronezh, where he passed away in April 1866.

A few months after his death in Russia, a rebellion broke out in Abkhazia. It began on July 26th 1866 at a popular meeting numbering 7,000 in the village of Lykhny. On this day the rebellious Abkhazians killed the head of the Sukhum Military Sector, Colonel Kon'jar, the officials Cherepov and Izmailov, four officers and 54 Cossacks.[5] The uprising promptly spread from the village of K'aldakh^wara to Dal and Sukhum. Up to 20,000 persons took part in it.

The main reason for the discontent was the preparation for the carrying out here of peasant-reform. A participant in these events, the son of the last ruler Mikhail, Prince Giorgij, wrote with regard to it: "The public declaration of the manifesto concerning serfdom, which did not exist among this people and was consequently inapplicable to them, was an utterly unforgivable error on the part of members of the administration . . . The people could in no wise understand from whom or what they were going to be liberated."

The administration's main mistake consisted of the fact that it did not deign to take note of the local particularities of this tiny country, the internal life of which, differently from Russia, Georgia and neighbouring Mingrelia, was free of serfdom. At the meeting in Lykhny the representatives of tsarist authority declared in a most rude fashion that the people would be freed from their master for a certain ransom. The peasants, deeming themselves to be already free, were perturbed, but the princes and nobles were insulted that they, it appeared, were "ruling" not free people but "slaves," with whom they had the most intimate bonds of milk-kinship.

News of this movement stirred up the entire Caucasus, especially the Kabardians, who announced to the authorities that "they themselves would follow the Abkhazians," i.e. rebel.

At the very height of the uprising on July 29th 1866 the rebels proclaimed the 20-year-old Giorgij Chachba as ruler of Abkhazia. However, the attempt to restore the princedom was not crowned with success. The uprising was put down by military force under the command of the governor-general of Kutaisi, Svjatopolk-Mirskij, and Prince Giorgi was expelled to the "army of the Orenburg Military District."

Following the uprising, a wave of repression descended upon Abkhazia. Part of the movement's leadership was executed; many prominent Abkhazians, including centenarian elders, were transported to central Russia and Siberia. But the most tragic consequence was the forced resettlement of Abkhazians to Turkey, an event well-known among the people under the name *amha'dzhyrra* (exile). From April to June 1867 almost 20,000 persons became *maxadzhirs* (exiles), the Abkhazian population vacating in its entirety the Dal valley and Ts'ebelda. Tsarism had a need of Abkhazia devoid of Abkhazians and insurgents, whilst Turkey had need of a warrior people.

Strengthening of the Russian colonial yoke led in 1877 to a new insurrection in Abkhazia. As is well known, it erupted not only here but also in the North Caucasus. These movements were evidently closely linked with events in the Russo-Turkish War of 1877-78. In May 1877 a Turkish squadron subjected Sukhum to bombardment and then landed a party which was composed basically of Abkhazian *maxadzhirs*. However, in August the Russian army retook the town.

The coming out of the Abkhazian population on the side of Turkey brought in its wake more serious political repressions than in 1866. For participation in this insurrection virtually the entire Abkhazian population was declared to be "guilty" (this stigma remained attached to them from 1877 to 1907). Abkhazians, with the exception of a few representatives of the highest estates, were forbidden to settle along the coast or to reside in Sukhum, Gudauta and Ochamchira. A Colonel Arakin proposed even to "group" the population, destroying the farmstead-character of the Abkhazians' dwelling-pattern (the *khutor*-system).

Active expulsion of rebels to the interior *gubernias* of the Russian Empire went on from 1877 to 1890. The policy of repression and colonisation led to a powerful new wave of enforced resettlement of Abkhazians to Turkey. Up to 50,000 persons were compelled in 1877 to abandon the homeland. Central Abkhazia from the River K'odor up to the River Psyrtskha was almost completely depopulated. Only one region remained untouched — the territory of Samurzaq'an, since it was solidly defended by Russian forces.

Up to the tragic events of 1877 Abkhazia consisted almost exclusively of its indigenous Abkhazian population. In a short span of years it was converted into a territorial patchwork in terms of its ethnic makeup. The Georgian social activist Ant'imoz Dzhugheli in the newspaper *Droeba* ('Time-being') of 1883 wrote in this regard: "After the latest war there was a decree that the Abkhazians were not to settle in places ranged between the rivers K'odor and Psyrtskha. Permission to settle here was granted to all but them."

Since 1864, after the abrogation of the Abkhazian princedom and the introduction of direct Russian governance, Greeks, Bulgarians, Armenians, Russians, Estonians, Germans and others, but most of all Mingrelians, had established their own villages here.

Georgia claims Abkhazia

At the end of the 1860s and the start of the 1870s there appear on the pages of Georgian periodical publications articles in which eminent representatives of the intelligentsia of Georgia incited their own people to assimilate Abkhazian lands denuded as a result of the exile. In these publications it is baldly stated that only Mingrelians, by right of being the neighbouring peoples, should colonise the territory of Abkhazia. And not only Abkhazia — as Georgian writers remarked: "The whole Caucasus is our land, our country." In 1873 Giorgi Ts'ereteli (a popular writer and, from 1871 to 1873, editor of the journal *K'rebuli* ['Collection']) urged the Georgians to occupy the whole coast of the Black Sea as far as the Crimea, to which "foreigners have attached themselves like leeches: Greeks, Tatars, Jews, and others." It is during this period that in Georgia there started to take shape an imperial consciousness, and the dangerous conviction became implanted in the minds of the Georgians of their exclusivity and special role in the Caucasus.

The first programmatic work in which one reads the suggestion that Abkhazia should be colonised by Mingrelians was the extensive article by the famous Georgian social activist and publicist, Iak'ob Gogebashvili, under the title 'Who should be settled in Abkhazia?'. It was printed in the *Tiflis Herald* newspaper in 1877[6] at the time of the Russian war with Turkey. In September to November 1877, when the Abkhazians were bleeding profusely and forced in masses to leave their homeland, Gogebashvili demonstrated all the advantages of the colonisation[7] of Abkhazia by Mingrelians. "'Mingrelians should be the first to deputise for the exiled Abkhazians," remarked the publicist.

Into central Abkhazia there gushed a torrent of 'safe' peoples. Among their number there were from the very start Mingrelians who settled together with Russians, Armenians and Greeks around Sukhum. These Mingrelians (with some Georgians), playing in Abkhazia the role that the Cossacks traditionally played as spearheads for Russia's imperial expansion in the North Caucasus, found themselves then in a privileged position thanks to their participation on the side of tsarist Russia in the war against the peoples of the Caucasus (1817-1864), including the Abkhazians. Distinguished representatives of the Tbilisi intelligentsia, who had received their education at Russian universities, unceasingly tried to persuade the government of Russia of the advantage and success that would accrue from conducting the colonisation of Abkhazia only with Mingrelians (and Georgians). For the sake of achieving this main goal of theirs they kept on expressing their feelings of loyal fidelity to the emperors of Russia, striving to gain from them the right to exclusive power over Abkhazia and its lands. Thus, Gogebashvili wrote: "In a political sense the Mingrelians are just as Russian as Muscovites, and in this way they can exercise influence over the tribe geographically closest to them . . ."

Without the slightest doubt one can say that it was the dependent territory of Georgia which gained the fullest measure of advantage from the fruits of the Russian military victory in Abkhazia in the 19th century. The temptation to take control of an Abkhazia that was being bled dry was so great that Gogebashvili in an appeal to the Russian authorities had recourse to the following formula: "The colonisation of Abkhazia by Mingrelians is a matter of state-importance." As a result, a mass of landless peasants from Western Georgia was planted in central Abkhazia, in the depopulated villages of Merkheul[8] (1879), Besletka (1881), Akapa (1882), K'elasur and Pshap (1883). In this way the ethno-demographic situation within Abkhazia during the post-war period altered radically, as explained in Chapter 15.

At this period the Georgian clergy unleashed a storm of activity, foisting on the autochthonous Abkhazian population a Georgian liturgy and the Georgian language, with which they were totally unfamiliar, whilst many Abkhazian surnames were registered by Mingrelian clerics in a Kartvelian form.[9]

In the final decade of the 19th century and at the start of the 20th, because of the endless flow of those resettled from Western Georgia, relations between Abkhazians and Kartvelians were becoming ever more complicated, reaching their lowest point during the revolutionary developments of 1905.

The politics of the 'cudgel'

The Abkhazian peasant, who lived in a world of patriarchal traditions, did not understand Marxism, the ideology of the working class, or social-democratic doctrine. Differently from other peoples with an orientation for commercial-financial relations, Abkhazians were not concerned with trade, seasonal work or working as day-labourers, considering such occupations "ignominious." They still preserved many characteristics inherent in the psychology of a warrior people. In 1906 one of the leading newspapers, *Outskirts of Russia*, stressed that "Socialism has not yet taken root among the Abkhazians, and so one can live with them."

The Abkhazian peasantry interpreted the events of the Russian revolution of 1905 in Abkhazia as a 'Georgian' revolution and viewed with distrust those who had so recently occupied the lands of their fellows and exiles and now appeared before them in the role of revolutionary agitators. With the aim of "preserving the Sukhum District," the champions of the official politics right on the eve of the revolution strengthened measures "against the influx into it of Mingrelians" who were "enslaving the area in terms of its economic relations." Such was the opinion of the governor-general of Kutaisi, Gershel'man, which he expressed to Tsar Nicholas II in 1900.

Those who had originally inspired the colonial doctrine, meeting in the shape of the transplanted Kartvelians a barrier on the path of widening their influence in Abkhazia, fashioned for them 'special rules': they limited their permits to Sukhum, Gudauta, and Ochamchira and made the procedure for acquiring real estate more difficult. All of this caused extreme annoyance among those resettled from Western Georgia, who were the fundamental motive force of the revolution. They controlled the land by right of tenant, basically around Sukhum and in the Samurzaq'an province, having quickly settled both places on the roads and different coastal points associated with vibrant trade. It was in just these regions that the 'revolutionary movement' appeared strongest.

The tsarist administration in the Caucasus, stirring up inter-nation discord in the spirit of the policy of divide and rule, with all its might sought to take advantage in its own interests of the lack of trust and the tension that had set in to complicate Abkhaz-Kartvelian relations in 1905-1907. In 1907 the Petersburg newspaper *New Time* observed: "Instead of a feeling of gratitude towards the Abkhazian population, amongst whom Kartvelian nationalists are living, there is brazen-faced exploitation . . . This accounts for the hatred the Abkhazians have for their economic and future political enslavers . . . Can we permit the Abkhazian people to be gobbled up by Kartvelian immigrants? . . . Is it not time to wake up? The tolerance of the Abkhazians might dry up. One Armeno-Tatar (= Azerbaijani) conflict in the Caucasus is enough — why do we need to create another Kartvelian-Abkhazian one!"

It was precisely at this time that L. Voronov published in Mosocow his booklet *Abkhazia is not Georgia* (1907), which aimed to counter attempted distortions of Abkhazian history with a restatement of the facts. (For a discussion of the ethnicity of the Samurzaq'anoans, see text 47 in Hewitt & Khiba [1997a].)

After three decades Tsar Nicholas on April 27th 1907 signed a proclamation on the remission of the charge of "culpability" against the Abkhazian people, in which was noted their loyalty to the government in the course of the Revolution. Especially stressed was the fact that "in the troubled times of 1905 the Abkhazians emerged from the experience with honour."

From the end of the 19th century the tsarist regime began to implement a new policy in regard to the Abkhazians. The politics of the 'cudgel', so characteristic for the period 1810-80, changed into the politics of the 'cake'. The authorities came to the conclusion that in place of the Russian colonisation planned in Abkhazia there had taken place a mass-Kartvelian settlement, whose representatives speedily appropriated into their own hands the economic levers in the region.[10] But organised administrative-political measures had not produced the desired results.

The fundamental danger to its interests was seen by tsarist Russia in the raging activity of the efforts of the Georgian church to spread its own influence over the Abkhazian population. Because of this, by decision of the Russian Synod in St Petersburg, the Commission for the Translation of Religious Books into Abkhaz was founded (1892). A group of Abkhazian clerics and teachers began to take shape from precisely this time.

In 1907 ceremonial worship in the Abkhaz language took place in the ancient cathedrals at Lykhny and Myk^w. The fact was that the Russian government was seeking under the cloak of church reform to carry out one of administration. The essence of it was that the frontiers of the Sukhum eparchate (incorporating within itself the whole territory of the Sukhum District, the Black Sea Gubernia, the town of Anapa and part of the Zugdidi region [= uezd]) was considerably more extensive than the frontiers of the Sukhum District (from 1883). But according to the make-up of the population, Russians were in a significant preponderance.

In connection with this situation, the Bishop of Sukhum in 1901 proposed to the Petersburg Synod a project to split his eparchate from the Georgian exarchate. However, the Russo-Japanese War (1904-5) and the developing Revolution hindered the implementation of this decision. The plan to divide off the eparchate as an independent one was raised several times in the years 1907-8, and again 1912-15. It is obvious that such independence for the eparchate would have isolated the district of Sukhum as well, protecting it from Georgian influence.

The first step towards these goals was taken by Prince Oldenburgskij (a relative of Nicholas II), who constructed in Gagra a beautiful weather-station (1901-1903), and in 1904 split off Gagra and its environs from the constituency of Sukhum District, annexing this territory (from the River Bzyp) to the Black Sea Gubernia. Later, in February 1914, the question of transforming the Sukhum District into an independent *gubernia* was raised before the Caucasian viceroy. The First World War again prevented the realisation of this reform.

It is hardly suprising that in the wake of the February Revolution in

Russia the question of the autocephaly of the Abkhazian Church was decided in Sukhum in May 1917 at an assembly of the clergy and voting laymen of the Abkhazian Orthodox population. The assembly appealed to the above-mentioned Synod as well as the transitional Russian government. However, the autocephaly of the Abkhazian Church, proclaimed in May, took no further shape.

During the years 1910 to 1917 there was a rapid growth in Abkhazian socio-political thinking. The major role in the awakening of national self-awareness among the Abkhazians was played by the native intelligentsia.

Conclusion

The Abkhazians were the only ethnic group resident in Transcaucasia to participate in the North Caucasian resistance to Russia's 19th century decades-long struggle to subjugate the Caucasian mountaineers and thus acquire total control over the whole Caucasus. As a result both of this and continuing disturbances after Russia's inevitable victory in 1864, entire swathes of Abkhazian territory were stripped of their ancestral inhabitants as much of the native population was expelled in various waves to Ottoman lands, giving rise to the large diaspora communities still surviving across the Near East. Despite this national tragedy, Abkhazia's union with tsarist Russia in 1810 has long been depicted as a voluntary act, thanks to the triumph of contemporary imperial propaganda; in addition, the Abkhazians themselves have lately been portrayed as innately pro-Russian.

The deserted state of such an inherently rich region after the expulsions gave impetus to inward migration, particularly from neighbouring Mingrelia, which in turn created the basis for a new myth: the 'Georgianness' of Abkhazia.

This chapter has introduced a necessary corrective into the historical record of Abkhazia's absorption into the Russian Empire and has explained the reasons why hostility directed towards Russia throughout the 19th century found a new focus as that century came to an end, given that thereafter the main threat to Abkhazia's well-being was to come from its neighbour to the south-east.

6
History: 1917-1989

Stanislav Lak'oba

After the dissolution of the Russian Empire Abkhazia entered the Union of United Mountain Peoples of the Caucasus (founded in May 1917), while in November 1917 at an assembly of the Abkhazian people in Sukhum a representative organ of power was set up. This was called the *Abkhazskij Narodnyj Sovet* (ANS)[1] or 'Abkhazian People's Council', and it was constituted earlier than the *Natsional'nyj Sovet Gruzii* (NSG) or 'National Council of Georgia'.

In the 'Declaration' of the Abkhazian People's Council taken at the assembly in November we read: "In the troubled times we are experiencing, when much is being destroyed to its foundations and much is being created anew, when radical change is affecting the conditions and state of life throughout Russia and, thus, Abkhazia, each people must keenly ensure that its rights and interests are not subjected to any encroachment and are not forgotten in the rebuilding of Russia on new principles. The Abkhazian people is convinced that its brethren, the mountain peoples of the North Caucasus and Daghestan, will support it in those circumstances when it is called upon to defend its rights. One of the main future problems for the Abkhazian National Council will be to work for the self-determination of the Abkhazian people."

Ten days later, on November 19th 1917, the chairman of the ANS, speaking in Tbilisi at the opening of the National Council of Georgia, stated: "I am delighted that the great honour has fallen to me of conveying to you warm greetings in the name of the Abkhazian People's Council. The Abkhazian people, a constituent part of the Union of United Mountain Peoples, congratulates beautiful Georgia on taking its first steps along the path to national self-determination . . . The Abkhazians, having entered a union with their northern brethren, are convinced therefore also that in the near future they will come together with the noble Georgian people in a general union of all the peoples of the Caucasus. And in this future union the Abkhazian people envisages itself as a member with equal rights of the Union of United Mountain Peoples."

Soon, at the invitation of the National Council of Georgia (Ak'ak'i Chkhenk'eli), a delegation of the first ANS visited Tbilisi. At a meeting on February 9th 1918 the Abkhazian delegation sought to have with "Georgia only good-neighbourly relations, as with an equal neighbour." That self-same day an agreement was struck between the ANS and NSG; in it Georgia gave recognition to "a single indivisible Abkhazia within frontiers from the River Ingur to the River Mzymta."

On May 11th 1918 a North Caucasian Republic ("The Mountain Republic") was declared. It was composed of Daghestan, Checheno-Ingushetia, Ossetia, Karachay-Balkaria, Abkhazia, Kabardia and Adyghea.

Fifteen days after this event, at the demand of Turkey and Germany, the Transcaucasian Democratic Federal Republic was disbanded, and on May 26th 1918 the Democratic Republic of Georgia was formed. At the moment when the Act on Georgia's independence was declared (May 26th) and signed, Abkhazia was outside the borders of its territory and formed a constituent part of the Mountain Republic (which had been in existence for about a year).

Taking advantage of the ambiguity of the so-called Treaty between Georgia and Abkhazia of June 8th 1918, at the signing of which the delegation from Abkhazia did not then possess plenipotentiary powers from the ANS, the Georgian army under the command of General Mazniev (Mazniashvili) occupied Abkhazia in the second half of June 1918. Mazniev declared the captured territory to be a "general gubernia" within Georgia. The Parliament of Abkhazia came out with a strong protest against such actions by Georgia, whilst the Abkhazian people rose up in battle against the occupiers. In answer the Georgian government twice (in August and October 1918) dismissed the ANS, arrested the deputies of the Abkhazian Parliament and imprisoned them in the Met'ekhi castle in Tbilisi.

After the dismissal of the second ANS, there set in a period (October 1918 to March 1919) of undisguised occupation within Abkhazia, and the country was governed with direct interference from Georgia. Abkhazia came to be ruled by 'Special Commissar' V. Chkhik'vishvili and 'Political Representative' Isidore Ramishvili, who were despatched from Tbilisi. Furthermore, the minister of internal affairs of Georgia recognised at that time that "only a sword of power" was in effect in Abkhazia. Under these conditions of blatant occupation and military edicts, Georgia set about electing the third ANS on "democratic principles." The extent to which the elections were "universal and equal" can be judged by the fact that amendments were introduced on their very eve. One of these stated: "As deputies to the

ANS only subjects of Georgia not resident in Abkhazia may be elected . . ." Only on the eve of the 'elections' were the former Abkhazian deputies released from the Met'ekhi prison at the request of the British high command.[2]

Meetings of the third ANS were held in Sukhum between March 18th and 20th 1919. The overwhelming number of deputies gave expression to the interests of the government of Georgia and passed the so-called 'Act on the Autonomy of Abkhazia', which remained a purely paper-document. It is interesting that, opening the first session of this Parliament, Ramishvili, Georgia's representative, declared: "We bear no resemblance to conquerors and have no need of land hereabouts" (the newspaper 'Our Word', March 21st 1919).

At that same time, on March 18th 1919, the writer and social activist Samson Ch'anba, from the group of Abkhazian deputies, the 'Independents', delivered a plain-speaking speech. "The Georgian Socialists," he said, "when they lived in Russia, followed the path of internationalism, but, having returned home to Georgia, decided to create their own state . . . A state, as is well-known, cannot exist without territory and human resources. For this reason, the Georgians are striving to extend the frontiers of their country. And tiny Abkhazia is for this a dainty morsel . . . We are not opposed to the self-determination of the Georgians and their republic — on the contrary, we welcome it. But at the same time we also have our self-respect. However sweet-sounding the words they articulate may be, their scheme to keep Abkhazia in their sights shines brightly through them."

The British interest

In the spring of 1919 the British expeditionary force under Major General William M. Thomson and General Anton Denikin, leader of the anti-Bolshevik White Russian forces, who was then in the Caucasus, were having great doubts about the 'democratic nature' of the elections in Abkhazia. Not only that, in May 1919 the British General Briggs declared in Tbilisi to the minister of foreign affairs of Georgia, Evgeni Gegech'k'ori: "The Abkhazians are dissatisfied with Georgian rule and declare that, if they are given weapons, they themselves will purge the district of Georgian troops. The Georgians are behaving there worse than the Bolsheviks: they are seizing homes and land, and they are conducting a policy of socialisation and nationalisation of property." In addition the general noted: "As for the Sukhum District, I have heard from other sources that a wish to unite with Georgia does not reflect the will of the population."

During the course of two years the third ANS proposed to Tbilisi three different drafts for a Constitution of Abkhazia, but not a single one of them was ratified. In September 1919 and November 1920 the exasperated deputies of even this obedient ANS directed sharp statements at the government of Georgia. The legislative rights of the ANS were completely infringed by the Constituent Assembly of Georgia, which rudely transgressed article 2 of the Act of Autonomy of March 20th 1919. Only on the day of the fall of the government of Georgia did the Constituent Assembly on February 21st ratify a constitution of Georgia with clauses on the 'autonomy' of Abkhazia.

However, this decision had no significance whatsoever, as it never came into force. Furthermore, it was in contradiction to the Act of March 20th 1919, which had been ratified at that time by the Constituent Assembly. Again in the spring of 1920 the Abkhazian people boycotted the elections to the Constituent Assembly of Georgia, which itself had no juridical basis for forming the so-called autonomy of Abkhazia. Besides, clause 107 of the constitution of Georgia was of a diffuse character, and it is difficult to understand what sort of autonomy (?cultural) is meant. Moreover, the "statute concerning the autonomy," mentioned in clause 108, was simply not worked out. Both these clauses read as follows in the officially published English-language version:

> (107) Abkhasie (district of Soukhoum), Georgia Musulmane (district of Batum), and Zakhathala (district of Zakhatala), which are integral parts of the Georgian Republic, enjoy an autonomy in the administration of their affairs; (108) The statute concerning the autonomy of the districts mentioned in the previous article will be the object of special legislation.

In 1921 there appeared in England the book *In Denikin's Russia and the Caucasus, 1919-1920*, in which the author, Carl Eric Bechhofer (Roberts), an English visitor to Menshevik Georgia, wrote thus: "The Free and Independent Social-Democratic State of Georgia will always remain in my memory as a classic example of an imperialist 'small nation'. Both in territory-snatching outside and bureaucratic tyranny inside, its chauvinism was beyond all bounds" (p14).

The aggressive politics of the government of Georgia towards Abkhazia occasioned extreme displeasure among the local Abkhazian, Armenian, Russian, Greek and a significant proportion of the Kartvelian peoples, which actually helped to facilitate the establishment of Soviet power in the region on March 4th 1921. Confirmation of the new authority, which coincided with the 'New Economic Policy' (NEP), was welcomed by the peoples of Abkhazia as a deliverance from the repression and meddling of the Georgian Republic.

The politics of this state was quite accurately characterised by one of its eminent activists, the jurist-internationalist Zurab Avalov (Avalishvili). In his book *The Independence of Georgia in International Politics 1918-1921* (Paris 1924) he remarked: "At the start of 1921 Georgia had in the person of its government and in the shape of the Constituent Assembly a simple creature of party-organisation . . . Georgian democracy 1918-1921, a form of social-democratic dictatorship (i.e. of the right wing of Marxism), was a period of preparation for the triumph in Georgia of Soviet dictatorship."

To begin with, the Bolsheviks allowed Abkhazia the freedom of political choice. This was realised by the declaration of an independent Abkhazian SSR (March 31st 1921). The unique feature of the political situation consisted in the fact that Abkhazia was called independent, and for about a year was independent of both Soviet Russia and Soviet Georgia.

However, in December 1921 under strong pressure from Stalin, Sergo Orjonik'idze and others, Abkhazia, under the leadership of Èfrem Èshba, was obliged to conclude with Georgia a "special union-treaty" (Constitution of Georgia 1922), ratified in February 1922, which established in essence the equality of status of the two Republics.[3] The character of the inter-state relations between Abkhazia and Georgia found its reflection in the Constitution of the Abkhazian SSR of 1925 and in the Constitution of the Georgian SSR of 1927, in which it is underlined that the Georgian SSR is a state constructed on federative principles (p2).

The first Soviet Constitution was adopted in Abkhazia in April 1925 by the All-Abkhazian Congress of Soviets. As with other 'union' republics, Abkhazia then adopted its own constitution — 'autonomous' republics did not have one. At this period the Abkhazian SSR according to its own status was not an autonomous but a union republic with the status of a sovereign state (p5 of the constitution). Therefore, the Constitution of Abkhazia of 1925 was not subject to confirmation in the structures of other states. The decision of the congress of the Soviets was deemed final as regards the relevant question. Abkhazia did not then enter into the make-up of Georgia but was in union with it. In October 1926 the session of the Central Executive Committee of Abkhazia added some supplements to the Constitution of Abkhazia of 1925, which found its reflection also in the new Constitution of Georgia of 1927 (federation and separate section on the Abkhazian SSR).

In 1924-25 the emblem and flag of the Republic of Abkhazia were confirmed, legislative acts of a constitutional character were ratified, and the codices of the Abkhazian SSR (relating to crime, citizenship, criminal court-proceedings, land and forestry) were put into action.

From 1922 to 1936 the government of Abkhazia was headed by Nest'or Lak'oba, who in every way possible resisted the introduction of collectivisation, having stated that in Abkhazia there was no *kulak*-class and that all estates here were equal. He did not carry out many of the Party directives, for which in 1929 he was subjected to strong criticism by Stalin. Still Lak'oba contrived to distribute financial allowances to many Abkhazian princes and noblemen at a time when people of this rank were being liquidated across the whole USSR. Under Lak'oba Abkhazia suffered none of the mass repressions so characteristic of the Soviet period.

Stalin, despite friendly relations with Lak'oba, demanded of him in 1930-31 the introduction of collectivisation regardless of the "particularity of the Abkhazian tenor of life." Being responsible for the destiny of the people and statehood of Abkhazia, Nest'or could not fail to appreciate to what collectivisation would lead. Stalin for his part, having become the sole master of the Kremlin, let it be known that he would hold back from its introduction in Abkhazia on one condition, namely the entry of the 'treaty-republic' of Abkhazia into the constituency of Georgia as an autonomous part thereof. Feeling incredible pressure from above and experiencing an organised opposition-movement within, which was clamouring for the immediate introduction of collectivisation and interpreted literally all the decisions of the Party, Lak'oba was forced to agree to entry into Georgia, seeing in this move the lesser of two evils.

What Stalin understood by collectivisation is well known. As a result of putting it into effect the Russian peasantry had found itself destroyed. What would have been the consequences for the small peasant land of Abkhazia? Half the population might have been transported to Siberia, while the other half would have been simply exterminated.

Abkhazia passes to Georgia

The question of Abkhazia's incorporation within the make-up of Georgia was considered at the Sixth Congress of the Soviets of Abkhazia on February 11th 1931, although it was not recorded on the agenda; later at the Sixth All-Georgian Congress of Soviets on February 19th 1931 a resolution on the transformation of the 'treaty' Abkhazian SSR into an autonomous republic within the make-up of the Georgian SSR was passed.

From the podium of the congress Lak'oba declared that the question had been decided, but at the same time he managed to urge the

Abkhazian peasantry to come out against such a decision. A general feeling of indignation took hold of the people. At Durypsh (D^wrypsh), Lykhny, Ach'andara and other villages a national gathering of the Abkhazian people lasting many days was constituted between February 18th and 26th 1931, which spoke out against entry into Georgia and against state-farms. Lak'oba's mother herself took an active part in this protest. Lavrent'i Beria, himself a Mingrelian from Abkhazia, head of the Transcaucasian Chekists (secret police), visited the Gudauta Region with a punishment squad and military equipment. Everything was set for bloodshed, but at the last moment the conflict situation was resolved.

As long as Lak'oba was alive, Abkhazia remained Abkhazia. In practice he was not subordinate to Beria, who, not without Lak'oba's assistance, had become head of the Georgian Communist Party from autumn 1931 and from 1932 head of the Communists for the whole of Transcaucasia. Between December 1935 and March 1936 Lak'oba declined a number of invitations from Stalin to transfer to Moscow and take over control of the NKVD (the replacement of the Cheka and predecessor of the KGB) in place of Genrikh Yagoda.

In December 1936 Beria summoned Lak'oba to Tbilisi where he acquainted him with a plan to transplant peasants from Western Georgia into Abkhazia. Nest'or was beside himself and refused point-blank. "Only over my dead body," was the reply he hurled at Beria . . .

The following day Beria poisoned him.[4] An unprecedented terror descended upon Abkhazia, which led to the total liquidation of the political and intellectual elite of the Abkhazian people. The policy of Georgianisation was conducted at a quicker tempo: the policy of importing non-Abkhazians to effect the assimilation of the region and deform the ethno-demographic pattern of the population was conducted with single-minded determination; original Abkhazian toponyms were Georgianised; the writing of Abkhaz was shifted to a Georgian graphical base (1938); the teaching of children at school was switched to Georgian from Abkhaz (1945).

Much later, the former secretary of the Central Committee of the Communist Party of Georgia, Eduard Shevardnadze, subjected the practice of those years to the following sharp criticism at the plenary session of the Communist Party of Georgia in June 1978: "It needs to be stated directly that in the past, in a period well-known to us, a policy was pursued in relation to the Abkhazian people which in practice can only be characterised as chauvinistic . . . Such acts as the closure of schools in the native language, the oppression of national institutes, the practice of distrusting cadre-policy, and other matters which are very well known to you cannot so easily pass into oblivion . . . When we speak of such conditions and complex processes as those in Abkhazia, we cannot escape the conclusion that we have to acknowledge the participation of our own people in the relevant problem and try to make another's pain our own, and then we shall not fall into error — at any rate, there will be fewer mistakes."

Over the period 1937-1953 tens of thousands of Kartvelians were transplanted from regions of Georgia into Abkhazia, which significantly increased their share of the population of Abkhazia.

An ideological facilitator of the policy of Georgianisation was the 'theory' propounded in the late 1940s by a range of Kartvelian scholars, such as P'avle Ingoroq'va and others, who declared Abkhazia to be an indigenous territory of Georgia and the Abkhazians to be one of the ethnic branches of the Kartvelians — for the history of this 'theory' and the subsequent use made of it from the late 1980s see the 'Introduction' to this volume.

Purges and 'reorganization'

An accurate characterisation has been given to the political situation of those years by the American sovietologist, Darrell Slider (in an article plublished in London): "Much of the political history of Abkhazia from 1931 until 1953 was dominated by Lavrentii Beria, a Mingrelian born in Abkhazia," he wrote in 1985. "There apparently was a deliberate policy, initiated by Beria . . . Leading Abkhaz Communists protested, including Nest'or Lak'oba, who was the Abkhaz Bolshevik leader. In 1937, a year after Lak'oba died mysteriously, Beria launched a purge of Abkhaz officials charging they had conspired to assassinate Stalin . . . The period after World War II until Stalin's (and Beria's) death in 1953 was an especially harsh one for the Abkhaz, as Beria launched a campaign apparently designed to obliterate the Abkhaz as a cultural entity. A so-called 'reorganization' of the educational system abolished all schools where the language of instruction was Abkhaz . . . Abkhaz language radio broadcasts ceased . . . Special land grants were issued in Tbilisi allowing Georgian collective farmers to settle in the Abkhaz coastal districts" (pp 52-54).

Despite the reversal of the most extreme and overt anti-Abkhazian measures described above, the demographic expansion of Kartvelians into Abkhazia, encouraged by Tbilisi, continued in a veiled form even in the post-Stalin period. Difficulties continued in the fields of access to higher education for Abkhazians and the publishing of works on the history of Abkhazia that failed to reflect the views of Tbilisi, while the long-term viability of the Abkhaz language and the culture of the Abkhazians was felt to be under threat, subject as it was to ongoing pressure. As for the economy, Slider again observed in 1985: "The Abkhaz, on the whole, appear to have benefited less from the development of Abkhazia than have other ethnic groups . . . The state budget for Abkhazia, an important source of centralized investment, has been about 40 per cent lower than that of the Georgian republic when measured on a per capita basis" (pp 57-58).

Mass meetings and demonstrations demanding the removal of Abkhazia from the make-up of Georgia took place in the republic in 1957, 1964, 1967, 1978 and 1989,[5] thereby demonstrating the continuing and widespread objection on the part of the Abkhazian people to their unrequested and unwanted inclusion within a Georgian state.

As the whole USSR was discussing the various draft-constitutions that were to mark Brezhnev's 1978 break with Stalin's constitutional legacy of 1936, 130 members of the Abkhazian intelligentsia wrote to the Kremlin on December 10th 1977 expressing the autonomous republic's dissatisfactions with its status of subordination to Tbilisi, making the point that "in Abkhazia at the present time there has developed a situation which demands radical measures for its solution. Already in their day the leaders of Abkhazia's revolutionary committee, Èshba, Lak'oba and others, in a document of March 26th 1921 addressed to Lenin and Stalin, remarked that 'Soviet Abkhazia should enter directly into the All-Russian Federation'. This idea has actually acquired a point today" (Marykhuba, 1994, pp 176-77).

The compilers of this epistle had earlier alluded to the untrustworthiness of Shevardnadze, then the relatively new (i.e. since 1972) Party Boss of Georgia, when they wrote: "Judging by the programmatic statements of the First Secretary of the Central Committee of the Communist Party of Georgia, Com. E. Shevardnadze, and other leaders of the Georgian SSR, one might have hoped that the mutual relations between Abkhazia and Georgia would finally proceed along the path of normalisation, along the path of regenerating the autonomous rights of the Abkhazian people. However, this did not happen. So overwhelming, it would seem, is the strength of historical tradition! While delivering words in strict compliance with the spirit and letter of our Party and declaring an implacable and resolute battle both against all who failed to comply with the Party-line and against all manifestations alien to our society, in point of fact the leaders of the Georgian SSR demonstrate strictness only in pursuance of the very tradition they censure. The further course of events irrefutably shows that the new government of Georgia . . . is even further aggravating the already well and truly unhealthy political and cultural relations between

Georgia and Abkhazia. With this aim in view it has outlined and is already carrying out a range of economic and socio-political measures. Today in the autonomous republic such a regime has been established, such reorganisations have been carried through, cadres have been put in place in such a way that Tbilisi can successfully and intensively effect as never before the georgianisation of Abkhazia. Indicative of this relationship is the former Gagra District, one of the main economic and historico-cultural regions of Abkhazia. At the present time this historic region of Abkhazia has in practice been liquidated by the Order of the Presidium of the Supreme Soviet of the Georgian SSR of April 5th 1973 entitled 'On the transformation of the regionally subordinate city of Gagra into a city of the Gagra District subordinate to, and governed by, the republic'. This was done without the involvement of any department of the Presidium of the Supreme Soviet of the Abkhazian Autonomous Republic" (ibid., pp 174-75).

All signatories to the letter were dismissed. But unrest, which on one night saw all Georgian road-signs in Abkhazia torn down or painted over, continued to grow in 1978. On May 21st, Ivan Vasilovich Kapitonov, secretary of the All-Union Central Committee, publicly acknowledged that "yes, in Abkhazia one meets traces of the Beria period in our life even today." Shevardnadze was forced to appear in Abkhazia, but, having begun to speak as follows in the presence of Kapitonov: "Dear brother Abkhazians! Apart from the secession of Abkhazia from Georgia, we shall do all you demand . . . ," he was hissed off the platform and rushed to take refuge in his official car (Marykhuba, 1994, p225). The small Pedagogical Institute in Sukhum was both enlarged and turned into Georgia's second university[6] — the Abkhaz State University — which, despite the name, was designed to serve the needs of the whole of western Georgia. Of its three sectors (Abkhazian, Russian, Georgian) it was the Georgian which was the largest. TV broadcasting in Abkhaz began (though with a paltry two half-hour programmes of mainly news per week). And a resolution was passed in Tbilisi entitled 'On measures for the further development of the economy and culture of the Abkhazian ASSR".

The type of difficulty facing those who wrote about the history of Abkhazia from an objective (i.e. not pro-Georgian) standpoint can be seen in the letter of a group of employees at the Abkhazian State Museum in response to the reaction aroused by the publication in 1976 of 'Questions of the ethno-cultural history of the Abkhazians' (in Russian) by Professor Shalva Inal-Ipa (d. 1995). The Russian text of the letter is included in Marykhuba (1994, pp 189-204); for an English translation see Hewitt (1996, pp 269-84).

One can also gain an appreciation of this grievance by reading the personal experience of the late Professor Yuri Voronov, a distinguished archaeologist and historian, as he described this in 1992: "Already in the 1930s the history of the peoples of the USSR was placed in the hands of the Academies of Sciences of the 15 Union Republics, where social scientists at once became appendages of the ideological structures whose purpose was to prove the superiority of the native peoples over the non-native, of the large nations over the small. In practical terms this led to the extinction of the more objective schools of Caucasology in Leningrad (St Petersburg) and Moscow. In each republic there became established standard variants of local history, and, when in the 1970s the need arose for a composite history of the countries of Transcaucasia, it became clear that the views about this history among leading representative academics in the respective republics were so divergent that such a jointly prepared general work on this theme was quite out of the question.

"The position of the Autonomous Republics within the Union Republics is that of third-class states. This gave life to yet another tier of historical elaboration, which re-cut the cloth of the history of these autonomies in accordance with the conception of the leading scholars within each Union Republic. Such manipulation of history took on the shape here and there of actual law. Thus, for instance, in Georgia in 1949 with the aim of keeping local materials out of the hands of Russian and foreign researchers a special law was promulgated according to which archaeological research on the territory of the republic was forbidden to all persons and organisations which have no relations with the Georgian Academy of Sciences. When in 1966 I began to concern myself with the study of Abkhazia, my first articles in Moscow scholarly journals resulted in the procurator issuing a search warrant against me and in further victimisation. Since I persevered in my investigations, matters reached such a pitch that the government of Georgia in 1979 obtained through the agency of Soviet Politburo ideologue Mikhail Suslov a special veto over the publication of my books in Moscow publishing houses on the grounds that my work was not in harmony with the 'achievements' of Georgian scholars!" (p259).

Yet again in 1985 three writers (Gennadij Alamia, Rushbej Smyr, Denis Chachkhalia) sent a further letter of complaint about the situation inside Abkhazia to the 27th Party Congress. The Russian original may be consulted in Marykhuba (1994, pp 374-82), while the following excerpt is taken from the translation in Hewitt (1996, pp 283-93): "In that year (1957) public disturbances took place in Abkhazia. These were repeated in 1967. Then again in 1978, after which the Central Committee of the Soviet Communist Party and the Soviet Council of

Ministers adopted the resolution, historic for the autonomous republic, 'On measures for the further development of the economy and culture of the Abkhazian ASSR'. This resolution is not being realised in its full dimension, and information about the course of its fulfilment deviates from the actual state of affairs.

"Take as an example just the construction of a TV centre in Sukhum. We know that a TV centre is no innovation for autonomous republics within the composition of the RSFSR (Russian Federation), but in Abkhazia every nest of culture is built only through incredible efforts on the part of the whole people. Every journal, every printed page published is the result of struggle . . .

"Abkhazian children today are losing their native language within Abkhazia itself. It is almost never heard in the street and in the school (unless the lesson is on the Abkhaz language and its literature). It is almost never heard in state offices . . .

"If in the first Soviet decades business in Abkhazia's organisations and institutions was of necessity conducted also in the Abkhaz language, today there is no such practice in a single urban institution (the only exceptions are in some rural ones).

"In the Constitution of the Abkhazian ASSR (article 70) it states: 'The Abkhazian ASSR guarantees the all-round development of the Abkhaz language and facilitates its usage and that of other state-languages in state and general organs, in institutions of culture, education and others.'

"True, in accordance with the Constitution the Abkhaz language is a state-language within the Abkhazian ASSR. But in what resides this status, if it is absent even on the official seals of the Abkhazian Regional Committee of the Georgian Communist Party, the Komsomol Regional Committee, Sukhum's Party City Committee and the Komsomol's City Committee?

"Over the 65 years of the existence of Soviet power in Abkhazia the printing of an explanatory dictionary of the Abkhaz language or of an Abkhaz-Russian dictionary has proved impossible to realise (N.B. a two-volume explanatory dictionary, including Russian equivalents, appeared finally in 1986 — *translator*): to the present day there has been no self-primer for the Abkhaz language. In compensation there is the resolution, adopted by the Abkhazian Regional Committee of the Party following the Central Committee of the Georgian Communist Party on the improvement of the study and teaching of the Abkhaz language . . .

"In a constant stream there flow into Abkhazia bureaucratic correspondence, edicts and telegrams in the Georgian language. And all this when the Georgian language is known to a certain extent essentially only by those Abkhazians who learnt to read and write it under fear of repression. The impression is given that in Tbilisi there is even now nostalgia for the times when Abkhazian children, choking with tears, used to repeat Georgian words they could not understand under the cudgel of the Beriaite 'enlighteners' . . .

"We would wish to forget that period, but we cannot. There is too much around us to remind us of that time . . . In Abkhazia there live and constantly reminisce people who participated in the closure of the Abkhazian schools, who took and take an attitude of scorn towards our culture, who were and are irritated by our language . . .

"Georgian nationalism, holding its ground even now, does a great deal even today to bring about a situation whereby the Abkhazians know their own history only in the form in which it is served up by certain 'scholars' from Tbilisi.

"Two years ago there was published in Tbilisi the encyclopaedic handbook *The Georgian SSR*, in which the history and culture of the Abkhazian people are distorted. Abkhazian society was perturbed at this insult. Our scholars and representatives of the creative intelligentsia informed the highest bodies about this . . . Nothing was altered. Moreover, this encyclopaedic handbook was given the distinction of a grade-one republican diploma as well as a financial prize. Thus are our feelings of indignation answered in Tbilisi."

Clearly the language-issue was still an open wound for Abkhazians in the mid-80s and was to figure again as the decade drew to its cataclysmic close. Taking advantage of Gorbachev's policy of *glasnost'*, a group of sixty intellectuals decided one final time to set out Abkhazia's detailed case for a return to its status of the 1920s. Their so-called 'Abkhazian Letter', consisting of 87 pages plus 12 pages of signatures and affiliations, republished in Marykhuba (1994, pp 383-439), was sent to Moscow on June 17th 1988. Meanwhile in Tbilisi, as the unofficial opposition was growing in strength on the back of its playing the nationalist card, the draft of a 'State Programme for the Georgian Language' was being prepared. This was published in November (and ratified into law in August 1989); its clauses stipulating the obligatory teaching of Georgian in all the republic's schools and that passing a test in Georgian language and literature would be a necessary qualification for entry into higher education throughout the republic had ominous implications for such minorities as the Abkhazians, where knowledge of Georgian was virtually non-existent among the relevant generation.

With the appearance of this draft-programme and news of the Abkhazian Letter filtering through to an ever-more nationalistically paranoid Tbilisi, the scene was set for the events of 1989 and beyond . . .

7
Soviet Abkhazia 1989: a personal account

Viktor Popkov

In the Darkness . . .

On Monday (July 10th) the Commission of the USSR's Supreme Soviet finished its work in Sukhum, deciding against the partition of the University on the basis of nationality, and on July 15th something happened.

It was about 10pm. Vadim Bzhania, scientific director of our expedition and director of the Department for the Preservation of Cultural Monuments of the Council of Ministers of the Abkhazian ASSR, had scarcely greeted me when he stunned me saying: "It's started! What we so feared has happened. We have just heard that fighting has broken out in Sukhum between Abkhazians and Kartvelians, probably involving firearms. I don't know how it will end, but we simply must be there with our people — there are so few of us."

At first Bzhania did not want to take me with him because of the danger, but I insisted — only one's own observations can fully guarantee accurate reporting, and certainly not second- or third-hand accounts. That is why I shall try below to rely on my own impressions, even if this leads to the loss of a certain completeness.

We left in darkness. From time to time our headlamps picked out little groups of people, evidently trying desperately to get into town too. Besides Bzhania and myself there were four others in the car. None knew what was going on in town or what was happening to their relatives and friends there. We hit a road-block just over 10km from town. At a narrow gap, left for traffic by a wagon that partly closed the roadway, only a trickle of cars was passing through, and the rest were resignedly turning back, as did our car. The lads explained that only cars with Kartvelian passengers were being allowed through. After some discussion of the chances of bypassing the road-block, Bzhania decided in view of the slender chances of success and the extremely alarming situation to go at once and bring out the detachment of our expedition working in the Gal District, where the population is predominantly Kartvelian. His decision was right, but I needed to get to town. So, I resolved to proceed on foot, if necessary.

Behind the wagon was a Highway Inspectorate (GAI) post, where the 'filtering' of cars was taking place. It seemed not to be the solitary, bewildered militia-lieutenant but a group of very determined men who were in charge. I cannot state the principles according to which they were controlling the flow of cars; it seemed that cars with Abkhazians were no longer even trying to approach, but not all the others were allowed through either. From snatches of conversation I formed the impression that at any rate they were trying not to let through cars with women and children. No one paid any attention to a lone pedestrian, and a middle-aged Kartvelian kindly offered me a lift to Sukhum when he realised I was from the magazine *Ogonjok*. We made off along the strangely deserted road, though in one place we had to reduce speed — a crowd of men with sticks, pieces of wood and even axes had dropped the sides of some carts and were hastily climbing into them. On arrival, we were allowed through freely, but even so we could not reach the centre of Sukhum as the road was blocked near the Apsny-cinema. I continued on foot.

People carrying automatic weapons caught my attention first. The very sight of the youngsters, mere boys, as I later learned, dressed in flak-jackets and helmets and carrying aluminium shields in the town, alarmed me more powerfully than any words.

I must confess that in Moscow, when thinking about the situation in Tbilisi or other areas where the State has been obliged to resort to force to restrain violence, the postulation that the use of force is inadmissible for the resolution of differences between people had always counted for a great deal with me. In principle this must be correct, though, as I now realise, it takes little account of local circumstances. Brute force is, alas, the only thing to which people, deafened and blinded by their respective pretensions, will pay attention. Force alone, naturally, will not open their eyes, but if people annihilate one another, no one will be left with eyes to open. This is why the leaders of the National Forum of Abkhazia (NFA), attempting to forestall such a train of events, turned more than once to the leaders of their own ASSR and of Georgia requesting the introduction of a curfew. Their pleas, however, went unheeded, or rather it was feared that they might be misinterpreted by public opinion both at home and abroad. Indeed, what need for a curfew when all was quiet, when nowhere was there — yet — physical violence, bloodshed or corpses?

I passed a lorry loaded with automatics and in 100 metres or so came to a little PAZ-bus with a small crowd around it. They were behaving oddly, savagely beating sticks against the batteries and other parts of the bus, which looked as if it had been in an accident, battered and with windows smashed. It transpired that Abkhazians had been riding in it, shooting, so people claimed, at passers-by. They had been stopped, I was told, only by the use of a heavy vehicle. Allegedly as a result, two of those in the bus had been killed. Fortunately, as the major in the cordon of the Internal Forces (IF) explained, no one shot at with those shot-guns had been seriously hurt. Indeed, that only two Abkhazians had been killed was amazing. If they had really opened fire on Kartvelians where Kartvelians are most numerous, it would have been pure madness, a form of suicide.

The bus faced the Apsny Cinema, and the wide square by the cinema was largely full of sturdy young men, many stripped to the waist, each having in his hands a stick, a piece of wood or an axe. The kerb was thinly lined with men from militia units, standing peaceably, though armed with automatics. Their lieutenant refused to be drawn into conversation, but the IF major explained that, in his view, the Abkhazians were entirely to blame for the situation that had arisen. They had come, he said, in a crowd 10,000 strong and wrecked the Georgian school in which the ill-starred branch of Tbilisi State University (TSU) had taken up residence in order to prepare for the holding there of the entrance-exams on July 16th.

"Come prepared," "planned extremist action" are typical accusations levelled at the Abkhazians — quite wrongly! I accept full responsibility for this statement, since everything I saw that night bore witness to the very poor, not to say non-existent, organisation of the Abkhazians. Otherwise, however, the major was near the truth. Both the information I obtained from the Muscovite Colonel Venjamin Kochergin (of the MVD [Interior Ministry] of the USSR) and the account of the Abkhazian university lecturer Niaz Gindia largely paint the same picture as the major regarding the incident at the school. To understand the motive, let us first consider Gindia's version.

"Following the Commission's decision about the inadmissibility of partitioning the Abkhazian State University (ASU), G. Enukidze, Georgia's Minister of Public Education, came out with a proposal for a federal structure for this educational establishment, with two rectors of equal standing, etc . . ."

Possibly this was equally bad, but in my view it offered, in the current situation, a perfectly reasonable temporary solution. But, unfortunately, . . .

". . . this proposal was rejected as unacceptable. Meanwhile, the branch continued accepting application forms, and it became known that the first exams were to take place on July 16th. Then, so as to disrupt these, a group of highly excited Abkhazians decided to blockade the building of Georgian School No. 1, having cleared their action neither with the leadership of the NFA nor with those of the ASSR (recall that these events occurred in 1989 when Soviet structures were still in place in Abkhazia, whose First Secretary was the ineffectual V. F. Khishba). That happened on the evening of July 14th. In response, the IF were called out, and they cordoned off the blockaders. News of the event spread all round town . . ."

By this time the question of preserving their university's integrity had, for the Abkhazians, long since become not a specific issue but a matter of principle, crucially linked with the question of preserving their nationality. Surprising as this yoking of matters apparently so heterogeneous may seem, we have not been in the Abkhazians' shoes; we have not had to suffer the Georgian press-campaign which had assigned to the Abkhazians the role of poor adoptive children forgetful of kindnesses shown to them; we have not been through the University-affair, which had been dragging on for more than two months, an affair full of disgraceful duplicity and unprincipled conduct on the part of the leadership of the ASSR, which decided to make clear its principled opposition to partitioning the university on a nationality-basis only on June 30th, by which time the disease was well and truly advanced and people were keeping watch round the clock in the Philharmonia, demanding that a Supreme Soviet Commission should come to investigate. Thus, I personally am not surprised that, when the news of the blockade of the branch spread round the town and beyond, . . .

". . . the Abkhazians were immediately drawn to it. Very soon a mass of them filled the surrounding streets, enveloping the school, the first ring of blockaders and the cordon.

"When the blockade started, there were in the building not more than 50 teachers and students of the Georgian sector. Later, some of these decided to leave and were let out unhindered, leaving 12 inside. These were, unquestionably, courageous people who acknowledged their responsibility for the safe-keeping of the school-leavers' documents. It cannot have been easy for them to have remained in such a siege-environment, but obviously they believed in something — presumably in the good sense of the Abkhazians and the probability of the republican leadership finding a solution. The Abkhazians too believed in this, especially as a rumour was going the rounds to the effect that Khishba, 1st Secretary of Abkhazia, had promised the 'elders' that, if an acceptable solution had not been found by 4pm on the 15th, he would resign. This deadline had now passed, but the question remained unresolved. Therefore, some time after 5pm Obkom-Secretary Tark'il read to the blockading Abkhazians a statement from the Rector of the TSU to the effect that entrance-exams for the branch would be held in the TSU itself, starting on July 20th . . ."

This decision, understandably, did not satisfy them. The situation started to get out of control. The besieged were the first to lose their nerve.

". . . They started encouraging one another to make a show of defiance with obscene gestures at the Abkhazians, who in rage attacked the school. Consequently, the teachers were driven out and the school wrecked; the safes supposedly containing the school-leavers' documents were removed. But even earlier a serious fight had broken out on Rustaveli Prospect, where there had been a confrontation between Abkhazians and Kartvelians waiting for Khishba's promised speech; about 800 were involved, armed with whatever came to hand, and a whole series of incidents ensued . . ."

Walking round Sukhum that night, I had been observing the consequences of these incidents and their further developments. It was now about 1am. The streets were completely free of cars and people, but, as I emerged onto Lenin Street, I saw at the far end, by Baratashvili Station, a crowd of cars and people; I also heard the occasional shot and burst of automatic fire. These were Abkhazians, armed with sticks and shot-guns and crowding together in expectation of a flank-attack. The forces of public order had made a feint with a dozen officers and MVD men, some armed with automatics. They fired occasional warning bursts into the air, but there had also been shots fired with hostile intent from the other side of the station, and people had been wounded. On my arrival, they naturally adopted a reserved attitude: what did this Russian want here? But when they discovered I was a journalist, they were sympathetic and tried not to expose me to fire unnecessarily. I watched this exchange of shots in the dark for a while then decided to make my way up to the NFA-headquarters, quite close on Frunze St., in the building of the Writers' Union. Here too were excited men, all armed. I entered with a group of elderly Abkhazians and went upstairs to the office of Aleksej Gogua, chairman of both the NFA and Writers' Union. Gogua was in an obviously depressed state. In the room's semi-darkness there were a number of men; the atmosphere was one of inconsolability and helplessness before the course of events. The only hope lay in the arrival of aircraft with units of the IF. All the talk was of their defencelessness, of the impossibility of opposing the Kartvelians' automatics with sticks and shotguns. Furthermore, in the view of the leadership of the NFA, the Kartvelians undoubtedly had at least the tacit support of MVD men of Kartvelian extraction. Indeed, it is hard to suppose that Kartvelians could move against Kartvelians in defence of Abkhazians. The facts, regrettably, fully justify this fear. Here is a statement taken by me from an old Abkhazian, Chama Gergia of the village of Kwitol (Kʷˈtʼol), on the evening of July 17th. He was clearly in a state of shock after what he had experienced, and it was hard to hear what he said, but the substance of his account is this:

"Returning home with my son and three nephews, our cars were stopped at Kʼelasur (just south of Sukhum) by a crowd of Kartvelians — about 3,000-4,000 people, old men and women among them, armed with sticks and knives. They made us get out, took our papers and started threatening us. I was jammed in the crush and immediately lost sight of my son and nephews; the cars vanished too. There were militia-men in the crowd, about 15 of them, officers with automatics. They were watching but not interfering. Suddenly I was amazed to see a familiar face among them — Colonel Andzhaparidze, the senior GAI-officer of Abkhazia."

"You mean he was in uniform?"

"Yes of course, like the rest of the militia. I said to him: 'We have done nothing; tell them to let us go and give us our papers and cars.' Andzhaparidze told them to give us our papers but said that I would get the cars back the next day from the GAI. He then vanished; not only did I not get my papers back but they threatened to 'weed me over' with their knives, and they put me in the cells."

"So where are the authorities when our militia-men are in with the Kartvelians like this, acting in collusion? Why are Abkhazians stopped and locked up?

"A while later they put another three Abkhazians in the cell with me, and two more later still. There were six of us, and only luck saved us. I speak a bit of Georgian, and I heard them say: 'They're coming, they're coming.' I looked through a crack — they were hiding their weapons in a hurry. It seemed that Russian soldiers had turned up. As they were going by, I shouted: 'Soviet soldiers! Save us, we are innocent in here!' One soldier heard, took a look, and we were let out. We went off with the soldiers, but I didn't see any of our captors arrested . . . Oh, I survived, but it would have been better if they had killed me. What is life to me at my age, when my only son and my nephews are gone?"

I myself had an opportunity to test the attitude of the Kartvelian militia, when I went to Abkhazia's MVD for information. It all began with them checking my papers and accusing *Ogonjok* and its editor, Korotich, of discrediting the Georgian nation in every issue. Baffled at first, I then realised they were referring to materials on the personality-cult of Stalin and stated that (the justifiably admired Georgian film) *Repentance* was anti-Georgian. They agreed and spent a long time explaining to me that the Kartvelians live on the edge of the Islamic world, which for hundreds of years had been trying to swallow them up. They were angry at our Russian interference in their internal affairs and asked whether I should not be at home in Moscow rather than writing articles 'stirring up nationalist discord'.

Yes, of course, I, as a Russian, cannot escape a feeling of guilt for our having tampered with the fate of nations. Yes, we Russians have been the involuntary tools of the imperialist policies of the State, and we ourselves have suffered acutely as a result of such policies, but that was largely through our own fault; how should we not feel shame? But this shame of mine causes me to do all that my ability and strength permit so as to give to all the nationalities of our multi-racial state the opportunity of recovering their loss, so that each of them may receive once more the chance of developing and of expressing itself. This goal requires some mutual rapprochement, and the call to such a rapprochement should not be taken to constitute interference in the sovereign affairs of nationalities. Does not the comfortable position 'Our affairs are our business; you attend to your own problems' fuel inter-ethnic conflict? It gives a chance to the ideologists of nationalities strong in numbers to drug their own people and pursue policies of repression against the less numerous.

To return to the events of July15th-16th. Everyone at the NFA-headquarters was anxiously awaiting the arrival of MVD IF-units. Outside, shots and bursts of automatic fire were occasionally heard. Inside, I failed to observe any activity pointing in any way to the proper organising-function of a headquarters; even the obtaining of information was treated very casually. In fact, we were completely uninformed, which dampened spirits even more. But at 3am we heard by telephone that at last a detachment of 400 men had arrived; things became calmer, and I, exhausted by it all, fell asleep on my chair. I awoke at 6.30. The shooting had stopped. I went to Lenin Square, where thousands of Abkhazians had spent a night of terror by the Government Building. Everyone had a stick, a piece of wood in his hands — their main means of self-defence against possible attack, against the automatics possessed by the Kartvelian extremists.

At 9am Igor' Markholia (Marykh^{w}ba), Gogua's deputy, urged those present to go home; by 10am the square was empty. Apart from a few food stores, shops were shut. Public transport was immobile.

About 7pm I returned to the Government Building, to which the headquarters of the NFA had now been transferred. Very bad news was coming in from Ochamchira, which borders on the mainly Mingrelian-speaking Gal District. Here the situation had been exacerbated by an attack carried out in West Georgia on a number of IF-detachments, which had given weapons to the extremists, and in Zugdidi prisoners had been set free and armed; the roads of the ASSR were completely closed to Abkhazians, as was a certain part of the town. The 400 men of the IF who had been sent were clearly inadequate to control the situation even in Sukhum, let alone the whole of Abkhazia. On the television, *Vremja* (Moscow's main evening news programme) spoke of 11 dead and 128 injured. Night was drawing on and terror creeping in.

Just after 2am we were awoken by the arrival of the Spetsnaz soldiers (specially trained commando units) from Moscow. It was a pleasure to see them. People smiled as they surrendered their sticks — their weapons of self-defence — and went out into the street. At first the order was to go home, but, praise be, a few minutes later, when realisation dawned of what people would be risking if they carried out this order, it was changed, and permission was granted after all to spend the night in the Government Building.

News kept coming in of fresh outbreaks of violence and even murders. On the evening of the 17th Tbilisi radio spoke of 14 dead and 13 seriously injured. Incidents grew of residents in various places being affected by the general atmosphere and starting to threaten their neighbours or unwarrantedly holding up transport. A rumour circulated among the Abkhazians that someone was marking their houses and flats, and again by nightfall fear was spreading. There was no curfew, which could have calmed people somewhat, and the introduction of which was most essential in the opinion of both Lieutenant-Colonel Kochergin and the Kartvelian major from the Obkom security ('Obkom' is a Russian abbreviation for regional committee). The major told me that a curfew was to be announced at 5pm, but that hour passed, as did 10pm, and the radio said nothing. After this Gogua went to the Obkom, where he had talks with both General-Colonel Jurij Shatalin, commander of the operation, and Otar Cherkezia, Chairman of Georgia's Praesidium of the Supreme Soviet. Shatalin expressed one straightforward view: on arrival he had realised the need for the imposition of a curfew. The decision, however, was not his to take, but depended on the leaders of Georgia. After discussion it emerged that Cherkezia too was in favour, but nevertheless it was only a 'Special Regime for the Conduct of Citizens' that was introduced with effect from 11pm on July 18th. That meant that Abkhazia had to endure another 24 hours of terror, to pay for the indecisiveness of the leadership with a number of lives, many injured, insulted and humiliated, and an indeterminate number of disappearances.

On July 18th I decided to visit Gudauta. In the region of the village of Lower Eshera my car was stopped by a large crowd from the village of Gvandra (Gʷandra). In the group that stopped us were: Abkhazian L. Agrba, Russian A. Kiseljov, Mingrelian P. K'ort'ava, Armenian S. Keshebian, Greek K. Murzidis, Tatar E. Bijazov.

I was particularly delighted that there was a Mingrelian, and I decided to tempt fate and test how far their friendship would go by asking what he thought of the Lykhny Declaration, which had caused in March so much fury amongst the Kartvelians in Georgia proper.

"Nothing out of the ordinary," was the reply.

Sukhum
July 18th 1989

Afterword

The Georgian media's account of the above events was not simply biased but, quite frankly, a pack of lies, peppered with a huge amount of disinformation. According to it, what had taken place had been the result of action well planned and prepared by the Abkhazian leadership against the Kartvelians — action in which the Abkhazians had presented a united front including both ordinary people (acting as blind instruments of the evil will of their leaders) and responsible individuals in official positions and Party-members. I, therefore, consider it necessary to bring forward the accounts of a number of eyewitnesses who paint quite a different picture. At the same time I must reiterate that to this day I am unaware of a single fact which shakes in any degree the conviction which I formed that very first night of the lack of any semblance of organisation or of any sort of preconceived extremist plans among the Abkhazians. From this it follows that either there really was nothing of the kind or that we have to deal with a thoroughly conspiratorial organisation comprising not only official and unofficial Abkhazian functionaries, but even personnel of the forces of public order of Georgia as well as officers of the IF, who, for some reason, did not report any such 'facts' either to me — and I spoke to them personally — or to anyone else.

*

I shall begin at the beginning, i.e. with the day of the events described above. In the first half of July there had been a smell of gunpowder in the air all over Abkhazia. The superficially obvious cause of this was the Abkhazian resolve not to accept legalisation of the partitioning of the University on the basis of nationality. But can it be inferred from the fact that many Abkhazians openly stated that they would not permit the TSU branch entrance exams to be held that they had plans violently to disrupt these exams by organising all-out violence against the Kartvelians? The Georgian media's reply to this question is "yes," which, without any corroborative evidence, is inadmissible. The mood of the masses is one thing, but the existence of a plot to turn this mood into plans for violent action is quite another. The very suggestion that the Abkhazians should possess plans for full-scale violence sounds quite absurd; even at home in Abkhazia they are today numerically much inferior to the Kartvelians, and in neighbouring Georgia there are several million Kartvelians! One would have to be quite insane deliberately to embark on a course leading to armed conflict under such circumstances.

But perhaps such fanaticism is a feature of the Abkhazian character? Take the episode with the bus, which I described earlier in the words of the IF major — did they not take just such a suicidal step there, opening fire into a crowd of Kartvelians? Let us see, however, how this incident looks as described by a participant, Abkhazian Edik' Lasuria, whose father and uncle were killed in the bus and who was himself beaten unconscious:

"On July 15th at 6pm we were told that officials were coming from Tbilisi to Sukhum to decide the question of the branch. My father and I got dressed and near the centre of the village of Kwitol stopped a bus driven by an acquaintance; it was carrying workers from the K'yndygh poultry-farm. We went along laughing and chatting."

"Did you have any weapons?"

"None. We reached the White Bridge (Sukhum) and met a road-block; a red Zhiguli 011, and a blue car on the other side, I don't know the make. There were some 2,000 people near the Apsny Cinema, stripped to the waist. A man was standing by a cabin saying something, and everybody was listening to him, except those in the street. When he had finished, the crowd left the square by the cinema and went along the street, up the hill. We had been standing there more than 10 minutes, and three chaps from T'amsh, Mingrelian-speakers, came to find out why people had assembled. They didn't rejoin the crowd, saying that they could see we were going to be killed and that, if they went back, they'd be killed too.

"So when the crowd from the cinema had gone up the street, the two or three cars held up in front of us were let through, and four men came to us and asked the driver where he was taking us. One of those subsequently killed told him to say that he was carrying workers from the poultry-farm. Two of them boarded the bus and looked at us. The driver said in Abkhaz: 'I'll have to use the handle, it won't start.' When he said that, the man by him shouted 'They're Abkhazians!' and the crowd attacked us. We started to fight. An empty Ikarus bus was standing nearby, and pistol-fire began to come from it, but not at us — just up and down; it was terrifying. The crowd ran away. Then shotgun fire started from the crowd — automatics, pistols, stones and bottles were thrown as well as sharpened weapons . . ."

"Sharpened weapons" — not highlighted in Edik"s account but worth dwelling on. The point is that home-made weapons of this kind were seen by Major Aleksej Grishchenko, Chief of Staff of the IF's Eighth Tactical Tbilisi Regiment, in Kartvelian hands near the cinema at about 6am on the 16th. According to him, they were among the weapons surrendered to the MVD. This is a hard fact, which speaks of work accomplished for a purpose — it takes time to produce such javelins — but by Kartvelians, *not* Abkhazians.

"Then they began to ram the bus with some heavy vehicle. We hadn't so much as a single gun. Someone came on the bus with a sawn-off gun and even let a shot off but was prevented from hitting anyone. By and large they couldn't get a shot at us — everything was in their way; a fight was going on. We fought for about 15 minutes. They were hitting us with weapons and bottles. I was hit with a spade — if I saw him again, I would recognise him, an elderly man of about 55, brown hair, two protruding front teeth . . . They were fighting one another; it was a real mix-up; they were hitting one another. At the time I knew nothing about who was hit or killed.

"Suddenly there was a shot and I was the only one left; someone else was being dragged off the bus. That's how it was — anyone unconscious was dragged off the bus and set upon by the women. They were all local women, wearing indoor clothes, aprons."

"And what time did all this occur?"

"Must have been 9.30pm. Oh, I forgot to say we saw militia-men nearby with automatics. They didn't interfere. While unconscious, my money and papers were taken. They cleaned me up at the hospital and wanted to admit me, but I refused and went to look for my father. At the hospital by Baratashvili militia-men with automatics started to threaten us. At Municipal Hospital No. 2 there were some militia, Kartvelians and an Abkhazian in a Zhiguli. They took us to the Republican Hospital, where Meskhi, a young Kartvelian doctor, was in charge. He saw that I was bleeding and told them to dress it. But at that moment four men came in and said: 'Since we failed to kill him out there, let's kill him here.' Meskhi threw them out and let us out by a back door, taking us to another building and telling us to hide. My younger brother came for me with a militia-man the next day and we learned that our father had been killed. At midday my brothers Gena and Avdik' took the bodies of our father Ivan and our uncle Nuria as well as that of one K'obakhia from the village of Beslakhuba (Beslakhʷba), who had been killed at Baratashvili, from the mortuary. At first we thought of taking the bodies out by helicopter, but the Kartvelian pilot said he wouldn't take Abkhazian bodies. On the suggestion of the NFA, we eventually got them out by boat."

Such is the account that I took down in Kwitol on July 25th. Of course, it is not possible on the basis of this alone to know who was speaking the truth, the Kartvelian major or Edik' Lasuria, but for my own part, as there is much detail in this account which matches what I have seen and heard from others, and by the simple logic of commonsense, Edik''s doleful tale evokes much the greater faith. Any public enquiry should also take account of the following.

Vladimir Chagava works as a driver of transport-column 1683 of Krasnodar. His Kamaz-lorry has the number 1588 KKR. On July 11th, returning from Erevan, he was stopped in the area of Kutaisi, capital of Imereti in West Georgia, between noon and 2pm at a control-despatch point. Apart from the GAI-man, there were two others in civilian dress. "When they had looked at my papers, they asked why I wasn't speaking Georgian," says Chagava. "I replied that I was an Abkhazian and that I speak to people I don't know in the all-Union language, Russian. An argument ensued, and in the end they went so far as to say that 'in a week, in a few days time, all you Abkhazians will be running to Krasnodar, just as the Azerbaijanis ran from us in the Marneuli region!' "[1]

It is easy enough to establish, on the basis of the precise evidence he gives of time and place, whether or not Chagava's statement is true. But the interesting point is that, according to him, responsible officials of the forces of public order in Georgia, hundreds of kilometres from Abkhazia, were certain of the likelihood of events happening there not long before they actually did occur. It is curious that, as its President, Ch'itanava, reported to the session of Georgia's Council of Ministers, there was an attack on a military depot on July 13th; a sentry was killed and a militia-man injured. All this cannot but urge one to the belief that some plan existed which anticipated events in Abkhazia. But neither these facts nor the business of the javelins are yet sufficient for such a stark conclusion . . .

Both in the spring of 1989 and in the period just preceding the recent tragedy, the leaders of Abkhazia's nationality movement made use of correct, purely parliamentary methods in the struggle in which they were engaged. Why, one wonders, is this practice not seen as an unquestionable indication of the lack of any extremist plans on their part? Just addresses to the Supreme Soviet, speeches at the Conference of Peoples' Deputies, demonstrations, acts of protest several days long in support of their demands for the coming of a commission, but not at the expense of working-hours, and, finally, extremely weak counter-propaganda in the form of practically total absence of any approach to the media — this is all they had at their disposal. And these methods have brought some success, such as the Supreme Soviet Commission's decision against partitioning the University. True, this did not lead to any corresponding change in Tbilisi's position, but, as long as Georgia is a constituent-republic of the USSR, the last word on a matter involving the interests of one of the nationalities must obviously remain in Moscow. To sum up, neither from the style nor the methods of the NFA nor from the situation itself is it possible to attribute to it extremist plans. And yet one cannot totally exclude the possibility of their existence; who knows, perhaps the sincere plans and methods of the NFA were simply a very deep plot, and its manifest activity merely a smoke-screen?

One could still just about accept such a postulation in the conditions of overwhelming distrust amongst the Abkhazians which existed prior to, say, July 14th-15th. But by July 16th, and more so later, it becomes absolutely untenable, for it is simply not corroborated by the facts of the matter.

July 15th. Disturbed at the mounting crisis, leaders of Abkhazia and Georgia, including Premier Cherkezia, the Secretary of the MVD plus lesser officials from Tbilisi and Moscow assembled in Sukhum. The building of the MVD itself was being guarded by militia-men from Tbilisi and other towns in Georgia. That measures were taken to re-inforce the forces of public order is in itself unremarkable; the question is, did these steps in fact contribute to the strength of these forces? The despatch of militia-units from Georgia rather than cooling the ardour of certain hotheads inflamed it — they saw in the presence of fellow-Kartvelians partners, albeit silent ones. Nor did it have a soothing effect on the Abkhazians, who saw it as a challenge — evidence of the determination of the Georgians to guarantee the holding of the exams at the TSU branch. This reduced the effectiveness of the call for restraint from the leaders of the NFA.

Nor, in my view, was it well-considered to reinforce the militia with men from other parts of Abkhazia: any conflagration would immediately spread throughout Abkhazia, and who would be in the districts to prevent it? Troops from Krasnodar should have been requested, but the leaders in Sukhum showed nothing but indecision and the like . . .

The Georgian school was attacked about 7pm, but, even before that, fighting had started on Rustaveli Prospect. Many believe that it was this and not the provocative gestures of the teachers in the makeshift branch of the TSU that served as the incitement to wreck the school; the blockaders were afraid, and not without cause, as we shall see, that a full-scale Kartvelian attack might be launched against them.

The actual fighting on Rustaveli started with a harmless incident: some Abkhazians decided to photograph the Kartvelian crowd. It must be said that both sides tried to obtain as much material of this kind as they could, and, as I experienced myself, such action did not always exactly arouse the sympathy of those being photographed! But now, with nerves strained, it evoked a storm of discontent — the enraged Kartvelians hurled themselves at the Abkhazians' car and beat up the photographer. Naturally, the Abkhazians rushed to his assistance, and the fight was on. At that moment there appeared from somewhere a lorry-load of stones, and everything assumed gigantic proportions. As for the militia in the vicinity, not only did they fail to take any steps to localise the incident, they preferred to vanish as soon as the affair changed from mere confrontation to hand-to-hand fighting!

At the school the militia-cordon did not flee but tried to separate the besieged from the Abkhazians and to ensure their evacuation. They failed to protect only one teacher who had been shouting obscenities, and he was soundly beaten up . . .

Now it was all over — the injured removed, the school and nearby streets cleared. Then, in the words of militia-captain Oleg Pilia, "three MAZs appeared with people stripped to the waist; they were Kartvelians. They broke through the thin cordon of militia who tried to stop them, and went towards the school. They had explosive devices and guns."

Information about Kartvelians possessing explosives — slabs of TNT with detonators, the preparation of which takes time — is confirmed by the Chief of Staff of the 8th Tbilisi Regiment. Yes, it is fearful to think what might have happened at the school if the Abkhazians, absolutely trusting and unarmed, had not managed to get away in time. Sad though it be, those hotheads who had decided after the fighting had broken out on Rustaveli that the time had come for positive action and that to delay was dangerous were proved quite right. The unarmed militia could scarcely have protected them — it was only thanks to their good fortune that they succeeded in defending the MVD.

"The soldiers blocked the road with their shields; but how can one stop heavy vehicles with shields? They had at once to open the MVD armoury and issue AKS automatic rifles held there without stopping to keep records. Anyone wanting one took it — Kartvelians and Abkhazians alike. With the help of these automatics, they managed to stop the MAZs."

July 15th-18th: the bridge over the Ghalidzga

The River Ghalidzga is on the edge of Ochamchira, itself the centre of the Ochamchira District. The territory on the other side is still Abkhazia, but the population there is predominantly Mingrelian. There is a mixed population in Ochamchira too. Therefore, on the fateful day the Ghalidzga unexpectedly became a frontier river.

*

The First Secretary of Ochamchira, Sergej Bagapsh, fully appreciated the potential danger which the regions of West Georgia offered to Abkhazia if aroused; their centre, Zugdidi, had become a focus for nationalistically minded elements. He realised that, if a flood of people in an anti-Abkhazian mood poured over from there, there would be no one but him to stop them. Before leaving for Sukhum, Bagapsh saw to it that on the bridge there was a GAI-post, which would not let through private cars or other suspicious forms of transport by which Kartvelian informals might get their men into Abkhazia. In case the GAI-forces proved inadequate, Bagapsh foresightedly arranged for a supply of heavy vehicles with which the bridge could be blocked, should need arise.

Daur Vouba of T'q'varchal (T'qʷ'archal) states: "We decided to stop the stream of traffic crossing from the Gal side around midnight and blocked the road with two MAZs and a cart. In about 15 minutes a crowd had formed on the far side; we had about 100 men. At that time no one thought of the possibility of shooting, and none of us had any weapons . . ."

Another T'qʷ'archalian, Genadij Cherigba, takes up the story:

"Soon there were bursts of automatic fire from across the river and shots from automatic rifles and shot-guns. Out of the crowd two men came to the bridge — one of medium height, even short, the other tall and well-built — and started shouting to their people, 'What are you doing?' But at that moment there was a shot from their crowd, sounded like a shotgun, and the smaller one fell; the crowd rushed at us. We threw stones, but then I fell, injured in the face and chest by light shot, and was taken to the Raikom. Even before the shooting, a heavy BELAZ came from their side, obviously taken from the Ingur hydro-electric station, and tried to move the dumper-truck. It was pelted with stones, and the driver jumped out, so that the bridge was even more solidly blocked."

Bagapsh returned to Ochamchira in the small hours, soon got his bearing and phoned the First Secretary of the Gal region to arrange a meeting at the bridge. But Bagapsh was fired on and withdrew, so the meeting never took place.

At 9am the First Secretary of the Zugdidi Gorkom (city committee), Guram Pipia, phoned Bagapsh with an identical suggestion. This again failed, as Pipia could not get through because of the blockade. Yes, too late did the local Party-chiefs think of this, when they were no longer able to control the situation without outside-help. From West Georgia an avalanche of vehicles was moving towards the Ghalidzga, now mainly occupied by armed men; they were convinced that in Abkhazia liquidation of Kartvelians was in full swing. Abkhazians too rushed to arms, even at the cost of illegal activity, in order to create an impassable wall to this avalanche. An extraordinary situation was developing, which demanded, many thought, extraordinary steps.

Militia Major Ruslan Ashuba reports: "I was at the bridge at 5am. There was shooting going on; automatic and shotgun fire was coming from the other side. When I arrived, there were not many people — about 100. But by 8am, there was a crowd of several thousand on the far side. People were arriving in dumper-trucks. There were wounded on both sides. I wept on seeing it. The militia could not restrain the fighting, and people took defence into their own hands."

But in order to "take defence into their own hands" they had to arm themselves. Only by returning the shotguns held in the State Bank was an assault on the militia station averted. Responsibility for this was accepted by regional procurator Valerij Gurdzhua, for which he now stands accused of grossly exceeding his powers. Consider what would have happened had Gurdzhua not exceeded his powers! Fortunately, thanks to his courage this did not happen. But in the regions of West Georgia, which were in any case under no immediate threat, militia-armouries were plundered and a great quantity of military weapons appeared in the hands of the population — pistols, automatics and carbines, taken from 28 militia units and SIZOs (Special Isolation Units) in Zugdidi; at the same time the prisoners were freed from the latter.

Colonel Aleksandr Zubarev reports: "We were called in and took off from Zaporozhe at 7.15am, July 16th, reaching Sukhum at 8.45. From there we moved in five helicopters at about 13.30 to 14.00 to the stadium at Ochamchira. We could hear firing and an explosion — a petrol-tanker had exploded at the bridge. At 5pm we were over T'amsh when we were told by radio to return to Ochamchira as a crowd of a couple of thousand was evidently on the move from the Gal District. We were told it was 5,000, but in fact it turned out that the crowd was of between 20,000-25,000 from various regions of West Georgia, as far away as Kutaisi."

As regards the appearance of a crowd of 25,000 a few hours after the military took control of the bridge, its size could just be a matter of chance, but I have data to the effect that during the afternoon vehicles which had brought people from Zugdidi were turning back to Gal and heading for other centres of population, allegedly because the main road was blocked. The outcome was that by a certain time, a build-up of living force, as it were, was taking place in the regions along the Ghalidzga, and this crowd was strategically concentrated at the bridge, where the leaders of the extremists considered it expedient. Why did they choose a moment when the military had already arrived?

It is hard to give a straightforward answer to this question, but the following is perfectly admissible as a working-hypothesis: it was an enforced step, caused precisely by the arrival of the military, who, it seems to me, were either not expected or at least not so soon. The original objective of the concentration of the forces from the regions of West Georgia consisted of the establishment not just of a concentration at the bridge, but of a massive armed confrontation which would have spread willy-nilly to the whole Gal District and which would eventually have led to a serious, almost uncontrollable, destabilisation of the situation in Abkhazia. The arrival of the military spoiled this plan. If they were to open the main road to traffic without delay, then people would be able personally to reassure themselves of the situation in Abkhazia and would calm down. And so, the decision was taken to concentrate at the bridge all those who were emotionally involved, so that this crowd would form an impassable obstacle on the main road.

July 17th and the following days: Ochamchira District
Report of Lt-Colonel Vladimir Lebedev (Leningrad): "I arrived as commander on July 17th. As First Secretary of Georgia's Communist Party, Givi Gumbaridze, and I were discussing our deployment, in rushed a man in a highly excited state, shouting that vehicles with armed men were in the vicinity and that everyone was shooting at one another. The office went into shock. I waited for orders but no decision was taken. Then I said I'd take some men and stop it. Near the village of Lakhut'i, we saw the silhouette of a drop-sided lorry, loaded with people. It was interesting that all of them wore white headbands; their average

age must have been 25-27, although one or two were over 35.

"At about 19.00 I was seeing Gumbaridze again for a conference. It had been in progress for about 10 minutes when another alarm was given. Two incidents, in Lakhut'i and Merk'ula (Merkʷ'yla), were neutralised."

Thus, while some excited persons were blocking the main road at the bridge, others had been sent along the right bank of the Ghalidzga to stir up trouble. Whatever the truth may be, the brief presence of the groups achieved its nefarious purpose, giving rise to rumours and complicating somewhat relationships between the Abkhazians and the military. The main goal of the military was the surrender of every weapon. But how could these be surrendered when armed groups of Kartvelians were on the loose? Rumours, however, need feeding, and the presence of the military, as the very first day showed, rendered impossible unopposed raiding by groups of any size. From this the next step to professionalisation is the establishment of small groups, hiding mostly in villages, carrying out occasional attacks, both conspicuous ones, so as to sustain fear in the Abkhazian section of the population, and quite small ones, so as not to bring themselves to the serious attention of the military. The chess-board pattern of Abkhazian and Kartvelian villages simplified the achievement of such tasks. For the formation of these groups declassified elements, including convicts freed from the SIZO in Zugdidi, could be used. Sudden strikes against Abkhazian houses, beatings, but in the main threats and demonstrations of their presence were their *modus operandi*.

Similar ethnic problems must exist in other countries, in some of which perhaps greater success in their resolution has been achieved; they have had longer experience than we. One feels that our law-enforcement agencies would have nothing to lose by copying such practices. Hitherto they have had to try to display, nonetheless, considerable variation and flexibility in dealing with similar situations. Thus, in Abkhazia, it seems to me, as the Abkhazian population no less than the Kartvelian is much given to patrolling and to mutual raids, it would be inappropriate to put the emphasis on unconditional total disarmament, which is simply unrealistic, rather than on the taking control of the potential forces for self-defence on both sides by forming a joint, three-sided (Abkhazian, Kartvelian, Russian) controlling body.

But today there is none of this; each side is doing as it pleases. The military are patrolling, observing, responding to signals; the Kartvelian extremists, as ever, are trying to prevent passions cooling, terrorising and tormenting the Abkhazians, while the latter are coming ever closer to taking counter-measures.

You will have realised by now that I have reached a simple conclusion: what has happened is by no means just the result of lack of reflection or short-sightedness on the part of the leaders of Georgia and Abkhazia. Above all else there is the feeling that some hand is guiding the process, quite consciously and thoroughly, in the direction that its owner wishes it to go. I could not have said that, knowing only of the javelins or armed groups, or of the fight on the Ghalidzga, but the whole panoply of facts points incontestably to such a conclusion.

T'amsh
September 12th 1989

*

Who was to blame?

"The situation in the ASSR remains tense" — this is the usual sentence with which the communiqués of the temporary press-centre of the USSR's MVD in Abkhazia and the press-centre of Abkhazia's MVD begin. And so it is, although it is not terribly obvious from a superficial sidelong glance on what such a disturbing conclusion is based. Trains run, buses run, shops open, coffee steams in coffee-shops, young men flirt, weaving around the very small number of tourists. According to the officers of the militia and IF-units, the main source of tension is the huge quantity of arms in the hands of the population, filched from the ravaged IF-units (mainly in the regions of West Georgia), arms-dealers, armouries etc or left over from the days of World War II.

This weaponry is dangerous, and even more so when it is in the hands of men blinded by hatred and fears, men under the influence of emotion rather than reason, and therefore vulnerable to anyone able to direct these emotions. Therefore, the existence of weaponry in Abkhazia and the surrounding areas, although it certainly aggravates the situation here, in itself does not at all cause tension; it would thus be wrong to withdraw the emergency-measures introduced here on such formal criteria as the return to the authorities of stolen weapons and the surrender of licensed shot-guns. A lot of responsible people, however, support such simplifications.

But perhaps I am dramatising this excessively; the very fact that all this weaponry in the hands of the population has so far, fortunately, not led to massive bloodshed is evidence that reason has not yet lost its restraining power. Yes, between July 15th and 17th emotions ran high, but then the calming effect of the military, it seemed, made people, if not feel ashamed of themselves and their conduct, for they will all produce their excuses, at least feel horror for all that happened, for neighbour raising hand against neighbour, fellow-countrymen against fellow-countrymen, nationality against nationality.

I am writing these lines in an Abkhazian village, shortly after returning from a tour of villages in the regions adjoining Abkhazia (Mingrelia and Upper Svanetia), and so I feel I can form an opinion of the moods and thoughts which govern the lives of local people. "We want to live in peace," they all aver. "What happened was madness." "We live side by side." "We are bound together not just by ties of neighbourliness but of blood. If not every family, certainly every clan has its blood-connections with an Abkhazian (or correspondingly Kartvelian) clan. We ordinary folk could have done without what has happened." "We ordinary people should get on with tilling the soil and earning our bread." "This has all been stirred up by the authorities — it is their little game."

But at the same time the Abkhazians are convinced that, whatever anyone says, it was the Kartvelians who started it, acting as the tools of those who hope, with their assistance, to "realise their anti-Soviet ambitions for the foundation of a single indivisible Georgia outside the USSR" and hope to pull off almost a "Fascist putsch" — "look at *Leninskoe Znamja* (the Soviet newspaper for the Red Army) (19th July) to see them mock the statues of our leaders." The Kartvelians are convinced that the Abkhazians are to blame, whose politicians had filled them with ideas about their special rights to land, who had obtained "by the stupidity, or rather the anti-nationalistic policies first of Russia and then of the Soviet State, an entirely bogus Abkhazian autonomy . . ."

So as to give you some idea of the consequences of these policies for Abkhazia, allow me to quote from Zurab Anchabadze's book *Essays on the ethnic history of the Abkhazian People* (Sukhum, 1976; in Russian):

". . . The migratory movement began immediately after the unification of Abkhazia with Russia . . . Nikolaj Marr (half-Georgian, half-Scottish philologist of the late Tsarist and early Soviet periods) wrote on this point, '(Abkhazia) was depopulated even in its central ethnographical region. Thus, all that was left of the Gumista region (now the regions of Sukhum and Gulripsh) were a few delapidated farmyards with fruit-trees, not a single Abkhazian, not a word of the language . . .' After the end of the Russo-Turkish war the Tsarist authorities beset the Abkhazians with cruel repressions . . . designating the vast majority of the Abkhazians as a 'guilty population', forbidden to live in the coastal area or less than 20 *versts* from Sukhum. The Abkhazians were designated 'temporary inhabitants' in their own land and for the least anti-governmental activity were threatened with evacuation from their homeland to the last man. The lands left by the Abkhazian chieftains started to be given out by the Tsarist government to military and civil administrators, who used them for colonisation, which, in the 1880s and 1890s, took on a widespread character. At the same period the movement from neighbouring regions, mainly Mingrelia, of peasants who had lost their land increased . . . In 1903 the Georgian (actually Mingrelian — *editor*) social reformer Tedo Sakhok'ia writes: 'Anyone who travelled here (i.e. in Abkhazia) 20 years ago will not believe how this country has changed in so short a time. The ethnic structure of the inhabitants has become mixed. You will hear Russian, Georgian, Greek, Armenian . . . Everything here has become confused' . . ." (pp 85-87).

"At the census of 1939 the population of the Abkhazian ASSR was made up of the following nationalities: Abkhazians 56,200, Georgians (i.e. Kartvelians) 92,000, Russians 60,200, Armenians 49,700, Greeks 34,600, Ukrainians 8,600, Jews 2,000, Others 8,600" (p136).

"According to the data of the 1970 census, nationalities more than 1,000 strong are listed as follows: Georgians (i.e. Kartvelians) 199,534, Russians 92,889, Abkhazians 77,276, Armenians 72,850, Greeks 13,144, Ukrainians 11,955, Jews 4,372, Belorussians 1,901, Estonians 1,834, Tatars 1,738, Ossetes 1,214. Abkhazians amounted to 15.9 per cent of the total population of the ASSR" (p162).

Thus, we see the tragic result of the truly anti-nationalistic policies of Tsarist Russia and, sad to say, of our State too, which has led to the historical land of the Abkhazians being usurped by other people. The title 'autonomous' has not so much resisted this process as merely masked it, permitting it to take place in the name of the Abkhazian people themselves.

Naturally, under the current system of the formation of elective governmental bodies, the Abkhazians are more and more excluded from these, which means from the control of the fate of their land, and this cannot fail, sadly, to be reflected in the culture of their nationality, the very existence of which must be in jeopardy. It may be said that I am becoming unnecessarily perturbed; one need only glance at the per centage of Abkhazians among the leaders to realise that they are not really so very constrained. I fully admit that this per centage is in fact higher than the Abkhazians might expect on a *pro rata* basis among the other nationalities, but it is more regrettable than cheering, for it indicates what is in fact the command-mechanism of promotion, which replaces the elective mechanism.

Nor do the Abkhazians derive any benefit from this, for it is not they who decide which of them is to rule, and these Abkhazian leaders do not have the interests of their own people at heart. This is a common failing. Frankly, I find it bitter and risible when cultural activists or leaders of the unofficial parties quote such per centages in speaking of the repressed state of their people. With the development of democratic means of governing society and the realisation of tendencies to the growth of the economic and political independence of republics, including ASSRs, these figures would certainly carry weight; then, I am sure, they would really start shouting.

Yes, the draft-programme of the Communist Party of the Soviet Union for nationality-questions may well be satisfactory from the point of view of those nationalities which are a majority within their administrative boundaries, but little will change in the situation of those who constitute minorities when the pre-eminence of another people starts to show in what was formerly their territory.

Vladimir K'vanch'iani of the Svan village Lat'ali says: "For centuries we have been living side by side. Now the Abkhazians have started to demand much from Georgia. They want their own republic, as though the Kartvelians were their worst enemies. It has been nearly five years since they started displaying hostility to the Kartvelians. Now the Abkhazians hate those Kartvelian experts who write that the lands on which the Abkhazians live are ancient Kartvelian lands. The experts know better who lived where, and where they live now. There has never been hostility between the Svans and the Abkhazians, but now the Svans are in the same position as the rest of Georgia. We have been in Sukhum just as long as the Abkhazians themselves."

I had another such depressing conversation with some young Kartvelian archaeologists working in Svanetia — all the more depressing for me as I already knew them from previous collaboration. I respect and like them, but, when we met recently, we hardly understood one another. They sincerely believed in the aggressiveness of the Abkhazians (although they had never been to Abkhazia!) and in the fact that they had no business raising the question of secession from Georgia; this autonomy was, they said, nonsense, since one could equally justify Armenian or any other autonomy in Abkhazia.

When I was in Zugdidi, demonstrations were still taking place there. The basic demands were the disarmament of Abkhazian extremists and the punishment of the guilty. In Abkhazia demonstrations are now prohibited, but people make their wishes known in meetings with Party- and military leaders. The main thrust of Abkhazian demands consists of the strengthening of law and order, including measures which will render impossible disinformation and the incitement of discord between nationalities by the media, an end to the repression of Abkhazian personnel. The Kartvelian hunger-strikers in the village of Ilori, near Ochamchira, insisted on the replacement of the 'extremist leaders' of their region. The same was demanded by activist strikers from a number of enterprises in this region. These demands were basically met: the Raikom office (office of the local regional committee) was effectively replaced, including all its secretaries; a new chairman of the Raispolkom (local regional executive committee) was chosen; the elected chief of militia and the procurator were replaced. And all this when the ordinary people, Abkhazian and Kartvelian alike, consider that the region has been very fortunate in having Sergej Bagapsh as head of the Raikom; under him the region has improved economically, become more orderly, and the town of Ochamchira itself had been transformed.

Zurab Partsvania, a post-graduate at the Tbilisi Polytechnic, told me: "Though we have nothing personally against Bagapsh and some of the other regional leaders, after what has happened none of the leadership has any right to stay here." When I asked whether he considered that this principle ought to apply to the leaders of other regions, including those of Georgia, such as Zugdidi, Zurab replied that this was of course so, but that it was the concern of those who lived there.

Even today in Ochamchira someone keeps constantly putting out flags of Independent Georgia (1918-21), with which the Abkhazians connect the dramatic events of the bloody repression of their own independence. I have seen these flags flying over literally all the village-soviets in the Gal District, whereas the Abkhazian villages are decorated with slogans demanding the recognition of the status of their Socialist Republic of 1921-31, together with an occasional flag of that republic.

If Tengiz Shanava, Second Secretary of the Zugdidi Gorkom (city committee), is persuaded that the cause of what happened lies in the unreasonable demands of unofficial Abkhazian organisations concerning the establishment of the branch of the TSU, which aroused in the final analysis the aggressiveness of the Abkhazians, including the Abkhazian leaders, Guram Pipia, First Secretary, said that he was unable to specify the causes of what happened and that one could only rely on official information. Shanava does this too, quoting in support of his arguments the figures published by the Georgian-language republican paper *The Communist*, which show that the Kartvelians suffered significantly more than the Abkhazians — it is odd that the MVD of the USSR press centre makes no analysis on a nationality basis so as not to cause a deterioration in the atmosphere, the information given being published with acknowledgement only to vague "reliable sources."

The Abkhazians interpret these figures as proof that the Kartvelians were the attacking side, for the attackers are bound to suffer greater losses. Shanava produced as proof of his viewpoint an interview with the

Procurator of Georgia, Vakht'ang Razmadze, in which he more or less accused the leaders of the Gudauta and Ochamchira regions of acquiring and issuing weapons. This statement, even if the facts it contains were true, is to say the least out of place, and in no way helps to normalise the position, to say nothing of the well known principle, especially applicable to members of the law-enforcement agencies, according to which guilt may only be determined in court. Furthermore, information at my disposal leaves practically no room for the possibility of the delivery of weapons to Ochamchira by boat. People, local inhabitants who had been trapped in Sukhum by the events, were taken out by boat, because the roads were blocked by the conflicting sides, but this was done, of course, in close liaison with the frontier-guards; people were not embarked in secret but publicly, right outside the Raikom, so that, if there had been any weapons, they would naturally have been seen and confiscated, but there were none — they have no existence outside Razmadze's interview.

However, whatever the cause, only Abkhazia and the adjacent regions of West Georgia are actually oversaturated with arms. This is, of course, potentially dangerous, but on the other hand the presence of these weapons has until now offered a barrier of sorts to the outbreak of open confrontation; people have to be strongly motivated before they will engage in a fight in which firearms may be used. The presence of units of the USSR's MVD and the state of emergency work in the same way. Such forceful factors, not in themselves constructive, do not of themselves encourage the opening of dialogue, but at least they inhibit the outbreak of physical violence and the shedding of blood, which would in no time at all erupt into flames of mutual hatred. But hatred can be born of things which seem much less offensive.

Let us take as an example the Georgian newspaper *Young Communist* (July 29th). This is what the writer Revaz Mishveladze writes: "Georgia stands on the brink of a real catastrophe — of extirpation. What devil ruled our minds, when we yielded up our land, gained inch by inch over the centuries, defended and soaked with our blood, to every homeless beggar that has come down from the fringes of the Caucasus, to tribes that have neither history nor culture? We must make every effort to raise the per centage of Georgians (Kartvelians in our terms — *editor*) in the population of Georgia (currently 61 per cent [a misprint for 71 per cent — *editor*]) to 95 per cent. The remaining five per cent must consist of only those who know Georgian, who have a proper respect for Georgia, who have been brought up under the influence of the Georgian national phenomenon. We must persuade other nationalities, who are multiplying suspiciously in the land of David the Builder, that ideal conditions for the development of their personalities are to be found only in their homelands. Apart from a peaceful announcement to that effect, it is possible to bring the law to bear upon those guests who eventually prove obdurate and slow to leave. The law will state clearly that land will be taken at once from those who have illegally possessed it, that any buildings erected there will be demolished without compensation . . . A few days ago a delegation from Georgia (which included the First Secretary of the Q'vareli Raikom) spent eight hours in nervous conversation with the leaders of Daghestan, trying to reach agreement on the return to their fatherland of part of the Lezgians (actually Avars — *editor*). Finally, after reminding them of their patriotic duty, of the possibility of actual danger, we succeeded in partially accomplishing our mission.

"Thus there lie before Georgia two urgent tasks: 1. to rescue the national organism of Georgia, i.e. the demographic regularisation of Georgia; 2. the attainment of the independence of Georgia. i.e. the restoration of the status quo of May 26th 1918."

Writer Mishveladze has every right to think whatever he likes; he is a man of emotion, not of learning (he is both a writer and a professor at TSU! — *editor*), and he may not even understand that salvation for a nation lies not in the achievement of statehood, which puts it in an exclusive position with regard to other nations, but in the formation of conditions which will allow it to live at peace with others. For the former gives birth to hatred and the threat of destruction, whereas the latter brings forth tolerance and the possibility of harmonious development of national culture. This latter can be achieved only in a social order of the democratic type.

Will Kartvelians become any happier by driving all other nationalities out of Georgia? It seems to Mishveladze that they will, and that is his affair, but it seems otherwise to the vast majority. Not without reason has such a policy, closely akin as it is to genocide, been condemned by world-opinion, which, by the way, has at the same time re-inforced the right of any man to choose freely where he will live, and by the laws of our country, which forbid the incitement of inter-ethnic discord, to which, without fail, such ideas must lead. These laws, moreover, have not been repealed, and therefore, it would appear, the publication of so nationalist, chauvinist an article must evoke an appropriate reaction if not, indeed, in those who bear responsibility for the publication of the paper, then at all events in those whose duty it is to ensure that the law is obeyed and to exact retribution for its infringement. Neither the one nor the other, however, has occurred, despite the tragedy in Abkhazia. What is this? — an oversight? fear of the informals, who have so taken possession of public opinion? or an attempt to shape public opinion? A long series of pieces in the Georgian media close in spirit to the article quoted above inclines one to the latter view. It is particularly annoying that even the most recent events in Abkhazia have not brought about, even temporarily, a cessation to the spreading of this drug. On July 26th the Russian-language newspaper *Dawn of the East* devoted more than half a column to the history of the mutual relationships of Democratic Georgia and the League of Nations.

On the 27th, alongside a lengthy article on the subject of whether the establishment of Soviet power in Georgia should be regarded as the result of annexation or of the 'export of a political system', appeared the interview with the Procurator of Georgia, Razmadze, in which the transporting of armed men from Gudauta to Ochamchira was 'confirmed.' Between the 28th and 30th, the same organ devoted four(!) columns to an analysis by Kartvelian experts of the 'Abkhazian Letter', addressed by 60 leading protagonists of Abkhazian culture to the Presidium of the 19th All-Union Party Congress . . . Objections may be raised: "Why nowadays, when the veils are parting a little over the secret, may a Party-organ not provide space for subjects which are unquestionably of vital interest and stimulate the nation?" But why touch upon these topics at the very moment when relationships between Kartvelians and Abkhazians are at breaking point? Why choose this particular time to embark on an exchange of views with Abkhazian cultural activists, to reveal the alleged imprecisions and distortions that they have tolerated without, however, having any effect on much that is really alarming in the ASSR by way of economic development, the structure of the national economy, the ecological and demographic positions, which is what has evoked so clear-cut a position among them? I am not saying that they were right in seeking their particular way out of the condition in which Abkhazia found itself; history is good for understanding tendencies in the development of society, for acquiring wisdom, but not at all as a source of ready-made examples to follow in building the future.

For that reason I cannot comprehend the Abkhazian demand to return to the 1921-31 position, any more than I understand the idealisation of the status of Democratic Georgia. What the Kartvelian and Abkhazian experts would find it worthwhile talking about is the joint-problems of their nations, how to resolve them by joint-efforts, rather than exchanging blows in public and compounding the problems even more. But no, another organ of the Georgian Communist Party, the (twice-weekly: once in Georgian, then in Russian) paper *National Education*, devoted four of its columns on July 30th to an analysis of the history of the mutual relationships between Georgia and Abkhazia from the 1890s to February 1931, when Abkhazia ceased to be a treaty-republic and became merely an autonomous republic within Georgia.

Leaving aside the wholly inappropriate time chosen for its publication, the piece is frankly biased. What is the value, for example, of the authors' insistence that "the Constitution of Democratic Georgia, confirmed by the Constituent Assembly on Feb 21st 1921, provided a just solution to the Abkhazian question"? — and this when, according to facts quoted in the same article, the delegation from the National Soviet of Abkhazia was present only as an observer!

The status of the Abkhazian Soviet Treaty Republic of 1921, it turns out, "played into the hands of the extreme nationalists and created, contrary to the interests of the two nations, preconditions for the deterioration of their fraternal historical links, which might on the one hand have been to the advantage of chauvinist circles in Russia, and on the other hand might have favoured the pan-Turkic tendencies of Turkey." One may speculate, if such were the consequences of the truncated equality that existed between Georgia and Abkhazia in the 1920s, to whose advantage was the unjust position in which Abkhazia found itself in the 1930s? Yes, all nationalities suffered from the policies of those years, but Georgian children, as distinct from Abkhazian, were nevertheless always educated in their native language, and Georgia was not covered deliberately with Russian villages, as Abkhazia was with Kartvelian villages in the 1940s! So if I were in the shoes of the Kartvelian experts, I would be reluctant to hold that out as an example of equality. But then what else can be expected from a Russian chauvinist like me?!

On August 13th writer Ak'ak'i Gelovani writes in the same paper: "It is surprising that on this occasion the minority displayed ferocity before an overwhelming majority . . . thanks to their weapons, their cunningly contrived plan and the protection of the authorities! It all started, as is well known, with a surprise armed attack, long-suppressed malice burst into flame, and then the attackers tried to blame those whom they had attacked (while themselves disappearing in good time) . . . Those injured and mutilated by illicitly acquired Turkish automatics and rifles and by iron bars begged for help . . ." That is to say, he is writing total falsehood, as I can testify as an eye-witness.

This is further borne out by the staff of the procuracy of Georgia and the men of the republican MVD — there were neither cunningly contrived Abkhazian plans, nor surprise armed attacks, nor Turkish automatics or rifles. And by the time this article was published a whole month had elapsed since the events, so that the editorial staff had had sufficient time to learn how to distinguish truth from malicious invention, to try, if not to see everything through the eyes of its own staff, at least to take an interest in competent sources of information.

I was told, for example, at the HQ of the Ochamchira District's tactical group that every time a gang was disarmed, there were in it Kartvelians who lived not locally but elsewhere. This answers the question who was threatening whom. But I do not exclude the possibility that elsewhere things were different. The main point is, I am very much afraid, that if this criminal line is maintained by the Georgian press, if furthermore — God forbid — it is supported by some decisions of a provocative sort — routine ones, to do with the TSU branch and the like — or provocative acts such as strikes, demonstrations, waving of banners, then we shall after all see armed groups amongst the Abkhazians. But perhaps this is what someone is trying to achieve? It is an unpleasant thought, but how else does one explain the impunity with which the media are fanning the flame of inter-ethnic discord, and those decisions, by no means the best possible, taken by the leadership of the republic in connection with events in Abkhazia?

How has First Secretary of the Abkhazian Obkom V. F. Khishba remained in office? It seems to me that he is untouched either because there is a fear that he might focus attention on the role of the Central Committee of Georgia's Communist Party in the situation that arose, which, broadly considering the undistinguished political background of the First Secretary seems less than likely, or because he was suitable for the policy which Georgia's Central Committee was, and still is, following. One can form an opinion of the nature of this policy from the publications of the republican party press, excerpts from which I have already set before you.

Leaving alone the obedient Abkhazian Khishba, Gumbaridze is strengthening the bureau of the Abkhazian Obkom with such strong leaders as the Secretary of Georgia's Central Committee, G. A. Anchabadze, who has become chairman of the Council of Ministers, and Doctor of Economics L. Ja. Khaburzania, who was formerly for a long time head of the economics department of Georgia's Central Committee and has now been appointed Second Secretary of the Abkhazian Obkom. Thus, the present membership of the bureau is not only, one assumes, satisfactory in terms of obedience, but also has a certain potential for the initiative sought by Tbilisi. One of the first decisions of this organ, a decision which stirred up the whole ASSR and caused the strike of miners in T'q'varchal, belongs entirely to him.

On August 3rd the bureau of the Abkhazian Obkom decided to suspend from duty all Heads of Departments of Internal Affairs, and at the same time to suspend Major-General M. A. Chulkov, minister of internal affairs. This decision is naturally restricted to the boundaries of the ASSR, but the great part of the weapons had been stolen outside it, where 28 internal affairs units had been robbed together with the SIZO in Zugdidi. The objection of the Abkhazian section of the population to this decision is therefore quite understandable, as it seemed to them clearly repressive and discriminatory. Apprehension arose among the people that they were being deprived of the few on whom they could count for protection, and secondly, that this was a continuation of the policy of flushing out non-corrupt officials at all levels.

Not long ago I learned in the republican procuracy that, whereas all the events stirred up in the Abkhazian ASSR by the happenings of July are being scrutinised in terms of their mutual relationship, everything that happened outside the boundaries of the ASSR (the suspiciously easy theft of weaponry from MVD units, attacks on sentries and armouries, the 'taking' of the SIZO in Zugdidi, inflammatory speeches at demonstrations, the use of State vehicles for the transporting of armed men to the river Ghalidzga, etc) is regarded as though it had been taking place in isolation and had nothing to do with the events in Abkhazia. This, surely, greatly complicates the task of unravelling the account of the possible preparation for the events, of their deliberate precipitation from the regions of West Georgia . . .

*

Conclusion

Unfortunately, each of us can only do what he is cut out for, whatever his abilities can achieve, and my artistic abilities are by no means great enough for me to venture to give a full account of the horror of the inter-ethnic conflict which I witnessed. I do not flatter myself that the reader will necessarily have much energy to spare more than a sidelong glance at this notice of the relevant events. Present-day inhabitants of Moscow, when they discuss the events in Abkhazia, just shrug their shoulders in incomprehension of the "imaginary fears" of the Abkhazians and Kartvelians.

Alternatively, they are filled with indignation: "What do they want to start trouble for? These people were living peacefully, it seemed, and now things have gone to pot — that's where perestroika gets you! No soap, no tea, rising crime-rate, trouble everywhere, somebody always wanting something, and now we can't even go down south for a bit of a quiet holiday!" But, if we do not realise that the problems of Abkhazia and Moldavia and the other unquiet areas are genuine and that these problems are ours too, even if this is not yet terribly obvious, and if we do not try to solve them by our joint efforts to everybody's satisfaction, then it will not be long before a trip to the cornershop becomes a risky business, let alone going off to the south, and our worthy neighbour assumes the appearance of a suspicious character, an enemy of the nation and of our families.

I think that considerable assistance has been given to the Kartvelians' confidence by a speech in Tbilisi by Shevardnadze, member of the USSR Politburo and Minister of Foreign Affairs, in which he, on behalf of Comrade Gorbachev, expressed satisfaction at the way in which the new government of Georgia (i.e. the one that came to power under Givi Gumbaridze after the April 9th killings in Tbilisi)[2] was dealing with the complex problems before it, including that of restoring the loss of faith in the Party and that of dialogue with unofficial organisations.

This procedure is fraught with deplorable consequences, with the threat of the fascisization of Kartvelian society, for, although Shevardnadze ended by stressing the need to acknowledge such realities as the irreversible tendency of a given people, however small it might be, to fight to the end for its culture and its preservation, I fear that his overall call may not have been understood as one for a more tactfully worded, sober approach to the fulfilment of the strategic wishes of the unofficial organisations in Georgia.

Quotations given above provide the reader with some indication as to their nature, and it is precisely by tacitly supporting these that the "new" leadership in Tbilisi is endeavouring to regain its "lost confidence."

T'amsh
September 13th 1989

8
History: the modern period
Jurij Anchabadze

The 1990s will remain in the history of Abkhazia not only as a period of grievous political ordeals and destructive cataclysms, but also as a decade of active struggle for national-state self-determination, and as an epoch of hitherto unseen solidarity and consolidation of the Abkhazian people and the concentration of its strength, spirit and historical aspirations.

The extraordinary event that occurred on March 18th 1989 was the precursor of this new stage in the history of Abkhazia. On this day a national assembly was held in the village of Lykhny on the initiative of the National Forum of Abkhazia — *Ajdgylara* 'Unity'. This assembly was attended by over 30,000 people; though the majority were obviously ethnic Abkhazians (roughly one third of the entire Abkhazian population of the republic), there were thousands of representatives of local Kartvelians, Russians, Armenians and Greeks (as reported on the pages of Ajdgylara's Russian-language paper *Edinenie* 'Unity', 1, of October 25th 1989). The assembly approved an appeal to the highest organs of power in the USSR requesting the restitution of Abkhazia's status as a Soviet Socialist Republic (i.e. Union Republic, separate from, and on a par with, Soviet Georgia and the other 14 then-existing Union Republics — *editor*).

The Centre (meaning the Kremlin), as usual, replied with silence. However, the Georgian reaction was quick to follow. After just a few days the leader of the Communist Party of Georgia, Dzhumber P'at'iashvili, speaking at a session of the republican Supreme Soviet, condemned the so-called Lykhny Declaration in harsh and menacing terms. After just a few days more the First Secretary of the Abkhazian Regional Committee of the Communist Party, Boris Adlejba, was dismissed — his signature was also appended to the Lykhny Declaration, and this caused extreme annoyance in Tbilisi. The Georgian national movement, already raging under slogans demanding restitution of the independence of a single and indivisible Georgia, received in those days a new impulse: henceforth Abkhazia took its place alongside Moscow as the main bogey of the Georgian nationalists. At stormy rallies in Tbilisi, together with calls to fight against the "Soviet empire" and "Russian occupiers" a powerful chorus voiced a demand for the immediate annulment of Abkhazian autonomy. The campaign to frighten and discredit Abkhazia was promoted also across the entire Georgian media.

Simultaneously, Georgian political organisations within Abkhazia itself were activated. From the end of March to July, almost without a break, there was held here a series of meetings, street processions, demonstrations, strikes, and other actions on the part of the local Kartvelian population, all of which were of a confrontational, anti-Abkhazian character. Abkhazia found itself hosting a constant stream of 'guests' from Tbilisi, principally representatives of the national-chauvinist wing of the Georgian movement, including its leaders, the Mingrelians Merab K'ost'ava and Zviad Gamsakhurdia, whose extremist statements inspired new waves of anti-Abkhazian hysteria.[1]

The single-minded division of organisations and enterprises along ethnic lines became one of the forms of political pressure: Kartvelians refused to work with Abkhazians, demanding the dismissal of those in authority — i.e. Abkhazians. In these conditions a split also occurred at the Abkhazian State University in Sukhum when Kartvelian teachers and students stopped going to work or their classes, demanding that a special university for Kartvelians be established in Sukhum. In connivance with Kartvelian activity in Abkhazia the authorities in Tbilisi proceeded to meet these demands, adopting in May a resolution on the opening in Sukhum of a branch of Tbilisi State University (TSU). This caused an extreme negative reaction amongst the Abkhazians, who began energetically to try to secure a change to this decision, seeing in the course of events not a humanitarian but an exclusively political sub-text.

From this moment the problem of the TSU branch in Sukhum became the main object around which the activity of both sides' national movements centred. For the Kartvelians the establishment to suit their wishes of a structure quite unwanted in Abkhazia symbolised the political domination and all-powerful position of their ethnic community in the republic; for the Abkhazians, who were unable to exert any influence in this matter, the situation became yet one more unambiguous confirmation of the way their ethnic rights were being strangled on their own soil. Tbilisi made no move to retreat even after June 21st when the Regional Committee and the Council of Ministers of Abkhazia officially declared its negative attitude to the intended opening in Sukhum of the TSU-Branch.

The July events in Abkhazia had a broad resonance in the North Caucasus, where public opinion and the positions of a range of ethno-

political organisations were unanimously pro-Abkhazian. The choice of Sukhum as the place to hold the First Conference of the Peoples of the Caucasus (August 25-26th 1989) was an expression of support. The conference saw the establishment of the Assembly of the Mountain Peoples of the Caucasus (subsequently transformed into the Confederation of [Mountain] Peoples of the Caucasus), which declared as its goal the political unification and the co-operation of all the peoples of the region. Membership of the assembly/confederation, which in a

Abkhazia abounds in tourist attractions, both old and new, from the lush resort of Gagra (facing page, bottom), to the ruins of the sixth century church at Tsandrypsh (centre) and the unique Pitsunda promontory set against a tall pine forest (top). Above on this page are three views of Old Sukhum.

short space of time became a political force in the region, had for the Abkhazians a far from insignificant psychological and practical meaning, sensing as they did allied support from neighbouring peoples.

Declaration of sovereignty

The year 1990 brought no relief from worry to Abkhazia. The weakening power of Communism lost its position of authority, yielding the political initiative to nationalist movements, which in both Georgia and Abkhazia were becoming the one and only expression of popular aspirations. It was, however, obvious that the political orientations of the Abkhazian and Georgian nationalist movements were of a radically divergent character.

On August 25th 1990 the Supreme Soviet of Abkhazia passed the

Declaration on the State Sovereignty of the Soviet Socialist Republic of
Abkhazia (for the text see either Amkvab & Ilarionova, 1992, pp 12-15,
or Marykhuba, 1994, pp 479-82). Within the framework of the still
existing USSR this was a purely declarative act, even though it
manifested one more time the goals of the Abkhazian movement. In
Tbilisi the Declaration gave rise to the next round of stormy indignation
from both the official Communist authorities, who smartly denounced
the Declaration as having no juridical force, and the national movement
that opposed the Communists; its leaders once more charged Abkhazia
with separatism and announced that they would not allow it self-
determination.

In Abkhazia itself the mutual relations between the Abkhazian and
Kartvelian communities continued in their state of tension, and there
were occasions when the situation attained an explosive character — for
example, at the start of August when in response to the preparation of a
peaceful march across the territory of Abkhazia by Meskhians (the so-
called Meskhetian Turks) wishing to return to their native areas in
southern Georgia's borderlands with Turkey whence they had been
deported to Uzbekistan in 1944 by Stalin, the Georgian side announced
that it would take up arms; or again at the start of October when armed
Georgian fighters came to Abkhazia accompanying the head of the
Georgian Orthodox Church, Patriarch Ilia II, who was visiting his
Abkhazian parishes.[2]

On December 4th 1990 Vladislav Ardzinba was elected chairman of
the Supreme Soviet of Abkhazia. Born in 1945, this young, energetic
politician's shoulder had no burden to bear of a past in the Communist
nomenklatura.[3] An intellectual, by profession a specialist in Hittite and
the history of the ancient Near East, Ardzinba acquired an extraordinary
popularity, thereby becoming the genuine leader of the Abkhazian
people. Coming to power in the republic at a difficult moment, he
resolutely and dynamically embarked on a course leading to the
construction of a new political future for Abkhazia.

Preservation of civic peace within Abkhazia was one of the main
problems facing Ardzinba. By demonstratively making a local
Mingrelian his deputy, the new head of the republic indicated that he
was determined to construct a polity that would operate by balancing the
mutual interests of the different communities; subsequently he showed
in practice that these were real advances.

Another anxiety for Ardzinba were the ever more aggravated
relations with Tbilisi, where in October 1990 the forces of the radical
opposition, headed by Zviad Gamsakhurdia, a Mingrelian from Abasha,
succeeded the Communists who had lost the parliamentary elections. To

the accompaniment of slogans like "Georgia for the Georgians" and "Georgia — God's chosen nation," which even the leading politicians and spiritual leaders of the new regime felt no shame in articulating, a suffocating wave of national chauvinist hysteria swept over the republic. Announcing the withdrawal of Georgia from the make-up of the USSR, Gamsakhurdia declared that he would permit in no shape or form the political self-determination of Abkhazia. Even during the final weeks of his hold on power, when he was in the process of being driven from his post by an opposition armed putsch, Gamsakhurdia did not change his anti-Abkhazian position, demanding of his compliant parliament extra powers to pacify by force of arms the recalcitrant republic.

Vladislav Ardzinba did not once visit Tbilisi, single-mindedly determined to keep his distance from the Gamsakhurdia regime with its political unpredictability, semi-fascist ideology and totalitarian practice. At the same time the Abkhazian leader actively supported the so-called Novo-Ogarevskian process,[4] Mikhail Gorbachev's last attempt to reform the USSR (in part) by democratising the national-state structure of the Union by means of equalising the statuses of the Soviet union-republics, on the one hand, and all the autonomous formations, on the other. Ardzinba's Novo-Ogarevskian policy found legitimacy in the results of the all-Union referendum that was held on March 17th 1991 on the question of the preservation of the USSR. The overwhelming majority of the Abkhazians and the other non-Kartvelian part of Abkhazia's population voted in favour of preserving the Union.[5] It was symptomatic that two weeks later the Abkhazians and the non-Kartvelians boycotted the referendum called by the Gamsakhurdian authorities on the question of Georgia's independence.

However, the August putsch in Moscow wrecked the signing of the new union-treaty, and a few months later in December 1991 the Soviet Union ceased to exist. The post-Soviet space split along the lines of the administrative frontiers of the former Union-republics, as a result of which Abkhazia formally remained within the confines of the (ex-Soviet) Georgian Republic. Abkhazia thus found itself in a new historical situation, which again made the problem of its political future all too real.

In these conditions what was crucial for the Abkhazian national movement was to consolidate its position in legally constituted structures of authority, so that the elections to the republican parliament became yet another battleground on which the ethno-political interests of Abkhazia's different national communities came into conflict. The Abkhazians strove to establish mechanisms which would grant them the right to be effectively represented in parliament as a demographic minority so as to be able, should the need arise, to oppose possible anti-Abkhazian initiatives from the body of Kartvelian deputies. With this end in view, the idea of a two-chamber parliament was proposed by the Abkhazian side with a quota-system of representation from all the ethnic communities of Abkhazia. However, this project was rejected by the Kartvelians. After long and difficult negotiations it was decided to secure in the future parliament 28 places for Abkhazians as the autochthonous population, 26 for the Kartvelians, and 11 for representatives of the other ethnic communities.[6] At the first session of the new parliament on January 5th 1992 Vladislav Ardzinba was again voted to be its chairman.

During those very days the putschists expelled President Gamsakhurdia. After his flight from Tbilisi on January 6th there came to power a Military Council. Soon afterwards, in March, Eduard Shevardnadze was invited to return to his former fiefdom to become effective ruler of the country as head of its State Council. At first this raised hopes in Abkhazia for positive changes in Georgia's position. However, no such changes occurred. Furthermore, the West immediately rushed with unseemly haste to recognise and establish diplomatic relations with Shevardnadze's Georgia, even though no veneer of legitimacy in the shape of elections could be organised before October 11th, by which time Georgia had even gained admission to the United Nations. Since Abkhazia, as we have seen, had not managed to divorce itself from Soviet Georgia, the precipitate recognition awarded to Georgia had the regrettable consequence that henceforth all discussion of the Abkhazian problem had to be set against the new dominating principle in international politics, namely the inviolability of the territorial integrity of recognised states.[7]

One of the first acts of the new authorities in Tbilisi was the substitution of the 1978 Georgian constitution by the revived pre-Soviet constitution of 1921. News of this development came as a shock to Abkhazia, for in the 1921 Georgian constitution Abkhazia was not mentioned as an entity with state-legal relations, as may be seen from the wording of the two relevant clauses quoted in Chapter 6. For this reason the developing situation was perceived in Abkhazia as the removal of the constitutional guarantees of Abkhazia's autonomous status. The oratorical declarations periodically enunciated by Shevardnadze to the effect that the autonomy of Abkhazia would remain inviolable convinced no one, the more so since in the following months a range of legislative acts was passed which completely ignored the interests of Abkhazia and its people.

Tension increased in Abkhazia itself. The political bifurcation in the Supreme Soviet rendered impossible any joint constructive work between the Abkhazian and Kartvelian deputations, which from the month of May effectively did not come together in joint sessions. Kartvelian national organisations were activated, and they paraded banners calling for the dissolution of the Supreme Soviet and the dismissal of Ardzinba. Strikes and other acts of civil disobedience on the part of the Kartvelian population began, and attempts were seen to create parallel ('Georgian') organs of authority and a militia. On the streets of Sukhum there appeared armed squads who declared themselves to be divisions of the Georgian National Guard. In Tbilisi there was no reaction to the several invitations from the Abkhazian side to initiate talks on a common future Georgian-Abkhazian state. It was plain that the Georgian government had decided to create a unitary Georgian state, liquidating Abkhazian autonomy.

In these circumstances the Supreme Soviet of Abkhazia adopted on July 23rd 1992 the resolution 'On the suspension of the 1978 Constitution of Abkhazia' (for the Russian text see either Amkvab & Ilarionova, 1992, pp 20-21, or Marykhuba, 1994, pp 488-89) and reinstated the Constitution of Abkhazia of 1925 (for the Russian text see Marykhuba, 1994, pp 489-502). It was this act which filled the constitutional-legal vacuum in which Abkhazia had found itself as a result of the unilateral actions taken in Tbilisi, since it was by the 1925 Constitution that Abkhazia's status as a state was enshrined. In the undertaking of this action there lay another historical sub-text: in the 1920s Abkhazia enjoyed union-treaty or, in essence, confederative relations with Georgia. The Abkhazian leaders deemed this form of mutual relationship between Sukhum and Tbilisi to be fully acceptable also in the modern period. A number of drafts for a mechanism of establishing federative relations with Georgia were prepared by the Abkhazian side. One of these drafts (for the Russian text see Amkvab & Ilarionova, 1992, pp 23-26; and Appendix 2 in this volume for the English translation) was to have been considered at its session on August 14th 1992 by Abkhazia's Supreme Soviet. However, the session never took place. At dawn that day Kartvelian forces (tanks, armoured troop-carriers, military helicopters) entered the territory of Abkhazia. Having decided upon an armed solution to the problem, it evidently seemed to Eduard Shevardnadze that he had spared himself forever the necessity of having to conduct with Abkhazia any kind of negotiations on federative relations.

The Kartvelian forces meet resistance

Officially the excuse for the invasion seemed wholly plausible, namely "defence of the railway." However, confident of success, Shevardnadze's entourage did not conceal that the main aim of the military operation was the overthrow of Ardzinba, the suppression of the Supreme Soviet they found so objectionable, the establishing of political control over Abkhazia, and the liquidation of its autonomous statehood. Initially everything went according to plan. Already by the afternoon of August 14th the Georgian military had entered Sukhum, capturing the government buildings, the TV centre, and the main lines of communication. Vladislav Ardzinba, the Supreme Soviet and the government were forced to abandon Sukhum and decamp to Gudauta. On August 15th a naval landing-party disbarked in the Gagra region, squeezing into the mountains the small coastal defence-squadron that was attempting to put up resistance.

However, later developments began not to unfold according to Tbilisi's scenario. On the very first day of the war the Kartvelian forces met resistance, and this continued to grow from day to day. Retreating from Sukhum, Abkhazian elements secured their positions on the left bank of the River Gumista, which marked the line of the western front and became the centre of a powerful partisan movement. The voluntary movement in defence of Abkhazia, which increased from the very first days of the conflict and continued to gather strength, became a most significant factor. One of the first to respond was the Confederation of the Peoples of the Caucasus, which formed a separate fighting division within the constituency of the Abkhazian armed forces. Adyghes and Kabardians (i.e. Western and Eastern Circassians respectively — *editor*), who are ethnically related to the Abkhazians, as well as Chechens, Ossetes, and Russians (including Cossacks)[8] poured in to the squadrons of the Abkhazian army. In defence of their historical homeland fighters came from the Abkhazian diaspora in Turkey and the Near East.

With every passing day the conflict more and more took on the character of an actual war. This compelled Russia, which hitherto had been calmly observing the unfolding events, to put forward a peace-making initiative. On September 3rd 1992 there was a meeting in Moscow between Boris Yeltsin, Eduard Shevardnadze and Vladislav Ardzinba. The tough negotiations ended with the signing of a summary document which provided for a ceasefire, the partial departure of the Kartvelian troops, an exchange of prisoners of war, the safeguarding of the return of refugees, and the restitution of power to the legal organs of power in Abkhazia. However, not a single point of the agreement was fulfilled, and in particular the Kartvelian troops stood their ground on the territory of Abkhazia. Military activity was renewed with all of its former intensity.

The Abkhazians soon experienced military success. As a result of bloody battles from October 2nd to 6th the Gagra bridgehead was liberated. The Kartvelian group that controlled it was utterly defeated, and Abkhazian detachments moved up to the Russian-Abkhazian border along the River Psou, thereby shattering the blockade-ring compressed around Gudauta. The victory had a deep political significance. It breathed new life into the Abkhazians and allowed the Abkhazian command to take full and effective advantage of its military, territorial and material resources, necessary for a war that had taken on a protracted character.

Later more lively military actions took place on the eastern front, where Abkhazian sections held the Kartvelian rear in a state of tension. At the end of October an offensive operation was undertaken here with the aim of liberating the town of Ochamchira. However, an unsuccessful attempt to disbark a landing-party in the environs of the town deprived the Abkhazian fighters of the necessary support — the unsuccessful offensive had to be suspended. Military actions continued also on the western front, but here too neither side enjoyed a decisive superiority.

The war brought innumerable miseries and ordeals to the peaceful population. From the very first days the savagest of occupational regimes was established in the territories under the control of the Kartvelian troops; its effect was to reduce the Abkhazians and the other ethnic non-Kartvelians there (Armenians, Russians, Greeks) to discriminated and victimised minorities. Human rights and civic liberties were for the Kartvelian military mere meaningless phrases.[9] The whole adult non-Kartvelian population found itself under total control; their movement away from place of residence was impeded; contacts with the outside-world via post and telephone were restricted on grounds of military expediency. Pillage, robbery and violence became everyday norms; arrests and executions without trial were carried out virtually every day.[10] In Sukhum the occupation forces rounded up males, who were despatched in convoy to the front-line to gather up the corpses of Kartvelian soldiers who had died there or to dig entrenchments. In October 1992 as a result of a deliberate act of wanton vandalism the National State Archive of Abkhazia and the Abkhazian D. Gulia Research Institute of Language, Literature & History were burned to the ground[11] — the Abkhazian nation was left with no documentary evidence of its historical past . . .

Victims of conflict

There were yet other victims of the war — the refugees. The first wave of refugees, saving themselves from the outrages and persecution committed by the Kartvelian soldiers, flooded over the River Gumista as early as August 14th 1992. After the consolidation of the western front, this path was sealed. Only one possibility of safety remained, and that was passage through the mountains. People would set out by night, in secret, united in groups or at times acting alone, in the uncertain hope of escaping to "our own folk," but under the all-too real threat that they would unexpectedly fall upon Kartvelian punishment-squads. Flight of people from the zone of Abkhazia under Tbilisi's control went on up to the very last days of the war.[12]

By the end of 1992 the situation in the mining-town of T'q^w'archal was acute. Since the start of the conflict this town had been effectively cut off from the rest of Abkhazia. Links with Gudauta were maintained only with the help of the humanitarian air-corridor along which helicopters ferried food and medicines to T'q^w'archal, taking away on their return-journey residents abandoning the blockaded town. Flights along this air-corridor were forced to fly over a zone under Kartvelian control. On December 14th a helicopter flying from T'q^w'archal was hit by a Georgian rocket. All 60 passengers, in the main women and children, perished in the flames.[13] The event came as a tragic shock for Abkhazia, and one more was to follow as a consequence: because of the danger that the incident might be repeated, flights along the air-corridor were suspended. But T'q^w'archal was not prepared for a total blockade. A real danger of starvation descended upon its residents.

The worsening situation pushed the Abkhazians into taking decisive actions. At the start of 1993 the military command in Gudauta made an attempt to alter the course of the war to its advantage. On January 5th a forced crossing was effected in the lower reaches of the River Gumista. It proved possible to liberate and secure a small bridgehead on the right bank. However, the initial success could not be consolidated. A new attempt to liberate Sukhum was undertaken in the spring. On March 16th a sub-division of the Abkhazian army crossed the Gumista, occupying on the right bank several strategic bridgeheads. Advance-parties carried the battle into the suburbs of Sukhum. However, disagreement on actions among the separate brigades as they pushed forward led to tragic consequences: the advance-parties became encircled. Beating off an enemy pressing hard against them, the Abkhazian detachments succeeded in returning to their original positions but suffering large manpower losses in the process.

In the summer military actions intensified. On July 2nd the Abkhazians put a landing-party ashore on a section of the coast on the eastern front. Uniting with elements fighting on the eastern front, they imposed control in the course of ten days over the strategic highway, blocking the enemy's military grouping in the direction of Sukhum. The successful operation on the eastern front was the signal for the start of actions on the western, and the front was breached. Forcing a crossing of the Gumista, the Abkhazian forces liberated one after another settled areas on the right bank to the north of Sukhum, advancing to the near-approaches to the Abkhazian capital.

The desperate situation in which the Kartvelian forces found themselves obliged the Russian government to apply pressure on the Abkhazian side. On July 27th an agreement was reached in Sochi on a ceasefire, which provided a real chance to end the war itself as the main point of the agreement was the understanding that the Kartvelian forces would be withdrawn from Abkhazia and that legitimate Abkhazian control would be restored over the territory of the republic. However, Tbilisi was in no hurry to fulfil the terms of the agreement. It became obvious that Eduard Shevardnadze was using the breathing-space to build up his forces and to uncoil anew military resistance. This placed the Abkhazian side in a hopeless situation.

On September 16th 1993 military actions were renewed. They began on the eastern front, where Abkhazian elements attacked Kartvelian positions. At the same time Abkhazian elements went into battle against Kartvelian forces on the western front, taking under their control the dominating heights above Sukhum. Keeping up their advance here, Abkhazian elements completely encircled the capital on September 20th and captured the airport on the 22nd. Liberation of the town's quarters proceeded in parallel. On September 27th Sukhum was retaken, and Shevardnadze, who was still there, took flight, being guaranteed safe-conduct out of the republic by the Abkhazian military command despite wild reports in the Western media, which in the final days of the war had suddenly developed an interest in Abkhazian affairs, that he was likely to be murdered. The Kartvelian forces retreated in utter confusion, as the Abkhazian army on September 30th advanced up to the Abkhaz-Georgian frontier at the River Ingur, whence just over a year earlier the invasion by Kartvelian troops had begun. The war was over, and a humiliating defeat had been inflicted on the invader.

On December 13th Abkhaz-Georgian negotiations on the settlement of the conflict got underway in Geneva, continuing later in Moscow and thereafter alternating between the two cities, under the auspices of the UN and with Russia as facilitator. A crucial stage in the negotiating process was reached in Moscow on April 4th 1994 with the signing of the agreement 'On Measures for a Political Settlement of the Georgian/Abkhaz Conflict' (see Appendix 3). The sides took upon themselves obligations not to resort to force in their mutual relations, appealing at the same moment to the UN with the request that peace-keeping forces be deployed in the zone of conflict — 3,000 CIS (Commonwealth of Independent States, though, in effect, largely Russian) troops were deployed in June 1994. The agreement defined spheres of joint state activity: foreign policy and foreign economic links; border-guard service; customs' service; energy; transport; communication; ecology and the alleviation of the results of natural disasters; safeguarding the rights and freedoms of the individual and national minorities. The same day saw the signing of the agreement 'On the Voluntary Return of Refugees and Displaced Persons' (see Appendix 4).

However, such a positive initial step forward towards peace did not gain any further impulse. Subsequent negotiations had no success. In Sukhum the conviction continues that the April 4th Agreement must be the basis of the negotiating process. With a view to making progress, the Abkhazian variant for a settlement proposes the union of Georgia and Abkhazia within the framework of a single union-state within which the mutual relations of two subjects of equal status, namely Georgia and Abkhazia, must be regulated by the terms of a treaty of union. Abkhazia absolutely rejects the granting to Tbilisi of any exclusive powers whatsoever, assenting only to those spheres of joint competence stipulated in the Agreement of April 4th.

But the stance of Tbilisi departs ever more widely from the stipulations of this document. Georgia sees Abkhazia only as a territorial and administrative part of itself. Thus, in Tbilisi they asseverate that a future Georgia might become a federative state in which Abkhazia will be offered broad rights of autonomous self-government. However, Abkhazians reject the Georgian proposals, pointing out that up to August 14th 1992 they themselves were offering Georgia federalisation of mutual relations. But after the war they desire to have more weighty guarantees of their security, the more so as the concrete Georgian proposals for the demarcation of powers between the federal centre and the autonomous periphery remind one rather of the classical pattern for the way administration was constructed during the period of Soviet totalitarianism than of any compromise programme for the democratisation of Georgia's internal structure.

The problem of refugees

A serious object of disagreement remains the problem of the Kartvelian refugees, which up to the present time has been only partly resolved. The Abkhazian authorities place no obstacles in the way of the return of refugees to one of the republic's districts, namely the Gal District, which before the war was compactly settled by Mingrelians. At the moment of writing (i.e. February 1997) over 80 per cent of this district's former population has returned to it.[14] The Georgian side is insisting only on a mass and simultaneous return of all (i.e. Kartvelian) refugees also to the other districts of Abkhazia. However, in this case the authorities in Sukhum demand strict observance of the gradual procedure as defined in the Agreement of April 4th 1994. The Abkhazian position emanates from the fact that, unlike the Gal District, the other regions of Abkhazia suffered intensely from military actions with the result that there is really nowhere for the refugees to return. The Abkhazians are also worried that a badly prepared repatriation procedure will provoke large-scale clashes between the Kartvelians and the Abkhazians, who not so long ago were separated by the trenches of war. Furthermore, it is clear that Abkhaz-Kartvelian clashes will play into the hands of the extremist wing of the Tbilisi government, which could use the incident as an excuse for a new attempt at armed invasion. But, this apart, any mass return of refugees could serve as cover for the infiltration of Kartvelian fighters into the territory of Abkhazia, which would indubitably mark the start of new military activity.

Meanwhile in Tbilisi voices are every more loudly heard (at least, they have not grown silent) calling for the necessity of the use of force in Abkhazia as the one and only means to return the republic to the jurisdiction of Georgia.[15] Eduard Shevardnadze has more than once demanded that policing functions be transferred to the peace-keeping contingent, even if the Abkhazian side should not agree to this change in their mandate. Russia, whose soldiers constitute the main contingent of the peace-keeping forces (even though the troops are nominally operating under CIS auspices), has thus far refrained from taking any such unilateral action.

However, Moscow has assented to another demand from Eduard Shevardnadze. In December 1995 Russia closed its border with Abkhazia at the River Psou, restricting the passage of people and goods. In May 1996 Russian naval border patrols made an attempt to close off for Abkhazia the sea-passage to Turkey, from where after the start of the blockade the republic received foodstuffs and industrial goods. However, the sharp reaction in Sukhum, which went as far as declaring military preparedness, forced Russia into a retreat. At the time at a meeting of the leaders of the CIS countries in January 1996 Shevardnadze demanded an even tighter blockade of Abkhazia. As a result of the measures adopted, the border along the River Psou became completely impenetrable. And one year on, Shevardnadze continues to press for more.[16]

The deteriorating situation aggravated the state of affairs within

Abkhazia, which even without this was desperate enough. Programmes to restore the shattered economy, the social infrastructure and support for those strata of the population with meagre means had to be curtailed. In the conditions of the really savage economic crisis in which Abkhazia found itself thanks to the blockade, the majority of the population was placed on the very verge of extinction. The government succeeded in coping with the burgeoning of criminal activity which ensued after the end of military operation. However, unceasing terrorist acts on the part of bandit-formations infiltrated onto the territory of Abkhazia from Georgia continue to remain a destabilising factor in political life.[17]

Abkhazia today is in terribly straitened circumstances, but it has no intention of changing its political course. In the autumn of 1994 its new constitution was ratified, which consolidated the post-war realities of the republic's state-building, whilst in the presidential elections that soon followed Vladislav Ardzinba again secured victory. On November 23rd 1996 elections were held in Abkhazia to the National Assembly (Parliament),[18] and at the present time the newly constituted highest legislative organ of the republic has already embarked on its work.

At the same time the conflict between Abkhazia and Georgia is still far from a mutually acceptable settlement and continues to remain one of the most potentially explosive hotspots in the whole post-Soviet space.

9
Military aspects of the war: the turning point

Dodge Billingsley

The battle for Gagra (in particular and the northern territory of Abkhazia in general) was a turning-point in the Georgian-Abkhazian war of 1992-93. More importantly, however, events at Gagra perfectly illustrated in microcosm the strengths and weaknesses of both protagonists throughout the 14 months of military engagement. Kartvelian forces were never able to become a cohesive fighting machine, as seen so glaringly at Gagra. A lack of unit and individual discipline not only cost them on the battlefield, but it also made the Kartvelian troops exceedingly unpopular amongst the local inhabitants. On the other hand, Abkhazian units surrounding Gagra were filled with outside volunteers but still managed to be much more cohesive. Though outnumbered, they were able to find common cause and make better use of their limited resources. These factors, repeated as they were for the duration of the war, had a telling effect on the outcome of the conflict.

On August 14th 1992 Kartvelian troops invaded Abkhazia in a two-pronged attack. Mechanised units raced across the River Ingur towards Sukhum, while an amphibious task-force landed in northern Abkhazia near the city of Gagra. After a brief stand-off at the Red Bridge leading into the centre of Sukhum, both sides agreed to pull their forces back. Abkhazian units moved adjacent to the River Gumista on the northern edge of the capital, while Kartvelian forces back-tracked to the southern approaches of the city. A couple of days later Kartvelian units broke the fragile truce, racing through the city centre and forcing all Abkhazian units north of the Gumista. The Abkhazian leadership moved its headquarters even further north to Gudauta, as a front began to materialise along the Gumista. Unable to break the stalemate that ensued, both sides focused on the northern territory and the city of Gagra. For the next few months the war would centre on this small resort-city. The outcome would, however, have an impact on the course of the war long after the smoke had cleared from Gagra itself.

The Gagra offensive

The battle for Gagra began on August 15th when Kartvelian forces landed near the Russian-Abkhazian border in Gʲachrypsh (Leselidze) in an effort to isolate the Abkhazian military and trap it between Kartvelian forces moving southward and those trying to fight their way northward from Sukhum. After securing the border, Kartvelian units turned their attention southward towards Tsandrypsh (Gantiadi) and Gagra. By nightfall of August 15th the village of Tsandrypsh had fallen to Kartvelian units. The same night there were skirmishes in Gagra, which resulted in casualties, including at least three Abkhazians killed in action.[1] By the end of the weekend Kartvelian forces were in control of Gʲachrypsh, Tsandrypsh and Gagra.[2]

Kartvelian forces deployed in Gʲachrypsh and on the Russian border were intended to guard the border with Russia to stop the flow of any outside-volunteers seeking to join the Abkhazian alliance.[3] While Shevardnadze dismissed statements by Abkhazian and Chechen officials regarding the deployment of volunteer-units from the North Caucasus to help Abkhazia, he was cautious enough to put the military in a position to defend Georgia's interests against such incursions. Outside-assistance from the North Caucasus or from ethnic Abkhazians from Turkey and elsewhere in the Middle East depended on an open border with Russia. The airport and ferryboat terminal in Sochi-Adler was a focal-point for volunteers arriving from abroad to help Abkhazia. The closing of the border was a must for Georgia.

But volunteers did arrive through the porous Russian border and mountain-passes. Strengthened by reinforcements from the North Caucasus, the newly established Abkhazian military began to encircle, or mass on the perimeter of, Gagra. They were soon ready to test the Kartvelian defences.[4] It is unclear which and where the first Abkhazian units attacked, but on the night of August 24th the Abkhazian Press Service announced that Abkhazian forces were assaulting Gagra.[5] The battle raged on the perimeter of the city into the morning of August 25th.[6] The strongest offensive-push was launched at 10pm on the night of the 25th. Kartvelian forces managed to hold despite running low on equipment and ammunition. Abkhazian units were able to make gains into the city, but on the whole, Kartvelian forces were able to hold them off, bolstered by fresh supplies of ammunition and reinforcements from a private Kartvelian militia known as the Mkhedrioni ('Cavalrymen').[7]

Fighting continued into August 30th. But by now the tide had turned and Kartvelian forces, still under fire, began to concentrate around the railway-station for an attempted break-out. On the afternoon of August 30th, at 2pm, Kartvelian forces launched a counter-attack southward in the direction of Pitsunda. But it too faltered and Kartvelian forces were compelled to retreat back to their previous position in and around Gagra. After a week of fierce fighting the battle-lines remained pretty much where they began at the beginning of the week.

Periodic fighting continued around Gagra for the next month and a half, but no clear advantage was recognised. However, Abkhazian units were consolidating their positions in the mountains surrounding Gagra. Peace-talks were held to find a political solution to the problems in Gagra, but they did not lead to any substantial changes.[8] On September 26th an agreement was reached that called for both Kartvelian and Abkhazian armed formations to withdraw from the city-limits and that all 'pickets' be removed from the city itself.[9] Kartvelian units were supposed to pull back north-west of Gagra while Abkhazian forces were to pull back to positions south-east of Pitsunda. It also called for the separation of both sides near the village of K'olkhida on the next day (September 27th) and the placement of four observation-posts along the River Bzyp.[10] The agreement was strikingly similar to the previous arrangement in Sukhum, in August, which called for each side to withdraw to the city-limits.[11]

However, on the very day the cease-fire and withdrawal-agreement was reached (September 26th) Kartvelian forces assaulted the village of Merk'ula (Merk^w'yla) in southern Abkhazia near Ochamchira. The battle itself was inconclusive, but Abkhazian officials used it as a pretext to call off the cease-fire and lift the restriction on volunteers from the North Caucasus, stating: "Since Georgia persists in violating the cease-fire agreement, the command of Abkhazia's militia decides to revise the time for the withdrawal of North Caucasian volunteers."[12]

With the agreement of September 26th to remove North Caucasian volunteers in a shambles, the stage was set for a major Abkhazian assault on Gagra. Abkhazians and Kartvelian officials both realised that holding Gagra and the road to the Russian border along the River Psou was critical to maintain control of the region and perhaps win the war. For Abkhazia an open supply-route from the north was essential to independence, whilst Georgia realised that without the ability to control the border they could never withstand the strength with which volunteers and supplies from the North Caucasus would provide Abkhazia.

Skirmishes around Gagra intensified on September 27th as both forces jockeyed for tactical advantage. Kartvelian forces were able to penetrate the Abkhazian held village of Okhtari (as given by FBIS), which is near Gagra, and evacuate 30 Kartvelian hostages. However, they were forced to retreat in an abortive attempt to break out of Gagra and seize a stategic hilltop on the approaches to the city. There were last-minute attempts to enact a cease-fire, but the whole charade was merely posturing by both sides for tactical advantage. Geographically speaking, Kartvelian units were severely lacking. Abkhazian units controlled all the high ground.

Abkhazian strategy to capture and hold the high ground surrounding the city to gain advantage for purposes of reconnaissance had been accomplished in preceding weeks. By October 2nd Abkhazian units held all the strategic heights. On that same day a combined Abkhazian force of local Abkhazian and North Caucasian volunteers lashed out at the Kartvelian perimeter around Gagra. The first objective was to cross the River Bzyp south of Gagra and occupy the strategically located village of K'olkhida.

The assault into Gagra itself was a three-pronged attack originating from the southern approaches of the city. One group followed the coastline and attacked the city from the beach and marsh areas, through a camp-ground located on the southern edge of the city. The other two Abkhazian spearheads fought their way through the city along parallel axes (along the old and new highways). There is only one major road into Gagra, and it runs parallel to the coast. However, on the edge of the city this highway splits in two, rejoining in north Gagra near the Ukraina sanatorium, to form the only highway to the Russian border. As the road splits, the old highway turns to the left towards the coastal edges of the city, passing the railway station, central market and police-station. The other road, known as the New Highway, continues straight ahead by way of an overpass hugging the hills along the eastern edge of Gagra.

The Abkhazian unit taking the Old Highway was ordered to fight its way into the city centre where it would link up with the unit following the seashore. The troops fighting along the new highway were ordered to cut a path through Gagra, racing to the northern end of the city to block any Kartvelian reinforcements that might arrive from the north. In this way Abkhazian units sought to trap the Kartvelian forces defending Gagra in a pincer-movement between Abkhazian forces advancing northward along the Old Highway and those barricading the highway at the northern end of the city.

The assault went as planned. By 6am on October 2nd the units fighting along the Old Highway had already broken through Kartvelian defensive positions around the overpass, meeting up with Abkhazian units fighting their way into Gagra from the seashore. Both units converged on Kartvelian forces holding the railway-station. The fire-fight for the railway-station lasted nearly three hours, but by 9am it had fallen to Abkhazian forces.[13] Abkhazian units continued to push through Gagra for the rest of the day. The next place of notable resistance was the sanatorium opposite the supermarket. Kartvelian soldiers deployed inside were able to hold off the advancing Abkhazian forces for some time, but this position was eventually surrounded and collapsed finally at 5.35pm. Other Abkhazian forces in the meantime continued down the old highway through the centre of town, and by 4pm all major Kartvelian positions were firmly under Abkhazian control, including the Hotel Abkhazia and the police station. An hour and a half later Gagra was totally under Abkhazian control.[14]

There were dedicated Kartvelian units. Initially, Abkhazian forces met stiff resistance. The units moving up the highway to K'olkhida were pinned down and could not move forward for some time. Eventually, they were able to break through but continued to meet stiff Kartvelian opposition at many points, most notably the railway- and police-stations. The battle at the police-station was unusually brutal, as it was defended by local Kartvelians[15] formed into a militia and members of the elite White Eagle unit.[16] Among the dead at the police-station were 12 members of the White Eagle unit — Kartvelian shock-troops.[17] Another fierce battle took place at the rehabilitation centre. There were high casualties, including many killed. Abkhazian units took 40 Kartvelian prisoners.

During the early morning hours of October 3rd Kartvelian helicopters arrived from Sukhum to blunt the Abkhazian assault, but it was too little too late. The Kartvelian defence of Gagra had turned into a large-scale, disorganised retreat. Questions remain regarding the Abkhazian strategy to cut off the retreating Kartvelian units fleeing Gagra. Abkhazian units earmarked to trap the Kartvelian units on the northern edge of the city were not effective. Empirical evidence suggests this may have been intentional. Abkhazian forces were not equipped to take large numbers of prisoners, and the main object was to secure Gagra not to kill or take prisoners, especially not thousands of them. The impending Kartvelian collapse in Gagra had caused a panic, and thousands of civilians also clogged the highway towards the villages of Gjachrypsh, Tsandrypsh and the Russian border in their desire to get out of Gagra before it was overrun.[18]

There seems to be validity to the Abkhazian claims suggesting that the escape-route was purposely left open. The road between the mountains and the sea is very narrow at the northern end of the city.[19] One concentrated blocking-force could easily have trapped the swelling northward migration of Kartvelians. To credit the Kartvelian side, efforts were made to keep the retreat-route open. On the afternoon of October

3rd SU-25 ground-attack planes bombed Abkhazian positions at the junction of the Old and New Highways at the Ukraina sanatorium, inflicting several casualties.[20]

Immediately after the collapse of Gagra, on October 4th, Kartvelian units began preparations for a counter-assault on the Sanatorium in Old Gagra. This began with the extraction of the White Eagles from Gagra on October 2nd and 3rd to the villages of Gjachrypsh and Tsandrypsh for reorganisation and refitting. Much of this reorganisation centred around the combining of two units, the White Eagles and the Orbi[21] Battalion.

On October 4th the hastily organised White Eagle/Orbi unit was given new orders. The objective was to attack the Ukraina sanatorium north of Gagra. The Abkhazian units occupying the sanatorium were in possession of heavy weapons, including captured Kartvelian tanks. Recapturing these weapons was given top priority. The sanatorium is located on the northern end of Gagra, between Gagra itself (often called New Gagra) and Old Gagra (which are separated by five to six kilometres).

The attack was intended to be a two-pronged assault. The objective of the White Eagle/Orbi unit, which consisted of 65 troops, was to circle around through the mountains and attack the sanatorium from high ground. Simultaneously, a much larger force, consisting of approximately 200 troops comprised primarily from the Military Police, Kutaisi Battalion and Avaza[22] Battalion were to advance southward on the highway, seize Old Gagra, and attack the sanatorium head on.

The planned assault collapsed nearly as fast as it began. The Kartvelian force making its way along the highway towards Old Gagra turned back to Tsandrypsh prematurely after seeing two ships 'full of Abkhazians' off the coast. Facing no opposition, whatsoever, the Abkhazian forces disbarked at Grebeshok and proceeded inland along mountain-paths to cut off the combined White Eagle and Orbi detachment.[23]

The next day, on October 5th, Abkhazian forces engaged the Kartvelian unit in a "very difficult mountain-place."[24] By 6pm the White Eagle/Orbi unit was trapped and on the defensive. Meanwhile, Abkhazian forces also attacked and broke through the hastily thrown up Kartvelian positions in Tsandrypsh. The Kartvelian collapse here resulted in additional chaos, and, as the White Eagle/Orbi unit lay pinned down in the mountains, thousands of Kartvelian civilians and military personnel were fleeing towards the Russian border. The retreat was completely unorganised, and Kartvelian units were scattered all over the nearby villages. Many left without their equipment. Abkhazian units continued mopping-up operations along the coastal highway, and at 6.40am on October 6th the Abkhazian State Flag was raised on the border with Russia.[25]

Meanwhile, in the mountains the White Eagle/Orbi detachment was in a desperate position, under attack from three sides.[26] The unit was trapped for 12 days. The Kartvelian unit suffered heavy casualties, including 30 killed. Among the dead was the commander of the White Eagles, Gocha Q'arq'arashvili.[27] Reinforcements did arrive. Amidst the chaotic retreat down on the coastal highway 30 troops from the Military Police unit were able to make their way to their embattled comrades. This brought the fighting-strength up to 62 combatants but did not enable the Kartvelian unit to break out.[28]

The situation in the forest continued to look bleak. However, in a stroke of luck a local Armenian villager happened upon the battle and was persuaded to travel across the border to Russia to relay the message of distress to the Kartvelian command in Sukhum. By telephone to Tbilisi he detailed the whereabouts and condition of the embattled unit. The Kartvelian command in Sukhum responded quickly by launching a rescue-mission of extraction. A single helicopter was despatched, which made two trips to extract the 62 fighters. The dead were left behind.

As the smoke cleared, the impact of the Kartvelian defeat started to become clearer. One manifest consequence of the victory was the tremendous boost of military equipment to Abkhazia. Accurate numbers are difficult to gauge, but Abkhazian units captured at least two tanks, 25 BMPs, six anti-tank guns, ammunition, radio-equipment and a small ship, which had been used to land Kartvelian forces.[29] However, the true importance of the battle was not immediately obvious.

The Kartvelian war effort crumbles

The defeat at Gagra was a terrible blow to the Kartvelian military and ultimately foreshadowed the eventual failure of the whole Kartvelian war effort. With the northern territory firmly in Abkhazian control, Georgia could not hope to stop the flow of men and equipment to Abkhazia from the North Caucasus. Moreover, the Kartvelian military (and the state) went into a bout of severe depression, which it could not shake. The Georgian government in Tbilisi established a special commission to determine the cause of the military debacle. Although veteran units of the battle still blame each other, the loss highlighted other deep-seated problems which would also remain characteristic of Kartvelian forces throughout the war.

On an operational level Kartvelian forces were just not trained for, or dedicated to, the art of war. The defensive positions protecting Gagra crumbled quickly after Abkhazian units were able to penetrate the perimeter of the city. Kartvelian forces did not employ a defence-in-depth, and their defensive action deteriorated into a rout once Abkhazian forces broke through. There was a substantial amount of house-to-house fighting, but this type of warfare hindered Kartvelian units from using heavy weapons, including their tanks and BMPs. Without heavy firepower, Kartvelian forces were easily driven from their positions. Others, usually small goups of ten to twenty, were trapped in buildings with no means of replenishment or communication with other units. There was also a severe lack of discipline amongst the rank and file, which increased the speed in which the Kartvelian positions crumbled.

To be sure, geography played a major role in the outcome in the Battle for Gagra. Abkhazian units did control the mountainous terrain surrounding the city, which made Abkhazian reconnaissance and spotting relatively easy. But Kartvelian forces should have had the advantage of being on the defensive. However, the mismanagement of Kartvelian forces and the lack of military preparation simply left too many open corridors into the city. Kartvelian forces were unable to defend them all and as a result were driven from Gagra and the northern territory.

Part of the communication breakdown was due to the nature of the Kartvelian military itself. By September 20th there were at least five independent Kartvelian military formations defending Gagra, totalling as many as 1,000 troops. Each unit was given its own sector to defend. However, command and control between units was non-existent. Each was simply tasked to take care of its own sector. While this may seem expedient on the surface, the many different militias represented various political parties and each had their own agenda and objectives. Throughout the war the Kartvelian forces were never able to become a cohesive army. There were continual divisions among units and unit-leaders. When the battle became intense, Kartvelian units were unable to come together and, as a consequence, crumbled into a rag-tag army blaming each other for the overall failure.

Abkhazian units, which included diaspora Abkhazians from Turkey, Syria, Jordan as well as North Caucasians, were much better prepared to fight together for a common cause. The presence of outside volunteers on the Abkhazian side prompted Georgia and many external observers to conclude Russian complicity in favour of Abkhazia. Many in Georgia and elsewhere feel that the war was really a Russian-Georgian conflict. This is a complicated issue. Technically, all volunteers from the North Caucasus were Russian citizens. The real question, however, centres on motivation and how the volunteers saw themselves. There were many indications that Chechen assistance to Abkhazia was stimulated by independent aspirations related to a pan-Caucasian federation rather than any Russian plot. The best known Chechen to fight against Georgia, Shamil Basaev (later deputy to Chechenia's President Aslan Maskhadov), stated that "as long as the small Abkhazian people suffered in the Georgian-Abkhazian conflict, his units would help them, but in the event of hostilities between Russia and Georgia, the volunteers would fight on the Georgian side."[30]

There were, however, verified cases of Russian assistance. Russian pilots were actually shot down by Kartvelian units, but the incidents were isolated and more likely reflected freelancing by rogue elements of the Russian military, a fact which has precedence elsewhere in the Caucasus, including the earlier Georgian conflict in South Ossetia.[31] Moreover, there were other indications that Russia (Yeltsin) knew of Shevardnadze's plan and was prepared to look the other way. Commenting on the unruly nature of the Kartvelian forces, Shevardnadze remarked that he was against sending his troops into Sukhum: "I wanted our military units to go around Sukhumi and move to Gagra . . . When I spoke to Yeltsin on the next day (after the beginning of hostilities), he told me: 'The generals can get out of control and you, as a smart man, should know it.' "[32] Russia did meddle in the conflict, but the factor that made the difference were the hundreds and hundreds of volunteers that made their way to the region to engage Kartvelian forces throughout the war. This is not to say that the volunteers might not incidentally have served the strategy of some circles in the Russian military-political arena. However, the volunteers, many of whom were Chechen, had their own reasons for helping Abkhazia, as the more recent war in Chechenia has demonstrated.

There is no doubt that volunteers from abroad did add to the quantity and quality of the Abkhazian military effort, but their numbers were still small. Although Abkhazian veterans claim that there were only 300 combatants on their side, it is more realistic that their numbers exceeded 500. However, Abkhazians never held an overall numerical advantage. Locally-based UN military observers substantiate these Abkhazian claims, suggesting that Kartvelian troops did indeed outnumber Abkhazian personnel but were so ill-disciplined that the Abkhazian victory at Gagra should have come as no surprise.[33]

What was a surprise was the ability of the Abkhazian movement successfully to incorporate volunteers from the North Caucasus and elsewhere, primarily Turkey, arriving to fight for Abkhazia. Abkhazia would prove most adept at this throughout the course of the war.

Military cohesion on an individual- and group-level was always better on the Abkhazian side. The reasons for this need to be explored in depth. However, it must suffice to say that this factor, illustrated so clearly at Gagra, was one of the most crucial determining factors in Abkhazia's success and Georgia's failure.

In many ways the battle for Gagra was the battle for Abkhazia itself. Once in control of the border and port-facilities in the northern corner of Abkhazia, the Abkhazian leadership was assured that supplies and manpower would get through. On the other hand, after the loss of Gagra, Georgia could only hope for a break-out on the Sukhum front. Reeling from the loss of Gagra, Kartvelian forces proved incapable of further large-scale offensive operations. There were only four more meaningful offensives undertaken that are worthy of note (January 1993, March 1993, July 1993 and the final offensive of September 1993), and all were conducted by the Abkhazian side.

A postcard from the exhibition 'Children of the Caucasus' in which 12-year-old Aksana G^wbaz depicts her brother and the house in which she says she wishes to live. Note the typical maize store (a'tsa) in the background.

10
Economy:
traditional & modern
Daur Bargandzhia

The modern economy of Abkhazia essentially took shape during the period when Abkhazia was part of the USSR. Those spheres of the economy for which the most favourable economic and climatic pre-requisites existed enjoyed priority of development; these were primarily subtropical agriculture, the processing industry intimately linked to it, the health-resorts as well as the associated infrastructure and services.

Up to the start of the 20th century the economy of Abkhazia had an overwhelmingly natural character and was based on agriculture and animal-husbandry. Maize, millet, wheat and kidney beans were cultivated here; there were also such technologically based cultures as tobacco, cotton and beet; viticulture, wine-making, horticulture, cattle-breeding, horse-breeding and bee-keeping had also been developed, as well as domestic industry and trades. Export of goods occurred in rare cases with the exception of the products of bee-keeping, namely honey and wax, which were basically produced not for home consumption but for the export market.

Growth of an economy

At the start of the 20th century substantial improvements began to take place in Abkhazia's economy. Tobacco became the main technological culture with a gross-yield of over 10,000 tonnes per year, for the highest quality sorts of export-tobacco grew in Abkhazia. Forestry and wood-working industry began to occupy a vital slot. Around ten enterprises processed such valuable local tree species as box, chestnut, oak, beech, walnut and yew, which began to take their place alongside tobacco as the most important export items. It was at the start of the 20th century that there also developed a completely new sphere — the health-resort and tourist industry. Many high-ranking persons, members of the royal family, eminent doctors and scholars as well as many businessmen acquired in Abkhazia large plots of land. Health sanatoria and hotels began to be built in the towns of Gagra and Sukhum. This was the same period when the first hydro-electric stations were constructed in Abkhazia; highways were built to join Abkhazia with Russia and the North Caucasus; regular shipping links were opened between Sukhum and other Black Sea port-towns.

In the 1920s and 30s the rural economy, which remained the bulwark of the overall economy, began to acquire an ever-more trading and commercial character. The foundations were laid for large tea-plantations and other long-term subtropical cultures, such as the growing of citrus and oil-bearing plants. Work began on studying the

Popular arrangement of buildings in a village homestead: main dwelling, often with external stairs, outhouse and replica of the ancient wattle structure (a'patsxa) in the foreground

mineral and other natural resources of Abkhazia. New health sanatoria went up. In the 1930s the mining-town of T'qʷ'archal was built; this was later transformed into the chief extractive and industrial centre of the republic. Industry's share in the gross national product reached 35 per cent. The urban population rose.

From the 1950s to the 80s, right up to the disintegration of the USSR and the Georgian-Abkhazian war of 1992-93, impressive structural advances were made in Abkhazia's economy. Dozens of modern industrial enterprises, two large and dozens of small power stations, multi-storeyed holiday, sporting and health complexes were constructed; a developed infrastructure was created. Laying of the transit railway-line was completed, and all main roads were resurfaced with asphalt; the seaport at Sukhum, several port points and the modern passenger-airport on the outskirts of Sukhum, one of the best in the former USSR, as well as a large military airport in the Gudauta District were built. According to data on means of transport and density of roads per capita of the population, Abkhazia held one of the first places in the former Soviet Union.

Abkhazia was transformed into a resort region of international significance. Splendid resort complexes meeting the standards of the day were constructed in Pitsunda, Gagra, New Athos, Sukhum and elsewhere. Millions of Soviet and tens of thousands of foreign tourists used to visit Abkhazia every year for their holidays.

As for the rural economy, tea, citrus fruits and also the production of tobacco and walnuts became the predominant cultures. Food production soared and attracted quite good equipment for the time; one can single out for mention investment in: tea, wine production, fruit conserves, oil-bearing plants, fish, confectionary, production of non-alcoholic beverages and so on. This production was developed in the main for the foreign market, as up to 95 per cent of it was sold beyond Abkhazia's borders, whilst one third of tobacco and half of the walnuts were exported outside the USSR on the world-market.

Meanwhile, Abkhazia remained dependent on imports for fuel, different kinds of machines and equipment, means of transport and also the main types of foodstuffs such as grain, butter, sugar, potatoes, etc.

The standard of living of Abkhazia's population during the Soviet period of its history was quite high, significantly higher than the average for the Union, only lagging behind, possibly, the standard of living in the Baltic states and large capital cities. This was explained by certain important particularities in Abkhazia's position, both political, economic as well as environmental and climatic.

High standards of living

Georgia, as a constituent part of which within the former USSR Abkhazia had the status of an autonomous republic (from 1931 only), found itself during Stalin's time in a privileged position thanks to the Georgian origin of the 'Leader[1] of Peoples' and also later because of the striving of the Soviet government to buy off with these privileges the separatist and anti-Russian sentiments that have always existed in Georgian society. Through the system of the centralised planning of the production and distribution of goods, Georgia, like no other region of the former USSR, received everything it needed, whilst what was produced in it, was centrally exported and marketed in other regions of the former USSR as well as overseas.

All this created for Georgia an economic base for effecting its own demographic expansion, which principally affected Abkhazia. Over many decades, for ever new generations of Georgian politicians, creating and increasing the numerical predominance of the Kartvelian population over the native Abkhazian population in Abkhazia and indeed the complete 'Kartvelianisation of the population' remained the main strategic goal of their actions. Economic progress was another tool to serve this purpose. The construction of any large entity, be it a mining

Harvesters collecting the most recent growth of leaves for the tea production that forms an important part of the economy in Abkhazia and neighbouring Mingrelia

or processing enterprise or some new resort complex, was inevitably accompanied by mass immigration of a Kartvelian workforce, which every time affected the demographic processes. The 'Kartvelianisation' of Abkhazia was, thus, as it were, the price forcibly levied for economic progress.

The chief factor facilitating the relatively high standard of living of Abkhazia's population was linked to the specifics of its geographical position and natural conditions. Situated in a subtropical zone, on the shore of a warm sea, Abkhazia, in the closed conditions of the former USSR that isolated it from world-markets and placed many obstacles in the way of the free movement of citizens across frontiers, was essentially transformed into one of the few regions which enjoyed a monopoly within the internal market in the production of subtropical species and the provision of resort and tourist services. Thus, for example, Abkhazia with a population of slightly more than half a million (or 0.2 per cent of the USSR's population) met up to 20 per cent of the USSR's demand for tea and annually welcomed up to one and a half million tourists. Exotic, subtropical fruits grew only in Abkhazia or a few other regions of the former USSR, such as citruses, figs, quinces, olives, persimmons, feikhoas, etc. Although these were hardly prime necessities of life in the Soviet period, there was a great demand for them, which meant their prices were high. This allowed the local population to reap extra revenues.

Finally, one other circumstance marked Abkhazia out from other regions of the former USSR and led to its higher standard of living: even during the period of very harsh centralisation there always existed here a quite broad and large private sector within the economy. Collective-farms, furthermore, never existed in Abkhazia in the classical form where members of a collective basically worked for the public sector. On the contrary, separate peasant-families widely rented

Maize is a staple of the Abkhazian diet, eaten daily in a polenta-like paste (a'bysta). Here maize stalks are hung over a tree to dry.

collective land and in effect thus enlarged the possibilities for their own private economy. Apart from this, for a whole variety of reasons there was hardly any construction of large industrial enterprises; the production of subtropical and other exotic species did not easily lend itself to wide-scale mechanisation and was for this reason in many cases concentrated in the private sector. Voluminous quantities of tourists also facilitated the development of the private sector, from the provision of living-quarters for the holiday-makers to the production of wares of folk art and handicrafts, different sorts of trinkets and to small street-trading.

Real Abkhazian backyard, with maize store (cobs inside, stalks on top and red chillies hung outside) and cart (awar'dyn) loaded with maize and children

Even during Soviet times certain traditions within the realm of free enterprise grew up in Abkhazia, and it is thus no coincidence that many modern-day, well known Russian businessmen hail from Abkhazia.

In summation, Abkhazia was a blessed region in terms of the living standards of its population when judged against the standards of the former USSR, for Abkhazia's average per capita annual income in the 1980s was $800. But one also needs to take into consideration that Soviet statistics, as a rule, did not take account of the private sector within the economy. The real income of Abkhazia's population was, thus, one and a half to two times higher.

Economic and political reforms

The break-up of the USSR at the end of 1991 caused radical change to all the conditions of existence for Abkhazia within a framework where infrastructure, economic relations and the division of labour across the former USSR had already begun to disintegrate. Like many other republics of the former USSR,

Time to harvest the local ak'a'ch'ych' black grape in the special cone-shaped wicker-backet (am'çʷ'yʃʷ)

Abkhazia set about economic and political reforms.

However, the Georgian-Abkhazian war of 1992-93 sharply altered the state of affairs. As a result of the war, which actually took place on Abkhazian soil and affected directly no less than 70 per cent of its territory, serious losses were sustained. To speak only of the direct economic sacrifice occasioned by military destruction and the plundering of property and belongings, this amounted to no less than $10 billion. In 1994, the first full post-war year, the fall in the general volume of industrial production was 93 per cent, in the output of electro-energy 60 per cent, and in the gross product of the rural economy 75 per cent. This was mirrored in other spheres too. Damage was inflicted on the key spheres of Abkhazia's economy. The resort- and tourist-complexes were almost completely deserted. Production and export of tea was reduced by a factor of 15, of citruses and tobacco by a factor of four, whilst that of walnuts halved.

The standard of living of the population also fell sharply. The average annual per capita income in the first post-war year of 1994 amounted to only $120, and, although it later rose and in 1996 stood at around $250, in absolute terms it remains extremely low. As a result of the victory gained in the war with Georgia, Abkhazia became a de facto independent state, though unrecognised by the international community. Over the several years since the end of the war in 1993 at

the present time in Abkhazia one can see an annual and substantial economic improvement (on average 30 to 40 per cent per annum). However, because of the extraordinarily severe fall during the war, the absolute economic indicators are still not high and fall sadly short of the pre-war level.

The situation is worsened yet more by the fact that the whole post-war period has seen Abkhazia subjected to a savage economic blockade and even isolation. This circumstance does not allow it to create favourable conditions for post-war revival and the reanimation of the economy. The large-scale assistance rendered to Georgia, the aggressor-state, by the international community, does not find its way into Abkhazia, which that same international community regards as part of Georgia; Abkhazia's borders with Russia, Georgia and the outside world, controlled by Russian borderguards, are almost completely closed not only for the movement of goods but also for the passage of individuals. All this, in addition to direct economic loss and political instability, prevents the movement of goods and capital and creates an unfavourable climate for investment, hindering the attraction of foreign investment in the country's economy.

At the same time, given the removal of external, purely political obstacles to economic progress, Abkhazia, despite its post-war ruin, could be an altogether attractive country in which there are quite wide possibilities for business and which in full measure could take advantage of all the privileges of the small country's geographical position.

First of all it is necessary to note that the main resort complexes situated in the towns of Pitsunda, Gagra and New Athos escaped the military activity. The resort-complexes, then, have survived and need relatively little expenditure for their improvement up to modern, international standards. Despite all the difficulties, even today each year sees a two- to three-fold rise in the number of tourists visiting Abkhazia. In 1996, despite the blockade, the figure reached 12,000, and in future similar increases are expected, insofar as Abkhazia's rich recreational resources are widely known, and every year of peaceful development will attract an ever larger number of tourists and holiday-makers.

Despite Abkhazia's mild sub-tropical climate, winters can be harsh enough to warrant protection for citrus trees

If favourable conditions for the export of the products of our subtropical agriculture could be created, it could be developed even further under those conditions. The fact is that Abkhazia is situated in the most northern part of the subtropical zone, and it can benefit from its geographical proximity to the southern regions of Russia, which give it a real advantage over its competitors from other regions of the world from where similar goods are sent to the Russian market (e.g. Greece, Turkey, Israel or Spain). The surviving strength of the food and reprocessing industries, given conditions of modernisation and up-to-date equipment, could also lend production a real competitive edge.

Abkhazia has at its disposal certain mineral resources which are large enough for its requirements, such as coal, oil, mercury, barytes, silver, lead-zinc ore, as well large industrial stocks of building materials — marble, limestone, dolomite, chalk, etc.

Of great value and the nation's property are Abkhazia's own water-resources. All the indicators on water-supply suggest that Abkhazia occupies one of the first places in the world. For every resident there is an average of over 50,000 cubic metres of water, whilst the total annual river-stock stands at around 14 billion cubic metres.

Taking into account that practically all the rivers are mountain-rivers and ecologically pure, Abkhazia's water-resources are suitable for both the large-scale development of hydro-electric energy and use as drinking-water. Abkhazia's potential average annual energy-resources are estimated to be roughly 25 billion kilowatts, whilst the resources of pure drinking-water, including mineral and spring-sources, are virtually limitless.

A serious source of future potential is the relatively well developed infrastructure, the presence of a network of highways, a through rail-line, ports and airports. This infrastructure might be used not only for Abkhazia but also to secure transit import-export from Russia to Transcaucasia and the Near East, as well as from other countries of the world to Russia and Transcaucasia.

Apart from this, given certain changes to legislation and a sensible customs' regime, Abkhazia, as has already been done in many small countries in Europe and elsewhere in the world, might be transformed into a unique tax- and investment-haven, guaranteeing a balance of interests in the region and capitalising at the same time on the advantageousness of its geographical and geo-political position.

11
Language
George Hewitt

Abkhaz, Circassian and the now extinct Ubykh form the small North West Caucasian language family. As far as one can ascertain, the dialect divisions for Abkhaz were: Sadz, Ahchypsy, Bzyp, Abzhywa, Ashkhar and T'ap'anta. Of these only Bzyp and Abzhywa are today still found in the Republic of Abkhazia, roughly spoken to the north(-west) and south(-east) of Sukhum respectively. The last two in the list are attested in the North Caucasian region of Karachay-Cherkessia, where they are viewed as dialects of the Abaza language. The majority of Abkhazians (including those who speak dialects no longer heard in Abkhazia) today live in Turkey, where knowledge of the language diminishes with the generations; there are also communities in Syria, Germany, Holland, Britain, Switzerland, and America.

Until at least the troubles of 1989 a small community also lived in the environs of Batumi in the Georgian province of Ach'ara/Ajaria; in 1970 this numbered 1,361, of whom 982 considered Abkhaz to be their native tongue (Kilba 1982). A short description of (T'ap'anta) Abaza can be found in Lomtatidze & Klychev (1989), whilst short accounts of (Abzhywa) Abkhaz can be found in Hewitt (1989b;[1] forthcoming b) and Hewitt & Khiba (1997a), whilst a full grammar is available in Hewitt (1979). See also Dumézil (1967), Spruit (1986), and Trigo (1992).

Though mutually unintelligible, the North West Caucasian languages display a remarkable uniformity of structure. Phonetically, members of the family are characterised by large numbers of consonant phonemes, produced not only by utilising all points of articulation from the lips back to the larynx (with the typically pan-Caucasian opposition of voiced vs voiceless aspirate vs voiceless ejective for obstruents) but by associating with plain consonants such secondary features as labialisation, palatalisation and (in the case of Ubykh and possibly Bzyp Abkhaz) pharyngalisation — Ubykh had a minimum of 80 consonantal phonemes. As would be predicted, these languages have minimal vowel systems, most commentators operating with just a vertical system of close /ə/[2] vs open /a/, though the status of Abkhaz [a:] is debatable — Allen (1956;

1965) discusses a further reduction. The literary form of Abkhaz, Abzhywa, has the 58 consonantal phonemes given in the chart below. Bzyp additionally has a full alveolo-palatal series with dʑ, tɕ, tɕ', ʑ, ɕ, z^v, ɕ^f, plus the two uvular fricatives χ and χ^w, which those who view the pan-Abkhaz back-fricatives as uvulars have to analyse as pharyngalised uvulars.

Consonantal phoneme chart for Literary Abkhaz (Abzhywa dialect)

Bilabial	b	p	p'			m		w
Labio-dental				f	v			
Alveolar	d	t	t'					
	d^b	t^p	t^p'					
	dz[3]	ts[4]	ts'	s	z	n	l	r
Alveolo-palatal	dz^v	tɕ^f	tɕ^f'					
Palato-alveolar	dʒ	tʃ[5]	tʃ'	ʃ[6]	ʒ[7]			j
				ʃ^w	ʒ^w			ɥ
Retroflex	ɖʐ	ʈʂ	ʈʂ'	ʂ	ʐ			
Velar	g	k	k'	x[8]	ɣ[9]			
	g^j[10]	k^j	k^j'	x^j	ɣ^j			
	g^w	k^w	k^w'	x^w	ɣ^w[11]			
Uvular			q'					
			q^j'					
			q^w'					
Pharyngal			ħ[12]					
			ħ^w					

The phonological feature of labialisation is phonetically instantiated in three ways: simple lip-rounding is indicated by a raised 'w',[13] labio-dentalisation by raised 'v' or 'f', and double bilabial-alveolar articulation by a raised 'b' or 'p' — for /ɥ/[14] there is a distinct constriction of the pharynx in the speech of some speakers, reflecting perhaps its origin in a labialised voiced pharyngal fricative, still preserved in Abaza.

Native roots typically consist of the simple structure C(V), with a high tolerance of homonymy. For example, with initial /a-/ the definite-generic article and /'/ marking stress, we have a-x^w 'price; wounded'[15] vs *a-'xʷy* 'part; portion of food; gift; hill; handle; hair; feathery down; throat' vs *'a-xʷa* 'ash; grey; bent; (meat-)worm'. Noun morphology is rudimentary, singular being distinguished from plural and, in Abkhaz, there being only one formally marked case (the adverbial/predicative, in *-s* or less commonly *-ny*). Most adjectives follow their nouns, and possession is marked by a pronominal prefix on the possessed nominal. This simplicity is counterbalanced by extreme polypersonalism in the verbal system, where such categories as finite vs non-finite, stative vs dynamic, tense vs mood, simplex vs causative are found, though there is no simple active vs passive opposition.

The functions of the NPs in a clause are indicated by the form and position of coreferential pronominal prefixes within the verbal complex; tripersonal verbs are common, though Abkhaz avoids four prefixes in one complex. The word order is predominantly SOV. Examples:

s-ab **s-an** **a-'para** **(Ø-)'ly-j-ta-Ø-jt'**[16]
my-father my-mother the-money (it-)her-he-give-PAST-FINITE
My father gave the money to my mother

s-an **s-ab** **a-'para** **(Ø-)'jy-l-ta-Ø-jt'**
my-mother my-father the-money (it-)him-she-give-PAST-FINITE
My mother gave the money to my father

r-'jʷyz-tçᶠa **r-an** **r-ab** **dy-l-dy-r-'dyry-Ø-jt'**
their-friend-s their-mother their-father him-her-they-CAUSE-know-PAST-FINITE
Their friends introduced their father to their mother

ʃʷy-tş-'ry-gy-ʃʷ-my-r-xa-la-n
your.PLURAL-self-them-late.for.you.PL-not-CAUSE-become-ITERATIVE-PROHIBITION
Don't in general (let yourselves) be late for them [lessons]!

Evliya Çelebi provides the earliest concrete linguistic evidence for North West Caucasian in his travel book of the 1640s; examples of Ubykh, Circassian and probably (as argued by Chirikba) the Sadz dialect of Abkhaz-Abaza, still then spoken in Abkhazia, feature in his word and phrase lists.

More extensive items of vocabulary were cited by Johann Anton

Güldenstädt in the description he wrote of his own travels in the Caucasus between 1770 and 1773. Though a manuscript of an early 19th century Abkhaz-Russian dictionary has been discovered in manuscript in a Tbilisi archive by Bernard Outtier, who will publish it, and though Georg Rosen included reference to Abkhaz in a paper delivered in 1845 on Svan, Mingrelian and Abkhaz, the first person to attempt a full-scale description of Abkhaz and provide it with a script was the Russian Baron Pjotr Uslar,[17] whose grammar of Abkhaz first appeared in lithograph format in 1862; it was printed in 1887, the final 27 pages being devoted to the only scholarly work on Ubykh to have been carried out while the Ubykhs still dwelt on their native soil.

Uslar studied the Bzyp dialect but did not manage to distinguish all its 67 consonant phonemes with his Cyrillic-based script of 55 characters. The first moves to publish materials in Abkhaz followed Uslar's pioneering efforts, and his script underwent a number of adaptations, the most successful of which was introduced by Andrej Ch'och'ua in 1909; this version also employed 55 characters and remained in use until 1926.

Nikolaj Marr employed his own staggeringly complex so-called 'Analytical Alphabet' with its 75 characters for his 1926 Abkhaz-Russian dictionary. Although this system was Roman-based, it was not adopted as the official Abkhaz script when the Soviet Union, in pursuance of its Romanisation drive for the 'Young Written Languages'[18] (i.e. those languages granted literary status by the Soviets and for which either scripts were first devised or recently devised orthographies received official approval), sanctioned in 1928 the 'Unified Abkhaz Alphabet' of the Russian caucasologist, Nikolaj Jakovlev.

Until this time most published works had been in the Bzyp dialect (such as the Gospels of 1912, reprinted with Ch'och'ua's original script in 1975 by the Institute for Bible Translation in Stockholm), but partly because most prominent writers of the day hailed from Abzhywa-speaking areas and also because Abzhywa is phonetically the simpler variety surviving in the Abkhazian homeland, from this time Abzhywa has served as the literary dialect — see Bgazhba (1964) for a description of Bzyp. With Stalin unassailable in the Kremlin and the Soviet borders secure, internationalism was abandoned, and this was reflected in the attitude towards scripts functioning inside the USSR — between 1936 and 1938 Cyrillic became the base for yet new orthographies for all the Young Written Languages, with two significant exceptions, both within Stalin's home republic of Georgia.

In 1931 Stalin had reduced the status of Abkhazia to that of a mere Autonomous Republic within the confines of Georgia, and South

Ossetia was an Autonomous Region therein. In 1938 new Georgian-based orthographies were approved for both Abkhaz and the Ossetic of South Ossetia (even though Cyrillic was introduced for the Ossetic of North Ossetia). Linguistically it cannot be denied that Georgian's is the best already established writing system to serve as base for the representation of any Caucasian language,[19] but this shift was primarily motivated not by linguistic considerations but in order to underscore Abkhazia's new subservience to Tbilisi.

As the repression of Abkhazian culture intensified under the sustained attempt by Beria and his successor in Tbilisi, the Svan K'andid Chark'viani, to georgianise Abkhazia, publishing of materials in Abkhaz diminished and dried up altogether when all Abkhaz language schools were closed in 1945-46 and replaced by Georgian language schools, in which children were beaten if overheard speaking Abkhaz — see the 1947 letter of complaint written by G. Dzidzarija *et al* (1992; English translation in Hewitt 1996).

With the deaths of Stalin and Beria in 1953 anti-Abkhazian activity was reversed: teaching of the language and publishing in it were restored, and for this a committee (sic!) devised a new Cyrillic-based script that is still in use. Although not all Cyrillic's characters are utilised, 14 non-Cyrillic items were incorporated. Even so, the script leaves much to be desired: it is not compatible with the Cyrillic-based orthography that Abaza has used since 1938; some graphs differ in phonetic realisation even between Russian and Abkhaz; it is inconsistent in marking the phonological opposition ejective vs non-ejective.

Since there is obviously no possibility of a Georgian base ever appealing to the Abkhazians, one might have thought that, had not the question of their very survival come on the agenda in 1992, the collapse of the Soviet Union would have been an appropriate time for the Abkhazians to introduce a more user-friendly, preferably Roman-based variant that could be easily written with a basic typewriter/computer-keyboard — for my own ideas on this theme see Hewitt (1995c). Whichever script finally serves post-Soviet Abkhaz, word stress should certainly be indicated, as it is by no means easy to predict.

The chart below presents the Cyrillic-based, introduced in 1954, and the preceding Georgian-based scripts; the order of the post-1953 alphabet is determined by that of Russian, but, when the Georgian-based orthography was in use, it was the sequence of the basic Georgian which determined the order of letters (see Dzhanashia's *Abkhaz-Georgian dictionary*, which, though it was published only in 1954, had been prepared in the late 1930s and thus uses the Georgian alphabet for both languages):

The Cyrillic and Georgian based alphabets for Abkhaz

Cyrillic	А,а	Б,б	В,в	Г,г	Гь,гь	Гу,гу	Ҕ,ҕ	Ҕь,ҕь	Ҕу,ҕу	Д,д
Georgian	ა	ბ	ვ	გ	გჲ	გჳ	ღ	ღჲ	ღჳ	დ
Phonetic	a	b	v	g	g^j	g^w	ɣ	$ɣ^j$	$ɣ^w$	d

Cyrillic	Дә,дә	Е,е	Ж,ж	Жь,жь	Жә,жә	З,з	Ӡ,ӡ	Ӡә,ӡә	И,и	К,к
Georgian	დჳ	ე	ჟ	ჟ	ჟჳ	ზ	ძ	ძჳ	ი	კ
Phonetic	d^b	e	ʐ	ʒ	$ʒ^w$	z	dz	dz^v	i/j	k'

Cyrillic	Кь,кь	Ку,ку	Қ,қ	Қь,қь	Қу,қу	Ҟ,ҟ	Ҟь,ҟь	Ҟу,ҟу	Л,л	М,м
Georgian	კჲ	კჳ	ქ	ქჲ	ქჳ	ყ	ყჲ	ყჳ	ლ	მ
Phonetic	$k^{j'}$	$k^{w'}$	k	k^j	k^w	q'	$q^{j'}$	$q^{w'}$	l	m

Cyrillic	Н,н	О,о	П,п	С,с	Т,т	Тә,тә	Ҭ,ҭ	Ҭә,ҭә	У,у	Ф,ф
Georgian	ნ	ო	პ	ს	ტ	ტჳ	თ	თჳ	უ	ფ
Phonetic	n	o	p'	s	t'	$t^{p'}$	t	t^p	u/w	f

Cyrillic	Х,х	Хь,хь	Ху,ху	Ҳ,ҳ	Ҳә,ҳә	Ц,ц	Цә,цә	Ҵ,ҵ	Ҵә,ҵә	Ч,ч
Georgian	ხ	ხჲ	ხჳ	ჰ	ჰჳ	ც	ცჳ	წ	წჳ	ჩ
Phonetic	x	x^j	x^w	ħ	$ħ^w$	ts	$tɕ^f$	ts'	$tɕ^{f'}$	tʃ

Cyrillic	Ҷ,ҷ	Ҽ,ҽ	Ҿ,ҿ	Ш,ш	Шь,шь	Шә,шә	Ы,ы	Ҩ,ҩ	Џ,џ	Џь,џь
Georgian	ჭ	ჩჳ	ჭჳ	შჳ	შ	შჳ	ჷ	ჳ	ჯჳ	ჯ
Phonetic	tʃ̣	ts	ts'	ʂ	ʃ	$ʃ^w$	ə	ɥ	dʐ	dʒ

A recent innovation, introduced since the end of the war in 1993, serves to standardise the marking of the feature of labialisation by use of the sign ә. This means that the sounds represented above by the digraphs гу, ҕу, ку, қу, ҟу, ху are now written as гә, ҕә, кә, қә, ҟә, хә. As a consequence, the script no longer needs to utilise the reverse apostrophe to distinguish a sequence of plain consonant followed by bilabial continuant from the labialised form of that same consonant (e.g. ик‘уеит vs икуеит = *jy-j-k'-'wa-jt* vs *jy-j-'kʷ'a-yt* = 'he seizes it/them' vs 'he filed/polished it/them', for the two verb forms would now be represented respectively as икуеит vs икәеит).

Teaching of Abkhaz was first introduced in 1892 on the basis of the 51-letter script of D. Gulia and K'onst'ant'ine Mach'avariani,[20] but in 1914-15 only ten per cent of the population was literate. At the time of the closure of Abkhaz language schools in 1945-46 Abkhaz served as the language of tuition up to Class 5, after which Russian replaced it. In

1966 there were only 91 Abkhaz language schools in the whole of Abkhazia (the number of all types of schools in 1980 was stated to be 365 by the Appendix to the 11-volume Georgian Encyclopaedia). The teaching plan for 1981-82 divided language and literature lessons as follows for Abkhaz language schools, where teaching was entirely in Abkhaz (apart from Russian language classes) up to the fourth class, after which the switch occurred to Russian, except for Abkhaz language classes:

Number of weekly lessons for language and literature in Abkhaz language schools

Year	I	II	III	IV	V	VI	VII	VIII	IX	X
Abkhaz Lg	7	6	6	3	3	3	2	2	–	–
Russian Lg	8	9	9	6	6	4	4/3	2	1	1
Abkhaz Lit	–	–	–	2	2	2	2	2	3	3
Russian Lit	–	–	–	2	2	2	2	3	3	2

The non-existence of appropriate text-books coupled with the political-economic-social disruption to life in the republic from 1992 will make any wider teaching in Abkhaz problematic. For further details of language planning in Soviet Georgia see Hewitt (1989c).

The paucity of Abkhaz language schools, the larger number of Russian language schools and the natural desire of parents to see their children proficient in the Soviet Union's (and Abkhazia's!) main lingua franca often meant that Abkhazian children were simply enrolled in Russian language schools.[21] Throughout Soviet Georgia the second language taught in Russian language schools was usually Georgian, but there is evidence that from at least the 1970s Abkhaz could be studied in not only Russian but even Armenian schools in the republic.[22] According to data from the 1979 Soviet census published in the Georgian journal *Ek'onomist'i* ('The Economist', 3, 1981, p74), 96.1 per cent of the Abkhazians considered Abkhaz to be their native tongue (with 2.4 per cent naming Russian vs 1.5 per cent naming Georgian); as for second-language knowledge, 73.9 per cent claimed fluency in Russian[23] (2.1 per cent citing Georgian, 0.4 per cent citing Abkhaz, and 0.1 per cent citing some other unspecified language). The first second language acquired by many Abzhywa Abkhazians for much of the 20th century (at least those in mixed Abkhazian-Mingrelian communities) was

Mingrelian.[24] Naturally, the southernmost region of Abkhazia, Gal (roughly equivalent to the former Samurzaq'an(o) district), was the first to experience this bilingualism, and indeed became thoroughly Mingrelianised quite early. Clear evidence for this dates from 1919 when the Georgian Shota Beridze was conducting fieldwork for the Mingrelian grammar he published in manuscript form in 1920:

> So Samurzaq'ano (from the Ingur to the Ghalidzga, north to the gates of Ochamchira) should be styled a 'Mingrelianised' region, for you will be unable to hear here the Abkhaz language, as you could 30-50 years ago; Mingrelian predominates. The intelligentsia ([in the towns of] Gali-Achigvara) know, or course, how to read and write in Russian, speak Mingrelian *and do not know Georgian* (p20, stresses added).

This observation vis-à-vis knowledge of Georgian continued to reflect the situation on the ground, for, apart from those educated during the closure of Abkhaz language schools, Abkhazians themselves tended not to learn Georgian. Nor was there any need: Russian was the natural second (or, in the case of Abkhaz-Mingrelian bilinguals, third) language for Abkhazians, and, since the bulk of the 239, 872 Kartvelian residents of Abkhazia in 1989 were Mingrelians who spoke Mingrelian amongst themselves or in the bazaars, even in those areas where Kartvelians predominated since Beria's importations of the 1930s, Georgian was rarely heard.

Until 1979, when the Pedagogical Institute in Sukhum was upgraded to a university (following disturbances in Abkhazia in 1978 connected with increasing dominance of Georgian and Kartvelians in the life of the republic), Georgia could boast only one university, that of Tbilisi (founded 1918), where a very small number of places were reserved each year for Abkhazians. From its foundation the Abkhazian State University consisted of three sectors (Russian, Abkhaz, Georgian), of which the largest was always the Georgian.

When the Kartvelian staff and students wrenched the Georgian sector away to form the rival (and illegal) Sukhum Branch of Tbilisi State University as part of the agitation that led to the inter-ethnic clashes of July 1989 (described elsewhere in this volume), the authorities at the Abkhazian State University made the most of this opportunity and opened an Armenian sector to replace the Georgian one — in 1989 there were 76,541 Armenians (14.6 per cent of the republic's population) in Abkhazia — this arrangement was resumed after the Abkhazian victory in 1993 and serves as an excellent indication of Abkhazian readiness to co-operate with other peoples living in their republic.

In addition to the Abkhaz-Russian and Abkhaz-Georgian dictionaries by Marr and Dzhanashia mentioned above, neither of which could claim to be at all exhaustive, a number of specialist dictionaries or lexicological works appeared from the 1960s (e.g. Bghaʒʷba 1968; Bghaʒʷba 1977; Khalbad 1977; Khalbad 1980; Aryṣ-pha 1980; Kvarchija 1981; K'aslandzia 1981; K'aslandzia 1985; K'aslandzia 1989; Mikaia 1985; Aryṣ-pha/Nach'qⁱ'ebia-pha 1986; Samandzhia 1987; Nach'qⁱ'ebia-pha 1988; Dzidzarija 1989), but it was only in 1986 that a reasonably comprehensive two-volume dictionary with both Abkhaz and Russian explanations appeared in Sukhum (Shakryl & Kondzharija 1986). Wim Lucassen and Albert Starreveld are producing an Abkhaz-English dictionary in Holland. F. Agrba of the Turkish diaspora community published an Abkhaz-Turkish dictionary in 1990. Bgazhba (1964a) produced a Russian-Abkhaz dictionary in 1964. For Abaza there is Zhirov & Èkba (1956) from Russian, and Tugov (1967) into Russian. Collections of Abkhazian proverbs are: Gulia (1939), Arch'elia (1986), and Bghaʒʷba (1983). See also Appendix 5 for a selection of proverbs and vocabulary items in semantic fields.

The long-term viability of Abkhaz will be precarious, given both the low number of speakers and the unfavourable linguistic environment, whatever the outcome of current political problems. Despite the larger numbers in Turkey, the long-term survival of Abkhaz (and indeed the other North Caucasian languages spoken there) must be regarded as being in similar jeopardy.

12
Literature
& linguistic politics
Vasilij Avidzba

The oral art of the Abkhazian people is multi-layered. Historically its character was polyfunctional. As with works of so-called pure art, stylised speech, which had a utilitarian significance, was practised on a wide scale. In particular, the art of oratory, which occupies a considerable place in the traditional culture of the Abkhazians, testifies to a special admiration for the word. Putting it another way, it is not only the thought and meaning of what was said which the Abkhazians valued but how colourfully and skilfully it is presented to listeners.

This circumstance naturally found reflection also in the oral-artistic creativity of the nation. Abkhazian folklore, which served as a prototype for Abkhazian belles-lettres, is of the utmost importance in both form and content. The heroic epic of the Narts, the mythical tale of the Ats'ans (Dwarfs), the fable of Abrsk'il (Abrskj'yl) and his fight with god, legends, novels, stories, ritual and seasonal poetry, etc, bear witness in the first place to the fact that the nation, the creator and bearer of such a cultural layer of artistic production, was involved in important events of world history, and, in the second place, to the fact that in the midst of these events it was able through the production of creative oral poetry to preserve its own ethnic identity and present to humanity its own artistic-ideological map of the world, one that is infused with national self-awareness.

In the history of the Abkhazians' cultural traditions, belles-lettres hold a significant place. Actual written Abkhazian literature came into being not all that long ago. The origins of its history are directly linked to the politics and processes of cultural enlightenment that occurred in the Caucasus and particularly in Abkhazia following the end of the Caucasian War (1864). To facilitate its own politics of colonisation in the Caucasus, Russia undertook and put into effect certain steps aimed at creating writing-systems for the Mountain Peoples. Thus, in 1861, an Abkhazian alphabet, which was attached to his monograph 'The

Abkhazian Language', was designed and later published by the Tsarist general and scholar-linguist Pjotr Uslar. In 1865 the first 'Abkhazian Primer' was published; it was composed under the supervision of another Russian general, I. Bartolomej. However, neither the alphabet nor the primer were put into proper practice. Work on the creation of an Abkhazian writing-system proceeded. In 1892 K'onst'ant'ine Mach'avariani together with Dyrmit' Gulia (Dyrmyjt' Gʷlyja — later to become the founder of Abkhazian belles-lettres) composed a new 'Abkhazian Primer'. In 1909 Andrej Ch'och'ua published a replacement, which was more successful methodologically. And it is essentially by means of this primer (with some insignificant changes) that Abkhazian children start out on their path to knowledge even today.

The birth of belles-lettres

The creation of a series of alphabets and primers for Abkhaz has been accompanied by a heightening awareness amongst the Abkhazian intelligentsia of their role as educators. Together these factors defined the character of the preliterary stage. However, the frequent alterations to the Abkhazian alphabet which also took place at a later period left a disagreeable imprint both on the general state of education and on the development of literature in particular.

From 1926 to 1954 the Abkhazian orthography was changed four times. Thus, in 1926, in place of the earlier Abkhazian alphabet composed on the basis of Russian graphics a new one was introduced that had been devised by Nikolaj Marr of the Russian Academy on the basis of Roman graphics and which was known as the 'Analytic' or 'Japhetic' script (Bgazhba, 1967, p58). However, this too was soon abolished and after two years was replaced by another Roman-based alphabet devised by Professor Nikolaj Jakovlev. Teaching based on this began in schools in 1929. But in 1937, solely in pursuit of the goal of the assimilation of the Abkhazian people, the alphabet was again subjected to alteration, the replacement being designed on the basis of Georgian graphics. And only in 1954 was the change to the current Abkhazian alphabet, based on Russian Cyrillic, effected. Nevertheless, despite the excessive and pointless number of changes in the graphic base of the orthography, this language saw the creation of artistic works which in spite of a panoply of obstacles were able to play a crucial historico-cultural role in the formation of a literature.

If one examines the origins of the birth of Abkhazian belles-lettres, then without a doubt one has to note the considerable role played by the Translation Commission that was established in Sukhum in 1892. The following participated in this at various times: Giorgi Shervashidze,

K'onst'ant'ine Mach'avariani, D. Adzhamov, L. Avaliani, Dyrmyjt' Gulia, N. Gublia (Gʷblyja), D. Margania (Maan), N. Ladaria, N. Patejpa, F. Èshba, and others.

This Commission in a relatively short period of time translated into Abkhaz a large quantity of books, in the first instance of an ecclesiastical-Christian nature, for example: *Prayers: The Ten Commandments and Ceremonial Oath* (1892), *Prayerbook* (1907), *The Divine Liturgy of John Chrysostom* (1907), *Servicebook* (a collection of books of divine worship), *The Main Festivals of the Orthodox Church* (1910), *Musical Notation for Abkhazian Liturgical Hymns* (1912), *The Holy Gospels* (1912) and a range of others.

The work of the Translation Commission indubitably played a role in the development of Abkhazian belles-lettres because already an active participation in it was being taken by the founder of Abkhazian literature, Dyrmyjt' Gulia. Firstly, in parallel with the translation of religious texts, he was involved in the gathering and publication of folklore-material. Thus, in 1907 he published the book *Abkhazian proverbs, riddles and tongue-twisters*. Secondly, the practices of textual construction acquired by him and his mastery of the habits of the technique of writing could not but serve as a double stimulus for his own creativity. It is surely no coincidence that Gulia's first works, dated to 1906, appear at precisely this period.

Truly Abkhazian belles-lettristic literature began in 1912 when Gulia published his first volume of collected works *(Poems and 'Chastushki')*.[1] From the moment of its birth to the present day around 200 poets, writers and playwrights have contributed to the creation of Abkhazian literature. Naturally, as with any other nation's literature, not all contributions are of equal value. But undoubtedly each participated in the formation and strengthening of our literature to the best of their talent and capacities.

Putting aside the different views of literary experts on the periodisation of Abkhazian literature, the most convenient would appear to be the one that treats its history as falling into two periods. The first period encompasses the years from 1912 to 1955, whilst the second runs from the latter half of the 1950s to the present day.

The first stage is characterised by the birth of literary genres, the presence of a didactic motif in writers' works, by the utilisation of folklore and by the significant influence of Russian literature. Thus, during the course of the said period there appeared in Abkhazian literature all the basic genres of poetry, prose and drama: verse (1912), narrative poem (1924), short story (1919), long ghost-story (1931), novel (1937), drama (1919).

The leitmotif of an important number of works were the probems of enlightenment — the direct call to receive instruction and gain an education. It is possible to reduce the way Abkhazian literature was used for purposes of enlightenment to roughly two fundamental elements: the first in connection with the rejection and often liquidation of the old way of life; and the second with propagating new ideas, mostly inspired by revolution. The distinctive peculiarity of Abkhazian enlightenment is also the fact that the motifs of instruction, as the new Communist

A page of text and an illustration from the 1962 edition of the Abkhaz version (sanitised!) of the pan-North Caucasian Nart epic

doctrine took a grip, were gradually transformed into peremptory didacticism and in this way surfaced in the language of the given epoch and were realised in the only forms possible in the historical situation that the country found itself.

However, the fact that Abkhazian literature of this period, thanks to its inexperience, was still unable to manage without a substantial input from the tradition of folklore and folk-poetry gave a certain scope to the creative freedom of poets and writers. Folklore indeed is detectable at all structural levels of literary production: plot and composition, aesthetics and tropes, ideology and themes. But over time the extent to which use is made of folklore gradually diminishes, or rather it starts to take on a different functional load. Undoubtedly relevant here is the fact that at this period Abkhazian oral-artistic creativity undergoes a demarcation and differentiation between two artistic systems: folklore with its national, collective element, and literature with its individual principle. The artistic individuality of the poets passes through a period of formation and, as it were, becomes distinct from the aesthetics of folklore as the role of the thinking, suffering *ego* and its 'self-scrutiny' (Èjkhenbaum, 1986), so characteristic of the lyric, begin to manifest themselves more strongly. On the linguistic level, despite the predominance in written works of common spoken language and the use of normal linguistic metaphor and epithets, one can observe their transformation as the 'individual-linguistic systems' of the writers became more complex.

As a result, a gradual departure from the poetics of folklore takes place. Characters become more varied in form and acquire lines of individuality. In addition, attempts are made (and not without success) to reveal the internal world of literary heroes; there is a striving to reflect the psychological struggle between their feelings and motives for action and the actions themselves (for example, the novel *Temyr*, by Ivan P'ap'askir [P'ap'askʲyr]). At the same time, starting from the 1930s, a move away from representation of the past is noticeable, and in works of this type contemporary life begins to dominate. There is a strengthening of the standing of the journalistic element. The adequacy of the artistic analogue of reality vis-à-vis the reflected picture of life in this situation depended on the degree to which authors were either forbidden or allowed by the ruling political system to raise problematical topics in their works. As everyone knows, during the period of Stalin's personality cult it was more a case of forbidding, and writers were compelled to 'tread on the throat of their own song' to devote their talents to the prevailing ideology.

The influence of Russian writers

A pivotal role in the establishment of Abkhazian literature belongs without doubt to Russian literature. This was primarily due to its linguistic accessibility; after all, the works of Russian writers were directly accessible to Abkhazian writers without the need for a translation. The works of their contemporaries enjoyed great popularity amongst Abkhazian writers, and this, in the circumstances described above, could not fail to condition at a certain level the ideological content of the works of Abkhazian literature. For the synchronic type of effect of Russian literature on Abkhazian literature (i.e. the influence of works composed in one and the same epoch), this is betrayed by a shared nucleus of morality and content and by appropriate characterisations. These parallels are especially notable in works devoted to the subject of state farming (for example, the transforming of rural economy to one based on collective farms).

There was also a diachronic aspect to the influence from Russian literature on Abkhazian literature. This was principally manifested in translations into Abkhaz of the classics of Russian literature. Translations appeared of such works as Pushkin's *The Captain's Daughter*, Gogol's *Marriage* and *The Government Inspector* and Tolstoy's *Hadji Murat*.

All the above factors taken together facilitated the assimiliation by a youthful Abkhazian literature of such essential belles-lettristic components as: the technique of mastering the art-form, the stabilisation of the unity of the subject-compositional structure of the work, the strengthening of the role of secondary conceptual thematisation, etc, without which the formation of a unified system of national literature would have been inconceivable.

Among the clearest representatives of Abkhazian masters of verbal art one can name Gulia, Samson Ch'anba, Iwa K'oghonia, and Ivan P'ap'askir; their contribution to the establishment of an Abkhazian literature was immense. The work of Gulia is multi-layered in both genre and thematic relations. Alongside works of a lyrical or lyrical-epic character he also composed in prose: the story 'Beneath an Alien Sky' (1919), the novel *K'amach'ych'* (1933-40), the play *Ghosts* (1949).

In *K'amach'ych'* Gulia strives to portray the life of Abkhazian society at the turn of the 19th-20th centuries. The poetic nature of this work in many respects also consists syncretically of the use of elements from differing genres. Thus, in its structural-compositional features, this novel absorbed within itself elements of the poetry of the Nart epic, of oral story-telling and of the ritual-performance forms of traditional, everyday culture, in particular various comic popular devices.

An important place belongs to the works of the founder of Abkhazian dramaturgy, Samson Ch'anba. From his pen came such works as the historical drama *Amhadzhir* (1919), the poem 'Maid of the Mountains' (1919-1925), the play *Apsny-Hanym* ('Lady Abkhazia') (1923), the tale 'Sejdyq'' and other prose-writings. Inherent in his output are a symbolic generalisation of forms ('Maid of the Mountains', 'Apsny-Hanym', 'Train No. 6', etc) and the ability to create portrait-like characteristics for his characters. The lyrical direction of Abkhazian literature was represented most plainly by Iwa K'oghonia. His poetry is distinguished by spirituality, sincerity and lofty but light linguistic arrangement. The subjects for his eight lyrical-epic works, or poems, K'oghonia took from the Abkhazians' folklore-epic legacy. Such human qualities as courage, devotion, self-control, are celebrated in them.

Three novels and a whole range of stories were composed by the first Abkhazian romantic, Ivan P'ap'askir. The first Abkhazian novel *Temyr* was published in 1937. The literary inheritance of P'ap'askir is redolent with elucidation of actual, contemporary problems — reflecting the process of forming the new man in the new historical conditions. Although his level of generalisation and power to penetrate the materials of the life under investigation proved to be somewhat limited, all the components and properties characteristic of maturity in artistic mastery are present — the author's well-plotted structure, his literary conventionality, and, as a corollary, the creation of colourful characters.

However, just as it was gathering strength and confidence, Abkhazian literature was forced to apply the brakes to its development. The political situation arising in the second half of the 1930s became a serious obstacle to its growth. After the elimination of the head of the Abkhazian Republic, Nest'or Lak'oba (poisoned in Tbilisi by Beria), from the political arena and the subsequent repression of practically all the members of the government, the turn came for the intelligentsia. On false, trumped-up charges the writers Ch'anba, Vladimir Agrba, Arushan K'aslandzia, Sh. Khok'erba (Khok'yrba) were shot. In different years the poet Shalva Ts'vizhba (Tçw'ydzhba) and the playwright and prose-author Mikhail Lak'erbaj (Lak'rba) became objects of repression, being shot or serving long terms of imprisonment.

Consequent upon this, even the Abkhaz language was subjected to persecution; its alphabet in 1937 was changed to a Georgian base. In 1945 the language of tuition in Abkhazian schools was also transferred to Georgian, which in practice meant the closure of Abkhazian schools.[2] In a word, everything was done to assimilate the Abkhazian people at the earliest possible date and to deprive them of their historical memory. Georgianisation was especially noticeable in the domination it achieved in the field of Abkhazian toponymy.

Another obstacle to the development of Abkhazian literature was the war of 1941-45. It took away the lives of both masters of belles-lettres, who had already lived long enough to make a name for themselves, such as the poet Lewarsa K'vits'inia (Kw'yts'nyja) and the prose-writer St'epan Kuchberia (Kwychberyja), as well as many young poets such as: Vladimir Chicheria, Mikhail Gochua, Rawfbej Dzhap'ua, Vladimir K'ap'ba, P. Anwa. Others, such as Ch'ich'ik'o Dzhonua, Aleksej Dzhonua, Mikhail Lak'erbaj and others, were obliged to interrupt their literary activity to participate in the war.[3]

Even at such a critical period for the history of the Abkhazian people and for the fate of Abkhazian literature the muse did not abandon her patriarch, Gulia; the talent of the young Bagrat' Shinkuba (Shynkʷba) began to manifest itself, and P'ap'askir continued to compose his novels.

A change for the better, which gave hope to the country, took place after the post-1953 condemnation (albeit partial) of Stalinism. At this period it became possible to a certain extent to overcome the enforced stagnation. Use of Abkhaz for teaching purposes was renewed in Abkhazian schools. And the results of positive socio-political changes were not long in coming. It was at this precise period, in the second half of the 1950s, that Abkhazian literature experienced an influx of a new generation of young, talented artists of the word who were destined, on the one hand, to secure the achievements of the national literature's preceding epoch and, on the other, to offer a new quality to its future course and complete the process of its formation.

Evolution in the 1950s

The cardinal changes that have occurred in Abkhazian literature, beginning with the second half of the 1950s, are primarily reflected in its greater emancipation and freedom (although by no means complete) from ideological diktat. And as a result, in works where the problem of the relationship between an individual and society predominated there appears a huge variety of models in the actual situations in which the characters find themselves. Striving to understand and portray spiritual values in their historical dynamic, on the one hand, and, on the other, to state their eternal and absolutely positive properties and merits, all this represents the problems which Abkhazian literature seeks to determine. Two fundamental directions are found at the focus of its attention: interest in the history of the nation and an investigation and analysis of the internal world of man.

An important evolution was achieved by Abkhazian poetry both in the realm of the development of rhythmical and metrical forms and also in diversity of genres, starting with lyrical versification and ending in verse-novels. On the other hand, the thematic composition of the works of Abkhazian poets starts to take on different shapes. In Abkhazian poetry of this stage we meet works imbued with a socio-publicist tone as well as philosophical and musical-melodic lyrics.

At this period Abkhazian literature is best represented by the talents of Shinkuba, Ivan Tarba, Anatolij Adzhyndzhal, Mushni Lasuria (Laʃʷryja), Taif Adzhba,[4] Rushbej Smyr and a range of others. The creative evolution of the poets had to some degree a general tendency, and in particular, if at the initial stage of creativity each of them naturally had a bent towards lyric, as their creative mastery and acquisition of experience grew, an inclination towards large-scale epic works manifested itself. Thus, in Abkhazian literature alongside lyric-epic works were composed four novels in verse. The most significant of these are Shynkᵂba's 'Song on the Rock' and Vladimir Ankᵂab's 'Abrskʲ'yl'.

Artistic prose developed on similar lines in Abkhaz. From the mid-1950s the first stage saw the publication of works of a small epic form, i.e. stories. Their authors — Aleksej Gogua, Dzhuma Ahᵂba, Aleksej Dzhenia, Nikolaj Hashyg and a range of others — sought to represent the changes that had taken place in the spiritual, psychological spheres of Abkhazian society, and artistically to generalise and form a model of the complex process of transformation in its consciousness. It is necessary to recognise that, on the whole, Abkhazian literature realised that the Abkhazian people were caught up amidst historical circumstances which, for objective-historical reasons, were compelling them to change many of their traditions, settled norms of behaviour and, in

Work table of the founder of Abkhaz literature, Dyrmyjt' Gulia, with a biblical illustration side by side a volume by Lenin

consequence, both their morality and general world-view. But, on the other hand, it also understood the perniciousness in unconditionally instilling the principles of the Communist social structure that was becoming dominant. And therefore, literature attempted (often in allegorical and coded terms) to indicate to the reader the tendentiousness and the flawed nature of the socialist system in which contemporary society was living along with the utopian quality of its central idea — the construction of an absolutely equal human society.

And in this way Abkhazian literature to a certain extent made it feasible for the Abkhazian people to preserve their own ethnic identity, their own world-view, and to this or that degree their traditional culture.

With the passage of time several trends in belles-lettres start to appear. We see this primarily in works of a journalistic character orientated towards contemporary reality. Another tendency was defined by works appealing to the historical past of the Abkhazian people. But differently from the works on historical themes from the earlier stage of literature, which had been composed in essence under the influence of oral poetry, these works were influenced by the development of Abkhazian historical scholarship. And, finally, a third trend in Abkhazian literature of the period from the 1950s to the 1990s is distinguished by the striving to bring to the fore the socio-psychological aspect of human existence.

With the increase in the quantity and importance of the problems raised, Abkhazian literature begins to gravitate towards more large-scale, epic genres, and, in particular, the use by writers of the genre-possibilities of the novel becomes noticeable. One can essentially, without any overstatement, style Abkhazian literature of the last quarter century as that of the novel. Over this period the number of works of this genre has reached fifty in number.

Among these an important place is held by *Last of the Departed* (Bagrat' Shinkuba; English translation by Paula Garb, published by Raduga in 1982), *Cleft Rock* (Shinkuba), *Halo*, *Heavy Snow* (Aleksej Gogua), *The Sun Rises amongst Us* (Ivan Tarba), *Scar* (Shaladija Adzhyndzhal), *Eighth Colour of the Rainbow*, *Amiran: Deity of Two* (Aleksej Dzhenia), *Golden Cart* (P'lat'on Bebia), *Ordeal* (Nikolaj Hashyg), *Moorage* (Dzhuma Ahʷba) and *King of Abkhazia* (Vitalij Amarshan).

The very fact that writers resorted to such a difficult genre as the novel testifies in a certain measure to the fact that literature had amassed a satisfactory level of professional expertise, which enables one to speak of a ready-shaped concept of the novel and thus of adequate literary maturity.

Traditional story-telling

In the best examples of Abkhazian literature an artistically convincing representation of reality and its psychological mechanisms is achieved. In them the writers frequently succeed in passing beyond the boundaries of socio-historical reality and in giving to their works a general-philosophical, in some ways universal conception of humanity, although the cultural-national milieu of the Abkhazian people remains fundamental to their core content.

For all the diversification and modification of genres, it may be noted that the basic compositional-narrative modes of the epic works of Abkhazian literature of the second stage are the traditional epic story-telling whereby the author 'sees' all the actions of the characters, their thoughts and emotional experiences. Subject-plot actions in works of this type are constructed, as a rule, in chronological order. The second type is story-telling in the first person, where one sees a rejection of the panoramic presentation of situations; it is filled with the internal monologues of the heroes, their recollections, wide use of retrospection and the device of montage. In such works the proportion of 'authorial narration' can be quite small. On the whole, the second stage of Abkhazian literature on the ideological-thematic level seeks to answer philosophical questions of existence and the concept of life by means of an artistic investigation into the mutual relationship between society and the individual, and between history and the present. Here writers appeal to, and seek anew to interpret, eternal themes — humanism, morality, liberty, patriotism, love, and so on.

Tangible changes have occurred also at the level of the development of the literary language. Artistic-figurative devices — epithets, metaphors, personifications — no longer have a folklore-oral character but appear to be the result of the author's associative thinking. But if an author also employs "stereotypical poetical features" (Dalgat, 1981), then they usually appear in a transformed guise and have some extra function, by which the author strives to express a definite thought.

At the turn of the 1980s and 1990s Abkhazian literature began to undergo serious changes in its thematic direction. The number of works saturated with a patriotic tendency increased strikingly. Strictly speaking, this was always a leading theme for Abkhazian writers. But previously it had been developed with the help of complex works, allegorically coded by the sub-texts. In the period under discussion patriotic thematisation took on an open, journalistic character. Such a phenomenon undoubtedly became possible thanks to the socio-political circumstances that had come about in the former USSR. As is well known, the politics of democracy and glasnost, declared in the mid-1980s, impelled the leaders of socio-political movements among many peoples towards self-determination. But by dint of the complexity of such a historical process, the battle for the freedom of one's people in several cases was accompanied by a yearning to enslave another and in this way, despite the logic of history, to legitimise the territorial boundaries of republics arbitrarily and unjustly drawn in the era of Stalin. In particular, Georgia, leaving a disintegrating Soviet Union, could not conceive that another people artificially incorporated within its own boundaries during the

1930s might have the right to choose. When this question was raised on the pages of the Georgian press and answered on the pages of the Abkhazian press, there flared up a political battle. Naturally, in this battle, alongside other representatives of the Abkhazian intelligentsia, Abkhazian writers occupied their own special niche. In journalistic articles and artistic works criticism was applied to the lack of objectivity in Georgian propaganda, and its essential mendaciousness was exposed. As is customary at such a period in the history of a people, poetry became by far the most effective vehicle. As for artistic prose, it too took serious steps to create epic œuvres relating the difficult but heroic fate of the people and its statehood (take the novel *King of Abkhazia* by Vitalij Amarshan).

However, Abkhazia and its people paid a high price for gaining their freedom. To put flesh on their aspirations and dreams, the Abkhazians found themselves having to defend their homeland, liberty and honour with blood in a war unleashed by Georgia. Thousands of the sons of Apsny laid down their lives in this war. But even in the darkest days of the war the pen of Abkhazian writers remained true to itself, and confidence in the ultimate victory of their people never wavered. The loud voice, forged in combat, of young poets and writers won through together with that of already established masters of their art. The literature from the period of the patriotic war in Abkhazia is distinguished by confidence that the justness of the struggle would inevitably prevail against the aggressor. It was during the war that a quite new type of poetry for Abkhazian literature, that of poet-bards, took shape. A. Altejba, who performed his songs at the war-front among actual fighters became the most famous of these. A collection of his songs was published after the war.

Over the last three years dozens of collections of verses or selected works of young and mature poets and writers have been printed. All this bears witness to the vitality of Abkhazian literature and to the perspectives for its future development. It is possible that the end of the 90s will see the beginning of the next period of Abkhazian literature. But today it is too early to speak of this, since shoots of a new manifestation in the national literature are still barely detectable; the works of those who might offer a new direction are not yet sufficiently strong — they are only just setting out on their creative journey. In this regard we can confidently speak only of the undoubted talent and giftedness of such poets as Gunda (Gʷynda) Sakania, Gunda Kʷ'yts'nia, and the poet and prose-writer Anatolij Lagʷlaa.

It is impossible not to remark on yet one more phenomenon of a literary nature directly related to the Abkhazian people. I am talking of the fact that sometimes ethnic Abkhazians compose their works in other languages. This phenomenon has deep historical roots. It is well known that the son of the last ruling prince of Abkhazia, Giorgij Shervashidze-Chachba, composed his works in Russian, Georgian, and French. Russian is the language in which Giorgij Gulia wrote his works, as do today Fazil Isk'ander, Eteri Basaria, Jurij Lak'erbaj, Stanislav Lak'oba, Denis Chachkhalia, Vitalij Sharia and others. The stylistic peculiarity of their output is that throughout their works an Abkhazian national flavour is present, and, with rare exceptions, all their writings are dedicated to Abkhazian themes. Then again there is the Abkhazian literature of the diaspora which is being developed principally by Abkhazians living in Turkey. However, this is as yet little studied, although it is possible to note that the most important figures are such names as Omar Begua and D. Harania.

In the 1930s such a genre as literary criticism was also born. In essence, the first professional Abkhazian literary critic was (the now professor) Khukhut' Bgazhba (Bghaȝᵂba). Doctor of history, Shalva Inal-Ipa (1914-95) produced many works of literary study and criticism. An especially rapid development in Abkhazian literary criticism is detectable from the 1960s. A new generation of scholar-researchers of linguistic creativity who later became mature scholars began their creative and investigative activity at that time. Among them are Shota Salaq'aja, Sergej Zykhba (Zykhᵂba), Vladimir Darsalia, Vladimir Ts'vinaria (Ts'naryja), Art'ur Anşba, Vladimir Agrba, Mushni Lasuria, Ruslan K'ap'ba, Vladimir Ankᵂab, B. Gurgulia (Gᵂrgᵂylyja). One can single out such collections of critical writings as: *Abyrtsk'al, What to Say and How to Say It?* (Ts'vinaria), *Abreast of Time* (Salaq'aja), *By the Paths of Growth* (Zykhᵂba), *In Response to Time* (Darsalia); literary-bibliographical works such as K'ap'ba's *Mikhail Lak'erbaj, Leont'i Labaxwa, St'ep'an Kwychberyja, K'aazym Agᵂmaa, Lewarsa Kᵂ'yts'nyja, The Writer and Folk Creativity* (Agrba).

As has been observed above, Abkhazian literature today is on the increase, but it is currently experiencing the ordeal of freedom. If in earlier times it was forced to be produced in spite of historical realities, overcoming prohibitions and impediments, then today this type of prohibition has been removed. Consequently, the future of Abkhazian literature depends on the talent and the capacity for work of the authors who compose it.

13
Art, handicrafts & architecture
Oleg Bgazhba

Art

The beginnings of art on the territory of Abkhazia find their roots in the Stone Age with elements of very simple line-ornamentation on artefacts of stone and bone as well as rock-drawings in the Agtsa cave.

In the Bronze Age ceramic plates were decorated with a variety of ornamentations achieved by cutting grooves or embossing. Daggers, axes, pins were decorated with corded relief and rows of notches in 'herring-bone' design. Unique is the female sculpture of the earth-mother made of limestone (in Otkhara, or in Abkhaz Wathara, which is in the north-west of the republic).

During the transitional period from the Bronze to the Iron Age engraved ornamentation, made on the surface of bronze artefacts by means of a steel chisel, came to dominate. In compositions the ancient masters included both traditional, early-agricultural ornamentation (waves, swastikas, solar circles, nets, meandering lines, etc) and representations of different animals (dogs, horses, deer, snakes, fish, birds, etc). A close link is observable with products of the Near Eastern art of that time (Urartu, Iran, Asia Minor). One can assign to the significant monuments of local art, for example, the drinking-horn of Bambora, decorated with the sculptured head of a billy-goat and ornamented with representations of snake, bird, 'dog-horse' and other elements. Deserving of special attention are the bronze figures of wine-drinker and earth-mother from Bambora and the aigrette-clasps showing representations of fighters, horses and dogs with specific features of stylisation and naturalism.

The composition of the small-sculptured products from Dzhantykha stand out for variety of subject-matter. Unique are the bronze axes from Dzhyrkhʷa and the clasps, encrusted with iron, from Krasnyj Majak. Alongside home-products, imported items also had great significance in the life of the local Heniokh tribes: a copper shield with representation of an eagle (Krasnyj Majak burial-ground), Pana-thenaean amphora with multi-subject black-figure painting (people, horses, etc) from Eshera, silver bowl with representation of the flight of birds (Akhʷyl-Abaa), and many other items, reflecting links with the Greek, Persian and Scythian cultural worlds.

During the period when the local population was in contact with Rome and later with Byzantium the Apsilians' ceramic table- and storage-ware stands out for originality and aesthetic charm. Ornamentation is charac-terised by variety of subject-matter and 'early-agricultural' symbols

Bronze cult daggers, spearheads and figurine of a dog (Late Bronze Age)

(vegetable and animal, 'rhombuses with hooks' and swastikas, five-pointed stars and little bands in relief, representations of sun and water, sculptured heads of rams and billy-goats). One should also mention the sculptured vessels of deer and bull, presumably, cult-objects. All this typifies Abkhazia's common archaeological 'Ts'ebelda (Ts'abal) culture' of the Late Antique and Early Byzantine periods. From imported goods one can mention: a gold plate (amulet) with Greek-Hebrew magical inscription, a medallion with Greek inscription and representation of the Gorgon Medusa, belt-buckles with sculptured tongues and clasps engraved or inlaid with variously coloured glass. The 'Apsilian' brooches and hair-slides of gold, silver and cornelian stand quite alone. On separate gems of cornelian (intaglio) representations of ancient deities (Fortuna, Nike), horses, woods and so on are present. Unique is the miniature paste-bead of Alexandrian production, ornamented with multi-coloured chess-designs and four representations of female faces. Clearly visible with strong magnification are the hairs, pupils, eyebrows, lips, and a mole on the neck, carefully delineated with different coloured glass. Popular too in local life was glass-ware: goblets, bowls, glasses, small glasses, horns, amphorae, decorated with blue solderings, crosses, vegetable-bands, etc.

During the time of Justinian elements of metropolitan jewellery-art developed widely among the local populace: silver medallion with representation of a female face, flower and lion; brooches in the form of a peacock; little spoons for grinding rouge; early-Christian golden and silver baptismal crosses; bronze, silver and golden cross-shaped clasp-fibulae, decorated with cornelian on mounts; gilded belt-buckles, the clasps of which are encrusted with variously coloured glass.

During the feudal epoch painted, glazed, monochrome, and polychrome ceramics, executed with graphite, brush, and grooving techniques, spread into daily use. These were prepared both locally and in Byzantium, the Crimea, Transcaucasia and the Near East. They are remarkable for their range of subject-matter: vegetable and geometric decorations were composed of animals, birds, people and hunting-scenes. Pride of place goes to such items as the gold cup from the Bedia church, decorated with representations of the saints against an appropriate decorative background; the bronze icon from Lykhny with representation of the Angel Gabriel; the silver icon with representation of the Virgin from Khᵂap. An obvious monument of book-art are the Mykᵂ Gospels of 1300, ornamented with magnificent

Marble relief from the fifth century BC, found in the bay at Sukhum, the site of ancient Dioscurias

miniatures. Among the jewellery-items of this period one can mention the gold and silver earrings from the churches of Ts'ebelda and the pins with bird-shaped heads from Akh^{w}yl-Abaa.

*

The art of the 18th century is as yet poorly studied. There is a spread at this period of Islamic epitaphs, Turkish painted ceramics of blue colour, richly ornamented clay-pipes for smoking.

As regards painting, the first professional Abkhazian artist was (Prince) A. Chachba (Shervashidze, 1867-1968); his work won international acclaim (Russia, Paris, London). While still in Abkhazia, he set up the first artist-studio in Sukhum. In their time the 19th century Russian artists I. Ajvazovskij and V. Vereshchagin worked in Abkhazia. The latter's name was given to one of the archaeological tumuli where he worked. A. Nesterov painted Mary Magdalene at the Pantelejmon Cathedral at the New Athos Monastery. With the support of the then-leader of Abkhazia, Nest'or Lak'oba, a two-year art school was opened in Sukhum in 1935, which was reorganised in 1937 into an art

The ethnographic song and dance ensemble known as The Narts ('Nartaa') has members whose minimum age must be 70 (with a reputed maximum of 120)

Abkhazian folk instruments, including the zither-like a'xymaa, and the two-stringed viol-like apxiar'tsa

college incorporating five years of study.

In 1939 the Union of Soviet Artists of Abkhazia was established. V. Bubnova exerted a notable influence on the artistic life of Abkhazia, for she had lived for 36 years in Japan before moving to Sukhum. Alongside thematic painting, an important place is held by landscape-painting (O. Brendel', I. Shengelaja, *et al*), portraiture (B. Bobyr'), portrait-sculpture (A. Razmadze, G. Rukhadze, M. Èshba, *et al*), applied art (N. Mastitskaja, K. Nikogosjan) among others.

Artists in Abkhazia have recently often turned to historical themes (S. Gabelija, Kh. Avidzba, S. Ts'vizhba, V. Lak'yrba, *et al*.); the genre of landscape has been developed (V. Shchelgov, N. Khalvash, *et al*.), still-life (A. Krajnjukov, N. Pisarchuk, V. Gagulija, *et al*.), sculptured portraiture and sculpting (G. Lak'oba, V. Ivanba, Ju. Ch'k'adua, A. Adlejba, *et al*.), graphics (T. Ampar, Z. Dzhindzholia, A. Dzidzarija, Z. Mukba, V. Delba, V. Orelkin, *et al*.), theatre design (E. Kotljarov, *et al*.), applied art (V. Shengelaja, L. Khurkhumal, A. Donchenko, S. Bagatelija, T. K'orsant'ija, B. Akhba, *et al*.). To the artist V. Gamgija belongs the authorship of the state symbol and flag of the Republic of Abkhazia (see illustrations on pp 20-21).

With their own manner of executing landscapes and portraits the following have entered the art arena: A. Sementsov, B. Jop'ua, S. Sangalov, A. Bojadzhan, L. Butba, R. Mukhamed-Galieva,[1] V. Arkanija, T. Kajtan, N. Logua, Akhra Argun, *et al*., who are known abroad. The works of G. Smyr, R. Pandarija, R. Bartsyts, V. Dzhindzholia, Diana

Vouba (who has exhibited in the West), et al. stand out for their originality.

Folk-dance ensembles, such as Sharatyn, and the Nartaa choir of centenarians (both of whom have appeared in the West) help to keep the traditions of music and dance alive — there are also such ensembles in Turkey amongst the diaspora. Traditional Abkhazian instruments (see Khashba 1979) include: the *apxʲar'tsa*, a small violin-like instrument, played like a viol; the *a'jʷymaa*, a harp-like instrument whose frame was curved in a v-shape, from which its name is literally 'two-handle(d)' from *jʷba* '2' and *'amaa* 'handle'; the *a'xymaa*, a zither-like instrument with two outer and one central frame, hence 'three-handle(d)' from *xpa* '3'. The CD *The Golden Fleece: Songs from Abkhazia and Ajaria* (PAN 2009CD, 1993) gives a flavour of Abkhazian folk-music.

Handicrafts

The ancestors of the Abkhazians were occupied with domestic industries from the earliest of times. The main forms were: pottery, metallurgy and both non-ferrous and ferrous metal-working. Special mention must also be made of weaving.

Ceramics appeared in Abkhazia during the Neolithic Age (sixth millennium BC). Vessels were originally shaped by hand (ribbon-technique); in the Bronze Age (third millennium BC) the hand-rotated potter's wheel made its appearance; during the Abkhazian Kingdom (eighth-tenth centuries) it was replaced by the foot-treadle as being more productive, though hand-wheels did not entirely disappear. Series of vessels already carried definite marks of the potters who worked in the market. After moulding, vessels in ancient times were fired directly on a bonfire, and only later in a special oven (in Abkhaz *at'nyra*). In the two-tier pottery ovens of Late Antiquity in Sebastopolis were fired not only crockery but also bricks and tiles. In the Middle Ages there was the Atara complex for ceramic production. There might have been parallel centres in other parts of Middle Age Abkhazia (Bagrat's Castle, Ochamchira, etc). Local clay was employed, both ordinary and kaolin, which served as surface-coating before firing (French *angobe*).

Amidst archaeological materials one finds ceramic rejects as well as 'crabs', remains of the legs of which are traceable on many vessels, which testifies to the local development of the potter's craft.[2] Local and imported ceramics are distinguishable in Abkhazia. Local ceramics are divided according to usage into the following groups: storage-ceramics (pithoi, amphorae, storage-pots with oval handles), table-ceramics (pots, tureens, salt-cellars), dining-ceramics (red-clayed pots with bowl-shaped nimbus, tureens, cups, pouring ceramics), building-ceramics (tiles,

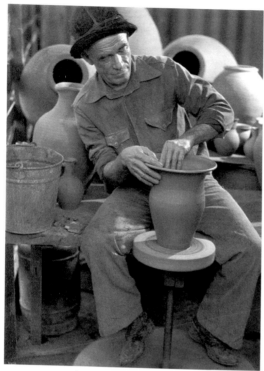

Potter (ahap'ʃardzjʷy or ahap'ʃaq'ats'ajʷy) at work

bricks). Very many imported ceramics appear in Early and Late Antique times — primarily Greek black-figured crockery (amphorae of the Panathenaean cycle), small bowls, large bowls, fish-dishes, Megaran cups, red-lacquered Roman plates, polished Alanian pots and tureens from the North Caucasus, etc. A characteristic peculiarity of the development of local ceramics consists of the fact that it knows no sharp change of ceramic types but rather exemplifies successive local development, adopting from abroad only individual details and technical methods. Even ancient colonising activity did not disturb this internal regularity of development.

Even today each rural family has large pithos-type pots (in Abkhaz *ahap'ʃa*) buried in the ground and filled with wine, as well as pots called *ap'hal* for water and *aj'rydz* for wine and water, or *aqʷ"dʒal* for beans, etc.

Metallurgy and metal-working

At the start there developed in Abkhazia non-ferrous metallurgy (of copper and bronze). The Bashkapsara copper-mines in the upper reaches of the River Bzyp were one of the oldest in the Caucasus, functioning from the third millennium BC to the eighth century AD. Thirteen units have been uncovered here, amongst which are open-cast workings, vertical shafts and multi-layered horizontal galleries with lateral chambers.

Ore was extracted by the fire-method and hewn off with stone-hammers. Bronze artefacts were usually prepared with the help of casting moulds. Casting in single moulds was the earliest metallurgical method. For the preparation of volumetrical items moulds consisting of two halves were involved. Several decorations were fashioned via wax-models. Forging moulds of axes and other implements have been found at various points in Abkhazia (Mach'ara, T'amsh, Kistrik, Tagilon), which speaks of the local production of these items. By no means rare are finds of crucibles, which helped in the pouring of molten metal into the mould.

Copper was smelted in special ovens (cf. the copper-smelting oven on Mount Sukhum) at a temperature of no less than 1,000°C, which was achieved during the combustion of charcoal with the aid of air-currents (either the older, natural method of wind in a valley or the more modern, artificial method using bellows). Bronze metallurgy and metal-working reached its zenith in Abkhazia during the florescence both here and in the whole Western and Central Caucasus of the Colchian-Koban culture, which had its local Abkhazian variant.

Abkhazian ferrous metallurgy and metal-working undoubtedly grew on the foundation of its non-ferrous predecessor. All the pre-conditions were in place: charcoal and ovens. But the main feature here were the ore-bases of iron: haematite, magnetite and limonite. Geologists single out Abkhazia as an ore-deposit zone. The appearance of the damp-blowing method for obtaining iron and the ways of working it only evolved thanks to the involvement of Asia Minor, where the Hattians (likely linguistic relatives of the Abkhazo-Circassians and the possible ancestors of the ancient Chalybes, or iron-workers) lived, and later of Urartu.

The Iron Age in Abkhazia began in the seventh-sixth centuries BC, although the first artefacts of this metal appeared here in the eighth century BC For comparison, in Egypt the Iron Age began roughly at this same time. Local ferrous metallurgy and metal-working developed at the juncture between the Scythian and Antique cultures. And so, the traditional technology of differentiated heat-treatment (toughening with tempering, soft toughening) was preserved. Scythian artefacts and those of Greek settlers were basically forged from iron and untoughened steel. The Abkhazian term *adz'ry ʒ^wra*, literally 'make drink water', signifies toughening and belongs, apparently, to the start of the Iron Age in Abkhazia. As toughening-medium might serve: water, oil, blood of a lamb (if not of a slave), urine of a fire-red lad or nanny-goat, air current, etc. Toughening in the early days was just part of the magical, traditional activities which often accompanied the work of local smiths precisely because, in all likelihood, it was not practised amongst the foreign circle of Scythian and Greek colonists.

One of the routes by which the iron industry penetrated Europe from Asia Minor (the home of iron) was the west Transcaucasian or east Black Sea Littoral route, which led through Abkhazia. During the Roman era they were acquainted here with damask steel. Of ten swords randomly investigated with the help of metallographic analysis five turned out to be of damask. These are the earliest (third-fourth centuries) swords of wrought damask discovered on former Soviet territory. The base of the blade of these swords had four types of pattern: linear, angular, doubly angular, and rose-shaped. Onto this base were welded the hardened steel blades.

In the middle of the century cementation (both part and full) or more rarely welding of the steel blade on an iron base was widely practised. During the Abkhazian Kingdom smiths were differentiated into the categories of: universal, knife-forging, axe-forging, weapon-forging, instrument-forging, lock-smiths, jewellers. There was in Abkhazia a kind of 'Apprenticeship School' for the smithcraft. It is reckoned that among no other Caucasian people was there observed such respect for the smithy, the work of smiths and smiths themselves. Up to the present sacred smithies, where rituals connected with the smithy-deity Shaʃʷy were conducted, have been preserved here.

Weaving

From ancient times this represented an important sphere of Abkhazia's national economy (exemplified by Neolithic earthenware and stone spinning-weights, later textile ceramics). Among archaeological materials near Sukhumski Mayak have been found rotted remains of flaxen linen of seventh-sixth centuries BC. In their own days Herodotus (mid-fifth century BC) and Xenophon (early fourth century BC) referred to the high quality of Colchian linen. Weaving here reached a high state of perfection before the arrival of the Hellenes. Judging by imprints on Heniokh fabrics, there were artefacts of wool and flaxen yarn from crude fabric to the most delicate of flaxen linen. Apparatuses for weaving (in Abkhaz *asyr'ty*) have long been known as well as every possible appliance for the preparation of felt-material (particularly for the heavy cloak known as *a'wap'a*), carpet-fabrics and other woollen, cotton, silk fabrics and knitted items.

The patterns of the Abkhazians' woven artefacts were varied: compositions of animal-shapes, geometric, plant and solar motifs. Common are representations of animals (deer, horse, dog, etc) or birds (pigeon, peacock, hoopoe, etc). One of the patterns was called *adʒaw'har*, the name of which was taken from the name of a style of sword of damask steel.

Wickerwork

There was a large variety of shapes and methods for wicker-work: plaiting based on the textile reworking of raw material (female task) and plaiting connected with the working of wood (liana plants) (male work). The roots of the art of plaiting go back to monuments of the Neolithic and Bronze Ages. Patterned plaiting stands out for its special artistry.

Alongside patterned weaving and plaiting, carving on wood had a wide currency in Abkhazia. Many methods of carving were known to master-craftsmen: graphic, relief, tracery, three-dimensional, carving by cauterisation, carving with inlay. Inlay with horn and bone was often combined with carving on wood. Horn and bone inlay was also employed as adornment for ladies' saddles, in trimming men's and ladies' belts, in decorating wooden shoes with their high platforms (still seen in some Abkhazian folk-dancing), and as trimmings for flint weapons and pistols.

Utilisation of flint and bone stocks in Abkhazia is witnessed by the archaeological materials of the cave-site of the Upper Palaeolithic period in the Cold Grotto (bone-harpoons with geometric ornamentation and 'the chief's baton' — the forearm of a cave-bear ornamented with a linear pattern and with an aperture polished by usage). Along with inlay and three-dimensional carving, saw-carving was also widely practised.

Judging by the artistic working of metal, there were masters of gold and silver works, which even found reflection in surnames: A'x'yjba = Khiba 'master of gold works', 'Ardzinba 'master of silver works', and 'Aȝyjba 'ironsmith'.

Architecture

The oldest architectural monuments of Abkhazia are the dolmens, or monumental graves of the Bronze Age (end of the third to the beginning of the second millennium BC), more than 2,000 of which are known in the western Caucasus, and of these about 80 are found in Abkhazia. They divide into tiled and trough-shaped (e.g. Eshera, Azante, Wathara, Mkhjalrypsh). Also famous in Abkhazia are cromlechs, another type of megalithic monument. If dolmens are reminiscent of little houses, cromlechs represent concentric circles. The monuments of the megalithic epoch in the village of Wathara, where a dolmen is surrounded by a cromlech, deserve special attention.

The architecture of the ancient period is characterised at the early stage by remains of wooden structures, typical of the life of both the Heniokh and Greek settlements of the region. These are primarily timbered frames, fences, wattled fences. The oldest stone-structures are the cyclopean walls of the Patskhirian fortress (Ts'ebelda) and the late-

Basket weaver (ak'alatşş'jʷy) displaying his skills outside his wattled outhouse, with heavy felt cloak (a'wap'a) and cherkesska (akʷ'ym'zhʷy) hung up behind him

Hellenistic ensemble of defence, residential and cult structures at the site of Eshera, where at the end of the second and start of the Ist century BC a mortar-solution was employed in the laying of walls. Buildings took shape with limestone columns and carved cornices, whilst roofs were covered with red-brown tiles.

The Apsilians' and Abazgians' close contacts with the Roman-

Byzantine cultural world (first-seventh centuries AD) were effected principally via the coastal fortress-towns of Sebastopolis and Pitiunt. In rural architecture the traditional wooden structures remained important. Sebastopolis and Pitiunt possessed perfect defence-works with towers, buttresses, and complex portal systems. Monumental dwelling, administrative and cult structures were located there. A watertight, cement-like solution, containing pounded brick, was poured over the floors. Trimmed limestone and marble were used for decoration. Worthy of special note are the mosaic floors, distinguished for diversity of subject, in civil and early-Christian church-structures at Pitiunt.

During Justinian's time in the second quarter of the sixth century a system of forts (Latin *cl(a)usura*), forming the internal 'Caucasian Frontier' that included Trakhea, Tsibilium, Ttsakhar, Shapky and others, was erected on the Eastern Black Sea Littoral to stave off coastal penetration by the Persians and their North Caucasian allies. Deep in the mountains Roman-Byzantine methods were widely utilised: *opus mixtum* (mixed brick and stone working); *opus quadratum* (laying of large, worked limestone-blocks); *opus incertum* (laying of crudely worked limestone with seams smoothed with mortar). Monumental multi-storeyed towers (circular, rectangular, pentagonal) were covered with low cupolas and box-like arches and were supplied with catapults and other projectile-launching mechanisms. Beyond the double walls, framed with merlons, were watch-areas for sentries, stairs, barracks, baths with three rooms (cold, warm, and hot), water-reservoirs, wine-presses, civil and religious buildings. Aqueducts were constructed for the fort; part of them function even today.

Large-scale building-works were carried out also in the fortress-towns of Sebastopolis and Pitiunt, which never formed part of the 'Pontic Frontier.' The Byzantines restored and used them.

It is well known that Abkhazia, as an early-Christian country, underwent, especially in the Justinian era, active church-building particularly of the Dranda Cathedral, the Tsandrypsh Basilica, and churches in Alahadzy, Sebastopolis, Ts'ebelda and Gyenos (Ochamchira). The walls were of stone and brick on a sold limestone base; a cement-like substance sealed the floor, whilst tiling covered the roof and shaped brick the eaves. Within, the churches were finished with marble (sometimes imported from the island Proconnesus), mosaics, frescoes, carved stones, colonnades, altars, reliquaries, rails, fonts, and church-plate consisting of gold, silver, copper and crystal. Abkhazian church-architecture of this period bears clear lines of influence from the different Byzantine architectural schools from Tsaritsin Grad (Yugoslavia) to Antioch (Syria).

The altar-rail of the Voronov Church (Ts'ebelda) is unique — these in effect are stone-icons from the second part of the sixth-seventh centuries. This 'Bible-in-stone' incorporated over ten sculptured scenes on themes from the Old Testament. The Ts'ebelda icons were fashioned on the spot under the influence of at least three schools (Byzantine, Syrian, Sassanian).

Fortificational art of Early Middle Age Abkhazia continues the building traditions of the preceding Roman-Byzantine times. The Anakopian fortress, the fundamental defensive line of which was erected in the second quarter of the seventh century, serves as an excellent example of this.

At this and the following period of the Abkhazian Kingdom the architecture of Anakopia exerted influence on the work of architects constructing fortresses in mountain-conditions (Gerzeul, Achapara, K'aldakh^{w}ara, Pskhu, Klych, etc). Civil architecture of Early Middle Age Abkhazia is characterised by complexes of dwellings and enclosures, known as *ats'an'g^{w}ara*. In the lowlands there were wooden structures, remains of which have survived. The oldest layer of building of the palace at Lykhnaşta, which is linked to the nearby church-ensemble, belongs to the Xth century.

In the special Abkhazo-Alanian school of Byzantine architecture the monuments of Christian architecture of Abkhazian churches of the tenth century (e.g. Pitsunda, Alahadzy, Bzyp, Lykhny, Msygkh^{w}a, Psyrtskha, North Zelenchuk Church) stand out. The walls were of brick, manufactured from limestone and sandstone. Basic attention was paid to the interior (brick-arches, crossed pillars, pre-altar colonnades). In the Myk^w Cathedral, for example, the floors and altar-section were adorned with marble and mosaics. Marble pillars and their capitals (in the shape of a cross, the sun, plants) have been found here. Preserved on the walls of the cathedral are exquisite graphite-murals, painted by masters of the art. It is worthy of special mention that masters from Abkhazia (the 'Obezy' of the Russian chronicles) took part in the building of the Sofia Cathedral in Kiev.

To the monumental architecture of the period of 'The Kingdom of the Abkhazians and Kartvelians' (11th-13th centuries) belong the upper part of the gate-tower with its colonnades at Anakopia, Bagrat's Castle, the Bedia Cathedral, the church at Elyr, the Besletian vaulted bridge, the altar-rail of the Ankh^{w}a Church with representation of St George, and others.

To the architectural monuments of the Late Middle Ages (14th-17th centuries) belong the large number of feudal castles (Zhabna, Mch'yshta, Durypsh, Merkheul, Lata, Dzhg^{j}arda, Tsarcha, etc), situated in the

The (renovated) Pitsunda Cathedral, which dates from the 11th century

mountain-region. Along the coast forts were built and functioned by the Genoese trading-posts (Psyrtskha, T'amsh, etc). Completed also were some sections of the K'elasurian (Great Abkhazian) Wall, the start of the building of which, perhaps, was linked to the Justinian epoch.

At the end of the 13th to the beginning of the 14th century many parish-churches and graveyards were constructed.

With the architecture of the 18th century it is possible to link the relevant building works on the Sukhum Fortress, which were occasioned by the presence in Abkhazia at that time of the Turks.

Between 1888 and 1900 the Pantelejmon Cathedral, the largest religious structure in Russia at that time, was erected at New Athos in Neo-Byzantine style; it can accommodate up to 3,000 people at one time.

Sukhum, Gudauta, Ochamchira and other places (including such resorts as Gagra, Gulrypsh) began to grow speedily at the end of the 19th and start of the 20th century. Individual large buildings went up: the former palace of Prince Oldenburgskij, the hotels 'Gagrypsh' and 'Rits'a' in Gagra, the rest-home 'Sinop' and the theatre in Sukhum, the sanatorium named after N. Smetskoj in Gulrypsh, dachas, villas, etc. Their style was eclectic or rigidly modern. Parks (in Gagra landscaped and coastal; in Sukhum dendrological) were laid out. In the 1930s the first general building-projects were put together in Sukhum, Gagra, and New Athos. To this period belongs the building of the hotel 'Abkhazia' (1938, I. Golubko, Ju. Shuko), the first section of Government House (1939, V. Shuko), the Council of Ministers' Resthome (1955, N. Severov), the Sanatorium 'Ukraine' (1936, I. Shtejnberg), etc. Construction of the new industrial centre of T'q^w'archal got underway. The city of Sukhum saw at this time the appearance of buildings in the constructivist style (State Bank, Fishkov's House). In Pitsunda a large resort-complex was constructed (1968, A. Mdojants, I. Popov, M. Posokhin, V. Svirskij, *et al*; Zurab Ts'ereteli supervised the decorative artwork). For touristic purposes the cave complex at New Athos, famed throughout the world, was tastefully laid out.

Abkhazia's climate in the main has not helped the preservation of wooden structures, although timber was widely used here in architecture from the most ancient of times — there are remains of rectangular and circular ancient dwellings. Timber retained its importance in the construction of Abkhazian dwellings right up to the start of the 20th century. However, few real data on the architectural details of timber-based buildings survive prior to the 19th century. Primarily these are circular cone-structures of wattled straw known as *a'k^{w}atᶜ^w*. The most widespread four-sided wattled dwelling in Abkhazia is the 'patskha' (*a'patsxa*), but timbered buildings of this type were known as *adʒar'g^{w}al*. Many Abkhazian yards even today have their own *a'patsxa*, where cheese and meat are smoked and home-made wine drunk. Part of the walls of the *a'patsxa* are regularly adorned with ancient artefacts. These structures are so durably plaited that one can spend time in them even in winter.

Single and double rows of timbered houses with one or several balconies on high stilts or a stone socle are known under the generic name *a'kʷ'askʲ'a.*

14
Religion[1]
Rachel Clogg

The Abkhaz historian Stanislav Lak'oba, when asked recently about the religion of Abkhazia, answered that the Abkhaz are 80 per cent Christian, twenty per cent (Sunni) Muslim, and 100 per cent pagan! While this was said partly in jest, it hints at an underlying truth. As Neal Ascherson (1995, pp 249-50) recently observed: "Trees matter to Abkhazians. Their two conversions to world religions, to Christianity in the sixth century and then to Islam under the Turks, have been less enduring than older ways of reverence for natural objects and for the dead." There are few census data, and estimates of religious affiliation vary from 20 per cent Muslim at the lower end of the scale to upwards of 40 at the upper end, leaving Christians the remaining majority. The ambiguity of numbers reflects a wider ambiguity; the Abkhaz would generally define themselves as either Christian or Muslim, yet this designation indicates little in terms of religious practice or belief. Few Abkhaz Christians are churchgoers, few Abkhaz Muslims follow the practice of circumcision or daily prayers, obey Muslim dress-codes, or have ever seen a Qur'an.

Religious practice in Abkhazia, however, is hardly 'pagan' in a traditional sense. It is rather a complex synthesis involving aspects of polytheistic worship and animism, which has evolved over time to include aspects of the two world religions with which the Abkhaz have come into contact. Over the centuries, a "peculiar mosaic of fragments of religious beliefs" has developed, in which "Christian ceremonies, Moslem rites and pagan observances are so closely interwoven that at times it seems almost impossible to separate them" (Benet, 1974, p92). Much of the social ritual of the Abkhaz has its roots in religious belief or superstition, and gatherings of the extended family, weddings, funerals, memorial services, and festivals sometimes still involve making sacrificial offerings. In this sense the Abkhaz approach toward religion is fairly homogeneous, and its ritual and custom are an important part of a collective identity. Generally, though, the Abkhaz lack any sense of exclusive dogma or fundamentalism; individual religious difference is respected, and belonging to different denominations is seldom a reason for antagonism. Indeed, it is not uncommon to find both Christians and Muslims in one family.[2]

Tolerance of, and to a certain extent assimilation to, religious beliefs and practices from outside, have been largely due to the Abkhaz lack of interest in the theology or dogma of either Christianity or Islam. Neither of these has been perceived as threatening to the social structure or daily practice of the Abkhaz, who have retained many elements of pre-Christian belief and practice, and adapted new practices to them. As the American anthropologist Paula Garb has said, ". . . in reality, the Abkhaz have never related seriously to either Christianity or Islam. They have stubbornly preserved their pagan customs, adopting from Christianity or Islam only those elements which did not contradict their ancient beliefs" (1986, p24).

The predominance of Christian or Muslim practices among the Abkhaz at different times, then, has been more a case of expediency than of 'conversion', an acceptance of religion as part of the politics of imperial power. Abkhazia officially adopted Christianity in the sixth century when the region formed part of the Byzantine Empire, and the primacy of Christianity continued through the Middle Ages before giving way to Islam and the Ottoman Empire in the 15th-16th centuries. As the Turkish influence declined and Abkhazia became a protectorate of Russia in the early 19th century, Christianity again came to the fore, before the Soviet period and the repression of explicit religious practice.

Christianity

The Apostles Andrew and Simon the Canaanite are said by some, on the basis of interpretations of the lives of the saints, to have first spread the word of Christianity in Abkhazia in the first century. There is more concrete evidence for the advent of Christianity in the fourth century, however, when the first community of Christians in the Caucasus came into being in Pitiunt,[3] made up of Christian martyrs exiled to Abkhazia by the Roman Emperor. In 325 the bishop of Pitiunt, Stratophil, represented this community at the first ecumenical council of the Christian Fathers at Nicea (Chachkhalia, 1994 pp 24-25).

The oldest churches in Abkhazia date from the fourth-fifth centuries and are located in the Pitiunt area, also the site of the first bishopric in Abkhazia (Lakoba (ed.), 1993, p64). The sixth century saw the expansion of the religious and political influence of Byzantium in Abkhazia. During the first half of the sixth century, church-building and proselytising increased; the Abkhazian prophet and missionary Euphratā was sent back to spread the word of Christianity in his country by the Byzantine

Emperor Justinian I; archbishoprics were established in both Pitiunt and Anakopia; and Orthodox Christianity was declared the official religion of Abkhazia — testimony of 11th century Eprem Mtsire, based on the *Ecclesiastical History* of Euagrios of Antioch.

The adoption of Christian beliefs and rituals by the population was gradual and not without resistance, yet the Christian presence in Abkhazia continued to grow. Toward the end of the eighth century the church in Abkhazia gained independence from Byzantium, and was represented at the council of Chalcedon as autocephalous (Smyr, 1994, p7). The Abkhazian church underwent many changes in the tenth century, as the influence of the Greek church waned and that of the Georgian rose. An independent Western Georgian Catholicos(ate) took shape in the second half of the tenth century and began to forge closer links with the Eastern Georgian Church. This led to their eventual union under the one Catholicos in Mtskheta.

This change in influence led to a gradual shift away from the use of Greek to Georgian for religious writings and services. Georgian inscriptions in eastern regions of Abkhazia have been dated to the ninth century, though further west there is no evidence for the use of Georgian before the end of the tenth century (Lakoba (ed.), 1993, p89). Greek continued to be used, though it became increasingly rare. Sources maintain that there were services still held primarily in Greek, though with some Abkhazian, in the 11th century (Smyr, 1994, p8), and inscriptions in Greek dating to the 14th and 16th centuries were found in the Lykhny church and Pitsunda cathedral respectively (Lakoba (ed.), 1993, p116). Another major development of the tenth century was the significant development of Abkhazian church architecture, most likely under the ruler Giorgi II. Many new churches were built, including those in Pitsunda, Lykhny, Alahadzy, Bzyp, Msygkh^{w}a, Psyrtskha, Arkhyz, and Shoana (the last two in the North Caucasus). These were followed by the outstanding Myk^w church, built in 966 under Leon III.

The Pitsunda church grew in prominence from the end of the 13th century to become the ecclesiastical centre of western Georgia and the western Caucasus. From 1390 Pitsunda had a separate Patriarch, the first of whom was Arsen, who had responsibility for Abkhazia, Mingrelia, Imereti(a), Svaneti(a) and Guria. It was in the 14th and early 15th centuries that the influence of Christianity was most widespread among the population in Abkhazia. Many smaller churches were built, older ones renovated, frescoes painted, and the Ts'ebelda monastery founded.

Sunni Islam

The first contact the Abkhaz had with Islam was through Arab raiders, from the eighth century on, and sources first mention Muslim inhabitants in Sevastopolis[4] in the 14th century. From 1451 repeated attempts were made by the Turks to win power in Abkhazia, until eventually they consolidated their hold along the coast. An official representative of the Turks settled in Sukhum in 1578, and Abkhazia became a protectorate of the Ottoman Empire. In the same year a flag was introduced in Abkhazia bearing Islamic symbols (Smyr 1994, p10). It was with this strengthening of Ottoman influence in the 16th-17th centuries that the gradual dissemination of Sunni Islam really began. This was a period of dramatic decline for Christian culture in Abkhazia, although in the early 17th century the Abkhaz were still paying the 'kharaj', a duty paid to the Ottoman Empire by non-Muslim subjects (Chachkhalia 1994, p25, col. 3). Many Christian priests were banished, and eventually, in the mid-17th century, the Abkhazian Catholicos was transferred from Pitsunda further east to Gelati in Imereti(a).

The first evidence of Abkhazian Muslims was given in the 1640s by the Turkish historian Evliya Çelebi, whose mother was an Abkhazian. On his travels he recorded that the Abkhazians had a mosque and that among them were "many Muslims." This Muslim population, according to Çelebi, was hostile to Christians, in spite of not recognising the Qur'an or being of any religious denomination. Other sources would seem to indicate, however, that although the Christian presence was on the wane, and the dissemination of Islam increasing, evidence of traditional Islam was more apparent among the higher levels of society by the end of the 18th century than among the population at large. The Abkhaz rulers were not in a position to decline Islam, a fact witnessed by the forced conversion of Shervashidze-Chachba, Abkhazia's ruling prince, to Islam in 1733, following the destruction by the Turks of Elyr, a pilgrimage-site of particular religious significance to the Abkhaz near Ochamchira.

Those Abkhazians who did identify themselves as Muslims interpreted Islam rather freely, adding it to the conglomerate of Christian and pagan belief, in the same way that Christianity had been adapted to encompass aspects of pagan ritual. Abkhazian Muslims were relaxed about the behavioural codes of Islam; most would drink wine, many continued to eat pork. They were known to practise many of the pagan rituals, to celebrate Christmas, Easter and other Christian festivals as well as Bairam, and to fast both for Ramadan and Lent (Tornau, quoted in Inal-Ipa, 1965, p374). Among the population of Abkhazia as a whole there was continued evidence of the practice of rituals pertaining to Christian worship when Abkhazia came under Russian protection in 1810. For example, each extended family, regardless of its religious persuasion, customarily made an annual sacrifice to Saint George (Ilorskij), most often on the first day of Easter, otherwise on any other sacred day throughout the summer (Zvanba, 1955, p56).

The second wave of Christianity

The shift in imperial influence after 1810 signalled a corresponding shift in religious attitude, the pendulum swinging back in favour of Christian Orthodoxy. The question of religion was even a condition of the protectorate, wherein the Abkhazian ruler agreed to resume the 'creed of our former faith' (Smyr, 1994, p12, quoting *Akty sobrannye Kavkazskoj arkheografitcheskoj komissiej (AKAK)*, vol. III, p209, no. 375). The Tsarist government set about reviving Christianity in Abkhazia, reopening the churches, almost all of which had fallen into disuse. In 1815 the ruler of the Abzhywa region of Abkhazia, Ali-bey Chachba, a Muslim by birth, converted to Christianity (thus becoming Aleksandr Chachba), and in 1831 the Abkhaz ruler Mikhail Chachba spoke of the importance of establishing a Christian mission in Abkhazia (Chachkhalia, 1994, p25, col. 3). In 1851 an Abkhazian diocese was established, and in 1860 the Myk^w Cathedral was repaired and restored, and a 'Society for the restoration of Orthodox Christianity in the Caucasus' (OVPKHK) was set up.

Following the Crimean War of 1853-56, Tsarist government treatment of the Muslims in Abkhazia became harsh; the practice of Islam was prohibited, as was the holding of Islamic burials, and Abkhaz Muslims were forbidden to marry Christians. Mullahs and mosques were banned, and some jobs were restricted to non-Muslims. The population as a whole was encouraged to be baptised; privileges were often bestowed upon those who complied, others who did not were sometimes forcibly baptised. Missionaries of the OVPKHK alone are said to have baptised 21,336 people between 1860 and 1877 (Smyr, 1994, p13, quoting *Obzor dejatel'nosti OVPKHK za 1860-1910*, Tbilisi, 1910, pp 172-73). Following the Tsarist annexation of the Caucasus, after the end of the Great Caucasian War in 1864, many Abkhazians fled their country. They were partly lured away by false promises of better treatment by the Ottoman Empire. Yet predominantly they left in fear of the Russians, a justifiable fear according to a British diplomat at the time: "Most of [the Abkhaz] have been plundered of everything by the Russians before embarking . . ." (Henze, 1992, pp 103-4, quoting Palgrave).

Although a sense of religious affiliation with the Turks may have been a motivating factor for some, the event of the 'exile' (*makhadzhirstvo*, or in Abkhaz *amhadʒrra*) also served further to

Islamicise many of the exiled Abkhaz. The territory which was left vacant by the Abkhaz was settled by Mingrelians, Russians and Armenians among others, another factor in the consolidation of Christianity in Abkhazia.

The programme of Christian revival continued, with the restoration of former churches and monasteries, and the foundation in 1875 of the New Athos Monastery, named after Mount Athos in Greece. Priests and translators from among the Abkhaz were prepared, the translation of church literature into Abkhaz began, and the first history of the church in Abkhazia was written in 1885 by the Russian archimandrite Leonid (Kavelin). In 1892, *The Ten Commandments and Ceremonial Oath* and *A Short Holy History* were the first ecclesiastical literature to be printed in Abkhaz. In 1907, the first services were held in Abkhaz since the decline of Christianity centuries before (Chachkhalia, 1994a, p26). Academician Nikolaj Marr, however, was doubtful as to the success of the Russian Orthodox clergy in Abkhazia, who could 'be more proud of their building of architectural monuments than of their building of religion in the souls of the Abkhaz' (Smyr, 1994, p14, quoting Basarija, 1923, p53).

Religion in Soviet times

In 1918, Abkhazia came under the control of the short-lived independent Georgian Menshevik government. The Georgian Mensheviks introduced a series of discriminatory policies towards non-Kartvelians. The discrimination extended to religious practice; almost all ecclesiastical literature in the Abkhaz language was destroyed, and the Abkhazian language, and Abkhazian clergy were excluded from the church. Several of Abkhazia's wooden mosques were destroyed, and pressure put on Abkhazian Muslims to leave the territory.

Although the Bolshevik suppression of the Menshevik regime in 1921 offered, in the early years, some respite to the Abkhaz from overt discrimination, the practice of religion was restricted almost from the beginning. Many churches were stripped of their valuables, and some destroyed. The purges of the 1930s and 1940s under Stalin and Beria hit hard at the Abkhazian clergy and members of the intelligentsia involved in both translation of ecclesiastical literature and documentation of church-history in Abkhazia. Following Stalin's death, restrictions on the research or publishing of the history of religion and belief in Abkhazia continued, the activity of the church was limited, and churches were closed, Abkhazians were not trained for the clergy, and services, when they were held, were conducted in the Georgian language only. What was left of Islam was also quashed; by the end of the Soviet period, there were no mosques in Abkhazia, and no overt practice of Islam, though some mullahs were left in the villages; they would still carry out burial and memorial rites locally when requested. Following their usual pattern of assimilation, the majority of Abkhaz defined themselves as atheist by the later stages of Soviet rule (Garb, 1986, p24).

The Soviet repression of 'official' religion failed significantly to affect Abkhaz religious practice in the same way that the earlier empires had been unable to adapt the ritual practices of the Abkhaz to their confessed religions. Soviet policies did deeply affect the Abkhaz way of life, yet the practice of religion, already a fairly unobtrusive private affair, continued fundamentally unaltered, despite the recorded prevalence of atheism among the Abkhaz.

The Abkhaz pantheon

The basic rituals of religion in Abkhazia have their roots in pagan polytheistic rituals and beliefs, and are inextricably linked to the structure of the extended family or lineage (all those who share a surname). Each lineage still has its own festivals and rituals, though few now observe the custom known as 'amṣ̌ara, the specific day or days each week when certain types of work and activity were forbidden for their particular family: when, among other things, they could not marry, perform funerals, or wash.

Traditionally, members of one lineage were buried close to one another, usually in a family burial ground, but increasingly in cemeteries in Soviet times. Though there did exist in earlier centuries the unusual custom of hanging the bodies of the dead in trees, either wrapped in skins or in wooden boxes, this tradition did not last. Funerals now are a complex ritual of mourning and celebration; the traditional displays of horsemanship are generally no longer held, but every funeral, both Christian and Muslim, involves a large gathering of people and a feast. Unusually, instances have been recorded when a burial has been carried out according to Muslim ceremony, and then according to Christian, the unique logic being that "if Allah cannot be of help, then perhaps Christ can" (Smyr, 1994, p15).

Each lineage also has its own sacred place, or a'nyxa. Though few families now have a specified god to whom they pray, in the past each lineage had its own protective spirits to whom sacrifices and prayers were made at an annual gathering. Some families still observe the practice of coming together once a year in their a'nyxa, though arguably the ritual has become a fairly secular affair, an occasion for meeting as a family and feasting, as opposed to offering sacrifices to the deities. These sacred places are natural locations, high up in the mountains, or in forest-groves, by springs or rivers, cliffs or sacred trees.

The Abkhaz generally were not in the custom of erecting idols or temples to their gods, and the *a'nyxa* took the place of a church or mosque, it being considered an inviolable sacred place. A place of prayer, it was also a location where one could seek refuge and the chance to absolve one's guilt.

Over time, the existence of these sacred locations has acquired a part-Christian mythology; said by some to be the places where St. George's bones were buried, churches have been built in the proximity of several of them. It is not unknown for family ceremonies to have been held inside Christian churches, and Easter (*'Amṣap*) and St George's day are important dates in the Abkhaz religious calendar. A wooden or iron cross was often placed in the *a'nyxa*, feasts were held, usually following animal-sacrifice, and other offerings made to the deities, in the form of wine or (more recently) prayer-ribbons tied to the trees.

Procopius of Caesarea wrote, in the sixth century, of the Abazgians (an Abkhaz tribe) that "in my time they still worshipped groves and trees [reckoning that] trees are gods" (Lakoba [ed.], 1993, p66). Travelling in the second half of the 18th century, another observer described a ceremony: "In the first days of May the Abkhaz gathered in a dense and dark sacred forest, the trees of which were considered inviolable for fear of offending some supreme being. In this grove, beside a large iron cross, there lived hermits who had gathered from the people significant remunerations for prayers for their health and success. Everyone who had come to the grove brought with them wooden crosses which they then placed anywhere they could find grass, and acquaintances meeting in the forest would exchange these crosses as a sign of friendship" (Lakoba [ed.], 1993, p131, quoting Jacob Reineggs).

Not only was each lineage in the practice of gathering, but the whole village would also gather over the course of the year to pray for a good harvest, among other things. In Soviet times, the focus of a sacred grove or tree for the village was seen as a potential threat to order, and attempts were made to control even the pagan elements of religious practice. Fazil Iskander, the well known writer (of three-quarters Abkhazian descent), refers to the anti-religious campaigns in the thirties in *Sandro of Chegem*, his satirical novel set largely in the Soviet period: "In the Kenguria district, there had never been a single mosque or church. But since the campaign (against religion) had to be waged, everyone did what they could. The chairman of the Chegem kolkhoz (collective farm), having consulted with his active members, decided to burn down the Prayer Tree as an object of superstitious worship" (p171 of vol. 1 of the 1991 Russian edition, or p137 of the 1993 Faber & Faber English edition).

Iskander's story makes a mockery of official attempts to control religious practice. For in spite of the secularisation of many 'religious' rituals, the Soviet period had a minimal impact on Abkhaz practice. More recently, some of the sacred locations, among which are Lykhny, Elyr, Dydrypsh, Pitsunda, Ach'andara, Psou and T'qʷ'archal, have risen to prominence as the focus of larger gatherings of Abkhazians drawn from a wider geographical area, including the urban centres.

These sites are endowed with particular spiritual significance for the Abkhaz, and are considered to be related to one another in a complex hierarchy of kinship-relationships (Inal-Ipa, 1965, p344). Traditionally the focus of religious worship, some of the sacred places have, thus, also become the scenes of mass-gatherings of elders and other members of the population to express social and political grievances. The Soviet emphasis on 'tradition' and 'ethnicity' as a rallying point for political aspirations has allowed for the combination of age-old religious practices with the more recent secular expression of national grievance. With the escalation of tension between Abkhazia and Georgia from the late seventies, for example, crowds of political protestors, sometimes thousands of them, would gather around the sacred oak tree at the Lykhny site.

Totemic and animistic beliefs and superstitions were at the foundation of the polytheistic religion which preceded Christianity in Abkhazia. In the past, many families worshipped their ancestors, believing that they were linked with an animal, plant, or element of nature, though all that is left of this today is an indication in some Abkhaz surnames that they may derive from the names of animals or plants. The numerous deities traditionally worshipped by the Abkhaz were also almost all associated with the natural world, or certain animals or elements within it.

The 'god of gods' in the Abkhaz pantheon is An'tçʷa, the creator, in whom all the other gods are contained. As with many other words connected with the spiritual life in Abkhaz, this term possibly begins with the Abkhaz for mother — an; it has been argued that the word derives from the plural form 'mothers' (today 'anatçʷa), and arose from the deification of ancestors (Janashia, 1937, p120) — note, however, that the initial vowel in an is part of the root, whereas it is not in the word for 'god'.

The first toast still to be given at feasts is one to An'tçʷa, in the form of "An'tçʷa, you give us the warmth of your eyes!" (Inal-Ipa, 1965, p368). Of the other deities, those associated with the hunt are generally male, and those with agriculture, water, and the earth, female. A'ʒʷejpʃaa is the god of the hunt, and the forest, A'jargʲ the god of hunting and war, and A'fy the god of thunder and lightning. Aj'tar is the god of reproduction and domestic animals, Dzhadzha ('ḓẓaḓẓa) the goddess of agriculture and fertility, 'Dzyzlan the goddess of water, Dzi'waw the rain-goddess, Anana-Gunda (A'nana-Gʷnda) the protectress of people, goddess of the hunt, bees and fertility.

Other deities represent animals (among them bears, snakes, dogs, and horses), the earth, sun and moon, mountain spirits, fire and the hearth, bronze and iron, Sha'ʃʷy being the smithy-god.

Religion in post-Soviet Abkhazia

During the war between Georgia and Abkhazia in 1992-93, both members of the Georgian leadership, and much of the international press, initially at least, portrayed events as the struggle between Orthodox Christianity in Georgia and the secessionist Muslim Abkhaz. In keeping with this, Shevardnadze underwent a very public 'conversion' to Christianity and was baptised

Aerial view of the New Athos monastery-church complex north of Sukhum. It was built in the 19th century.

in the Georgian Orthodox Church as Giorgi a few months after the war began.

This perhaps was intended to play on Western geo-political fears of the spread of Islamic influence in the post-Soviet space, but in actual fact, religion played no part in the war. The Abkhaz were careful to stress this from the start, holding the opinion that "the Islamic factor, supposedly influencing Abkhazia, is a myth created by the pro-Georgian lobby in the Moscow press" (Smyr, 1994a, p42, quoting S. Ivanov). This was borne out by the 'rainbow coalition' against the Georgians which emerged during the war, for it included Muslim and Christian Abkhaz, Muslim Abkhaz from Turkey, North Caucasians, Russians, Greeks and Armenians.

However, questions concerning the position of religion in Abkhazia have become more acute, both because of the inter-ethnic conflict with Georgia and the redefinition of post-Soviet Abkhazian identity, and also due to the potential for tension with the Abkhazian diaspora if and when they do return. Generations of Abkhaz — whose ancestors migrated in the 1860s and after — live predominantly in Turkey. They tend to be practising Muslims and outnumber the Abkhazians in Abkhazia about four to one. According to Grigorij Smyr in 1994, there has been an "increase in the religiousness of the population," following the war between Georgia and Abkhazia in 1992-93 (Smyr, 1994, p19).

This is, to some extent, borne out by an increase in religious language; for example, a recent article chronicling the history of the church in Abkhazia until 1922, has as an afterword a comment on the war: "God was with us in the cruel war for our country against the Antichrist. Our Saviour helped us! Let us confirm our faith in him, pray for salvation and the strengthening of the Christian church in Abkhazia. Amen!" (Chachkhalia, 1994a, p26).

Certainly, the publication of such books as Smyr's *Religioznye Verovanija Abkhazov* ('The religious beliefs of the Abkhaz'),[5] and others on Islam in Abkhazia indicates that religious identity is undergoing a resurgence of interest. A mosque has recently opened in Gudauta, several Abkhaz have entered Orthodox seminaries in Russia for training, and efforts are being made to acquire ecclesiastical literature and copies of the Bible and the Qur'an in Abkhaz.[6] Gatherings at the sacred places continue, baptisms have increased, and there are also plans to introduce religious education in the schools, an interesting project when the Abkhaz are "simultaneously pagan, Christian, Muslim and atheist" (Smyr, 1994, p20).

On the whole, however, religious revival is not being stressed. And if the post-Soviet years are heralding some revival of interest in, and discussion of, religion, then it is a revival of the typically relaxed and heterogeneous, non-dogmatic religious belief and practice which has characterised the Abkhaz in the past. The emphasis placed on tolerance and the absence of religious rivalry or fundamentalism is evident in a brief excursion on the historical symbolism of the state flag of Abkhazia, following its adoption in July 1992. The sequence of green and white stripes is taken from the flag of the North Caucasian Republic of 1918, but is said to symbolise religious tolerance, Islam peacefully co-existing with Christianity.[7] In 1995, one minister of the de facto Abkhazian Parliament even included among plans for the restoration of Sukhum the building of a cathedral and a mosque on opposite sides of a square in the centre of town as a symbol of continued peaceful coexistence.[8] While perhaps astute political rhetoric, appealing to Western liberal values, this tolerance also reflects the general attitude toward religion in Abkhazia.

This tolerance largely extends to religions and denominations other than Orthodoxy and Islam in Abkhazia. There has long been a presence of Jews, Armenians, and Catholic communities in the traditionally heterogeneous mix of people along the Black Sea coast of Abkhazia. Professor S. Karpov, talking of the 14th and 15th centuries writes about the inhabitants of late medieval Sukhum: "The population of Sebastopolis was . . . ethnically variegated. Alongside Greeks and Abkhazians there lived many Jews" (Voronov, 1992, p264). Certainly, there is evidence which indicates the presence of Jewish communities in Gagra in the 11th century, and in Sebastopol in the 14th (Voronov, 1993, pp 16-17).

Catholicism was introduced with the establishment of trading posts along the Black Sea coast, and increasing links with Genoa from the 14th century onwards. Evidence of a Catholic community can be found in a letter written in 1330 by the Catholic bishop Peter from Sebastopol wherein he complains that the Genoese Catholic community was being oppressed by the local Orthodox inhabitants. By the beginning of the 14th century, there was a Catholic episcopal see in Sebastopol, and a Catholic cemetery (Voronov, 1993, pp 16-17). There is little evidence of the fate of the minority religious groups in Abkhazia following the 1992-93 war with Georgia. Large numbers of the Greek, Armenian and Jewish populations were evacuated, but small communities have remained, together with Catholics, Baptists, Seventh Day Adventists and Krishnaites. The post-war increase in the popularity of smaller denominations and sects has given rise to an element of religious intolerance, and the banning of Jehovah's Witnesses in Abkhazia.

In conclusion, the complex synthesis of paganism, Christianity and Islam which forms the basis of religious practice in Abkhazia is not prominent in the current discourse of Abkhaz identity. Indeed, the notion of 'religion', which has always been approached somewhat idiosyncratically by the Abkhaz, has merged to a great extent with the notion of *'apswara* (i.e. what it is to be an Abkhazian). This is a code of ethics, a secular description of the fundamental essence of Abkhaz identity, one not of belief, but of 'mentality'. Incorporating as it does the concepts of 'goodness, fairness, honour and conscience' (Inal-Ipa, 1984, p44), and allowing for freedom of religious belief, *'apswara* plays a far more significant role than religion as the conscience of the people.[9]

15
Demography: ethno-demographic history, 1886-1989

Daniel Müller

Demography has many aspects. With regard to the Abkhaz, their famed longevity comes immediately to mind. However, it is difficult to prove just how old one is when, at the supposed time of one's birth, registration was the exception rather than the norm. It has been noted that in the (January 15th) 1970 All-Union Census the number of people in some higher age cohorts was actually larger than had been the size of corresponding (eleven year younger) cohorts in the (January 15th) 1959 Census. Unless we assume a pensioner-invasion of the USSR in between, this must caution us to realize that some people may have a tendency in old age to advance more rapidly in years than the rest of us![1]

However, we shall not deal with this interesting matter here, nor with any other of the more classical topics of demography. What we shall restrict ourselves to here is what is in Russian so aptly termed ethno-demography (ètnodemografija). This issue is controversial. Generally, Georgian and pro-Georgian writers try to prove the largest possible per centage of 'Georgians' (strictly Kartvelians) in the territory that today is Abkhazia throughout history, whereas Abkhaz and pro-Abkhaz writers perform the process from an opposite point of view. We shall narrow our focus in the main to Abkhazia, treating the Abkhaz diaspora only in a cursory manner. Concentrating on the topic of Kartvelian versus Abkhaz dominance, we shall also allocate less space to the many other groups in Abkhazia's history than would be desirable if space were no problem.

Our focus in time will be the period from 1864 until 1989; in fact, the first good source we can use is for 1886. Not that we lack sources; there are literally many thousands of them. We will here restrict ourselves to: a) what may be called the canonical sources, i.e. those used in normative Soviet scholarship, namely census results for 1897, 1926, 1939, 1959,

1970, 1979 and 1989; and b) a few of the 'non-canonical' sources shunned by the Soviets and thus regularly overlooked by Westerners.

The theoretical and methodological pitfalls in writing the ethno-demography of Abkhazia are awesome indeed. We cannot even try to list them here; hopefully we shall soon do so elsewhere. For a useful introduction to the Russian and Soviet Censuses in general, see Clem (1986). Suffice it to say here that it is certainly not enough to grab a book from a shelf, open it and take out an isolated figure or two, as is so often done when the pseudo-objectivity of numbers is employed (more often than one would believe, even such shortest of quotes will on close inspection turn out to be patently false). Figures have a context, which is often very complex and must be considered. If this were not so, future historians might indeed conclude that hordes of pensioners actually did descend on the USSR between 1959 and 1970.

Figures before 1864

The Russian Empire incorporated the territory that today is Abkhazia only after the end of organized West Caucasian resistance in 1864. Before that, no real administration existed, although some Russian presence had intermittently been maintained, namely on the coast, rising and falling with the ebb and flow of Russian fortunes on the Black Sea, having been very low as late as the Crimean War. 'No administration' means 'no reliable figures'. Despite or because of this, we have a large number of demographic figures for this period. To call these estimates would be to accord honour where none is due. None of the authors of our sources could or did claim to have counted the people, or at least to have visited all inhabited places, many of them inaccessible, some accepting no outside authority at all. The figures, even when compiled by people in a (semi-)official capacity, were based as much on hearsay as not. Before 1864, neither Russians nor Ottomans nor any other power, local or otherwise, were in a position to make anything like a realistic estimate of the population. To give any of these guesses (for that is what they are) precedence would be quite arbitrary.

What can be surmised is ethnographic rather than demographic in nature; namely, that the population consisted mainly of people speaking Abkhaz; in the north, the boundaries with speakers of other West Caucasian tongues, i.e., Ubykh and Circassian, were ill-defined, as bi- or possibly trilingual groups lived and moved in the area. Not far away (closer than today) were also bands of Abazinians, plus some hordes of Turkic-speaking Noghais. To the east, high altitudes made for a clear boundary with Turkic Karachays and Kartvelian Svans, although it need not necessarily have conformed to modern borders. In the south, the strip of land known as Samurzaq'an(o) was a bone of contention between the ruling houses of most of Abkhazia, and of Mingrelia; the locals were largely Georgian Orthodox and probably to a large degree bilingual in Abkhaz and Mingrelian. It would prove difficult to decide whether these were Abkhaz in the process of Mingrelianisation or vice-versa.[2]

Beyond the Ingur began Mingrelia proper. Only in some of the tiny coastal towns was the population somewhat more mixed. Besides people from the hinterland, there were Turks and other Ottoman Muslims, as well as possibly some Greeks, Armenians, Jews or Persians. Presence of Russians was limited to places where, and times when, their garrisons were in place. Due to the slave trade, for which Abkhazia provided entrepôts, there may have been some Africans.

The slave trade was also responsible for what one could euphemistically call out-migration. The tradition of Abkhaz men being sold was old, the ethnonym *Abha:z* appearing, for example, in medieval Mamluk sources. Another form of this export delivered females to Ottoman harems. The dimension of this body-drain is unclear. The Abkhaz were also decimated through risings, wars, epidemics and abysmally low living standards, which between them may have more than offset natural growth for longish periods.

From 1864 until 1886

Even before 1864, the out-migration of Abkhaz accelerated. In 1864, it reached considerable proportions, then declined until the end of 1866, when a doomed Abkhaz rising that lasted well into 1867 led to a second wave. Another lull followed until the Russo-Ottoman war of 1877/1878, when Ottoman troops landed in Abkhazia and were supported by local irregulars. Russian victory meant heavy casualties and the outflux of probably an actual majority of the population; wide areas were totally depopulated.

Again, we will not attempt here to grapple with the many figures of how many Abkhaz actually left. The Ottoman authorities generally indiscriminately counted all the Caucasian arrivals under a single heading; when Abkhaz are listed separately, they often may have been, or included, either Abazinians or Ubykhs. Finally, the appalling loss of life *en route* meant that only a portion of the out-migrants from the Russian Empire ever became immigrants into the Ottoman realm; some entered the country illegally by land and sea (for example being smuggled in as slaves) and were thus not counted at all. The Russians, who were in a better position to count, were not too interested.

Numbers were, however, dramatic, especially between 1864 and 1878. A trickle continued long afterwards, in fact outlasting both

Empires. There was also a considerable remigration of Abkhaz unhappy with life in the Ottoman Empire, although in size it was just a fraction of the out-migration. Some Abkhaz who had gone to the Batumi area were reincorporated into Russia without bodily returning, being annexed in 1878 with their new homes, although many chose to leave for the Ottoman interior.

The Abkhaz diaspora in the Ottoman successor states today bears witness to the scale of these forced migrations; the greatest number live in Turkey, where Abkhaz as a language was last mentioned in the published results of the 1965 census, although due to what seems to have been the customary combination of bureaucratic incompetence and Turkish nationalism, reported numbers were ridiculously low: just 4,563 first and 7,836 second language speakers (see Andrews, 1989, p167)). Another sizeable community lives in Syria, where before 1967 its homes lay mainly on the Golan, from where practically all were driven out by the Israelis. Since World War II, a secondary 'outer' diaspora has sprung up, as *inter alios* Abkhaz from Turkey came to Germany, Golan Abkhaz to the USA, etc.; not using Turkish or other non-Russian sources, we shall restrict further remarks on the diaspora to the 'inner' groups inside Russian/Soviet/former Soviet territory.

The departing Abkhaz were replaced by newcomers from all over the Russian Empire and even abroad. The most obvious new arrivals came from Mingrelia, where serfdom had been finally abolished in 1867. Population-densities there were high and many newly freed peasants stranded landless; in Abkhazia, population-density was very low in huge fertile areas, the health hazards of which (like malaria) the neighbouring Mingrelians were additionally better prepared to brave than people from other climes.

The Cameral Description of 1873

After the Russians took military control of the Western Caucasus in 1864, it was a long time before they actually established a more or less efficient administration. The numerous figures released after the occupation in any case closely resemble those before in their inexactitude. Of these post-1864 statistics, we want to single out for scrutiny the so-called Cameral Description of 1873. At present I only have results of this in the doctored version which Nikolaus von Seidlitz, an official statistician, wrote for the 1880 volume of a German learned journal. It would be interesting to consult the original results (see Seidlitz, 1880, pp 340–47). The German version gives four components for Sukhum territory: the town of Sukhum, the counties of Ochamchira and Pitsunda, and (the prefecture of) Ts'ebelda.

1. Supposed population of the Sukhum territory (1873)

	Sukhum town	Ochamchira	Pitsunda	Ts'ebelda	**Total**
Population	1,500	32.179	7,080	605	41,364
Mingrelians	?	26,475	0	0	26,475
Abkhaz	0	5,700	6,900	605	13,205
Russians	?	0	138	0	138
Turks	0	4	42	0	46
Greeks, Armenians	?	0	0	0	?

In Sukhum town, the population is said to consist mainly of Russians, including the garrison, plus some Greek, Armenian and Mingrelian traders. For the whole territory, 64.0 per cent not including those in Sukhum town would have been Mingrelians, just 31.9 per cent Abkhaz. It is strange that, as far as I know, Georgian authors do not use these figures, given their being so well suited to their purpose; the only reason I can see for this is that they have never come across this source.

As it is, rounded figures, quite untypical of a source where rounding is not generally employed, nurture suspicion, which is found to be well grounded: the figures are admittedly not those for 1873, having been tampered with, as from a footnote we learn that besides these Abkhaz a further 32,000 plus 847 Kabardians from near Gagra near Pitsunda had emigrated to 'Turkey' (the Ottoman Empire) in the war of 1877/78. This would leave us with a figure of *74,211 for 1873, *45,205 of whom or 60.9 per cent would have been Abkhaz, 35.7 per cent (plus some in Sukhum) Mingrelians.[3]

The figures only begin to make sense when we realise that the Samurzaq'anoans are here treated as Mingrelians, not Abkhaz. Even so, outside the southern fringe of Abkhazia, i.e., Samurzaq'an(o) (here under Ochamchira), there were practically no Kartvelians, whereas Abkhaz were living all over the territory, except for Sukhum, where they were rarely and barely tolerated by the authorities (although four Abkhaz were reported in Tbilisi).

The Family Lists of 1886
In 1886, the authorities compiled so-called Family Lists, giving the population of even the tiniest hamlets in Transcaucasia. The figures were published officially in a volume of more than a 1,000 pages (albeit without pagination) in Tbilisi in 1893, and there were many subsequent

publications. In the Sukhumskij Okrug, roughly corresponding to modern Abkhazia, 145 settlements are listed, the smallest of which, Pshauri, was reported to have just 13 inhabitants. People are listed according to: a) nationalities (*narodnosti*); b) religious affiliation; and c) estates.[4]

Both sexes as well as households are indicated separately for each category. Because of the ease with which this source allowed itself to be falsified by contemporaries who only had to visit a few villages to check the accuracy of the figures, these Family Lists are our first serious source. It is not without its shortcomings, of course: We may suspect that the 11 Shi'ite Muslims registered in the village of Aradu (1,879 Abkhaz, five Mingrelians, no other nationalities) were actually Persians or Tatars (i.e. modern 'Azerbaijanis'), or indeed Alevi Turks or Turkmens, but none such are listed in all the okrug; nor are Ottoman Turks and other groups one strongly suspects did actually live there. Probably these were generally regarded as non-permanent residents and thus excluded.

2. Nationalities in Sukhumskij Okrug (1886)						
	Samurzaq'an(o) uchastok	K'odor uchastok	Gudauta uchastok	Gumista uchastok	Sukhum town	Ochamchira town	**Total**
Population	30,529	15,821	14,887	6,609	412	515	68,773
Samurzaq'anoans	29,520	1,108	0 (!)	12	0	0	30,640
Abkhaz	0 (!)	14,525	13,404	391	3	0	28,323
Mingrelians[5]	984	172	41	2,277	84	0	3,558
Greeks	0	0	9	2,047	93	0	2,149
Armenians	0	0	1,037	0	53	0	1,090
Russians	4	0	361	606	119	0	1,090
Estonians	0	0	0	637	0	0	637
Georgians[6]	0[20]	0[13]	0[29]	0	0	515	515[577]
Germans	0	0	0	245	0	0	245
Moldavians	0	0	0	148	0	0	148
Ukrainians	0	0	0	126	0	0	126
Bulgarians	0	0	0	95	3	0	98
Imeretians[6]	20[0]	13[0]	29[0]	0	22	0	84[22]
Poles	0	0	1	5	17	0	23
Circassians[7]	1	3	5	7	3	0	19
Jews	0	0	0	4	6	0	10
Latvians	0	0	0	9	0	0	9
Gurians[6]	0	0	0	0	9	0	9

Comparing '1873' (or rather, 1878) with 1886, we see that Seidlitz took the Samurzaq'anoans for Mingrelians. Whether this and subsequent natural growth of the Abkhaz population bolstered by thousands of returnees is enough to explain his low figure for the Abkhaz, we leave undecided.

It is in any case easy to see that, and why, the Samurzaq'anoans are the bone of contention between Abkhaz and Georgians. According to the Family Lists, they were actually the most numerous group of all. Some (pro-)Abkhaz scholars have stated the per centage of Abkhaz in Abkhazia for 1886 to have been 85.7 per cent; that clearly is an addition of Abkhaz plus Samurzaq'anoans (30,640 + 28,323 = 58,963 or 85.7 per cent of 68,773). On the other hand, some (pro-)Georgian scholars have claimed that actually they, the 'Georgians', were in a majority of 50.6 per cent, clearly arriving at this by adding all Kartvelians (Mingrelians [and some Laz for Sukhum town] + Georgians [including Imeretians and Gurians] to the Samurzaq'anoans (30,640 + 3,558 + 515 + 84 + 9 = 34,806 or 50.6 per cent of 68,773).

Presentation of figures should always be supported by explanation of how they are calculated. While the (pro-)Abkhaz may be criticized for the form they choose, they are quite justified in the essence: the very source itself compiles additional summary tables, and in these, Samurzaq'anoans are not listed, but the number of Abkhaz in *Kutaisskaja Gubernija* is given as 60,432. Now, in Batumi (city and okrug), 1,469 Abkhaz were listed; thus 58,963 remain — clearly, these are the Abkhaz plus the Samurzaq'anoans in our okrug!

Besides the proof offered by the table, we have additional evidence in the fact that Samurzaq'anoans and Abkhaz are kept apart quite neatly. Only in two villages in Gumista, far from Samurzaq'an(o), are both listed side by side; elsewhere, it is either one or the other: Abkhaz in the rest of Gumista, in Gudauta and in K'odor (minus one large village of Samurzaq'anoans with no Abkhaz), Samurzaq'anoans in Samurzaq'an(o). Clearly the authorities had trouble distinguishing Abkhaz and Samurzaq'anoans,[8] going by territorial divisions instead. On the other hand, they seem to have had little difficulty distinguishing Mingrelians and Samurzaq'anoans, who are regularly listed living side by side.[9]

Finally, look at the sex-ratio of the Kartvelians: 142 males to every 100 females for Mingrelians (including a few Laz), 207:100 for Georgians (including Imeretians and Gurians). Look also at the restriction of non-Mingrelian Kartvelians to a few settlements (515 in Ochamchira alone, although we suspect some may actually have been Mingrelians; 355 of them male); combining these facts, one must realise that we are dealing here with a recently arrived settler population.

Outside the okrug, the source lists Abkhaz only in *Batumskij okrug* (554 in the city, 915 in villages), and in one town of the *Karskaja oblast'* (just 12).

The First All-General Census of 1897

The so-called First All-General Census of Russia, conducted to represent the state of the population as of January 28th, 1897 (old style; new, February 9th), was the only one ever to cover all the Empire, except the Central Asian protectorate Khanates and the Grand Duchy of Finland. It is strange (but little wonder, considering the unwelcome results) that Georgian scholars often do not even mention this source. Its peculiarity, often ignored, was that no question on nationality was included, questions on language, religion, estate or place of birth serving as partial substitutes. While insisting that it is not synonymous with nationality, we will concentrate on language.

3. Mother tongue ('rodnoj jazyk') in Sukhumskij Okrug (1897)[10]

Population	106,179	no language indicated	18
Abkhaz[11]	58,697	Avar & Andi Languages[12]	26
All Kartvelian	25,873	Kjurinian [i.e. Lezgian proper][13]	21
of which:		Assyrian [i.e. Aramaean]	17
Mingrelian	23,810	Circassian	16
var. Georgian dialects & Laz[13]	1,830	Chuvash	15
Imeretian [Georgian dialect][11]	141	Ingush	11
Svan	92	Ossetian	11
Armenian	6,552	Bashkir	6
Greek	5,393	Darginian[12]	6
Russian	5,135	English	6
Turkish	1,347	Kumyk	5
Ukrainian	809	Italian	3
Estonian	604	Turkmen	3
German	406	Cheremiss [i.e. Mari]	2
Polish	234	French	2
Persian	186	Kabardian	2
Tatar [incl. modern Tatar & Azerbaijani]	171	Kurdish	2
'Jewish' [i.e. Yiddish][14]	136	Talysh	2
Romanian (Moldovan)	133	Abyssinian [probably Amharic]	1
Lithuanian	72	Arabic	1
Belorussian	67	Chechen	1
Czech [probably incl. Slovak]	63	Karachay	1
Latvian	51	Kazikumyk [i.e. Lak] & others[13]	1
Bulgarian	38	Mordvinian	1
Kist [Chechen dialect]	31	Udi[12]	1

Looking at Tables 2 and 3, we must be careful to avoid one-to-one comparison of *nationality* with *language*. Probably some people earlier listed as Samurzaq'anoans were now registered as Mingrelian by language, athough, asked for nationality, they might still have stated 'Samurzaq'anoan' or indeed 'Abkhaz': as late as 1926, 8,755 persons in Abkhazia reportedly professed a Kartvelian *mother tongue* but Abkhaz *nationality (narodnost')*. It is thus hard to tell whether to attribute the numerical decline of 266 (from 58,963 to 58,697), in the absence of large-scale out-migration and allowing for natural growth, to actual mingrelianisation or to the new statistical method. Probably both factors were present.

But the census also tells us of continuing immigration not only of a wide range of groups from further afield, but also indeed of Mingrelians, through the birthplace question. 7,957 persons had been born abroad, 7,610 of them in 'Turkey' alone (Greeks, Armenians, Turks); in all, there were no less than 9,671 foreigners, 9,349 of them subjects of the Porte. Another 6,416 had been born inside the Empire, but outside *Kutaisskaja Gubernija*. These would, for example, include Eastern Slavs, Poles and Balts, of course excepting children already born in the okrug. Especially among the 284 people born in the Tbilisi Gubernia, there must have been some Georgian immigrants too.

Finally, 16,528 persons were born inside the gubernia but outside the okrug. The gubernia was heavily Kartvelian, except for the Artvin Okrug (dominated by Turks) and the industrial city and ethnic hotch-potch of Batumi, itself a magnet for settlers and not likely to send out (m)any. It is thus almost indisputable that almost all the 16,528 non-local Kutaissians in the okrug would be Mingrelians, (western) Georgians and Svans, numerically leaving just *9,345 locally born Kartvelians (minus some non-Kartvelians born in Kutaisi, but outside Sukhum, but plus some Kartvelians born outside Kutaisi altogether). It is thus beyond reasonable doubt that at most some 10,000 or so of mother tongue Kartvelians counted in the okrug had actually been born there. These would include assimilated Samurzaq'anoans as well as locally born children of settlers. The sex-ratio of Kartvelian speakers is also revealing: 15,122 males to 10,751 females or 141:100; for Mingrelian alone, it is 131:100, whereas in Mingrelia proper, Zugdidi (101:100) and Senak'i (98:100) *uezds*, it shows almost too perfect a balance for male-dominated Caucasia, thus further indicating migration.

Outside Abkhazia, figures in the Batumi area declined dramatically from 1,469 Abkhaz in 1886 to just 687 Abkhaz speakers in 1897 (from 554 to 58 in the city itself). In the 1890s, Abkhaz were forcibly removed by the authorities. Barred from returning to Abkhazia, most emigrated to the Ottoman Empire (see text 26 of Hewitt and Khiba (1997)). In the North Caucasus, Abkhaz speakers must in the main have been modern-day Abazinians, 12,481 of them in the Kubanskaja oblast' alone. Outside these units (Batumi & Sukhum okrugs plus Kubanskaja oblast'), the diaspora was just 264 (83 of them elsewhere in Kutaisi) to make it 72,123 speakers of Abkhaz for all the Empire. However, outside Caucasia Abkhaz was generally counted with Circassian, thus there may have been a few more Abkhaz speakers included under that heading.

The Caucasian Calendar

The next good source regularly quoted is the first All-Union Census of 1926. Anything but good, though much quoted, is another source, to which we now turn: the *Caucasian Calendar* (CC). This yearbook was published under the auspices of the viceroy in Tbilisi until 1916, when the final CC for the year 1917 appeared, carrying demographic figures compiled for January 1, 1916 (old style; new, January 14). In the same manner, the CC for 1914, published in 1913, has figures for January 1, 1913, and so forth.

4. Nationalities ('narodnosti') in Sukhumskij Okrug (1913 & 1916)[15]

Population	1/I/1913 181,947	sex-ratio (m.:100 f.)	permanent population	1/I/1916 209,700
Russians, Orthodox [incl. Ukrainians & Belorussians]	18,043	184:100	66.1%	25,300
Russians, 'sectarians'	54	391:100	100.0%	100
Other European peoples [i.e. Poles, Germans, etc.]	13,784	173:100	56.7%	6,600
Kartvelians, Orthodox	69,799	158:100	79.2%	49,400
Kartvelians, Muslim [i.e. Laz, Ajars, etc.]	315	(just 3 f.)	(none)	1,000
Armenians, Gregorian [i.e. Armenian Apostolic]	13,034	137:100	24.6%	20,700
Armenians, Orthodox	37	118:100	100.0%	0
Armenians, other beliefs [i.e. Uniate, Protestant?]	132	169:100	100.0%	50
Caucasian mountaineers, Muslim	29,186	104:100	79.2%	200
Caucasian mountaineers, other beliefs [?]	16,919	118:100	96.3%	200
Other Asiatic peoples, Christians	5,528	112:100	45.1%	103,200
Other Asiatic peoples, Shi'i Muslims	1,597	298:100	34.9%	200
Other Asiatic peoples, Sunni Muslims	13,071	676:100	2.4%	2,400
Jews	448	126:100	99.1%	300

Preposterous categories like 'Other Asiatics' are useful for manipulative purposes only. Taken with crude territorial divisions employed (no figures below *uezd* level), these categories make the CC a caricature of ethno-demography. An eye-opener to CC believers should be a 13/16 comparison, my reading of the bewildering data being this: almost all the mountaineers reported in 1913 were actually Abkhaz, as may have been the Christians among the 'Other Asiatics'. In 1916, these three categories were merged as Christian 'Other Asiatics', to which further may have been added thousands of Greeks possibly represented in 1913 under 'Other Europeans' as well as 20,000 or so Samurzaq'anoans listed in 1913 as Kartvelians; finally, thousands of refugees from Anatolia (Greeks?) must have boosted this category. Whereas 1886/1897 sources depict the Abkhaz as 93 per cent and 84 per cent Orthodox, in 1913 30,000 were Muslims, but almost none in 1916!

Sex-ratios are again revealing: even among the permanent Christian Kartvelian population, the quota is more than 144 males to 100 females. In the light of the CC's defects, the practice of short quotations from it is not helpful and should be abandoned. A detailed study of all CC figures on Abkhazia would of course be very welcome.

The Agricultural Census of 1917
In 1917, the Provisional Government ordered an Agricultural and Soil Census to be completed by September 1st, following the tsarist one in 1916; results appeared in 1923.

5. Agricultural Census 1917					
	Samurzaq'an(o) uchastok	K'odor uchastok	Gudauta uchastok	Gumista uchastok	Sukhumskij okrug
Population	42,201	26,581	25,106	37,347	131,235
Georg. (all Kartv.)	40,959	3,882	276	9,643	54,760
Abkhaz	1,161	20,022	17,993	739	39,915
Greeks	18	375	1,160	15,727	17,280
Armenians	0	2,227	4,386	7,224	13,837
Russians	27	21	1,221	1,365	2,634
Germans	0	0	0	339	339
Persians	0	0	22	0	22
Jews	0	9	0	5	14
Others	36	45	48	2,305	2,434

A decline of the population from 209,700 in 1916 to 131,235 in the summer of 1917, thus *before* the war started in earnest for Abkhazia, is unlikely. Actually, as an explanation it is quite unnecessary, as after all it was an *agricultural* census that excluded urban populations. Thus, the per centage of both Kartvelians and Abkhaz is here high, as they were concentrated on the land, the Abkhaz even more so. As late as 1917, Kartvelians were still heavily outnumbered in K'odor, Gudauta (by Abkhaz) and Gumista (by other settlers, especially Greeks), forming an overwhelming majority only in tiny Samurzaq'an(o), where it is of course only explained by another switch in the way the Samurzaq'anoans were listed: once again as Kartvelians.[16]

Two typical examples from the press of the period
Exactly as the supply of reliable information dried up, with the U-boat actions, landings, uprisings, revolutions, counter-revolutions and civil war of 1917-22, demand for figures reached an all-time high, and even after the demise of what little of doubtful use the collapsed administration had offered in the form of the CC, supplies for this brisk demand were not slow in coming forth. Figures one finds in archives or print for the period under inspection turn out to be at best mangled repetitions of the CC.

Thus *Kavkazskoe Slovo* reported in its No. 107 of May 29th, 1918, that Georgia had 2,761,000 inhabitants, of whom 4.6 per cent were Abkhaz; that would imply some 127,000 Abkhaz! Perhaps this is a result of faulty calculations based on the CC. Even more remarkably, *Vozrozhdenie* had this to offer in its No. 104 of June 1: "In Sukhum, there were 180,000 natives: 50,000 Abkhaz, 60,000 Mingrelians, 70,000 Georgians; besides, 20,000 Greeks, 22,000 Armenians, 16,000 Estonians and 12,000 others."[17]

The All-Georgian Census of 1922/23
Before the Soviets conducted their first All-Union Census (1926), they carried out a number of restricted censuses, e.g. an urban census in 1923, which was explicitly not held in Georgia, because one had just taken place there on November 30th, 1922. Rural parts followed in 1923 to conclude the first and only All-Georgian Census in Soviet times. As late as 1925, the results on the nationalities in the rural population had not been officially published. My best guess is they actually never were. With the publication of the first All-Union Census, the All-Georgian Census de facto became unquotable. What little had been published was regularly ignored.

6. Towns (1922)					
	Gal	Ochamchira	Gudauta	Sukhum	urban pop.[18]
Population	230	2,669	2,843	17,426	23,168
Georgians (all Kartv.)	223	1,576	612	3,706	6,117
Greeks	0	251	720	4,992	5,963
Russians	3	171	711	4,467	5,352
Armenians	1	78	304	1,889	2,272
Abkhaz	0	453	186	426	1,065
Jews	0	5	9	1,012	1,026
Persians	0	0	44	203	247
Poles	0	0	39	204	243
Germans	0	0	31	127	158
Azerbaijani Turks	0	0	12	5	17
Ossetians	0	0	0	10	10
Other Caucasians	0	0	4	12	16
Others	3	135	171	373	682

Georgians (i.e. Kartvelians) had a plurality of just a good quarter of the urban population in 1922. If we add these figures to those of the rural population from the Agricultural Census of 1917, we find that Kartvelians (including the Samurzaq'anoans) would make up just 39.4 per cent of the population of Abkhazia, whereas the Abkhaz (without the Samurzaq'anoans) would numerically still be 26.5 per cent of the population.

In 1926, the first volume of the *Great Soviet Encyclopaedia* was printed, including the entry for the Abkhaz SSR (note in passing that at the time nominally it was not, as erroneously or mischievously often stated, an ASSR, but an SSR). This entry mentions the population of the five *uezd* centres, Sukhum (17,426), Ochamchira (2,920), Gudauta (2,834), Gagra (1,075), and Gal (849). Whereas the figure for Gudauta may be a misprint for 2,843, the figure for Sukhum is clearly derived from the Census of November 30th 1922; the differences for Ochamchira and Gal may be explained by administrative expansion of both towns between 1922/23 and 1926.[19]

Besides these figures, the entry gives figures for the whole population of Abkhazia, stating that out of a population of 174,126, 83,794 and thus 'around 50 per cent' (actually 48.1 per cent) were Abkhaz, Georgians 18.4 per cent, Greeks 12.8 per cent, Armenians 10.2 per cent, Russians 5.9 per cent, Persians 2.2 per cent and others, including Jews, Estonians, Germans, Turks and Poles, less than 1 per cent (each). Put into absolute figures, we thus receive this picture:

7. Population of Abkhazia according to the 'Great Soviet Encyclopaedia' (for 1922/23?)

Population	174,126	lowest possible	highest possible
Abkhaz	83,794	—	—
Georgians (18.4%)	*32,039	31,953	32,126
Greeks (12.8%)	*22,288	22,202	22,375
Armenians (10.2%)	*17,761	17,674	17,847
Russians (5.9%)	*10,273	10,187	10,360
Persians (2.2%)	*3,831	3,744	3,917
others (each 1%)	*4,140	3,707	4,572

I actually suspect that the figures stem from the census of 1922/23 (as obviously does the figure for, say, Sukhum), although proof is lacking, and they may well be from another source, as yet unknown. Be that as it may, according to the most authoritative source imaginable, where not a single word was printed without approval from the highest bodies, Abkhaz once again heavily outnumbered Kartvelians as late as 1926. Obviously, the Samurzaq'anoans were here once again counted as Abkhaz.

The All-Union Census of 1926

In discussions of the first All-Union Census of (17 December) 1926, the foreign subjects are regularly forgotten. That is a pity, as at 7.5 per cent of the population (15,012 persons) they were more important here than anywhere else in the USSR except for the Far East, where foreigners made up 8.2 per cent. To avoid confusion, we follow the custom of listing only Soviet citizens, but add foreigners in brackets.

8. Nationalities ('narodnosti') in the Abkhaz SSR (1926)[20]

Population: 186,004 Soviet citizens +15,012 foreigners, thus 201,016

Georgians, i.e. Kartvelians	(+509) 67,494	Ossetians	20
of whom:		Assyrians [i.e. Aramaeans]	(+1) 19
Mingrelians	(+1) 40,989	Czechs & Slovaks	(+1) 16
Georgians proper	24,576	Mordvinians	13

Svans	1,875	Central Asian Jews	11
Laz	(+508) 42	Hungarians	(+4) 10
Ajars	12	Circassians	10
Abkhaz	(+4) 55,918	Albanians	(+1) 9
Armenians	(+2,323) 25,677	French	(+1) 9
Greeks	(+10,802) 14,045	Romanians	8
Russians	(+1) 12,553	Finns	7
Ukrainians	(+1) 4,647	Chinese	7
Ottoman Turks	(+652) 1,115	Karelians	5
Estonians	779	Mountain Jews	4
Jews	702	Komi	4
Germans	(+478) 672	Karachays	3
Belorussians	406	Uzbeks	3
Poles	(+7) 357	Chuvash	3
[Azerbaijani] Turks	(+68) 276	Kalmyks	3
Georgian Jews	215	Chechens	2
Crimean Jews	152	Ingush	2
Persians	(+145) 147	Swedes	2
Bulgarians	(+1) 127	Dutch	2
Latvians	(+1) 112	Kabardians	1
Moldovans	(+1) 97	Kirghiz	1
Lithuanians	(+3) 57	Gypsies	1
Kazakhs	54	Udmurts	1
Karaims	(+1) 39	Finns of Leningrad	1
Italians	(+3) 30	Serbians	(+1) 1
Tatars	29	Britons	(+2) 1
Lezgians [probably incl. var. Daghestani groups]	22	others	(+1) 4
Kurds	22	no nationality indicated	77

Omitting the foreigners thus means playing down the size of the Greek (by more than 10,000 people), Armenian, Ottoman Turk, Laz, German, Persian and (Azerbaijani) Turk communities. Of 550 Laz, only 42 were Soviet citizens.

Comparing figures from the Encyclopaedia (1926) and the 1926 census, the Abkhaz decrease by 27,876, whereas the Kartvelians increase by something like *35,455! Clearly, the Samurzaq'anoans, some 30,000 or so, are once again listed as Kartvelians; that Abkhaz losses are somewhat lower and Kartvelian gains somewhat higher may easily be explained by natural growth for both plus some immigration for the Kartvelians. Very useful is a look at a combination of some language/nationality figures:

9. Nationality and mother tongue in the Abkhaz SSR (1926, Soviet citizens only)

Nationality	Mother tongue					
	Mingrelian	Abkhaz	Georgian	Svan	Laz	Others
Abkhaz	8,736	47,053	19	0	0	110
Mingrelians	40,228	78	542	1	2	138
Georgians proper	17,412	36	6,957	1	0	170
Svans	10	0	4	1,860	0	1
Laz	0	4	0	0	17	21
Ajars	0	0	6	0	0	6

Table 9 in two ways significantly enlarges and changes the picture of Table 8. We learn that 15.6 per cent of all listed Abkhaz actually had Mingrelian listed as their mother tongue . This obviously represents a strong hint on mingrelianisation, past and ongoing. No less significant: 70.8 per cent of all 'Georgians' proper have Mingrelian registered as their mother tongue.

Thus, we may safely assume, they were Mingrelians who (out of a mixture of inclination towards their own 'high culture', which for long had been Georgian, and of nationalist pressure, the balance of which factors we are not in a position to decide) declared themselves 'Georgians'. The number of Kartvelians giving Georgian as their mother tongue is just 7,509 (undoubtedly, western dialects would here predominate), or 3.7 per cent of the population of Abkhazia, if that: some of those Mingrelians more strongly influenced (or pressured) by Georgian nationalism may have given both Georgian nationality and Georgian language, as seems quite possible. The figure for Georgians would then have to be further lowered accordingly.

Using the language-data, we can see two processes at work: linguistic mingrelianisation of part of the Abkhaz and ideological Georgianisation of part of the Mingrelians. When we compare 47,307 first-language speakers of Abkhaz (including non-Abkhaz) registered in Abkhazia in 1926 with 58,697 counted in 1897, we see how assimilation and the upheaval of 1917/22 have taken their toll.

The census results for 1926 contain a list of nationalities by village-soviet (95 of them plus 4 towns) virtually inviting a detailed comparison with the Family Lists of 1886, which space however does not permit here; we restrict ourselves to *uezd* level and to juxtaposing Kartvelians and Abkhaz.

10. 'Uezd' figures (1926)

	Sukhum	Gal	Gudauta	K'odor	Gagra	Abkhazia
Population	77,097	50,086	30,800	33,086	9,947	201,016
All Kartvelians	20,619	36,802	1,374	6,762	1,934	67,491[21]
of whom:						
Mingrelians	14,739	19,018	579	5,729	924	40,989
Georg., Ajar, Laz	4,068	17,748	?	?	?	(24,630)
Svans	1,812	36	?	?	?	(1,875)
Abkhaz	2,189	12,963	17,846	21,762	1,158	55,918

Gal is the only *uezd* dominated by Kartvelians; however, dominance is nothing like that supposed in the Agricultural Census of 1917, where 'Georgians' nominally made up 40,959 of 42,201 rural inhabitants of Samurzaq'an(o) *uchastok* (as Gal *uezd* then was). The Abkhaz, then just 1,161 of them, are again a substantial 12,963. What we see here is that the final statistical assimilation of the Samurzaq'anoans is not yet complete. In 1926, only 5,295 persons in all Gal *uezd* had Abkhaz listed as their mother tongue . Numerically, something like *7,668 Abkhaz in this *uezd* alone thus had Kartvelian languages. In only six village-soviets of the *uezd* was Abkhaz mother tongue to more than a 100 people (led by Bedia I at 1,673). The next stages were that Kartvelophone Abkhaz became Mingrelians, whereas several of the still Abkhazophone Abkhaz villages (including Bedia I) were administratively separated from Gal and joined to K'odor, thus completing the mingrelianisation of Gal *uezd* (see Lezhava, 1989, pp 20f.). It should be added that in Gal, pressure on the Mingrelians was also high. Although officially only 574 people spoke Georgian as first language, numerically *17,748 people were listed as Georgians proper, a figure which may include some (at most 54) Ajars and Laz. Thus, while almost 8,000 Abkhaz were linguistically mingrelianised, more than 17,000 Mingrelians were ideologically georgianised in Gal *uezd* alone (note that we do not know which part of the process was of their own choosing).[22]

The census provides another glimpse of the diaspora: in the USSR, there were reportedly 56,957 Abkhaz; 110 were listed outside Georgia, 929 inside Georgia but outside Abkhazia (of which 779 in Ajaria around Batumi, and 72 in Tbilisi).

The All-Union Censuses of 1937 and 1939

In 1932 the USSR experienced a census I have seen dubbed 'experimental' at a later time.[23] Perhaps it was; or else it received the

name only after misfiring one way or the other, to justify that results
were not published. Be that as it may, they never were, as happened for a
half-century with the next census of (January 6th) 1937. Published data
for this from 1990/91, while duly noting the ethnic composition of every
oblast in the RSFSR, still fail to give a nationality-breakdown for
Abkhazia.

Abkhaz numbered just 55,561 in the USSR (55,409 of them in
Georgia). Thus, from 1926 to 1937, the Abkhaz in the USSR reportedly
declined from 56,957 to 55,561; a net loss of 1,396 or 2.3 per cent only,
but still astonishing when compared to the quarter million (15.2 per
cent) growth of neighbouring Kartvelians.[24] This is the period when
Abkhazia was demoted to ASSR status (1931) and separate Mingrelian,
Svan, Laz (by 1937) and Ajar (1939) identities were abolished (besides,
21,471 Georgian Jews were listed in the USSR in 1926, but just ten (!) in
1937; by 1939, they were listed as Jews or Georgians, as the category
disappeared). We cannot dwell on these matters here, but certainly this
is a context to be remembered: it means that Samurzaq'anoans who had
personally opted to declare themselves or been reclassified as
Mingrelians were *in toto* reclassified as Georgians. Results of the (January
17th) 1939 census were also published restrictedly. Only in the 1990s did
we get fuller accounts.

11. 1939 census data (compared with 1926)[25]

	Abkhazia, 1926	Abkhazia, 1939	growth, Abkhazia	growth, USSR
Population	201,016	311,885	55.2%	—
Georgians (all Kartvelians)	67,494	91,967	36.3%	23.5%
Russians	12,553	60,201	379.6%	28.0%
Abkhaz	55,918	56,197	0.5%	3.6%
Armenians	25,677	49,705	93.6%	37.3%
Greeks	14,045	34,621	146.5%	34.0%

The growth of the Abkhaz population is small, whereas other groups
experienced dramatic immigration, Russians now outnumbering Abkhaz.
Kartvelian immigration was not very strong from 1926 to 1939, growth
being just some *8,500 faster than would be expected through natural
growth as experienced by all Kartvelians; part of this growth may be
explained by continued assimilation of Abkhaz, especially of those 8.755

or so (in Abkhazia) who had Kartvelian mother tongues listed in 1926. However, of all 59,003 Abkhaz in the USSR, still only 52,347 had Abkhaz listed as their mother tongue (808 Russian, 5,878 other languages, including Kartvelian ones). Interestingly, 670 non-Abkhaz had Abkhaz listed as their mother tongue .

For the first time since emigration across the Black Sea petered out, we have strong out-migration of Abkhaz. 2,806 were registered outside Abkhazia, 1,608 of these inside Georgia, but already 1,198 elsewhere, compared to just 152 in 1937.

The All-Union Census of 1959

Between 1939 and the All-Union Census of (January 15th) 1959, the picture was again changed by force. Most of the Greeks (especially those, called Urum, who spoke Turkish) were collectively deported during the war, as were others, including some Abkhaz. Reclassification continued apace, sometimes influenced by fear of deportation. Thus, several Laz families reportedly escaped a cold war deportation in 1949 by passing themselves off as Abkhaz (communication by Wolfgang Feurstein); possibly some Greeks for similar reasons 'became' Georgians or Russians. In this period the Abkhaz (surpassed also by Armenians in 1959) were under immense pressure of Georgianisation, their cultural institutions being all but destroyed. We cannot here deal with sources mentioning Kartvelians being, often against their will, dumped in truckloads by Beria's henchmen in the Abkhazian countryside. The figures speak for themselves and bolster the reports: the rise of the Georgians cannot be explained by natural growth and the assimilation of some Abkhaz and possibly some Greeks; there must have been significant immigration as well. Numerically, there were *48,172 Kartvelians more in Abkhazia in 1959 than would be expected through natural growth since 1939, given that overall rates were similar.

	Abkhazia, 1939	Abkhazia, 1959	growth, Abkhazia	growth, USSR
12. 1959 census data (compared with 1939)[26]				
Population	311,885	404,738	29.8%	—
Georgians (all Kartvelians)	91,967	158,221	72.0%	19.7%
Russians	60,201	86,715	44.0%	14.6%
Armenians	49,705	64,425	29.6%	29.5%
Abkhaz	56,197	61,193	8.9%	10.9%
Greeks	34,621	9,101	−73.7%	8.0%

The All-Union Censuses of 1970, 1979 and 1989

The nearer we come to the present, the more there is consensus — albeit on the facts of demography only. We will thus treat the figures for (15 January) 1970, (17 January) 1979 and (12 January) 1989 together.[27]

13. Population of Abkhazia				
	1959	1970	1979	1989
Population	404,738	486,959	486,082	525,061
Georgians (all Kartvelians)	158,221	199,595	213,322	239,872
Abkhaz	61,193	77,276	83,097	93,267
Armenians	64,425	74,850	73,350	76,541
Russians	86,715	92,889	79,730	74,914
Greeks	9,101	13,114	13,642	14,664
Abkhaz diaspora outside	2,552	3,791	5,630	9,455
and inside Georgia	1,685	2,173	2,188	2,586
(of whom in Ajaria)	(1,157)	(1,361)	(1,508)	(1,636)

By 1979, immigration of Russians and Armenians had turned to net out-migration, offsetting natural growth and still heavy Kartvelian net immigration to result in an actual decline in overall population between 1970 and 1979. Abkhaz out-migration also accelerated; by 1989, only 88.6 per cent of all Soviet Abkhaz were living in Abkhazia. Outside Georgia, there were 7,239 in the RSFSR, 990 in the Ukraine, 333 in Kazakhstan, 163 in Azerbaijan, 149 in Belarus, 129 in Uzbekistan, 102 in Armenia, 90 in Latvia, 63 in Turkmenistan, 52 in Kirghizia, 51 in Moldova, 44 in Tajikistan, and 25 each in Estonia and Lithuania.[28]

A few words may be appropriate on linguistic assimilation. In 1989, of 105,308 Abkhaz 98,448 claimed Abkhaz as mother tongue, 5,135 admitted Russian and 1,725 named other languages. As this has to be taken with a grain of salt (the true extent of linguistic russification being certainly larger, if not dramatic), we refrain from going into detail; as for the present, reliable statistical data later than for 1989 are not available to me.

Conclusion

As stated at the outset, demography has many aspects. We hope to have proven this at least, if nothing else. If one deals with the ethno-demography of Abkhazia, it is not enough merely to state that Abkhaz

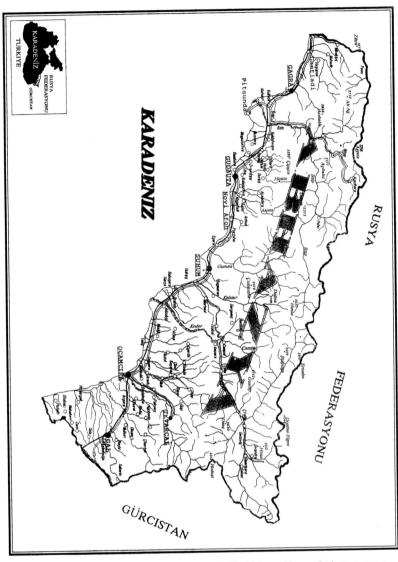

1990s map of Abkhazia from Turkey, with Turkish spellings of place names

numbered just 17.8 per cent of the population in 1989, whereas 'Georgians' numbered 45.7 per cent. Historical processes must be interpreted.

There are at least five (in themselves complex) phenomena to be studied: the net out-migration of Abkhaz; the immigration of Kartvelians (until the recent war); the assimilation of the intermediary group of Samurzaq'anoans, who may have been either Abkhaz or Mingrelians originally, by the Mingrelians; the inner-Kartvelian ideological georgianisation especially of the Mingrelians; and the movements (of bodies and minds) of other groups. While we have reasonably good studies for all processes, it is a comprehensive view on all phenomena that alone can help explain the bewildering data of canonical and non-canonical sources alike. We may refer to the fact that Greeks may at times have been counted with the Abkhaz (CC for 1917), at others partly with the 'Georgians' (1959).

Surely, the picture is not as simple as both sides, Georgians and Abkhaz alike, try to paint it, although the Abkhaz naturally have the stronger position, as no one in their right mind can deny the Abkhaz majority up to 1878.

The Samurzaq'anoan problem as the heart of the matter takes us to the limits of what ethno-demography, relying on official Russian sources, can achieve. Surely here another complementary approach, using all available sources in any language, but also (where still possible) methods of oral history, ought to be employed to augment our knowledge.

Offering a toast (a'nyhʷaṭs'a) is an integral part of Abkhazian feasting, though not always in a drinking horn ('aҫʷxla). Perhaps the toastmaster is saying: an'ҫʷa 'anasyp 'ʃʷitaajt' "May God grant you happiness!"

16
Ethnic culture
Jurij Anchabadze

The basic characteristics of the Abkhazians' ethno-cultural makeup bring them close to the mountain-peoples of the North Caucasus, especially to their Circassian relatives (Kabardians, Adyghes, Cherkess). At the same time long proximity to, and contacts with, the Transcaucasian peoples have introduced into the culture of the Abkhazians some original features which have become an integral part of their life and mentality. The Abkhazians' ethnic culture is conspicuous for its large number of traditions, preserving to the present day not a few archaic elements whose origins pre-date the Christian era. The Communist authorities fought persistently and methodically against Abkhazian traditionalism in an unsuccessful attempt to substitute the ethnographic realities of national life with 'progressive' Soviet innovations. However, the Abkhazians unfailingly adhered to their ancient traditions, instinctively fearing to lose along with them the very foundations of their ethnic identity.

Village life
Abkhazian national culture knows no sharp distinction between town and village. Urban traditions started developing in Abkhazia comparatively recently, and so differentiation in respective cultural standards have not occurred. Important too is the fact that the majority of urban Abkhazians have kept to the present day strong roots in the countryside: there they have their ancestral country-seat, and numerous kinfolk live there, whom they often have to visit. Additionally the insignificant distances separating Abkhazian villages from Sukhum, Gudauta, and Ochamchira render intercourse and mutual influence between town and country tight and constant.

The external appearance of Abkhazian villages is quite noteworthy. They are extraordinarily sparse, spread out, and bereft of any clear planning to boot. Houses, surrounded by gardens, vegetable-plots and arable areas stand at remote distances from one another, such that a foreign traveller might even not consider himself to be in the centre of a village at all rather than in some uninhabited territory. Ancient Abkhazian dwellings were wicker structures plaited from lissom twigs of hazel or rhododendron — compactness of wattling preserved warmth in winter and coolness in summer. From the end of the 19th century houses started to be made from wooden planks; according to the fashion in vogue at that time, a spacious verandah was run along the front of the house, the wooden elements of which were skilfully decorated with carving. From the 1950s wood was finally supplanted by more robust building-materials. However, when erecting new houses the Abkhazians did not abandon the construction of balconies along the facade, which is a distinguishing feature of their village-architecture. A further tradition was also preserved: in front of an Abkhazian house, which is usually situated in deep grounds, a

Shashlyk is as popular in Abkhazia as elsewhere in the Caucasus

capacious grass-lawn is always laid out. This not only serves an aesthetic purpose but is also the place for holding many ritual ceremonies, such as weddings, burials, meetings with honoured guests.

Working the land has long been the fundamental economic activity of the Abkhazians. The main grain crop, millet, was supplanted in the 18th century by maize, fields of which still occupy the main areas under tillage. In each Abkhazian homestead there is a vine and vegetable-plot with varying sets of cultivated vegetables and greens. The economic significance of the one-time most important sphere of cattle-breeding drastically declined in later times, although even today many Abkhazians keep, in the main, small horned cattle, which in summer they drive into high-mountain, alpine pastures. In the 20th century the Abkhazians developed the cultivation of tobacco, tea, and citrus fruits, with which they were occupied while working on the collective farms. However, as a result of destruction during the Georgian-Abkhazian war, these truly high-income spheres fell into decline and desolation. Hunting had great importance in olden times, replenishing significantly the food-rations of the family. Today hunting is nothing more than a favourite pastime for men.

Abkhazian food is distinguishable for its variety.[1] Pride of place is taken by a dish of boiled maize-flour known as *a'bysta* 'grits', which serves as both an everyday and ceremonial meal. Boiled beans (*a'q^w'yd*) are widely eaten. Of equal importance is milk, especially in the form of yoghurt, as are milk products, particularly cheeses, which are not only eaten on their own but also serve as the main ingredient in the preparation of a range of dishes. Among the meat ration of the Abkhazians one finds goat, which is specially esteemed for its tasty qualities, as well as beef, mutton and the meat of domestic fowl. A characteristic particularity of Abkhazian cuisine is the variety of bitter sauces and seasonings as well as *a'dʒyk'a*, a mixed paste consisting of ground chillies, garlic and other herbs.[2] The most popular drink is wine from grapes, whilst honey is the favourite sweet item. Abkhazian traditional cuisine has been preserved practically unchanged to our own day.

Dress,[3] on the other hand, has undergone quite an evolution. Its traditional forms were in large measure identical to the mountain-variant of Caucasian costume. Men wore the *cherkesska* (Abkhaz *ak^w'ym'ʒ^{w}y*). This tightly fitted the torso whilst fanning out freely in the lower part that reached the knees. Narrowing trousers were tucked into high, soft-leather boots. On the head they wore a shaggy woollen cap, or a 'bashlyk' (*axta/yr'pa*), a strip of woollen material bound up in a special way. Essential components of male dress were the belt (*ama'q'a*) and the dagger (*a'q'ama*), bereft of which it was impossible to appear out of doors. The cut of a woman's dress emphasised the waist. Over the bosom there was a low cut which was tightly closed with broad, silver fasteners.

The head was covered with a shawl, the ends of which rested on the shoulders. From a certain age girls began to wear a cloth-corset (*'ajlakɨ*). Preventing excessive development of the mammary glands, it shaped the bodily appearance of the future woman in accordance with traditional aesthetic standards. From the start of the 20th century active europeanisation of dress got underway, which led in practice to the complete expulsion of traditional styles from daily usage. Of the old ways there has remained only the habit of women to wear subdued, muffled, dark colours.

'Apswara

The fundamental constructive element in Abkhazian national culture is the concept of *'apswara*, which might be loosely rendered 'Abkhazianness', 'Abkhazian view of the world', 'Abkhazian ideology." Principally it is the code of unwritten moral, ethical, behavioural norms, the pursuance of which is prescribed by custom and general opinion. Conforming to the norms of *'apswara*, an Abkhazian can select the correct course of action in all of life's vicissitudes, for *'apswara* has broadly and voluminously accommodated within itself the rich variety and nuances of the socio-cultural relations at the centre of which an individual may find himself. These relations encompass even the world of nature, both flora and fauna, contacts with which, particularly in olden times, were also subject to the laws of *'apswara*. Finally, *'apswara* not only embodied behaviour but also stereotypes of thought, feelings and psychological reactions to common situations and circumstances.

The Abkhazian State Dance Troupe

Part of the concept of *'apswara* is the representation of the ideal person. Thus, a man must be honest, magnanimous, restrained in manifesting both positive and negative emotions, and a hospitable host. Highly valued of old were the ability to master a weapon and skill in horsemanship; it was also important that one have the reputation of being heroic and brave, although boasting of one's military exploits was deemed reprehensible. A woman had to be modest, affable, with the ability to get on with her numerous relatives, including those on the husband's side. The main requirement of a woman was chastity and virtue — frivolous behaviour and adultery met with universal and unreserved condemnation.

Clan solidarity is strongly developed in Abkhazian society. All persons bearing the same surname are considered relatives and to the best of their ability render help and support to one another, acting, when necessary, for the honour and interests of their representatives. Blood-feud might once have been the response to an insult — there was an example of this recorded as recently as the 1930s.[4] An offender is no longer killed, but even today an Abkhazian will not tolerate an affront to

Abkhazian dances are performed to the accompaniment of accordion and drums

his personal or familial dignity. Such cases are fraught with the danger of serious conflicts, into which the clans on both sides are usually drawn.[5]

Abkhazians place an especially high value on the honour of the family. In olden times family life was distinguished for its far-reaching patriarchal structure. Mutual relations within the household were subject to strict rules, chief amongst which were the set of restrictions imposed on communication between a family's daughter-in-law and the parents or elderly relatives of her husband. At the present time this practice of 'shunning' is virtually eradicated having been transformed into a restrained but specially deferential relationship between the daughter-in-law and her parents-in-law. Family-life is permeated also with the principle of honouring one's elders. According to this, the younger must always subordinate themselves to the older, even if the difference in age, for example between brothers, is a mere one or two years.

In the life of society this principle developed into the present cult of the aged. Persons belonging to old-age groups enjoyed in Abkhazian society unquestioned authority, respect, esteem, and a certain share of power. Even today in Abkhazia old age is wrapped in respect. The norms of etiquette associated with *'apswara* demand that the younger ones be courteous in the extreme towards the old: when they appear, the younger ones must greet them standing; it is impossible to sit down without their permission; when communicating with them it is essential

Preparation of bean-sauce (a'qʷ'ydchapara) at the traditional Abkhazian hearth (axʷyṣtaa'ra)

to observe a spatial distance. In the presence of the elderly a range of activities — smoking, loud laughter, slovenliness in posture and dress, etc — are not tolerated.

The rules of communion between the old and their juniors are only a part of the general moral complex that is *'apswara*, which in its traditional forms both spiritually and in concrete details resembled the courtly manners of European chivalry in the Middle Ages. The domestic life of the Abkhazians even today shows several ceremonial features. At times this gives rise to a number of inconveniences, but at the same time it wonderfully elevates and improves daily life. By way of an illustration of refined Abkhazian ceremonial one can adduce the etiquette of the table. This is thoroughly regulated by, and subordinated to, strict rules which vary depending on the occasion of the meal (wedding, memorial, in honour of an esteemed guest, etc), the age and social standing of the participants, the degree of mutual acquaintance, and

Aṭsyr'xʷmarra: a popular Abkhazian ball game played on horseback

many other factors, which makes it extremely difficult for the uninitiated to comprehend.[6]

The Abkhazians are very hospitable.[7] In ancient times welcoming a guest was almost the main event in the life of a family or even of a whole village, if an honoured guest, especially one from far away, visited a local resident. In those days the normal business of the household was, as it were, suspended, as everything was henceforth subordinated exclusively to the problem of entertaining, servicing and providing diversion for the guest. Even today Abkhazians love welcoming guests, viewing hospitality on the whole as an indivisible part of their ethnic culture and national character, the more so as here and there in Abkhazia the longstanding conviction is still preserved that the appearance of a guest in a house is a sign of the favourable disposition of the higher powers.

Abkhazian moral consciousness

Though the question of religion has already been addressed in another chapter, it needs to be re-emphasised that the religious tolerance and indulgence of the Abkhazians always surprised visiting travellers, who noted with amazement how they had been struck by the habit of the local residents of praying both in churches and in mosques as well as to their pagan deities. Religious pluralism is preserved among the Abkhazians even today. True, the influence of Islam at the present time is minimal (the main mass of Abkhazian Muslims having settled in Turkey as a result of the great exile at the end of the 19th century), but a peaceful synthesis of Orthodoxy and traditional pagan attitudes remains the fundamental element of the Abkhazians' religious sentiment. Furthermore, during the Georgian-Abkhazian war a strong revival of religiosity was noticeable among the Abkhazians. At one of the most baleful and unsuccessful periods of military activity a collective act of worship was conducted at the sacred mountain of Dydrypsh, whilst at that time the number of worshippers in Orthodox churches increased.

In general, the Georgian-Abkhazian war, which was a huge shock for Abkhazian society, exerted a massive influence on its moral consciousness. Faced with blatant aggression from Georgia, with attempts to destroy Abkhazia's national statehood, with cultural genocide, the Abkhazians in the darkest period began to seek spiritual support, including among the traditional, moral roots of their contemporary culture. This moral distinctiveness continues to be for Abkhazians' self-awareness an adequate proof of the independence of their own history and inalienable right to live in accordance with their own cultural standards. In defending itself and its land, the Abkhazian nation is striving to establish itself in the post-Soviet world as a full member of the modern international community, endowed with the self-same rights as other nations.

Further reading

Mountain range sections of the Abkhazia region

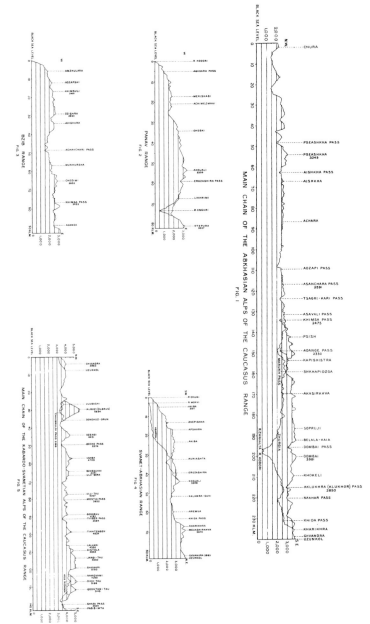

References
& general bibliography

The number of works dealing with Abkhazia in accessible languages is not large, and I hope that the bibliography attached to this volume omits no essential titles. Also listed there, of course, are some works referred to in the body of the book which are decidedly *not* recommended reading (such as Chervonnaya, 1994; or *Georgia: a report*, produced in January 1992 by the London-based NGO International Alert). Indeed, it would perhaps be more appropriate for this volume to have by way of epilogue a section entitled 'Further non-reading', given the amount of biased and/or uninformed material that has been produced in print or on the Internet about Abkhazia, Abkhazians or Abkhazian aspirations since most of the world was alerted to the existence of the country and its inhabitants, which happened for most people only with the war of 1992-93.

It is my hope that the 16 chapters in this volume will serve as a necessary corrective for anyone who may have come under the influence of such writings.

EDITOR

Abdokov, A., *K voprosu o geneticheskom rodstve abkhazsko-adygskikh i nakhsko-dagestanskikh jazykov* [On the genetic relationship of the Abkhazo-Adyghe and the Nakh-Daghestanian languages], Nal'chik, 1976.

Abdokov, A., *Vvedenie v sravnitel'no-istoricheskuju morfologiju abkhazsko-adygskikh i nakhsko-dagestanskikh jazykov* [Introduction to the comparative-historical morphology of the Abkhazo-Adyghean and Nakh-Daghestanian languages], Nal'chik, 1981.

Abdokov, A., *O zvukovykh i slovarnykh sootvetstvijakh severo-kavkazskikh jazykov* [On the phonetic and lexical correspondences of the North Caucasian languages], Nal'chik, 1983.

Abkhazija v tsifrakh [Abkhazia in figures], Sukhum, 1984.

Achugba, T. (ed.), *Ètnicheskaja 'revoljutsija' v Abkhazii: po sledam gruzinskoj periodiki XIXv.* [The ethnic 'Revolution' in Abkhazia: on the tracks of Georgian periodicals of the 19th century], Sukhum, 1995.

Adzhindzhal, E., *Iz istorii abkhazskoj gosudarstvennosti* [From the history of Abkhazian Statehood], Sukhum, 1996.

Adzhindzhal, I., *Iz ètnografii Abkhazii* [From the ethnography of Abkhazia], Sukhum, 1969.

Adzinba, I., *Arkhitekturnye pamjatniki Abkhazii* [Architectural monuments of Abkhazia], Sukhum, 1958.

Afanas'ev, K., *Sobor v Mokve i arkhitektura Kievskoj Rusi* [The cathedral at Mykʷ and the architecture of Kievan Rus], Moscow, 1968..

Agafij [Agathias], *O tsarstvovanii Justiniana* [On the reign of Justinian], Moscow, 1953.

Agrba, F., *Apswa Byzȷ̌ʷa Atyrkʷ Byzȷ̌ʷa A ȝʷar* [Abkhaz-Turkish dictionary], Istanbul, 1990.

AKAK, *Akty, sobrannye Kavkazskoj arkheograficheskoj komissiej* [Acts gathered by the Caucasian Archaeographical Commission], vols. 1-12, 1866-1904..

Akhobadze, V., *Abkhazskie pesni* [Abkhazian Songs], Moscow, 1957.

Al'bov, N., 'Resul'taty botanicheskikh issledovanij Abkhazii [Results of botanical research in Abkhazia]', in *Trudy S.-Pb. obshchestva estestvoispytatelej, t.23* [Works of the St Petersburg Society of Naturalists, vol. 23], 1893.

Allen, W. S., 'Structure and system in the Abaza verbal system', in *Transactions of the Philological Society (1956)*, 1956, pp 127-76.

Allen, W. S., 'On one-vowel systems', in *Lingua 13*, 1965, pp 111-24.

Amichba, G., *Abkhazija i Abkhazy v srednevekovykh gruzinskikh povestvovatel'nykh istochnikakh* [Abkhazia and the Abkhazians in Georgian narrative sources of the Middle Ages], Tbilisi, 1988.

Amkvab, G. & Ilarionova, T., *Abkhazija: khronika neob"javlennoj vojny* [Abkhazia: chronicle of an undeclared war], Moscow, 1992.

Anchabadze, Z., *Iz istorii srednevekovoj Abkhazii (VI-XVII v.v.)* [On the history of Abkhazia in the Middle Ages (sixth-17th centuries)], Sukhum, 1959.

Anchabadze, Z., *Istorija i kul'tura drevnej Abkhazii* [The history and culture of ancient Abkhazia], Moscow, 1964.

Anchabadze, Z., *Ocherk ètnicheskoj istorii abkhazskogo naroda* [Sketch of the ethnic history of the Abkhazian people], Sukhum, 1976.

Andrews, P., *Ethnic groups in the republic of Turkey*, Wiesbaden, 1989.

Apakidze, A. (ed.), *Didi P'it'iunt'i: arkeologiuri gatkhrebi bich'vint'ashi* [Great Pitiunt: archaeological excavations at Pitsunda], vols. 1-3, Tbilisi, 1975/77/78.

Arch'elia, A., *Apswa ӡᵂapq'akᵂa* [Abkhazian proverbs], Sukhum, 1986.

Ardzinba, V, 'Nekotorye skhodnye strukturnye priznaki khattskogo i abkhazo-adygskikh jazykov [Some parallel structural markers between the Hattic and Abkhazo-Adyghe languages]', in *Peredneaziatskij Sbornik. III. Istorija i filologija stran Drevnego Vostoka* [Asia Minor Collection. III. History and philology of the lands of the Ancient East], 1979, pp 26-37.

Ardzinba, V., 'K istorii kul'ta zheleza i kuznechnogo remesla (pochitanie kuznitsy u abkhazov) [On the history of the cult of iron and the smith's craft (adoration of the smithy among the Abkhazians)]', in *Drevnij Vostok: ètnokul'turnye svjazi* [The ancient East: ethnocultural links], Moscow, 1988.

Argᵂyn, I., *Iaxjatᵂ'i Apswaa Rybzazaʃei Rk'ult'urei* [The lifestyle and culture of today's Abkhazians], Aqᵂ'a, 1976.

Arrian Flavij [Arrian Flavius], *Peripl Ponta Èvksinskogo* [Voyage round the Pontic Euxine], See V. Latyshev *Izvestija drevnikh pisatelej grecheskikh i latinskikh o Skifii i Kavkaze. Latinskie pisateli. T.11, vyp.1* [Reports of ancient Greek and Roman writers on Scythia and the Caucasus. vol. 11, issue 1], St Petersburg, 1904.

Aryṣ-pha, N., *Araxᵂaadzaratᵂ' T'erminkᵂa Rӡᵂar* [Dictionary of animal husbandry terms], Sukhum, 1980.

Aryṣ-pha, N. and Nach'qj'ebia-pha, S., *Dyrmit' Gᵂylia jybyzʃᵂa Aӡᵂar* [Dictionary of Dmitri Gulia's Language], Sukhum, 1986.

Ascherson, N., *Black Sea*, London, 1995

Ashuba, B., Bushina, N., Gulija, A. and Lagvilava, R., *Problemy razvitija regional'nogo khozjajstvennogo kompleksa Abkhazskoj ASSR* [Problems of the development of the regional economic complex of the Abkhazian ASSR], Tbilisi, 1982.

Avaliani, S., *Krest'janskij vopros v Zakavkaz'e, t.2* [The peasant question in Transcaucasia, vol. 2], Odessa, 1913.

Avalov, Z., *Nezavisimost' Gruzii v mezhdunarodnoj politike, 1918-1921* [The independence of Georgia in international politics, 1918-1921], Paris, 1924.

Bakradze, Z., *Ist'oria sakartvelosi* [History of Georgia], Tbilisi, 1889.

Balkarov, V., 'Leksicheskie vstrechi adygskikh jazykov s dagestanskimi [Lexical parallels between Adyghean languages and those of Daghestan]', in *Uchenye Zapiski Kabardino-Balkarskogo Nauchno-Issledovatel'skogo Instituta, 20* [Scholarly Reports of the Kabardino-Balkarian Scientific-Research Institute, 20], 1964.

Balkarov, V., 'Adygo-vejnakhskie jazykovye vstrechi [Adyghe-Veinakh linguistic parallels]', in *Izvestija Checheno-Ingushskogo Nauchno-Issledovatel'skogo Instituta, 8, vyp.2* [Reports of the Chechen-Ingush Scientific Research Institure, 8, issue 2], 1966.

Barach, G., *Ryby presnykh vod Abkhazii: materialy k faune Abkhazii* [Abkhazia's freshwater fish: materials on the fauna of Abkhazia], Tbilisi, 1939.

Basarija, S., *Abkhazija v geograficheskom, ètnograficheskom i èkonomicheskom otnoshenii* [Abkhazia in relation to geography, ethnography and economics], Sukhum(-Kale), 1923.

Bebija, S. et al., *Pitsunda-Mjusserskij zapovednik* [The Pitsunda-Mjussera reserve], Moscow, 1987.

Bechhofer, C. E., *In Denikin's Russia and the Caucasus, 1919-1920*, London, 1921.

Benet, S., *Abkhasians: the long-living people of the Caucasus*, New York, 1974.

Beridze, Sh., *Megruli (Iveruli) ena* [The Mingrelian (Iberian) Language], Tbilisi, 1920.

Bgazhba, O., *Material'naja kul'tura srednevekovoj Abkhazii (VI-XIIIv.v.)* [The material culture of Abkhazia in the Middle Ages (sixth-13th centuries)], Avtoreferat, Moscow, 1972.

Bgazhba, O., *Ocherki po remeslu srednevekovoj Abkhazii (VIII-XIV)* [Essays on the handicrafts of Abkhazia in the Middle Ages (eighth-14th centuries)], Sukhum, 1977.

Bgazhba, O., *Po sledam kuznetsa Ajnara* [On the tracks of Smith Ajnar], Sukhum, 1982.

Bgazhba, O., *Chernaja metallurgija i metalloobrabotka v drevnej i srednevekovoj Abkhazii (VIIIv. do n.è. — XVv. n.è.)* [Ferrous metallurgy and metal-working in ancient and medieval Abkhazia (eighth century BC–15th century AD)], Tbilisi, 1983.

Bgazhba, O., *Istorija zhelezoobrabatyvajushchego proizvodstva v Zapadnom Zakavkaz'e (I tys. do n.è. — seredina II tys. n.è.)* [History of iron-forging production in Western Transcaucasia (first millennium BC–mid-second millennium AD)], Avtoreferat of Doctoral Dissertation, Moscow, 1994.

Bgazhba, Kh., *Bzybskij dialekt abkhazskogo jazyka* [The Bzyp dialect of the Abkhaz language], Tbilisi, 1964.

Bgazhba, Kh., *Russko-abkhazskij slovar'* [Russian-Abkhaz dictionary], Sukhum, 1964a.

Bgazhba, Kh., *Iz istorii pis'mennosti v abkhazii* [On the history of writing in Abkhazia], Tbilisi, 1967.

Bgazhba, Kh., *Ètjudy i issledovanija* [Studies and investigations], Sukhum, 1974.

Bgazhba, Kh., *Trudy — v 2-x tomakh* [Works — in 2 vols], Sukhum, 1987-88.

Bgazhba, Kh. & Salakaja, Sh., (eds.) *Ocherki istorii abkhazskoj literatury* [Essays on the history of Abkhazian literature], Sukhum, 1974.

Bghaჳʷba, M., *Ardʷyna A[ʷa Abʷojt'* [The blackbird sings], Sukhum, 1968.

Bghaჳʷba, M., *Apsydzkʷa* [Fish], Sukhum, 1977.

Bghaჳʷba, Kh., *Apswa ჳʷapq'akʷa* [Abkhazian proverbs], Sukhum, 1983.

Bigvava, V., *Obraz zhizni Abkhazskikh dolgozhitelej* [The lifestyle of Abkhazia's long-living people], Tbilisi, 1988.

Bihl, W., *Die Kaukasus-Politik der Mittelmächte. Teil II*, Vienna, 1992.

Bleichsteiner, R., 'Zum Protohattischen', in *Berichte des Forschungs-Institutes für Osten und Orient*, Bd.III, 102-106, 1923.

Braun, J., 'Khattskij i abkhazo-adygskij jazyki (èkskurs po tablitsam) [Hattian and Abkhazo-Adyghean languages (excursus by tables)]', in *The Nart epic and Caucasology*, Maikop, 1994, pp 352-357.

Braund, D., *Georgia in Antiquity: a history of Colchis and Transcaucasian Iberia 550 BC-AD 562*. Oxford, 1994.

Bronevskij, S., *Novejshie geograficheskie i istoricheskie izvestija o Kavkaze, ch, 1* [The latest geographical and historical reports on the Caucasus, part 1], Moscow, 1823.

Butba, V., *Plemena Zapadnogo Kavkaza po 'Ashkharatsujtsu' (sravnitel'nyj analiz* [The tribes of the Western Caucasus according to 'Ashkharatsujts' (comparative analysis)], Avtoreferat, Moscow, 1990.

Chachkhalia, D., 'Khronika abkhazskoi tserkvi [Chronicle of the Abkhazian Church]', in newspaper *Abkhazija*, 1 (29), 1994.

Chachkhalia, D., 'Khronika abkhazskoi tserkvi [Chronicle of the Abkhazian Church]', in newspaper *Abkhazija*, 2 (80), 1994a.

Chachkalia, D., *Abkhazskaja pravoslavnaja tserkov'* [The Abkhazian Orthodox Church], Moscow, 1997.

Chanba, R., *Zemledelie i zemel'nye otnoshenija v dorevoljutsionnoj Abkhazii* [Land division and land relations in pre-revolutionary Abkhazia], Tbilisi, 1977.

Chervonnaya, S., *Conflict in the Caucasus*, Glastonbury, 1994.

Chichurov, I., *Vizantijskie istoricheskie sochinenija: 'Khronografija' Feofana, 'Breviarij' Nikofora* [Byzantine historical works: Theophanis' 'Chronography', Nikophor's 'Breviary'], Moscow, 1980.

Chirikba, V., 'On the etymology of the ethnonym *áрҕwа* "Abkhaz"', in *The Annual of the Society for the Study of Caucasia*, 3, 13-18. Chicago, 1991.

Chirikba, V., *Common West Caucasian: the reconstruction of its phonological system and parts of its lexicon and morphology*. Leiden, 1996.

Chkhetija, Sh. (ed.), *Dokumenty po istorii Gruzii (1862-1917), t, 1, ch, 1* [Documents on the History of Georgia (1862-1917), vol, 1, part 1], Tbilisi, 1954.

Chumalov, M. (ed.), *Abkhazskij uzel: dokumenty i materialy po ètnicheskomu konfliktu v Abkhazii* [The Abkhazian Knot: documents and materials on the ethnic conflict in Abkhazia], Moscow, 1995.

Chursin, G., *Materialy po ètnografii Abkhazii* [Materials on the ethnography of Abkhazia], Sukhum, 1957.

Clem, R. (ed.), *Research guide to the Russian and Soviet censuses*, Ithaca, 1986.

Clogg, Richard, 'Abchasien und Georgien: Der vergessene Krieg', in *Pogrom. Zeitschrift für bedrohte Völker 178*, Aug/Sept, 37-39, 1994.

Clogg, Rachel, 'Documents from the KGB archive in Sukhum: Abkhazia in the Stalin years', in *Central Asian Survey 14, 1*, 155-189, 1995.

Dalgat, U., *Literatura i fol'klor* [Literature and Folklore], Moscow, 1981.

Danilov, S., 'Tragedija abkhazskogo naroda [The tragedy of the Abkhazian people]', in *Vestnik Instituta po Izucheniju Istorii i Kul'tury v SSSR* [Herald of the Institute for the Study of History and Culture in the USSR], 1, Munich, 1951.

Darsalia, V., *Abkhazskaja proza 20-60-x godov* [Abkhazian prose in the years 1920-60], Tbilisi, 1980.

Dbar, D., *Iz istorii abkhazskogo katolikosata* [On the history of the Abkhazian Catholicosate], Moscow, 1997.

Demokraticheskoe pravitel'stvo Gruzii i anglijskoe komandovanie [The democratic government of Georgia and the British Command], Tbilisi, 1928.

Denikin-Judenich-Vrangel' [Denikin-Judenich-Wrangel], Moscow-Leningrad, 1927.

Diakonoff [Diakonov], I. & Starostin, S., *Hurro-Urartian as an Eastern Caucasian language*, Munich, 1986.

Diakonov, I., *Jazyki drevnej Perednej Azii* [The languages of Ancient Asia Minor], Moscow, 1967.

Diakonov, I., *Predistorija armjanskogo naroda* [The prehistory of the Armenian people], Erevan, 1968.

Djubua de Monperè, F. [Dubois de Montpéreux, François], *Puteshestvie vokrug Kavkaza, t, 1* [Journey around the Caucasus, vol, 1], Sukhum, 1937.

Dobrynin, B., *Terrasy Abkhazii: uchenyj zapiski MGU, vyp.5* [Abkhazia's terraces: scientific reports of Moscow State University, issue 5], 1936.

Dokumenty i materialy po vneshnej politike Zakavkaz'ja i Gruzii [Documents and materials on the foreign policy of Transcaucasia and Georgia], Tbilisi, 1919.

Dubljanskij, V. & Iljukhin V., *Krupnejshie karstovye peshchery i shakhty SSSR* [The largest karstal caves of the USSR], Moscow, 1982.

Dubrovin, N., *Istorija vojny i vladychestva russkikh na Kavkaze, tt.I & VI* [History of the war and dominion of the Russians in the Caucasus, vols. 1 & 6], St Petersburg, 1871 & 1888.

Dumaa, K., *Nositel' jashika pandory* [The bearer of Pandora's Box], Sukhum, 1995.

Dumézil, G., *Etudes comparatives sur les langues caucasiennes du nord-ouest (morphologie)*, Paris, 1932.

Dumézil, G., *Introduction à la grammaire comparée des langues caucasiennes du Nord*, Paris, 1933.

Dumézil, G., *Documents anatoliens sur les langues et les traditions du Caucase, III: Nouvelles Etudes Oubykh*. Paris, 1965.

Dumézil, G., *Documents anatoliens sur les langues et les traditions du Caucase, V: Etudes Abkhaz*. Paris, 1967.

Dunaevskaja, I., 'O strukturnom skhodstve khattskogo jazyka s jazykami severo- zapadnogo Kavkaza [On the structural resemblance of the Hattic language with the languages of the north-west Caucasus]', in *Issledovanija po istorii kul'tury narodov Vostoka: Sbornik v chest' akademika I. A. Orbeli* [Researches on the history of the culture of the Oriental peoples: collection in honour of Academician I. A. Orbeli], Moscow-Leningrad, 1960, pp 73-77.

Dzhanashia, S., 'O vremenii i uslovijakh vozniknovenija Abkhazskogo tsarstva [On the time and conditions of the development of the Abkhazian Kingdom]', in *Shromebi 2* [Works 2], Tbilisi, 1952, pp 322-41.

Dzhavakhishvili, I., *Kartveli eris ist'oria, 1* [History of the Georgian people, 1], Tbilisi, 1960 [1913].

Dzhavakhishvili, I., *Kartuli da K'avk'asiuri enebis tavdap'irveli buneba da natesaoba* [The original nature and kinship of the Georgian and Caucasian languages], Tbilisi, 1937.

Dzhonua, B., 'K khronologii Kartvelizmov v Abkhazskom jazyke [On the chronology of Kartvelianisms in the Abkhaz language]', in Hewitt, 1992c, 1992, pp 240- 43.

Dzidzarija, G., *Bor'ba za Abkhaziju v pervom desjatiletii XIX veka* [The battle for Abkhazia in the first decade of the 19th century], Sukhum, 1940.

Dzidzarija, G., *Narodnoe khozjajstvo i sotsial'nye otnoshenija v Abkhazii v XIX veke* [The national economy and social relations in Abkhazia in the 19th century], Sukhum, 1958.

Dzidzarija, G., *Makhadzhirstvo i problemy istorii Abkhazii XIX stoletija* [The exile and problems of the history of Abkhazia in the 19th century], Sukhum, 1975.

Dzidzarija, G., Shinkuba, B. & Shakryl, K., 'V tsentral'nyj komitet vsesojuznoj kommunisticheskoj partii (bol'shevikov) [To the Central Committee of the All-Union Communist Party (of Bolsheviks)]', in B. Sagarija, T. Achugba, & V. Pachulija (eds.), 1992, 1992, pp 531-36.

Dzidzarija [Dzaria], O., *Morskaja leksika v Abkhazskom jazyke* [Sea-vocabulary in the Abkhaz language], Sukhum, 1989.

Èjkhenbaum, B., *O proze, o poèzii* [On prose, on poetry], Leningrad, 1986.

Erckert, R. von, *Die Sprachen des kaukasischen Stammes*. Leipzig, 1895.

Ermolov, A., *Zapiski* [Notes], Moscow, 1991.

Èsadze, B., *Letopis' Gruzii. Jubilejnyj sbornik k 300-letiju tsarstvovanija Doma Romanovykh — derzhavnykh pokrovitelej gruzinskogo naroda, 1613-1913, vyp, 1* [Chronicle of Georgia. Jubilee-Collection for the 300-year Tsardom of the House of the Romanovs — Ruler-protectors of the Georgian nation, 1613-1913, issue 1], Tbilisi, 1913.

Èsadze, B., *Pokorenie Zapadnogo Kavkaza i okonchanie Kavkazskoj vojny* [The subjugation of the Western Caucasus and the end of the Caucasian War], Tbilisi, 1914.

Fadeev, A., *Rossija i Kavkaz pervoj treti XIX v.* [Russia and the Caucasus in the first third of the 19th century], Moscow, 1960.

Fedorov, J., *Istoricheskaja ètnografija Severnogo Kavkaza* [The historical ethnography of the North Caucasus], Moscow, 1983.

Fejzba, Ja., *Èkonomicheskie osobennosti ispol'zovanija trudovykh resursov Abkhazii* [The economic particularities of utilising Abkhazia's labour resources], Sukhum, 1988.

Fernández-Armesto, F. (ed.), *The Times guide to the peoples of Europe*, 1994. Paperback-edition 1997.

Forrer, E., 'Die acht Sprachen der Boghazköy-Inschriften', in *Sitzungsberichte der Preussischen Akademie der Wissenschaften, Phil.-hist. Klasse*, Nr. LIII, 1029-1041, 1919.

Freshfield, D., *The Exploration of the Caucasus*, 2 vols., 2nd. edition, London, 1902.

Gachechiladze, R., 'Geographical and historical factors of state building in Transcaucasia', in Stephen Jones (ed.), 1996, 1996, pp 24-36.

Garb, P., *Where the young are old: long life in the Soviet Caucasus*, Palo Alto, 1987 (published in Russian as *Dolgozhiteli* [The long-lived ones], Moscow, 1986).

Giorgadze, G., 'K voprosu o lokalizatsii i jazykovoj strukture kaskskix ètnicheskix i geograficheskikh nazvanij [On the question of the localisation and linguistic structure of the Kaskian ethnic and geographic names]', in *Peredneaziatskij Sbornik: Voprosy khettologii i khurritologii* [Asia Minor Collection: Questions of Hittitology and Hurritology], Moscow, 1961.

Gordeziani, R., *Kavkaz i problemy drevnejshikh sredizemnomorskikh jazykovykh i kul'turnykh vzaimootnoshenij* [The Caucasus and problems of the oldest Mediterranean linguistic and cultural mutual relations], Tbilisi, 1975.

Grossgejm, A., *Rastitel'nyj pokrov Kavkaza* [The vegetative cover of the Caucasus], Moscow, 1948.

Gulia, D., *Apswa ӡʷapq'ak^wei, atsufarak^wei, aӡʷartstsak't^wk^wei, aomonimk^wei, aomografk^wei, ӡʷlar amҭҁ^wg'a eilk'aashas irymowi, amts xats'arak^wei, at^wh^wak^wei reizga* [Collection of Abkhaz proverbs, riddles, tongue-twisters, homonyms and homographs, folk bad weather predictions, folk-beliefs, and spells], Sukhum, 1939. (In Georgian script; reprinted as part of vol. 5 of Gulia's *Collected Works* in 6 volumes, 1985, in Cyrillic script. Parts first published in Cyrillic in 1907, others in Georgian script in 1939.)

Gulija, Ch., *Zemlepol'zovanie v Abkhazii* [Land-use in Abkhazia], Sukhum, 1972.

Gunba, M., *Atarskie goncharnye pechi* [The pottery ovens of Atara], Tbilisi, 1985.

Gunba, M., *Abkhazija v pervom tysjacheletii nashej èry* [Abkhazia in the first millennium of our era], Sukhum, 1989.

Gvozdetskij, N., *Fizicheskaja geografija Kavkaza. Kurs lektsij, vyp, 1* [The physical geography of the Caucasus: lecture-course, issue 1], Moscow, 1954.

Harvey, Mrs. (of Ickwell Bury), *Turkish harems & Circassian homes*, London, 1871.

Henze, P. B., 'Circassian resistance to Russia', in M. Bennigsen Broxup (ed.) *The North Caucasus barrier: the Russian advance into the Muslim World*, London, 1992.

Hewitt, B. G., *Lingua Descriptive Studies 2: Abkhaz (in collaboration with Z. K. Khiba)*. Amsterdam, 1979. Since published by Croom Helm and also Routledge.

Hewitt, B. G., '"Savsed q'opnis" gamokhat'va ramdenime K'avk'asiur enashi (k'erdzod Megrulshi) [The representation of 'to be full' in some Caucasian languages (especially Mingrelian)]', in *P'irveli saertashoriso Kartvelologiuri simp'oziumis masalebi* [Materials of the First International Kartvelological Symposium], Tbilisi, 1988, pp 119-27.

Hewitt, B. G., 'Einige kaukasische Ausdrücke für "voll sein"', in *Georgica 11*, 1989a, pp 22-23.

Hewitt, B. G., 'Abkhaz', in B. G. Hewitt (ed.), 1989d, 1989b, pp 37-88.

Hewitt, B. G., 'Aspects of language planning in Georgia (Georgian and Abkhaz)', in M. Kirkwood (ed.), *Language Planning in the Soviet Union*, London, 1989c, pp 123-144.

Hewitt, B. G. (ed.), *The Indigenous Languages of the Caucasus 2: North West Caucasus*, New York, 1989d.

[Hewitt, B. G.], '"Guests" on their own territory', published anonymously in *Index on Censorship*, 19, 1, pp 23-25, 1990.

Hewitt, B. G., 'Languages in contact: a Transcaucasian example', in *Zeitschrift für Sprachwissenschaft und Kommunikationsforschung (ZPSK)*, 44.3, 1991, pp 295-300.

Hewitt, B. G., 'Languages in contact in N. W. Georgia: fact or fiction?', in G. Hewitt (ed.), 1992c, 1992a, pp 244-58.

Hewitt, B. G., 'Another case of the influence of Abkhaz on Mingrelian syntax?', in C. Paris (ed.), 1992, 1992b, pp 405-9.

Hewitt, (B.) G. (ed.), *Caucasian Perspectives*, Unterschleissheim, 1992c.

Hewitt, B. G., 'The valid and non-valid application of philology to history', in *Revue des Etudes Géorgiennes et Caucasiennes, 6-7, 1990-1991*, 247-263, 1993a.

Hewitt, B. G., 'Abkhazia: a problem of identity and ownership', in *Central Asian Survey, 12.3, 1993*, 1993b, pp 267-323. See also J. Wright, S. Goldenberg & R. Schofield (eds.) *Transcaucasian Boundaries*, UCL Press, 1997, pp 190-225.

Hewitt, B. G., 'Peoples of the Caucasus', in F. Fernández-Armesto (ed.), 1994, pp 366-84. Paperback 1997.

Hewitt, B. G., 'Demographic manipulation in the Caucasus', in *The Journal of Refugee Studies*, 8, 1, 1995a, pp 48-74.

Hewitt, B. G., 'Yet a third consideration of *Völker, Sprachen und Kulturen des südlichen Kaukasus*', in *Central Asian Survey, 14.2*, 1995b, pp 285-310.

Hewitt, B. G., 'A suggestion for Romanizing the Abkhaz alphabet (based on Monika Höhlig's *Adighe Alfabet*)', in BSOAS, LVIII, 1995c, pp 334-40.

Hewitt, B. G., 'Appendix to "Documents from the KGB archive in Sukhum. Abkhazia in the Stalin years (Central Asian Survey, 14, 1, 1995, pp 155-189)"', in *Central Asian Survey, 15.2*, 259-297, 1996.

Hewitt, B. G., 'Post-war developments in the Georgian-Abkhazian dispute', to appear in *Contrasts and solutions in the Caucasus*, eds. Sefa Yürükel & Ole Høiris, Aarhus University Press, forthcoming a.

Hewitt, B. G. 'Abkhaz', in A. Harris & R. Smeets (eds.), *The languages of the Caucasus*, Curzon, forthcoming b.

Hewitt, B. G. & Khiba, Z. K., *An Abkhaz newspaper reader*, Dunwoody Press, 1997a.

Hewitt, B. G. & Khiba, Z. K., 'Male dress in the Caucasus (with special reference to Abkhazia and Georgia)', in N. Lindisfarne-Tapper & B. Ingham (eds.), 1997b.

Ierusalimskaja, A., *Velikij shelkovyj put' i Severnyj Kavkaz* [The Great Silk Road and the North Caucasus], Leningrad, 1972.

Inal-Ipa, Sh., *Abkhazy* [The Abkhazians], Sukhum, 1965.

Inal-Ipa, Sh., *Voprosy ètno-kul'turnoj istorii abkhazov* [On the ethno-cultural history of the Abkhazians], Sukhum, 1976.

Inal-Ipa, Sh., *Apkhazuri mts'erloba gushin da dghes* [Abkhazian literature yesterday and today], Tbilisi, 1978.

Inal-Ipa, Sh., *Ocherki ob abxazskom ètikete* [Observations on Abkhazian etiquette], Sukhum, 1984.

Inal-Ipa, Sh., *Sadzy* [The Sadzians], Sukhum, 1995.

Ioanidi, N., *Greki v Abkhazii: ocherki istorii grecheskogo naselenija Abkhazskoj ASSR* [Greeks in Abkhazia: essays on the history of the Greek population of the Abkhazian ASSR], Sukhum, 1990.

Iskander, F., *Sandro iz Chegema* [Sandro of Chegem], Moscow, 1991. (English version currently available from Faber & Faber, trans. Susan Brownsberger, 1993.)

Ivanov, V., 'Ob otnoshenii xattskogo jazyka k severo-zapadno-kavkazskim [On the relationship of Hattic with North West Caucasian]', in *Drevnjaja Anatolija* [Ancient Anatolia], Moscow, 1985, pp 26-59.

Janashia [Dzhanashia], N., 'The religious beliefs of the Abkhasians', in *Georgica: A Journal of Georgian and Caucasian Studies*, vols. 4 & 5, 1937, pp 117-53.

Jones, S. (ed.), *Caucasian Regional Studies*, 1, 1996.

K'aslandzia, V., *Apswa byzⱡʷa asinonimkʷa jaazyrk'atṣ'u rʒʷar* [Short dictionary of the synonyms of the Abkhaz language], Sukhum, 1981.

K'aslandzia, V., *Anemets-Apswa frazeologiat^w' z^war* [German-Abkhaz phraseological dictionary], Tbilisi, 1985.

K'aslandzia, V., *Apswa byz{^{w}a afrazeologiat^w' z^war — akt^w'i ax^{w}ra: A-F* [Phraseological dictionary of the Abkhaz language – first part: A-F], Aq^w'a, 1989.

Katsija, R., *Ital'janskie kolonii na Chernomorskom poberezh'e Kavkaza i ikh vzaimootnoshenija s mestnym naseleniem (konets XIII-XV v.v.)* [Italian colonies on the Black Sea littoral of the Caucasus and their mutual relations with the local population (end of 12th to 15th century)], Avtoreferat, Moscow, 1986.

Khagba, V., *Agressija gruzii i mezhdunarodnoe pravo* [Georgian aggression and international law], Gagra, 1995.

Khalbad, T., *Alingvistik'at^w' t'ermink^{w}a rz^war* [Dictionary of linguistic terms], Sukhum, 1977.

Khalbad, T., *Autratyxaaryxrat^w' t'erminologiat^w' z^war* [Terminological dictionary of vegetable-growing], Sukhum, 1980.

Khashba, I., *Abkhazskie narodnye muzykal'nye instrumenty* [Abkhazian folk musical instruments], Sukhum, 1979.

Khiba, Z., 'A contribution to Abkhaz lexicography: the secret language of the hunters', in *Bedi Kartlisa: Revue de Kartvélologie, 38*, 1980, pp 269-77.

[Khiba, Z.], *Ioann iq'ynt^w' az^wa bzia* [Good News from John = The Gospel according to St. John], translated from Russian and published anonymously by the Institute for Bible Translation, Stockholm, 1981. Translations of the remaining Gospels, 'Life of Jesus' and a children's Bible remain unpublished.

Khiba, Z., 'An Abkhazian's response', in *Index on Censorship, 19.5*, 30-31, 1990.

Khrushkova, L., *Skul'ptura rannesrednevekovoj Abkhazii V-X vv.* [Sculpture of early medieval Abkhazia in the fifth-tenth centuries], Tbilisi, 1980.

Khrushkova, L., 'O religioznykh verovanijakh apsilov (IV-VI c.c.) [On the religious beliefs of the Apsilians (fourth-sixth centuries)', in *Izvestija Abkhazskogo Instituta Jazyka, Literatury i Istorii, t.XII* [Reports of the Abkhazian Institute of Language, Literature and History, vol. 12], 76-87, 1983.

Khrushkova, L., *Tsandripsh; materialy po rannesrednevekovomu stroitel'stvu v Abkhazii* [Tsandripsh: materials on early medieval building in Abkhazia], Sukhum, 1985.

Kilba, È., *Osobennosti rechi batumskikh abkhazov* [Particularities of the speech of the Batumi Abkhazians], Tbilisi, 1982.

Klimov, G., *Vvedenie v kavkazskoe jazykoznanie* [Introduction to Caucasian linguistics], Moscow, 1986.

Kolakovskij, A., *Flora Abkhazii, tt. I-IV* [The flora of Abkhazia, vols. 1-4], 1938-49.

Kolakovskij, A., 'Osnovnye fitolandshafty primorskoj nizmennosti juzhnoj Abxazii [The main phyto-landscapes of southern Abkhazia's coastal depression]', in *Trudy Tbilisskogo bot. instituta, t.XII* [Works of the Tbilisi Botanical Institute, vol. 12], 1948.

Kopeshavidze, G., *Abkhazskaja kukhnja* [Abkhazian cuisine], Sukhum, 1989.

Kudrjavtsev, K., *Materialy po istorii Abkhazii* [Materials on the history of Abkhazia], Sukhum, 1926.

Kuftyreva, N., Lashkhija, Sh. & Mgeladze, I., *Priroda Abkhazii* [The natural world of Abkhazia], Sukhum, 1961.

Kuznetsov, V,. *Zodchestvo srednevekovoj Alanii* [Architecture of medieval Alania], Ordzhonikidze, 1977.

Kvarchija, V., *Zhivotnovodcheskaja (pastusheskaja) leksika v Abkhazskom jazyke* [The vocabulary of animal-husbandry (shepherding) in the Abkhaz language], Sukhum, 1981.

Kvarchija, V., *Èkonomika sel'skogo khozjajstva Respubliki Abkhazija* [The economics of the rural economy of the Republic of Abkhazia], Sukhum, 1995.

K'vit'ashvili, M., 'Teiranis k'onperentsia [The Teheran Conference]', in *Lit'erat'uruli Sakartvelo, 37, 38, 39* [Literary Georgia, 37, 38, 39], Sept 14, 21, 28, 1990.

Lakoba, S., *Krylilis' dni v Sukhum-Kale* [Winged days in Sukhum-Kale], Sukhum, 1988.

Lakoba, S., *Ocherki politicheskoj istorii Abkhazii* [Essays on the political history of Abkhazia], Sukhum, 1990.

Lakoba, S., 'On the political problems of Abkhazia', in *Central Asia and Caucasus Chronicle*, 9, 1, 16-18, 1990a.

Lakoba, S. (ed.), *Istorija Abkhazii* [History of Abkhazia], Sukhum, 1991 [2nd edn, Gudauta, 1993].

Lakoba, S., *Stoletnjaja vojna Gruzii protiv Abkhazii* [The Hundred Year War of Georgia against Abkhazia], Gagra, 1993.

Lakoba, S., 'Abkhazia is Abkhazia', in *Central Asian Survey*, 14, 1, 1995, pp 97-105.

Lavrov, L., 'Dol'meny Severo-Zapadnogo Kavkaza [The dolmens of the north-west Caucasus]', in *Trudy AbIJLI*, XXXI [Works of the Abkhazian Institute of Language, Literature and History, 31], Sukhum, 1960.

Lejberov, I., *Rossija, Kavkaz, Abkhazija: istoricheskie stat'i i ocherki* [Russia, the Caucasus, Abkhazia: historical articles and essays], St Petersburg, 1995.

Lekvinadze, V., 'Pontijskij limes [The Pontic frontier]', in *Vestnik Drevnej Istorii, 2* [Herald of Ancient History, 2], Moscow, 1969.

Lezhava, G., *Izmenenie klassovo-natsional'noj struktury naselenija Abkhazii (konets XIX v.—70-e g.g. XX v.)* [Change to the class-national structure of the population of Abkhazia (end of the 19th-seventies of the 20th century)], Sukhum, 1989.

Lindisfarne-Tapper, N. & Ingham, B. (eds.), *Languages of Dress in the Middle East*, Curzon, London, 1997.

Loginov, V., *Keramika i keramicheskoe proizvodstvo Abkhazii v pozdneantichnoe i rannevizantijskoe vremja (II-VII vv n.è.)* [Ceramics and the ceramic industry of Abkhazia in late Antiquity and early Byzantine times (second-seventh centuries AD)], Avtoreferat of Candidate Thesis, Moscow, 1987.

Lomtatidze, K. & Klychev, R., 'Abaza', in B. G. Hewitt (ed.), 1989d, 1989, pp 89-154.

Mach['javariani, K['], *Opisatel'nyj putevoditel' po gorodu Sukhumu i Sukhumskomu okrugu* [Descriptive guide to the city of Sukhum and the Sukhum district], Sukhum, 1913.

Malija, E., *Narodoe izobrazitel'noe iskusstvo abkhazov (tkani, vyshivka)* [Folk fine art of the Abkhazians (fabrics, embroidery)], Tbilisi, 1970.

Malija, E. & Akaba, L., *Odezhda i zhilishche Abkhazov* [Clothing and dwellings of the Abkhazians], Tbilisi, 1982.

Maq'ashvili, A., *Bot'anik'uri leksik'oni* [Botanical dictionary], Tbilisi, 1949.

Markovin, V., *Dol'meny Zapadnogo Kavkaza* [The dolmens of the Western Caucasus], Moscow, 1978.

Marr, N., 'On the religious beliefs of the Abkhasians', in *Georgica: A Journal of Georgian and Caucasian Studies*, vols. 4-5, 1937, pp 157-80.

Marr, N., *O jazyke i istorii abkhazov* [On the language and history of the Abkhazians], Moscow-Leningrad, 1938.

Marykhuba, I. (ed.), *Abkhazija v sovetskuju èpokhu: Abkhazskie pis'ma (1947- 1989). Sbornik dokumentov, tom 1* [Abkhazia in the Soviet epoch: Abkhazian letters (1947-89). Collection of Documents, vol. 1], Nal'chik, 1994.

Melikishvili, G., *K istorii drevnej Gruzii* [On the history of ancient Georgia], Tbilisi, 1959.

Melikishvili, G., *Urartskie klinoobraznye nadpisi* [Urartian cuneiform inscriptions], Moscow, 1960.

Melikishvili, G., *Politicheskoe ob"edinenie feodal'noj Gruzii i nekotorye voprosy razvitija feodal'nykh otnoshenij v Gruzii* [The political unification of feudal Georgia and some questions of the development of feudal relations in Georgia], Tbilisi, 1973.

Mikaia, Dzh., *Apswa byz\u{j}ʷa arts'agatʷ' ȝʷar* [Pedagogical dictionary of the Abkhaz language], Sukhum, 1985.

Nach'qj'ebia-pha, S., *Apswa byz\u{j}ʷa aomografkʷa r ȝʷar* [Dictionary of the homographs of the Abkhaz language], Sukhum, 1988.

Nadareishvili, T., *Genotsid v Abkhazii* [Genocide in Abkhazia], Tbilisi, 1996.

Nekrasov, V. (ed.), *Berija: konets kar'ery* [Beria: end of a career], Moscow, 1991.

Nikolaev, S. L. & Starostin, S. A., *A North Caucasian etymological dictionary*, Moscow, 1994.

Novosel'tsev, A., *Genezis feodalizma v stranakh Zakavkaz'ja* [The genesis of feudalism in the countries of Transcaucasia], Moscow, 1980.

Overeem, P., 'Report of a UNPO coordinated human rights mission to Abkhazia and Georgia', in *Central Asian Survey, 14, 1*, 1995, pp 127-54.

Palgrave, W., *Essays on Eastern Questions.* London, 1872.

Paris, C. (ed.), *Caucasologie et mythologie comparée*, Actes du Colloque international du CNRS — IVe Colloque de Caucasologie (Sèvres, 27-29 juin), 1992.

Petermann, A. (ed.), *Geographische Mittheilungen (Gotha)*, 26, 1880.

Petermann, A. (ed.), *Geographische Mittheilungen (Gotha)*, 43, 1897.

Plinij Starshij [Plinius Major], *Estestvennaja istorija* [Naturalis Historia], in 5 vols, 1870-98.

Potto, V,. *Utverzhdenie russkogo vladychestva na Kavkaze, t.III, ch.II* [Confirmation of Russian rule in the Caucasus, vol. 3, part 2], Tbilisi, 1904.

Procopij iz Kesarii [Procopius Caesariensis], *Vojna s gotami* [War with the Goths], Moscow, 1950.

Q'aukhchishvili, S. (ed.), *Kartlis Tskhovreba I, II, IV* [Life of Kartli (= Georgia) 1, 2, 4], Tbilisi, 1955/1959/1973.

Rcheulishvili, L., Nekotorye aspekty gruzinskoj arkhitektury Chernomorskogo poberezh'ja [Some aspects of Georgian architecture on the Black Sea coast], in *Srednevekovoe iskusstvo. Rus'. Gruzija* [Medieval art: Russia, Georgia], Moscow, 1978.

Russell, J., *The Georgians: a Minority Rights' Group update*, London, 1991.

Rybinskij, G., *Sukhumskij okrug: Abkhazija v sel'skokhozjajstvennom i bytovom otnoshenii* [The Sukhum district: Abkhazia in relation to village economy and way of life], Tbilisi, 1894.

Sagarija, B., *Natsional'no-gosudarstvennoe stroitel'stvo v Abkhazii (1921-1931)* [National state building in Abkhazia (1921-31)], Sukhum, 1970.

Sagarija, B., *O "belykh" i "chernykh" pjatnakh v istorii Abkhazii* [On the "white" and "black" spots in the history of Abkhazia], Gagra, 1993.

Sagarija, B., Achugba, T. & Pachulia, V., *Abkhazija: dokumenty svidetel'stvujut 1937-1953* [Abkhazia: documents bear witness 1937-53], Sukhum, 1992.

Sakhok'ia, T., *Mogzaurobani* [Travels], Batumi, 1985.

Samandzhia, L,. *Apswa byz]ʷa aomonimkʷa rʒʷar* [Dictionary of the homonyms of the Abkhaz language], Sukhum, 1987.

Satunin, K., *Fauna Chernomorskogo poberezh'ja Kavkaza: trudy obshchestva izuchenija Chernomorskogo poberezh'ja Kavkaza, t.2* [The fauna of the Caucasus Black Sea coast: works of the Society for the Study of the Caucasus Black Sea Coast, vol. 2], St Petersburg, 1913.

Schuchardt, H., 'Zur Geographie und Statistik der kharthwelischen (südkaukasischen) Sprachen', in A. Petermann, 1897.

Seidlitz, N. von, 'Ethnographie des Kaukasus', in A. Petermann, 1880, 340- 347, 1880.

Severnyj Kavkaz [The North Caucasus], September 1937, no. 41., Warsaw.

Shagirov, A., *Ètimologicheskij slovar' adygskikh (cherkesskikh) jazykov, I, II* [Etymological dictionary of the Adyghean (Circassian) languages, 1 & 2], Moscow, 1977.

Shakryl, K. & Kondzharija, V., *Apswa byz]ʷa aʒʷar* [Dictionary of the Abkhaz language], 2 vols., Sukhum, 1986.

Shamba, G., *Axat]t]arxʷ — drevnij mogil'nik nagornoj Abkhazii* [Axat]t]arxʷ — the ancient burial-ground of mountainous Abkhazia], Sukhum, 1970.

Shamba, G., *Èsherskie kromlekhi* [The Esheran cromlechs], Sukhum, 1980.

Shamba, G., *Raskopki drevnikh pamjatnikov Abkhazii* [Excavations of the ancient monuments of Abkhazia], Sukhum, 1985.

Shamba, G., *Apsny arkheologiatʷ' baq'akʷa* [The archaeological monuments of Abkhazia], Aqʷ'a, 1988.

Shamba, O. & Fejzba, Ja., *Sredstva proizvodstva Respubliki Abkhazija v uslovijakh perekhoda k rynochnoj èkonomike* [The Republic of Abkhazia's means of production in the conditions of moving to a market economy], Sukhum, 1995.

Sharija, V. (ed.), *Abkhazskaja tragedija* [The Abkhazian Tragedy], Sochi, 1994.

Shervashidze, G., 'Tak pishetsja istorija [Thus is history written]', in newspaper *Zakavkaz'e* [Transcaucasia], *June 5th, 6th*, 1910.

Shervashidze, L., *Izobrazitel'noe iskusstvo v Abkhazii za 40 let Sovetskoj vlasti* [Fine art in Abkhazia during 40 years of Soviet power], Tbilisi, 1961.

Shervashidze, L., *Srednevekovaja monumental'naja zhivopis' v Abkhazii* [Medieval monumental painting in Abkhazia], Tbilisi, 1980.

Shynkʷba, B. (ed.), *Nart Sasryqʷ'ei pḻynjʷa ʒʷi ze ʒʷjʷyk iara iaᶘtćʷei. Apswa ʒʷlar rep'os* [Nart Sasryqʷ'a and his 99 brothers: the national epic of the Abkhazian people], Aqʷ'a, 1962.

Slider, D., 'Crisis and response in Soviet nationality policy: the case of Abkhazia', in *Central Asian Survey*, 4.4, 1985, pp 51-68.

Smyr, G., *Islamskij faktor v Abkhazii i na Severnom Kavkaze* [The Islamic factor in Abkhazia and the North Caucasus], Gagra, 1994a.

Smyr, G., *Religioznye verovanija abkhazov (istoricheskaja èvolutsija i osobennosti)* [The religious beliefs of the Abkhazians (Historical evolution and particularities)], Gagra, 1994b.

Solov'ev, L., *Pamjatniki kamennogo veka abkhazii* [Monuments of Abkhazia's Stone Age], Tbilisi, 1987.

Spruit, A., *Abkhaz Studies*, doctoral publication, Holland, 1986.

Starostin, S., 'Kul'turnaja leksika v obshche-severno-kavkazskom slovarnom fonde [Cultural lexics in the Common North Caucasian lexical fond]', in *Drevnjaja Anatolija* [Ancient Anatolia], 74-94, 1985.

T'ap'aghʷywa, Dzh., *Apswa byzᶘʷa atćʷa ʒʷaratʷ' wyrok'kʷa* [Abkhaz language conversational lessons], Aqʷ'a, 1973.

Taracha, P., 'Zum Stand der hattischen Studien: Möglisches und Unmöglisches in der Erforschung des Hattischen', in *Atti del II Congresso Internazionale di Hittitologia a curo di Onofrio Carruba — Mauro Giorgieri — Clelia Mora. Studia mediterranea. 9. Iuculano Editore*, Pavia, 1995, pp 351-58.

Tardy, L., 'The Caucasian peoples and their neighbours in 1404', in *Acta Orientalia Academiae Scientiarum Hung. Tomus XXXII (1)*, 1978, pp 83-111.

Tarnava, M., *Kratkij ocherk istorii Abkhazskoj tserkvi* [A short sketch of the history of the Abkhazian Church], Sukhum, 1917.

Toria, Y. (ed.), *Pitsunda conference: the role of international organizations in the process of post-conflict peace building in Abkhazia*, Sukhum, 1996.

Tornau, F., *Vospominanija kavkazskogo ofitsera, ch.I-II* [Reminiscences of a Caucasian officer, pts. 1-2], Moscow, 1864.

Trapsh, M., *Drevnij Sukhumi. Trudy II* [Ancient Sukhum: works 2], Sukhum, 1969.

Trapsh, M., *Kul'tura Tsebel'dinskikh nekropolej* [The culture of the Tsebeldan Nekropoleis], in *Trudy v 4-kh tomakh, t.III* [Works in 4 volumes, vol. 3], Tbilisi, 1971.

Trigo, L., 'Abkhaz stress shift', in G. Hewitt (ed.), 1992c, 1992, pp 191-235.

Trubetzkoy, N., 'Les consonnes latérales des langues caucasiennes septentrionales', in *Bulletin de la Société de Linguistique de Paris*, t.23, fasc.3 (no.72), 1922, pp 184-204.

Trubetzkoy, N., 'Nordkaukasische Wortgleichungen', in *Wiener Zeitschrift für Kunde des Morgenlandes*, Bd. XXXVII, heft 1-2, 1930, pp 76-92.

Tsulaja, G., *Abkhazija i abkhazy v kontekste istorii Gruzii (domongol'skij period)* [Abkhazia and the Abkhazians in the context of the history of Georgia (Pre-Mongol period)], Moscow, 1995.

Tsvinarija, I., *Novye pamjatniki dol'mennoj kul'tury Abkhazii* [New monuments of Abkhazia's dolmen culture], Tbilisi, 1990.

Tsvinarija, V., *Abkhazskoe stikhoslozhenie* [Abkhazian versification], Sukhum, 1987.

Tugov, V., *Abazinsko-russkij slovar'* [Abaza-Russian dictionary], Moscow, 1967.

Tylecote, R., *A history of metallurgy*. London, 1976.

Uslar, P., *Ètnografija Kavkaza: Jazykoznanie — Abkhazskij jazyk* [Ethnography of the Caucasus: Linguistics – the Abkhaz language], Tbilisi, 1887.

Uturashvili, I., *Dimit'ri Q'ipiani*, Tbilisi, 1989.

Vereshchagin, A., *Istoricheskij obzor kolonizatsii Chernomorskogo pribrezh'ja Kavkaza* [Historical survey of the colonisation of the Black Sea coast of the Caucasus], St Petersburg, 1885.

Vereshchagin, N., 'Zoogeograficheskoe rajonirovanie Kavkaza [Zoo-geographical regionalisation of the Caucasus]', in *Zhivotnyj mir SSSR, t.5* [The animal world of the USSR, vol. 5], Moscow-Leningrad, 1958, pp 506-14.

Voejkov, A., *Osadki Chernomorskogo poberezh'ja Kavkaza: doklady XIII s"ezda russkikh estestvoispytatelej i vrachej* [Precipitations of the Caucasus Black Sea coast: reports of the 13th Meeting of Russian Naturalists and Doctors], 1914.

Vorob'ev, N., *O neosnovatel'nosti pritjazanij gruzin na Sukhumskij okrug (Abkhaziju)* [On the groundless claim of the Georgians to the Sukhum District (Abkhazia)], Rostov-on-Don, 1919.

Voronov, L., *Abkhazija — ne Gruzija* [Abkhazia is not Georgia], Moscow, 1907.

Voronov, Ju., *Arkheologicheskaja karta Abkhazii* [Archaeological map of Abkhazia], Sukhum, 1969.

Voronov, Ju., *Tajna Tsebel'dinskoj doliny* [Mystery of the Ts'ebelda Valley], Moscow, 1975.

Voronov, Ju., *V mire arkhitekturnykh pamjatnikov Abkhazii* [In the world of the architectural monuments of Abkhazia], Moscow, 1978.

Voronov, Ju., *Dioskuriada — Sebastopolis — Tskhum* [Dioskuriada — Sebastopolis — Tskhum], Moscow, 1980.

Voronov, Y [Ju.]., 'Review of Mariam Lordkipanidze's "The Abkhazians and Abkhazia" (in Georgian, Russian and English), Tbilisi, 1990, *Ganatleba* (75pp)', in G. Hewitt (ed.), 1992c, 259-264.

Voronov, Ju., *Abkhazy — kto oni?* [The Abkhazians — who are they?], Gagra, 1993.

Voronov, Ju. 1985. Iskusstvo apsilov: 1. keramika; 2. ukrashenie; 3. arkhitektura [Art of the Apsilians: 1. ceramics; 2. decoration; 3. architecture], in *Apsny Aq'azara*, 4, 5, 6 [Art of Abkhazia, 4, 5, 6] respectively.

Voronov, Ju. & Bgazhba, O., *Glavnaja krepost' Apsilii* [The main fortress of Apsilia], Sukhum, 1986.

Voronov, Ju. & Bgazhba, O., 'Krepost' Tsibilium — odin iz uzlov kavkazskogo limesa justinianovskoj èpokhi [The fortress of Tsibilium — one of the hubs of the Caucasian frontier of the Justinian epoch]', in *Vizantijskij Vremennik, 48* [Byzantine Chronicler, 48], Moscow, 1987.

Voronov, Ju., Florenskij, P. & Shutova, T., *Belaja kniga Abkhazii: dokumenty, materialy, svidetel'stva, 1992-1993* [The White Book of Abkhazia: documents, materials, eye-witness reports, 1992-1993], Moscow, 1993.

Vvedenskij, A., Abkhaztsy (azega). Po povodu sochinenija g. Dubrovina 'Ocherk Kavkaza i narodov ego naseljajushchikh', *Sbornik svedenij o Kavkazskikh gortsakh, vyp.VI* [The Abkhazians (Azega). In connection with Dubrovin's work 'Essay on the Caucasus and the People who Inhabit it', *Collection of Testimonies on the Caucasian Mountaineers, issue VI*], Tbilisi, 1872.

Yagan, M., *I come from behind Kaf Mountain*, Vermont, 1984.

Yagan, M., *The Caucasian book of longevity and well-being*, Vermont, 1988.

Zhirov, Kh. & Èkba, N., *Russko-abazinskij slovar'* [Russian-Abaza dictionary], Moscow, 1956.

Zhordanija, N., *Moja zhizn'* [My life], Stanford, USA, 1968.

Zvanba, S., *Ètmograficheskie ètjudy* [Ethnographical essays], Sukhum, 1955.

Appendices

Appendix 1

Constitution of the Abkhazian People's Soviet

Adopted at an Assembly of the Abkhazian People
(November 8th 1917)

1. The Abkhazian People's Soviet is a national-political organisation uniting the Abkhazian people.
2. The Abkhazian People's Soviet represents and expresses the will of the Abkhazian people in relations with governmental and administrative departments and with socio-political organisations.
3. The Abkhazian People's Soviet is responsible primarily to the Abkhazian people personified by a general assembly.
4. The aims of The Abkhazian People's Soviet are:
   a. the defence and strengthening of the now won revolution; the political education and organisation of the popular masses; the struggle against anarchy and counter-revolution;
   b. the defence of the national and cultural-economic interests and the political rights of the Abkhazian people;
   c. preparatory work for the self-government for the Abkhazian people;
   d. supporting and strengthening the Abkhazian people's link with the Union of Caucasian Mountaineers, and putting into effect the political slogans, resolutions and measures of the Central Committe of the Union;
   e. work on current questions demanding the manifestation of the will of the Abkhazian people.
5. The District Committee, commissars and other administrative departments and persons reserve for themselves the former functions of government, but the work and activity of all administrative and other departments and persons — insofar as this work and activity concerns Abkhazia — must be conducted in contact with The Abkhazian People's Soviet in the interests of achieving fruitful results.
6. The Abkhazian People's Soviet recognises the power and competence of relevant administrative departments and socio-political organisations to the extent that the principles of democracy and self-determination of the nation are observed by these departments and organisations.
7. For the purpose of safeguarding the interests of national minorities, questions affecting the interests of others must be decided either by the District Committee or by a general assembly of the region or by an assembly of interested parties.
8. The Abkhazian People's Soviet shall have its own representatives in the District Committee and, as may be required, in remaining places of administrative and socio-political organisations.
9. The Abkhazian People's Soviet must put into effect the resolutions adopted by the General Assembly of the Abkhazian people.
10. The Soviet will give an account of its activity to the General Assembly of the Abkhazian people.
    Note. While demonstrating personal initiative on current questions and on questions demanding immediate decisions, the People's Soviet is nevertheless obliged to give an account to the Assembly of its activity also regarding these questions.

11. The Soviet shall have the right of co-optation, but co-opted members until they are approved by the General Assembly shall have only an advisory voice.

12. The Soviet shall select from its membership a presidium consisting of a chairman, three deputy-chairmen, a secretary and treasurer. The presidium shall then be approved by the General Assembly.

13. As may be necessary, the Soviet shall select from its membership sub-committees to deal with different special questions: for example, questions on schools, religion, finance, land and other matters.
    Note. In the work of these sub-committees, apart from their members other persons invited by the Soviet may also take part.

14. Half of the general number of the members of the Soviet (including the chairman) shall be deemed to form a quorum, and decisions shall be carried by a simple majority vote.
    Note. In the case of a tie the chairman shall have the casting vote.

15. The Soviet must itself compose the detailed mandate and charter of its internal regulations without deviating from the general paths noted in the declaration and constitution adopted by the Assembly.

16. All members individually and the People's Soviet as a whole accept the obligation to take the declaration and constitution as basis for their own activity.

President of the Assembly: Simon Basaria.
Secretaries: Tsaturia, Alania, and Tarnava.
Speaker: Sheripov.
Adopted 8 November 1917 in the city of Sukhum.
(Newspaper *Vpered* 'Forward', no. 146, 8 December 1917).

Appendix 2

Draft treaty (1992)

The following is a translation of the draft-treaty of alliance between Abkhazia and Georgia, which was drawn up by the Abkhazian T'aras M. Shamba (Doctor of Law) in the summer of 1992. The original Russian text may be consulted on page 2 of the newspaper 'Abkhazia' (23) for the week June 29th–July 4th 1992.

TREATY
on the Principles for Mutual Relations between the Republic of Abkhazia
and the Republic of Georgia
(Proposal for the Project)

In accordance with the Declaration of the State Sovereignty of Georgia and the State Sovereignty of Abkhazia, until the adoption of new Constitutions, the official delegations of both republics, hereafter referred to as *The Sides*, have as a result of talks agreed to the following:

1. The Sides declare their wish to:
    strengthen the mutual respect and friendship of the Georgian and Abkhazian peoples;
    develop the socio-economic and cultural ties;
    expand co-operation into all spheres of life on equal and mutually beneficial conditions;
    strictly observe human rights and liberties, including the rights of national minorities;
    prohibit hostility and international discord, use of force or threat to use force;
    refrain from interference in each other's internal affairs;
    respect territorial integrity;
    cater for the satisfaction of national, cultural, spiritual, linguistic and other

requirements of all the peoples living on the territory of Georgia and Abkhazia.

2. The Sides recognise Georgia and Abkhazia as sovereign states and full and equal participants of international and foreign economic relations, as well as agreements with other republics and regions of the Russian Federation and the other members of the Commonwealth of Independent States.

The Sides shall independently conclude treaties and agreements with other countries, which should not cause damage or be directed against the other Side.

3. The Republic of Abkhazia of its own free will unites with the Republic of Georgia and possesses all legislative, executive and judicial power on its own territory apart from those plenary powers which are assigned by the Constitutions of Georgia and Abkhazia to the jurisdiction of the Republic of Georgia.

In the Constitutions are listed those plenary powers which are effected jointly by the organs of state-power of Georgia and Abkhazia.

4. The territory and status of the two sovereign states cannot be changed without their consent, expressed by their supreme organs of government or by a plebiscite (referendum).

5. The land, its mineral wealth, waters, flora and fauna are the property of the peoples living on the territory of Abkhazia.

Questions concerning the possession, use and exploitation of the natural resources are regulated by the laws of Georgia and Abkhazia and also are settled on the basis of bilateral agreements.

6. The governmental bodies of the Republic of Abkhazia shall take part in the realisation of the plenary powers of the Republic of Georgia and have their own representation in its organs of power.

7. On questions of joint-authority the organs of governmental power shall issue the Fundamentals (general principles) of the legislative system in accordance with which the organs of power of Abkhazia shall independently effect legal regulation.

Projects for the Fundamentals of the legislative system shall be sent to Abkhazia, and her suggestions shall be taken into account when they are revised.

8. The Constitution and laws of Abkhazia shall enjoy supremacy on the territory of the Republic of Abkhazia.

The laws of Georgia in matters which are under the jurisdiction of the Republic of Georgia are mandatory on the territory of Abkhazia, provided they do not contradict the Constitution and laws of Abkhazia.

The Fundamentals for the legislative system of Georgia, issued on questions of joint-management, shall come into power on the territory of Abkhazia after their approval by the supreme organs of state-power of the Republic of Abkhazia.

9. The Republic of Georgia recognises the citizenship of the Republic of Abkhazia.

The Sides guarantee to their citizens equal rights, liberties and responsibilities, declared by the Universal Declaration of Human Rights and reflected in international-judicial acts and in the Constitutions of Georgia and Abkhazia.

Discrimination on the basis of national identity, religion or any other difference is prohibited.

Each Side shall protect the rights of its citizens irrespective of the place of their residence or sojourn, providing them with comprehensive help and support. In this the Sides shall co-operate with each other.

Matters concerning the acquisition or loss of citizenship of one of the Sides by persons living on the territory of the other Side are regulated by the laws of citizenship of Georgia and Abkhazia.

10. The Sides confirm the agreement reached previously concerning the creation on the territory of Abkhazia of the unified multi-national Abkhazian Guard, subordinated to the Supreme Council of Abkhazia and, at times of general threat to or attack upon them, to the Ministry of Defence of Georgia.

The Sides commit themselves not to create any military formations on nationality lines and directed against the other Side.

11. In case of disputes the Sides commit themselves conscientiously and in the spirit of co-operation to make every effort to settle them in the shortest possible time on the basis

of legislation actually in force or, in the absence of such legislation, on the basis of the principles and norms of international law.
The procedure for the settlement of disputes shall be determined by the Sides arising out of the prevailing circumstances.

12. The Abkhazian Side declares its readiness to participate in the drawing up of a new Constitution for the Republic of Georgia and the constitutional laws resulting therefrom. The Georgian Side regards this declaration with understanding and considers the participation of the representatives of the Republic of Abkhazia as well as the representatives of the other nations and peoples residing on the territory of Georgia essential in the drawing up of the new Constitution and constitutional laws of the Republic of Georgia.

13. The Sides have agreed to have permanent plenipotentiary representations — the Republic of Georgia in the city of Sukhum, the Republic of Abkhazia in the city of Tbilisi.

14. The Sides do not exclude the possibility of additional inter-parliamentary, inter-governmental or other treaties and agreements concerning specific questions of co-operation and mutual relations between the Sides.

15. The present Treaty comes into effect from the moment of signing and remains in force up to the formation of new supreme organs of state-power and governance in the Republic of Georgia, after which the process of negotiation shall be continued.

Appendix 3
Moscow Agreement
(April 4th 1994)

Translation of the Agreement signed in Moscow on 4th April 1994
"Declaration on measures for a political settlement of the Georgian/Abkhaz conflict"

1. The third round of negotiations on a comprehensive settlement of the Georgian-Abkhaz conflict took place from 22 to 25 February 1994 in Geneva, from 7 to 9 March 1994 in New York and from 29 to 31 March in Moscow under the aegis of the United Nations with the facilitation of the Russian Federation and with the participation of representatives of the Conference on Security and Co-operation in Europe (CSCE) and the United Nations High Commissioner fro Refugees (UNHCR).

2. The negotiations were held in accordance with Security Council resolutions 849 (1993) of 9 July 1993, 854 (1993) of 6 August 1993, 858 (1993) of 24 August 1993, 876 (1993) of 19 October 1993, 881 (1993) of 4 November 1993, 892 (1993) of 22 December 1993, 896 (1994) of 31 January 1994, 901 (1994) of 4 March 1994 and 906 (1994) of 25 March 1994.

3. By signing this declaration, the parties hereby commit themselves to a strict formal cease-fire from this date and also reaffirm their commitment to the non-use of force or threat of the use of force against each other as expressed in the Communiqué of 13 January 1994.

4. The parties have agreed to and signed a quadripartite agreement, a copy of which is attached to the present Declaration, on the repatriation of refugees/displaced persons. The agreement provides for the return of refugees/displaced person in accordance with existing international practice, including the practice of UNHCR.
A special commission on refugees/displaced persons, which shall include representatives of the parties, UNHCR, the Russian Federation, and CSCE in an observer capacity, shall begin its work in Sochi in mid April 1994. The implementation of the agreement will begin upon the deployment of a peace-keeping force.

5. The parties reaffirm their request for the early deployment of a peace-keeping operation and for the participation of a Russian military contingent in the United Nations peace-keeping force, as stated in the Memorandum of Understanding of 1 December

1993 and the Communiqué of 13 January 1994. The plan for carrying out the peace-keeping operation will be agreed upon with the parties to the conflict.

The realization of the peace-keeping operation should also promote the safe return of refugees/displaced persons.

The parties again appeal to the United Nations Security Council to expand the mandate of the United Nations Observer Mission in Georgia (UNOMIG).

6. Abkhazia shall have its own Constitution and legislation and appropriate state symbols, such as anthem, emblem and flag.

7. The parties held discussions on distribution of powers on the understanding that any agreement on this issue is part of a comprehensive settlement and will only be reached once a final solution to the conflict has been found.

At this stage, the parties have reached mutual understanding regarding powers for joint action in the following fields:

a) Foreign policy and forging economic ties;

b) Border guard arrangements;

c) Customs;

d) Energy, transport and communication;

e) Ecology and elimination of the consequences of natural disasters;

f) Ensuring human and civic rights and freedoms and the rights of national minorities.

8. The parties agree to continue energetic efforts to achieve a comprehensive settlement.

The parties will set up an appropriate committee, which will work on a standing basis, taking into account the decisions of the Security Council under the chairmanship of the United Nations, with participation of representatives of the CSCE and the Russian Federation and with the involvement of international experts. This body will meet alternatively in Moscow and Geneva. Its first meeting will be held in Geneva on 19 April 1994. A phased action programme will be worked out and proposals on the reestablishment of state- and legal relations will be elaborated.

9. The parties decided to take additional measures in connection with the search for missing persons and the reburial of the dead.

10. The parties, based on the fact that there is no statute of limitations applicable to war crimes, agreed to intensify efforts to investigate war crimes, crimes against humanity and serious criminal offences as defined by international and national law and bring the perpetrators to justice.

Inevitable punishment shall also be inflicted on persons who try or will try to undermine the peace process in Abkhaz by resorting to arms.

For the Georgian side: A. Kavsadze;
For the Abkhaz side: S. Dzhindzholia;
From the United Nations: E. Brunner;
From the Russian Federation: B. Pastukhov;
From the Conference on Security and Co-operation in Europe: A. Manno.
Moscow, 4 April 1994

Appendix 4

Quadripartite Agreement on Voluntary Return of Refugees & Displaced Persons (Annex II)

Signed on 4 April 1994
(Official English Version)

The Abkhaz and Georgian sides, hereinafter referred to as the Parties, the Russian Federation and the United Nations High Commissioner for Refugees,
Recalling Security Council resolutions 849 (1993) of 9 July 1993, 854 (1993) of 6 August

1993, 858 (1993) of 24 August 1993, 876 (1993) of 19 October 1993, 892 (1993) of 22 December 1993, 896 (1994) of 31 January 1994, 901 (1994) of 4 March 1994 and 906 (1994) of 25 March 1994,

Recognizing that the right of all citizens to live in and to return to their country of origin is enshrined in the Universal Declaration of Human Rights and the International Covenant on Civil and Political Rights,

Noting conclusions 18 (XXXI) and 40 (XXXVI) of the Executive Committee of the Programme of the Office of the United Nations High Commissioner for Refugees, which constitute internationally agreed principles governing the repatriation of refugees,

Acting in accordance with the Memorandum of Understanding signed by the Parties on 1 December 1993 and especially paragraph 4, under which Parties expressed their willingness to create conditions for the voluntary, safe and dignified return of displaced persons to their permanent places of residence in all regions of Abkhazia,

Recalling that resolution 428 (V) of 14 December 1950, by which the General Assembly of the United Nations adopted the statute of the Office of the United Nations High Commissioner for Refugees, ascribes to the High Commissioner the function of providing international protection to refugees and of seeking permanent solutions for the problems of refugees, *inter alia*, by promoting and facilitating their voluntary repatriation,

Given the responsibility entrusted to the United Nations High Commissioner for Refugees to act, under the Secretary-General's authority, as the international lead agency for the repatriation of displaced persons to Abkhazia,

Noting the desire of the Parties to co-operate with each other to achieve full observance of the principles and safeguards governing voluntary repatriation,

Considering the need, therefore, to establish a framework to define modalities of such co-operation for implementation of the repatriation,

Noting that the Parties agree that a repatriation operation to Abkhazia will imply, prior to its implementation, that the security and living conditions in the areas of return are guaranteed,

HAVE AGREED ON THE FOLLOWING PROVISIONS:

1. The Parties agree to co-operate and to interact in planning and conducting the activities aimed to safeguard and guarantee the safe, secure and dignified return of people who have fled from areas of the conflict zone to the areas of their previous permanent residence.
2. For the purpose of the present agreement, the Parties will guarantee the safety of refugees and displaced persons in the course of the voluntary repatriation and rehabilitation operations to be organized.
3. In implementing this voluntary repatriation programme, the Parties undertake to respect the following principles:
   (a) Displaced persons/refugees have the right to return voluntarily to their places of origin or residence irrespective of their ethnic, social or political affiliation under conditions of complete safety, freedom and dignity;
   (b) The voluntary character of the repatriation shall be ascertained and respected through appropriate arrangements;
   (c) Displaced persons/refugees shall have the right to return peacefully without risk of arrest, detention, imprisonment or legal criminal proceedings.
   Such immunity shall not apply to persons where there are serious evidences that they have committed war crimes and crimes against humanity as defined in international instruments and international practice as well as serious non-political crimes committed in the context of the conflict. Such immunity shall also not apply to persons who have previously taken part in the hostilities and are currently serving in armed formations, preparing to fight in Abkhazia.
   Persons falling into these categories should be informed through appropriate

channels of the possible consequences they may face upon return;

(d) The Parties shall ensure that returnees, upon return, will enjoy freedom of movement and establishment including the right to return to the areas where they lived prior to leaving the conflict zone or to the area of their choice;

(e) The Parties shall ensure that refugees and displaced persons, upon return, will get their expired documents (*propiska*, passport) extended and validated for their previous place of residence or the elected place of return;

(f) The Parties shall ensure that repatriants, upon return, will be protected from harassment, including unauthorized charges or fees and threat to life and property;

(g) Returnees shall, upon return, get back movable and immovable properties they left behind and should be helped to do so, or to receive whenever possible an appropriate compensation for their lost properties if return of property appears not feasible.

The Commission mentioned in paragraph 5 below will establish a mechanism for such claims. Such compensation should be worked out in the framework of the reconstruction/rehabilitation programmes to be established with a financial assistance through the United Nations Voluntary Fund;

(h) Displaced persons/refugees who choose not to return to Abkhazia shall continue to be assisted and protected until acceptable alternative solutions are found for such cases;

(i) In accordance with the fundamental principle of preserving family unity, where it is not possible for families to repatriate as units, a mechanism shall be established for their reunification in Abkhazia. Measures shall also be taken for the identification and extra care/assistance for unaccompanied minors and other vulnerable persons during the repatriation process;

(j) The Parties agree that refugees and displaced persons will be guaranteed unimpeded access to all available information on the situation in the areas where repatriation will take place. Such an information should be provided in the framework of a campaign to be launched by the Commission as mentioned in paragraph 9 (b) below.

4. For the purpose of the implementation of voluntary return of displaced persons and refugees to Abkhazia, a quadripartite Commission is hereby established.

5. The principal tasks of the Commission shall be to formulate, discuss and approve plans to implement programmes for the safe, orderly and voluntary repatriation of the refugees and displaced persons to Abkhazia from Georgia, the Russian Federation and within Abkhazia, and for their successful reintegration. Such plans should include registration, transport, basic material assistance for a period of up to six months and rehabilitation assistance.

In order to create the conditions for the return of refugees and displaced persons, the Commission will establish a working group of experts to undertake an assessment of the level of damage to the economic and social infrastructure in Abkhazia, the availability of housing and the extent of damage to houses in the areas of return as well as the projected needs in rehabilitation/reconstruction, with financial implications. This survey should be undertaken region by region according to the plan of return to be worked out and accepted by the Parties, bearing in mind that the Parties have agreed to start the repatriation operation with the Gal[i] Region.

6. The Commission shall be composed of four members, one being designated by each of the Parties and two representing the Russian Federation and the United Nations High Commissioner for Refugees.

In addition, the Conference on Security and Co-operation in Europe (CSCE) will designate a representative to attend the Commission's meetings in an observer capacity. If circumstances do not allow the designated CSCE representative to attend such meetings, the Commission will keep the CSCE mission in Georgia informed on a regular basis on the progress of the Commission's work.

7. Any member of the Commission may, when attending any meeting of the Commission, be accompanied by such advisers as the Party designating that member may deem necessary. Where a member of the Commission is unable to attend any meeting of the Commission, the Party concerned may designate a substitute.
8. The Commission shall meet as often as required, but no less frequently than once every month. Meetings of the Commission may be convened at the request of any of the members and shall be held on the territory of the Russian Federation, except as the members of the Commission may otherwise agree. The Parties agree to guarantee the personal security of the members of the Commission and personnel involved in the activities agreed.

   The first meeting of the Commission shall be scheduled as soon as possible and no later than one week after the adoption by the Security Council of a resolution on a mechanism ensuring the security conditions in the areas of return.
9. During its first meeting, the Commission will set out the modalities of the assessment mentioned in paragraph 5 above and will establish a plan concerning:
   (a) The areas where repatriation will be primarily conducted according to the level of guaranteed security and preparedness;
   (b) The implementation of an information campaign among the displaced person/refugee population to encourage voluntary return;
   (c) The registration process of persons expressing their willingness to return;
   (d) The activities needed to safeguard the safety of returnees based on the principles set out in paragraph 3 (a) to (j) above;
   (e) The needs for financial, transport and basic material assistance to displaced persons/refugees as well as projected needs of rehabilitation/reconstruction of the areas of return as mentioned in paragraph 5 above.
10. The Parties agree that representatives of refugees and displaced persons shall be provided with facilities to visit the areas of return and to see for themselves arrangements made for their return.
11. In the event of disagreement within the Commission regarding the application and interpretation of this Agreement, where such disagreement cannot amicably be settled among the members of the Commission, the Commission shall refer such disagreements to the Parties and to the Russian Federation and the United Nations High Commissioner for Refugees.

THE PARTIES, THE RUSSIAN FEDERATION AND THE UNITED NATIONS HIGH COMMISSIONER FOR REFUGEES FURTHER AGREE AS FOLLOWS:

(a) UNHCR shall have direct and unhindered access to all displaced persons/refugees from Abkhazia in order to undertake activities essential to the discharge of its mandate and operational and monitoring responsibilities;
(b) Travel shall be facilitated between and within all areas where refugees and displaced persons are located and areas of return for the personnel of the United Nations and other relevant international and non-governmental agencies co-operating with the United Nations in repatriation, reintegration and rehabilitation programmes. It shall include the free use of airspace and authorized airstrips and airports for relief flights and the exemption from taxes and duties of all goods imported for use in the voluntary repatriation programmes of displaced persons/refugees from Abkhazia and for the provision of relief integration and rehabilitation assistance to the Abkhazian region by the United Nations and co-operating agencies, as well as the expeditious clearance and handling of such goods;
(c) The Russian Federation will guarantee unimpeded transit of humanitarian supplies through its territory for the purposes of the present Agreement;
(d) UNHCR shall establish local offices, as deemed appropriate, at locations to be approved by the Parties concerned, to facilitate voluntary repatriation, reintegration and rehabilitation;

(e) The security of the staff and property of the United Nations and the co-operating agencies shall be guaranteed;

(f) The allocation and continued use by the Parties, the United Nations and the co-operating agencies of particular designated radio frequencies for radio communication between their offices, vehicles, and staff, in areas where refugees and displaced persons are located and in areas of return, shall be provided.

This agreement shall enter into force with immediate effect and shall remain in force for the period required for the effective voluntary return of the displaced persons/refugees.

In witness whereof, the authorized representatives of the Abkhaz and Georgian sides, the Russian Federation and the United Nations High Commissioner for Refugees, have signed the present agreement.

Done at Moscow, this fourth day of April 1994 in four originals, three in the Russian language, and one in the English language, the four texts being equally authentic but the English text being authoritative for interpretation purposes.

For the Abkhaz side: S. Jinjolia [Dzhindzholia]
For the Georgian side: A. Kavsadze
For the Russian Federation: B. Pastukhov
For the United Nations High Commissioner for Refugees: J. Amunategul

Appendix 5

Selected proverbs & vocabulary items in semantic fields

Proverbs

'adʒma z'tɕʷədzəz 'amsgʲə jə'tɕʷədzəjt'
—Whoever has lost a goat has lost the entire day too.

wan 'bzəja dəw'bozar, adẕʷ jan dəwmətɕʷ'ħan
—If you love your own mother, don't swear at anyone else's.

a'dẕʷə jə'zən 'aẕra zzəz ja'ra d'taħajt'
—He who dug a hole for someone else fell into it himself.

'ats'abərg wə'ħʷar, a'psə dar'gəlojt'
—If one speaks the truth, it will raise the dead.

ma'la tʷ'a'ra 'ats'kʲ'əs, ma'la 'nəqʷ'ara 'ejɣʲəwp'
—Better running in vain than sitting in vain.

'amɥa 'jaşa wəzəʃ'tsəlam 'ats'kʲ'əs, wəzəʃ'tsəlow 'amɥa xʷa'xʷa aaj'gʷɔwp'
—A zigzag road known to you is shorter than an unknown straight one.

'asas dətɕʷgʲarxʷxʷ'ɥəwp'
—A guest immediately notices defects.

ɥkʲ'an'ts'aak' adəw'nej jəkʷəjbar'dzoməzt'
—Two dwarfs couldn't find room in the world for each other.

a't'ə 'abla ana'jow, 'adʒəmʃ, 'adʒəmʃ a'ħʷon
—When the owl acquired eyes, it started asking for eyebrows.

nxaцts'as k'ər'wə aamsta'ts'as k'rəf
—Work like a peasant — eat like a lord.

zəbza'ra ţşejm jəpsra'gʲə ţşejm
—He who has a lousy life has a lousy death too.

ap'ħʷəs 'aaʃa 'ləmʂʃara ratɕʷa'xojt'
—A lazy woman gets to have many days appointed for non-work.
*(N.B. reference is to the tradition whereby certain types of activities
were forbidden on certain days of the week — see Chapter 14 above)*

wə'dʒam zlam wəm'ħatɕʷʲ 'alowmts'an
—Don't put your spoon into anything that does not have your bowl beneath it.
(The translation equivalent would be: "Don't poke your nose into another's business.")

awa'цə jəbz awa'цə jə'zə jəxʷʲʃʷəwp'
—A person's tongue is his medicine.

awa'цə baa'psə dej'tʃərtʃaцxojt'
—A bad person is the cause of discord.

a'psadgʲəl zmam, ntɕʷa'gʲə 'dəjmam
—Whoever has no homeland has no god.

a'psadgʲəl a'zə jə'psəz dəps'dzam
—He who died for his homeland is not dead.

awaц'ra ztsəm a'xats'ara p'a't'əwdarowp'
—Manliness without humanity is dishonourable.

'aləməs zmam awaцra'gʲə 'jəlam
—Whoever has no conscience has no humanity.

'apswa jəmtʃ tɕʷwəɣʷk' jəʃt'naxwejt', 'jələməs ʃʷk'am'baʃk' jərzərts'əs'wam
— A pair of bulls can lift the strength of an Abkhazian, but 100 buffalo cannot shake his conscience.

'apswa 'jələməs awp' d'mərdzkʷ'a daaz'go
—It is thanks to his conscience that an Abkhazian survives and exists.

awaц 'jəbz ja'ra ja'ɣowp'
—A person's tongue is his enemy.

a'mal arħa'ra marə'jowp', awaц'rowp' zərħa'ra tɕʷgʲow
—The acquisition of wealth is easy — humanity is what it is difficult to acquire.

ax'ʂəц zts'am apʂ'ra 'başowp'
—Appearance is nothing without intelligence.

'bzəja 'ejbabo a'tɕʷħʷəraţş'gʲə ejtsən'xojt'
—Those in love can live together even in a desert.

a'pa də'bzəjaxar, 'aʒʷlar dər't'ʷ'əwp'; dətɕʷgʲa'xar, 'janəj 'jabəj dər't'ʷ'əwp'
—If a son turns out well, he belongs to the people; if he turns out bad, he belongs to his parents.

Vocabulary items

I published in *Bedi Kartlisa XXXIX* (pp 256-67) a list of Abkhaz kinship terms (alongside those of Georgian and Mingrelian). My paper 'Contribution to the lexicography of Abkhaz' appeared in *Proceedings of the Conference on Northwest Caucasian Linguistics (10-12 October 1994)* (ed. Sumru Özsoy, pp 128-32), with a comprehensive list of terms for parts of the body. Below is a selection of vocabulary for weekdays, trees, comestibles, and creatures:

Days of the week

Sunday a'mtҫ̌ǝҫ̌a		*Thursday* a'pʃaҫ̌a
Monday aʃʷa'xʲa		*Friday* a'xʷaҫ̌a
Tuesday a'ɥaҫ̌a		*Saturday* a'sabҫ̌a
Wednesday 'axaҫ̌a		*week* 'amtʃǝbӡ

Trees (etc)

tree 'ats'la	*box* a'ҫ̌ǝts	*chestnut* 'axʲa[ts'la]
oak adӡ	*beech* aʃʷ	*walnut* a'ra[ts'la]
yew aa	*maple* a'mtʃ'a	*pine* 'apsa[ts'la]
birch a'ts'aats'la	*elm* 'araҫ̌	*alder* al
hornbeam 'axʲatsa	*apple-tree* a'tҫ̌ʷ'ats'la	*edible thorn* abǝr'tʃ'man
holly a'dǝɣadӡa	*fern* a'tǝras	*grass* aħa'skʲ'ǝn
tobacco ata'tǝn, atǝ'tǝn	*nettle* 'axʷats	

Comestibles

fruit a'ʃʷǝr	*apple* a'tҫ̌ʷ'a	*pear* a'ħa
plum ab'ħʷa	*peach* at'a'ma	*apricot* a'tҫ̌ʷ'at'ama
medlar a'batҫ̌ʷ	*grape* aӡ	*fig* ala'ħa
crab-apple a'tҫ̌ʷ'aҫ̌a	*cherry* 'atsa	*cucumber* a'naҫ̌a, akʲ'ǝn't'ǝr
watermelon aħabǝr'zakʲ'	*maize* apҫ̌, adӡǝ'kʷrej	*coriander* 'axʷǝsxʷa
millet 'axʷdz	*bread* a'tʃa	*cheese* aʃʷ
yoghurt axar'tҫ̌ʷ'ǝ	*wine* a'ɥǝ	*salt* a'dӡǝk'a
pepper ap'ǝr'p'ǝl	*meat* a'kʷ'ats	*beans* a'qʷ'ǝd
milk axҫ̌	*butter* 'axʷҫ̌a	*grits* a'bǝsta
nut ara'sa	*blackberry* amaa'xǝr	*strawberry* ats'ǝ'ts'ǝndra
honey 'atsxa	*egg* akʷʲ't'aɣʲ	

Creatures

animal aps'tʷ'ǝ	*bird* a'psaa, a'ts'ǝs	*dog* a'la
bitch a'laps	*puppy* alas'ba	*cat* ats'gʷǝ
kitten ats'gʷǝpҫ̌ka	*pig* a'ħʷa	*sow* a'ħʷan, a'ħʷaps
piglet 'aʃǝʃ, aħʷa'ts'ǝs	*cow* aӡʷ	*bull* atҫ̌ʷ
calf a'ħʷǝs	*horse* a'tҫ̌ǝ	*stallion, colt* a'tҫ̌aba
mare a'tҫ̌an	*foal* atҫ̌'ts'ǝs	*goose* a'q'ǝz
chicken akʷʲ't'ǝ	*hen* 'arts[ǝ]na	*cock(erel)* 'arbaɣʲ
chick akʷʲ'tʃ'ǝʃ	*swallow* 'aӡʷts'[ǝs]	*blackbird* 'ardʷǝna
sheep, ewe awa'sa	*ram* awa'sabaɣʲ, a'tǝ	*lamb* a'sǝs
frog 'adaɣʲ	*lion* 'alǝm	*snake* 'amat
bear amʃʷ	*female bear* 'amʃʷaps	*bear-cub* amʃʷ'ħʷǝs
wolf abga'dǝw	*fox* abgaxʷǝ'tʃ'ǝ	*quail* 'atʃa
eagle a'warba[ӡʷ]	*duck* a'kʷ'ata	*fish* a'psǝdz
deer a'ʃabǝsta	*female deer* a'tҫ̌a	*fawn* atҫ̌a'ħʷǝs
mouse a'ħʷǝnap	*rat* a'ħʷǝnapdǝw	*mosquito* akʷʲ'ǝ'brǝ
donkey atҫ̌a'da	*male donkey* atҫ̌a'dabaɣʲ	*donkey mare* atҫ̌a'daps
donkey foal atҫ̌ad'ħʷǝs	*goat* 'adӡma	*male ibex* a'bɣab
female ibex a'bɣadӡma	*pigeon* a'ħʷǝħʷ	*wasp* a'ҫ̌xǝrtҫ̌ʷ'aɣʲ
fly amts'	*bee* 'aʃxa, 'aʃxǝts	*lizard* 'ajntҫ̌ʷ[']ǝҫ̌
toad 'adaӡʷ	*turkey* aʃʷǝj'ʃʷǝj, a'gʷagʷǝʃ, a'kʷ'akʷ'ǝʃ	

Contributors

Jurij Anchabadze (b. 1953, T'q^w'archal), Candidate of Historical Sciences, studied at Sukhum's Pedagogical Institute and the Moscow Institute of Ethnology, where, since 1986, he has been senior researcher in the Caucasian Department. He is the author of a number of works dealing with questions of the ethnic history of the Caucasus, such as the 1993 Moscow publication *The ethnic history of the North Caucasus (16th-19th centuries).*

Vasilij Avidzba (b. 1958), Candidate of Philological Sciences, works at the Abkhazian Institute for Humanitarian Research (Sukhum), specialising in literature.

Daur Bargandzhia (b. 1958), Candidate of Economic Sciences, holds the title of Doctor at the Abkhazian State University and is the author of 20 scholarly works dealing with the concentration of capital and monopolisation of the market.

Oleg Bgazhba (b. 1941), Doctor of Historical Sciences, is a leading scholar at the Abkhazian Institute for Humanitarian Research (Sukhum) and is the author of seven books, amongst which are: *Essays on the handicrafts of Medieval Abkhazia* (Sukhum, 1977), *On the tracks of the smith Ajnar* (Sukhum, 1982), *Ferrous metallurgy and metal-working in ancient and medieval Abkhazia (eighth century BC–15th century)* (Tbilisi, 1984), *The main fortress of Apsilia* (Sukhum, 1986), plus a range of other publications. He was the first to uncover the earliest swords made from Damask steel on the territory of the former USSR; these were found in Abkhazia. He also researches ancient and medieval monuments.

Dodge Billingsley (b. 1962) took his BA at Columbia and his MA at the Department of War Studies at King's College (London), where he co-founded the *War Studies' Journal*. He has visited Abkhazia and Georgia several times and has written many articles (including for *Jane's Intelligence Review*) on the conflict there. One-time recipient of the MacArthur Fellowship for regional security in the Caucasus, he currently works as documentary producer for Video Ordnance (New York).

Vjacheslav Chirikba [Chrygba] (b. 1959, Gagra), studied English at Kharkov University (1977-82), becoming a postgraduate in Caucasian languages at the Linguistics' Institute (Moscow), where he remained until 1991, defending his Candidate's thesis (a phonetic study of Abkhaz and Circassian) in 1986. Further study in Leiden led in 1996 to the award there of a doctorate based on his now published dissertation *Common West Caucasian: the reconstruction of its phonological system and parts of its lexicon and morphology* . With the books *Aspects of phonological typology* (Moscow, 1991), *A dictionary of Common Abkhaz* (Leiden, 1996), and some 20 other articles to his name, he is currently preparing a book on the Georgian-Abkhazian conflict for the Dutch Institute of International Relations 'Clingendael', published by Curzon.

Rachel Clogg (b. 1969) is currently a postgraduate student at Wolfson College, Oxford. She is completing her doctorate on Fazil Iskander in the context of Abkhazian cultural history. Iskander is an Abkhazian regarded by some as one of the leading writers of Russian prose currently active. She graduated with Honours in Russian and Spanish from Clare College, Cambridge, and has travelled widely in Abkhazia and the Caucasus.

Roman Dbar (b. 1957), Candidate of Biological Sciences, is the author of a range of publications dealing with questions of ecology, specifically the insect world.

Brian George Hewitt (b. 1949), Doctor of Philosophy (Cambridge, where he initially read Classics as an Open Scholar of St John's College), is Professor of Caucasian Languages at the School of Oriental and African Studies (London) and is the author of grammars of both Abkhaz and Georgian as well as of numerous articles on the languages and politics of the Caucasus. He is married to an Abkhazian, and their *Abkhaz Newspaper Reader* appeared in 1998. They have two daughters.

Stanislav Lak'oba (b. 1953), Candidate of Historical Sciences, is a leading scholar at the Abkhazian Institute for Humanitarian Research (Sukhum) and is the author of seven books, amongst which are: *Winged days in Sukhum-Kale* (Sukhum, 1988), *Essays on the political history of Abkhazia* (Sukhum, 1990), *The history of Abkhazia: text-book* (Sukhum, 1991, which he edited), plus a range of other publications on the history, politics and culture of the Caucasian peoples.

Daniel Müller (b. 1969, Münster) has studied, in both Bochum and Dortmund, Eastern European history, oriental studes and journalism (Diploma 1995; research assistant at the Institute for Journalistic Studies, Dortmund University since 1996). He is currently preparing his doctorate in the field of Caucasian ethno-demography in the 19th and 20th centuries.

Viktor Popkov, one-time freelance journalist and archaeological photographer. He was met by British journalist Anatol Lieven in a cellar during a Russian air-raid on Grozny (Chechenia), who described him thus in the *The Times* (London, 27 Dec 1994): "He gave me his card and told me he was Magister Viktor Popkov, leader of the Omega Inter-Ethnic Inter-Confessional Society for Justice and Well-being in Moscow. As shells and bombs sent tremors through the floor under our feet, he said he had come to Grozny 'to fix the principles for the avoidance of war between nations.' For want of any other description, I must classify him as a saint. I hope he does not suffer martyrdom for his principles."

Giorgij Shamba [Şamba] (b. 1940), Doctor of Historical Sciences, is head of the Department of Archaeology at the Abkhazian Institute for Humanitarian Research (Sukhum) and is the author of several books. His doctorate was defended in 1987 at the Institute of Archaeology and Ethnography of the Academy of Sciences of Armenia in Erevan.

Notes

Introduction

1. cf. Аҧсуаа/Аҧсацәа *'Apswaa/'Apsaçᵂa*, the collective and distributive plurals respectively of the singular Аҧсуа *'Apswa*.

2. Аҧсны *Aps'ny*.

3. Аҟуа (or Аҟәа since the post-Soviet spelling-adjustment) *'Aqᵂ'a* (Dioscurias or Seb/vastopol(is) in antiquity).

4. The final '-i' of the variant Sukhumi is the Georgian ending of the nominative case and was introduced in the late 1930s as part of the intensive drive to Georgianise Abkhazia, which explains why its use is no longer tolerated by Abkhazians.

5. The mountains come almost to the sea just to the north of this town, leaving a very narrow stretch on which the railway-line and the road have been constructed. The most likely etymology (by Valerij K'varch'ia [Kʷ'arch'yja]) derives the toponym from *'a-ga* 'the sea(-coast)' + *a-k'-'ra* 'holding it.'

6. Known to the Abkhazians as Аҧсуа бызшәа/Аҧсшәа *'Apswa byzˢʷa/'Apsˢʷa*).

7. Those who believe Stalin to have rejected his Georgian identity and to have been totally Russified may like to ponder why, after brutally expelling the entire Karachay and Chechen (plus other) peoples to Central Asia in 1943-44, he bestowed parts of their eponymous lands, then wiped off Soviet maps, upon his native republic; why, as described in his memoirs by a Georgian officer in the British army who was present at the Big Three wartime-conference in Tehran, Stalin's inner bodyguard was made up of Kartvelians (Merab K'vit'ashvili, 1990); and why Donald Rayfield (Queen Mary Westfield College, London), a specialist in Russian and Georgian literature, should have characterised the period in Georgia from the late 1980s as "not so much a de-Stalinisation of Georgia as an attempted de-Georgianisation of Stalin" (SOAS talk, March 6th 1990).

8. That the intelligentsia in Georgia was not naturally pre-disposed to anti-Abkhazian sentiment at the time of the mass migrations of the 1860-70s is evidenced by the views some of their number committed to print, as with the following on 'Abkhazians and Abkhazia' by Sergei Meskhi (*Droeba* 'Time-being', issue 158, 6.8, 1878, reprinted on pp 20-21 of vol. 3, 1964, of his collected works, and part-translated into Russian in Achugba, 1995, pp 38-39): "Abkhazia and in general the whole of this Caucasian Black Sea littoral is one of the most beautiful and richest of spots on the earth . . . We must hope that our government will not hinder but rather permit those Abkhazians who may wish to return to and settle anew their own land to do so. Apart from feelings of philanthropy, this is demanded both by justice and indeed self-interest, for undoubtedly it is better to have people like the Circassians and Abkhazians as friends than as enemies." Sadly, new attitudes were not long in forming.

9. The earliest edition of this work that I have seen containing this passage is the seventh, which appeared in 1892.

10. The noted scholar of Abkhaz, Ketevan Lomtatidze, was an honourable exception.

11. The street in Tbilisi on which stands the Institute of Linguistics has since been renamed Ingoroq'va Street.

12. The best known devotee of Ingoroq'va, the Georgian academician Tamaz Gamq'relidze, entered the fray in 1991 with yet another linguistically-based defence. My 1993a article is a detailed rebuttal and is preceded by my English translation of Gamq'relidze's 1991 Georgian original; my 1992a article is a response to Oniani.

13. Dzhavakhishvili was himself unwise enough later to deviate from his main discipline, producing in 1937 754 pages (with many dubious etymologies) designed to demonstrate that all the autochthonous Caucasian languages derived from a single source, which is no longer a tenable hypothesis (at least as far as the inclusion of the Kartvelian group is concerned).

14. Unfortunately, he went on to spoil the observation by detecting a Mingrelian derivational prefix *do-* (e.g. *do-xor-e* 'palace, area of residence' < *xor-ua* 'living' — how *t'u-* developed is unexplained) in combination with roots he interpreted as deriving from *Apswa*

— in fact, the Circassian toponym is analysable exclusively in terms of Circassian (t^w'*y* '2', *psy* 'water').

15. Hence the necessity for Nadareishvili to add (also on p7): "Certain toponyms or hydronyms on the territory of historical Colchis once regarded as Circassian (*Supsa, Maltaq'va*) turned out to be Georgian." Naturally, no reference is given for the relevant 'proof' of their Georgianness.

16. Some critics respond to this argument over the length of time the Abkhazians have resided in Abkhazia by asking what difference their length of residence (200 or over 2,000 years) makes to their right to remain in place today, and the point is valid — to a degree. Given that relative shortness of tenure is palpably so critical in shaping Kartvelian attitudes (otherwise they would not invest so much energy in manufacturing a history for the Abkhazians), it is important for purely scholarly reasons to reassert the facts as often as may be necessary — this in no way implies that more than two millennia of residence is to be regarded as bestowing greater territorial claims than one of two centuries, as is implicit in such criticism. What is the role of scholarship if not to establish the truth and then to buttress it when it is abused?

17. At least two Internet sites are devoted to Abkhazia. Their addresses at the time of printing are: www.abkhazia.org
www.gse.uci.edu/abkhazia/homepage.htm

Chapter 1

1. Malaria was a severe problem, making Abkhazia a difficult place for non-Abkhazians to live, until the relevant swamps were drained as part of Russia's colonisation-programme after the Caucasian War in the 19th century. — *(Editor)*

Chapter 3

1. Among these was the young Abkhazian archaeologist Mushni Khvartskia, awarded the title 'Hero of the Republic of Abkhazia' after laying down his life for the freedom of his country in 1993.

2. Khandzia too fell in the liberation of Sukhum in 1993.

3. This derives from the word 'Colchis', which term was first introduced as a geographical concept by the Ancient Greek poet, Eumelus of Corinth, in the eighth century BC.

4. Agathias' original Greek text is quite unambiguous in linking the Apsilians and Missimians both culturally and linguistically. At IV, 15 he refers to the Apsilians as ὄντας ὁμοδιαίτους καὶ ἀγχιτέρμονας "being related to and neighbouring (the Missimians)." However, careless translation of another passage at III, 15 might easily lead the unwary to think that Agathias is there drawing a distinction in terms of customs and language between the Apsilians and Missimians, whereas the Greek text is incontrovertibly drawing this contrast between the Missimians and the so-called 'Colchians' (presumably the ancestors of today's Kartvelian Laz and Mingrelian peoples). Sadly it was apparently reliance on just such an inadequate translation that lead the classicist David Braund (1994, p310, note) into error concerning "Agathias, 3, 15.8, noting the linguistic and cultural gulf between the Misimiani and Apsilii and, *a fortiori*, the Lazi." Since it is not in the interests of Kartvelian nationalist historians that the Missimians should be linked by the ancient witnesses with the Apsilians, for they wish to argue this tribe were Kartvelians in order to establish a Kartvelian presence on historical Abkhazian territory in ancient times (and thus, they would contend, strengthen their claims to have Abkhazia deemed part of 'Georgian' territory), it is naturally the (deliberate?) mistranslation of Agathias than one so often finds in their works, as illustrated by the following baseless assertion: "Although Agathias underlines the relatedness of the Apsilians and Missimians, he also stresses that their languages as well as their customs were different" (Mariam Lordkipanidze writing in *Svobodnaja Gruzija* ('Free Georgia'), Aug 9th 1991, p3), and in similar vein Tsulaja (1995, p21). — *(Editor)*

Chapter 4

1. The Alans were the ancestors of today's Ossetians, who speak an Iranian language.
2. The traditional dividing line between western and central/eastern Georgia.
3. Q'aukhchishvili, on p636 of vol. 2 of his 1959 edition of these Chronicles, glosses the term 'Apsars' as "one of the Georgian tribes in Western Georgia," for which interpretation he adduces no evidence whatsoever, and, of course, there is none. — *(Editor)*
4. The family is known in Georgian as Shervashidze or Sharvashidze, and in Mingrelian as Sharashia. See Anchabadze's discussion (1959, pp 190-95). — *(Editor)*

Chapter 5

1. "Charter given February 17th 1810 by the Emperor Alexander I to the ruler of Abkhazia, Prince Georgij Sharvashidze . . . We, Alexander the First, Emperor and Autocrat of All Russia . . . Ruler and Sovereign of the Iberian, Kartlian, Georgian and Kabardinian lands . . . offer Our Imperial grace and favour to the Ruler of the Abkhazian land, Prince Georgij Sharvashidze, Our amiable and true subject. In consideration of your request to enter into permanent subjecthood of the Russian Empire and not doubting your devotion to Our supreme throne as expressed in your letter of commitment despatched in Our Royal Name, we confirm and recognise you, Our loyal subject, as the hereditary Prince of the Abkhazian domains under the protection, power and defence of the Russian Empire, and incorporating you, your family and all the inhabitants of the Abkhazian domains within the number of Our subjects, we promise you and your descendants Our Imperial grace and favour . . ." (Frontispiece of the collective *History of Abkhazia* (in Russian), Sukhum, 1991). — *(Editor)*
2. Note how even a Kartvelian evidently perceived the western provinces of Guria and Imereti as distinct from Georgia proper as late as 1913. — *(Editor)*
3. This word appears in the vocabulary list appended to his two-volume *Journal of a residence in Circassia during the years 1837, 1838, 1839*, by the English visitor J. S. Bell in 1840 with the meaning 'slave'. It happens to be the Abkhazian ethnonym for 'Mingrelian' (based on the -gr- radical element seen in the Mingrelian self-designation *ma-rg-al-i* or the Georgian equivalent *me-gr-el-i*) and this secondary sense is an excellent indication of the status of Mingrelians who found themselves in Abkhazia prior to the influx that began at the close of the 19th century, as described later in this chapter. — *(Editor)*
4. Britain actually had a vice-consul, Charles Hamer Dickson, in Sukhum from January 12th 1858 to March 25th 1865, followed by an acting vice-consul until consular presence ended on November 2nd 1866 — information supplied by Peter Roland, formerly of the Foreign & Commonwealth Office's Research Department. — *(Editor)*
5. For an Englishman's almost contemporary account see Palgrave (1872, pp 250-70). — *(Editor)*
6. Republished in vol. 1 of his collected works in 1952, pp 90-120, and again in vol. 1 of a five-volume collection of his writings from 1989, pp 366-99. — *(Editor)*
7. As Hewitt (1993b, p319, note 52) noted: "The 1952 editors felt it necessary to gloss this term on p93 thus: 'Gogebashvili here and below uses the word *coloniser* not in its modern sense but to mean the persons settled there.' Obviously they sensed some discomfort over one of the leading Georgians of the 1870s describing Kartvelian settlers on territory that had been by 1952 long and strenuously argued to be Georgian soil as *colonisers!*"
8. Birthplace in 1899 of Beria. — *(Editor)*
9. Abkhazian surnames are typically rendered with the ending *-ba* (cf. *jy-'pa* 'his son' vs *jy-'pha* 'his daughter'), while Mingrelian endings are typically *-ia, -ua, -ava, -aia*; Georgian names usually end in *-shvili* or *-dze*; and Svan endings are *-(i)ani*. — *(Editor)*
10. These Russian attempts to counter the unfortunate and unforeseen results of their colonial policy in Abkhazia are typically glossed today by Kartvelian commentators in words similar to the following by Georgian geographer, Revaz Gachechiladze: "A definite increase in Georgian national self-awareness and the rapid integration of the different Georgian sub(-)ethnic groups into one nation occurred in the second half of the 19th century. *This made the imperial government rather suspicious and as a counter(-)measure Abkhazian nationalism was*

encouraged on the eve of the 20th century and deliberately directed in an anti-Georgian way" (1996, p32, stresses added). — *(Editor)*

Chapter 6

1. In the years 1917-21 there functioned within Abkhazia three completely different ANSs. The first existed from November 8th 1917 to April 1918, the second from May-June to October 10th 1918, the third from March 18th 1919 to March 1921.

2. A British expeditionary force was operating in the Caucasus at the time. Based in Baku (to protect the oil-fields), its aim was to try to prevent Bolshevik expansion into Transcaucasia. — *(Editor)*

3. Contrast this actual sequence of events with the all-too-typical re-interpretation of history by scholars in Tbilisi as represented by the following recent claim from geographer Revaz Gachechiladze: "After the Russian Bolsheviks . . . incorporated the Transcaucasian states . . . they re-delimited (sic) their borders, but did this in such a way as if to leave 'delayed action mines' (that actually blew up 70 years later) . . . The imperialist mentality in Russia . . . uses 'delayed action mines', i.e. the autonomous units created in the 1920s" (1996, pp 28 & 35). — *(Editor)*

4. When Lak'oba's body was returned for burial to Abkhazia, all the internal organs were discovered to have been removed. — *(Editor)*

5. The author, Stanislav Lak[']oba, ended his contribution at this point. In order to present readers with a fuller understanding of events between the death of Stalin and the tragedy that began to unfold in 1989, I have inserted suitable material, largely from Abkhazian sources — *(Editor)*

6. Batumi, the capital of the Ajarian Autonomous Republic, had previously been designated as the site of Georgia's second university. In the event, no further universities were established in Soviet Georgia.

Chapter 7

1. Reference is to the fighting that had preceded the events here described by a few days between Kartvelians and members of their Azerbaijani minority in this district of southern Georgia. — *(Editor)*

2. This was when a huge demonstration that had paralysed the main square and thoroughfare in Tbilisi was broken up by Soviet troops at the cost of some 20 lives. The operation was sanctioned by the Georgian government of Dzhumber P'at'iashvili and approved by the Kremlin, but whether Gorbachev and Shevardnadze were party to it has never been clarified to everyone's satisfaction. — *(Editor)*

Chapter 8

1. A local Mingrelian who had for some years been producing *samizdat*-material often unfavourable to the Abkhazians, Boris K'ak'ubava, was active on behalf of K'ost'ava and Gamsakhurdia at this period. On April 1st 1989 he appeared with K'ost'ava and another leading member of the movement, Irak'li Ch'avch'avadze, at an unsanctioned meeting in Gechripsh (Gjachrypsh) near the Abkhazian-Russian frontier, where such slogans as the following were paraded: "Georgia for the Georgians," "Liquidation of Abkhazian Autonomy," "Abkhazia is an Inseparable Part of Georgia," "Abkhazians are simply Georgians," "Long Live the Territorial Integrity of Georgia!" — *(Editor)*

2. The entourage was stopped on the main highway near Lykhny, and the occupants of the escorting car were relieved of five Uzi automatic weapons. — *(Editor)*

3. Despite this undeniable contrast with the decidedly unsavoury record of the Georgian leader, Eduard Shevardnadze, it has paradoxically been Ardzinba and the Abkhazian leadership who have been portrayed (and thus implicitly condemned) as "Communist sympathisers" by the largely pro-Georgian (or, at least, pro-Shevardnadze) Western media. — *(Editor)*

4. The name derives from the country house, Novo-Ogarevo, near Moscow where the

meeting between President Gorbachev and the leaders of nine of the Slav and Muslim republics (including Yeltsin) met on April 23rd/24th 1991 to discuss the concluding of a treaty for a 'Union of Sovereign States." Georgia, Armenia, Moldava, and the three Baltic states did not participate. — *(Editor, with thanks to Rieks Smeets for information supplied)*

5. Boycotted by Kartvelians throughout Soviet Georgia, 52.3 per cent of Abkhazia's total electorate did vote, with 98.6 per cent of these saying 'yes' to remaining within a union of sovereign republics — this meant that an absolute majority of over 51 per cent of the electorate in Abkhazia effectively voted NOT to back Gamsakhurdia in his determination to leave the Union, which was entirely natural in the climate of ethnic hatred that had been stirred up amongst the bulk of the Kartvelian population. The resulting treaty was due to be signed by the union-republics in mid-August, with Ardzinba later adding his signature on behalf of the Autonomous Republic of Abkhazia, which would thereby have achieved the union-status it desired. — *(Editor)*

6. Much has been made of this division of seats over the years by Kartvelian propagandists. Take, for example, the following passage from the English version of a distasteful, albeit relatively subtle, example of the genre, namely Chervonnaya (1994, p91): "By blackmail and demagogy, juridical trickery and with the connivance of Gamsakhurdia, Ardzinba and his colleagues managed to push the electoral law of July 9th 1991 through the Georgian (sic) Parliament. This permitted the creation of prerogatives and restrictions on a solely ethnic basis in the formation of the new electoral districts.

Shevardnadze wrote later that: 'The electoral law of July 9th 1991 totally ignores the norms and practice of modern parliamentarianism. What is this if not apartheid *de jure*, the striving of the minority to dictate its will to the majority, deliberately provoking the threat of inter-ethnic clashes? . . . This was pure racial discrimination and the establishment of an ethno-dictatorship.' " — A certain Professor Levan Aleksidze not only contributed some pages to this work but spoke at its London launch, where he again emphasised this specific matter.

But if one delves a little further, something interesting is uncovered, just as it was by the mission to Abkhazia and Georgia of the Unrepresented Nations and Peoples' Organisation (UNPO) of October 1993. The details are given in Overeem's report (1995, p147): "According to the Georgian authorities this law endangered the sovereignty of the Georgian state and is the most important legal basis for allegations of the Abkhaz genocide against the Georgian people. This law proved (they alleged) that the policies of the Abkhaz political elite from 1988 onwards were aimed at the creation of a mono-ethnic Abkhazia. *It should be noted, however, that the personal adviser to the Georgian president, Levan Alexidze (=Aleksidze), was the co-author of this law, which was accepted by the Abkhazian authorities at the suggestion of President Gamsakhurdia"* (stresses added); see *Central Asian Survey*, 12.3, 1993, pp 325-45 for UNPO's first report. — *(Editor)*

7. The significance of this principle, as opposed to that of self-determination, comes out in a letter of February 18th 1997 from the UK's junior minister at the Foreign and Commonwealth Office with responsibility for Transcaucasia, Sir Nicholas Bonsor, in answer to a complaint about the unwillingness of the West to consider the Abkhazian position: "The Abkhaz will no doubt continue to consider the international community to be one-sided but that is an unavoidable result of the international community's position on the territorial integrity of Georgia under the OSCE principles." The essential inhumanity of this arbitrary stance resulted in almost total silence on the part of Western governments when the two North Caucasian peoples, the Abkhazians and the Chechens, were subjected to unspeakable brutality by the central authorities in Tbilisi and later Moscow bent effectively on aggressive territorial integrationism using territorial integrity as their justification. — *(Editor)*

8. Georgian propaganda and apologists for the Georgian cause have consistently argued by way of excuse for the eventual Abkhazian victory that Russia won the war for them, and this has become received wisdom, though the Abkhazians strenuously deny it, pointing out that, whilst they may have acquired weaponry from Russian sources, they, unlike Georgia, had to pay a great deal of money for this. However, virtually no attention is paid to the involvement of Ukrainians on the Kartvelian side. Clear evidence of this is contained, no doubt inadvertently, in Chervonnaya's Kartvelian apologia (1994), for illustration 7 shows a

Ukrainian vessel disgorging tanks and armoured troop-carriers on the shores of Kartvelian-occupied Abkhazia. See also Chapter 9 of this volume. — *(Editor)*

9. Rather than help the Georgian government address the roots of its widespread problem of minority-rights to the mutual advantage of both the minorities and the central authorities, one Western reaction has been to imagine that the best solution is to give military training to government troops, possibly in the conviction that professionally trained troops are less likely to commit atrocities and that any such would be penalised by the local judiciary. Consider, for instance, these words of Dr Charles Fairbanks (Professor of International Relations at John Hopkins Foreign Policy Institute) voiced during the question and answer session at a briefing before the Commission on Security and Co-operation in Europe (Monday, October 25th 1993, Washington DC): "If one gave arms to the most westernized and youngest elements of the population and created an army that had some discipline, that really obeys the government, that had a chain of command, to begin with, it wouldn't commit atrocities this easily . . . And if one has professionalization of armies in these areas, one will greatly reduce the level of human rights violation."

However, reports issued as late as early 1997 by international human rights groups, such as Amnesty International, continue to allude to allegations of the use of torture and the denial of due process in Georgia's legal system, the US State Department even noting: "The judiciary is subject to executive pressure." With specific reference to the Abkhazian war, the second UNPO Mission noted in its report (Overeem 1995, pp 145-46) that, while on the Abkhazian side "persons suspected of crimes, including human rights violation, have been arrested and tried. Several Abkhazians responsible for crimes against Georgian civilians have been prosecuted or are awaiting trial in Sukhum," on the other side the "Georgian authorities in Tbilisi were unable to provide the mission with evidence of data concerning the prosecution of Georgians, Mingrelians, Abkhazians or others who committed human rights violations and other crimes during the time the Georgian authorities controlled parts of Abkhazia . . . The mission had the strongest impression that this issue is not given priority by the Georgian prosecutor-general." Given this background, the response to Fairbanks from journalist Thomas Goltz could be more germane to a Western-trained Georgian army let loose among non-Kartvelian (or even non-Georgian) discontents: "I think both the Germans and the Japanese were well ordered and had very good armies and I think they committed a lot of atrocities" (*Current Situation in Georgia and Implications for US Policy*, October 1993, pp 13-15). — *(Editor)*

10. For details of human rights abuses see Voronov et al. 1993. But as an illustration of how all non-Kartvelians were abused at this time consider the following from Richard Clogg, who in his article 'The Greeks and the war in Abkhazia' (*The Greek American*, 26, March 1994) observes: "Much of our knowledge of the plight of the Abkhazian Greeks is due to Vlasis Agtzidis . . . He accompanied operation 'Golden Fleece', the dispatch in August 1993 by the Greek government of a ship to evacuate just over a thousand ethnic Greeks from Sukhum to Greece . . . Agtzidis carried out interviews among a sizeable proportion of these refugees. His initial findings were published in *Eleftherotypia* (August 29th 1993) and he has now produced a much more detailed report on the consequences of the war for the Greeks of Abkhazia. This report makes grim reading. Take, for instance, the case of Xanthi Kyriazova from Sukhum. She was overpowered one night by a group of seven armed Georgian paramilitaries, who proceeded to extract five gold teeth with pliers. They tortured and murdered her 70-year-old aunt, whose children had earlier fled to Greece. Afterwards she was killed and buried in the yard of her house. This was seized by a Georgian family who dug up her aunt's corpse. A.P. had the lobe of her ear shot off when she tried to resist a group of Georgians bent on rape. (A photograph of her damaged ear was published in *Eleftherotypia*)." — *(Editor)*

11. Compare the general ignorance in the West of this grievous blow with the coverage afforded to the burning down of the National Library in Sarajevo and the subsequent calls for international support to restock this cultural resource (see Clogg, 1994). — *(Editor)*

12. And there was not one word of condemnation of the horrors inflicted by Georgia's invasion on this peaceful population during 13 and a half months of occupation; in sharp and indicative contrast, ever since the end of the war no Western government or (semi-)

governmental agency (up to and including even the Council of Europe) can mention the Georgian-Abkhazian conflict without evincing sympathy (translated into huge amounts of aid to the Shevardnadze regime) for the plight of the subsequent wave of exclusively Kartvelian refugees, who fled across the Ingur into Mingrelia or over the mountains into Svanetia in advance of the arrival of the forces of the victorious Abkhazian alliance. — *(Editor)*

13. Shevardnadze justified this crime by saying that the helicopter might have been carrying arms — only the pilot's revolver was found among the wreckage. — *(Editor)*

14. These Mingrelians are often the targets of (*pace* most commentators) Kartvelian terrorist acts, effected in order to destabilise the area. As one small step to cater for the cultural needs of these Mingrelians, the Abkhazians instituted a trilingual (Mingrelian, Russian, Abkhaz) newspaper, *Gal*, in the summer of 1995, which contrasts sharply with the standard attitude to Mingrelian amongst Georgians proper, for Mingrelian has effectively been banned as a literary tool in Georgia since the late 1930s. — *(Editor)*

15. Consider the following excerpt from an Interfax report on the conflict from February 24th 1997: "In an interview in the Georgian paper *Akhali Taoba* ('New Generation') the leader of the 'White Legion', Zurab Samushia, declared that 'the partisan-formation known as the White Legion' is conducting an armed struggle against 'a puppet, separatist regime' . . . Samushia maintained that the 'White Legion' . . . will continue to carry on the armed struggle against the current authorities in Abkhazia until there is complete restoration of Georgia's jurisdiction in this republic." — *(Editor)*

16. Consider the following from a letter sent by Abkhazian Foreign Minister, K'onst'ant'in Ozgan, to Deputy Foreign Minister of Russia, Boris Pastukhov, on February 25th 1997: ". . . as practice demonstrates, the Georgian side uses negotiations to create merely a semblance of using civilised methods to decide the conflict. The basis for this assertion are the practical actions of Georgia — it simply ignores understandings already reached. Regrettable too is the fact that several actions which go against existing agreements receive the support of the facilitator in the negotiations, i.e. the Russian Federation. In particular, on February 15th 1997 an agreement was signed in Tbilisi between the ministries of communication of Georgia and the Russian Federation according to which it is proposed to switch off the remaining channels of communication linking Abkhazia with the outside-world," telephone-lines having been reduced by the relevant Russian ministry on April 5th 1996 from 223 to a mere 16 — in mid-April 1997 all lines were severed. — *(Editor)*

17. The Interfax report of February 24th 1997 quoted above ends with this observation: "According to information from Abkhazia's defence service, 38 acts of terrorism and sabotage were committed in the republic during 1996, while in the first half of the present month no fewer than ten have already been committed." — *(Editor)*

18. The report of one Western observer, Lord Eric Avebury, chairman of the British Parliamentary Human Rights' Group, can be consulted on the Internet (www.abkhazia.org).

Chapter 9

1. Press release from the Press Service of the Supreme Soviet of the Republic of Abkhazia, August 18th 1992.

2. 'Shevardnadze: Sukhumi curfew possible', FBIS-SOV-92-159, August 17th 1992, p39.

3. 'Shevardnadze: Sukhumi curfew possible', FBIS-SOV-92-159, August 17th 1992, p39.

4. 'Mountain peoples take up positions', FBIS-SOV-92-164, August 24th 1992, pp 58-59.

5. Official statement, Press Service of Abkhazia, September 25th 1992.

6. 'Abkhazian reservists mobilized', FBIS-SOV-92-165, p50.

7. 'Georgian troops killed in Gagra attack', FBIS-SOV-92-166, p54. The Mkhedrioni would play a major role in the development of Georgia's military during the war. However, they were very independent-minded and often set their own agenda. They were very difficult to integrate with other Kartvelian units and in many ways were a hindrance to the war effort.

Shevardnadze spent a great deal of time trying to neutralise their influence during the war.

8. 'Agreement reached on Gagra situation', FBIS-SOV-92-159, August 17th 1992, p38.

9. 'Agreement reached on Gagra situation', FBIS-SOV-92-159, August 17th 1992, p38.

10. 'Tripartite Commission observers arrive in Georgia', FBIS-SOV-92-189, September 29th 1992, p51.

11. 'Tripartite Commission observers arrive in Georgia', FBIS-SOV-92-189, September 29th 1992, p51.

12. 'Volunteers' withdrawal delayed', FBIS-SOV-92-188, September 28th 1992, p55.

13. *Tragedy of Abkhazia* (in Russian), compilation published in Sochi, 1994.

14. *Tragedy of Abkhazia* (in Russian), compilation published in Sochi, 1994.

15. Many local Mingrelians were involved in the defence of Gagra. Kartvelian numbers were boosted later in the war by the arrival of between 700 and 1,000 Ukrainian volunteers. Abkhazian Armenians tended to fight for Abkhazia, while Armenians from Georgia were reported on the Kartvelian side.

16. The dedication of local Kartvelian units was noticeable in comparison with other Kartvelian units operating in Abkhazia. However, dedication was one factor, training quite another. In this regard these units too were inadequate.

17. Equivalent to US Army Rangers but not as well trained and certainly less well equipped. Interview with member of Abkhazian artillery battalion in Sukhum, June 1995.

18. Just as happened south-east of Sukhum after the final rout of the Kartvelian forces in September 1993 *before* the arrival of forces in the Abkhazian alliance. — *(Editor)*

19. Recall the proposed etymology of Gagra discussed in note 5 of the Introduction to this volume. — *(Editor)*

20. Interview with member of Abkhazian artillery battalion in Sukhum, June 1995.

21. A type of vulture (*Gyps fulvus*) in Georgian. — *(Editor)*

22. 'Leopard' (*Acinonyx jubatus*) in Georgian. — *(Editor)*

23. Interview with member of Abkhazian artillery battalion in Sukhum, June 1995.

24. *Tragedy of Abkhazia* (in Russian), compilation published in Sochi, 1994.

25. *Tragedy of Abkhazia* (in Russian), compilation published in Sochi, 1994.

26. Interview with member of the Georgian White Eagle Unit, Tbilisi, July 1995.

27. He was the brother of Gia, commander of Kartvelian forces in Abkhazia, whose TV appearance on August 25th was reported in the Georgian newspaper 7 *Dghe* ('7 Days') (No.31, September 4th-10th 1992, p3): "On August 25th Gia Q'arq'arashvili, general of the National Guard stationed in western Georgia appeared on Abkhazian television. He issued an ultimatum to the Abkhazian side: if within 24 hours they should not lay down their arms and hand themselves over to members of the State Council, 'the Abkhazians would have no one left to carry on their race; 100,000 Georgians would be sacrificed for the 97,000 (27,000 is printed in error — *translator*) Abkhazians, but Georgia's borders would remain intact.'" — *(Editor)*

28. Interview with member of the Georgian White Eagle Unit, Tbilisi, July 1995.

29. Interview with member of the Georgian White Eagle Unit, Tbilisi, July 1995.

30. 'The Georgian Chronicle', Monthly Bulletin, Center for Peace, Development and Democracy, March-April 1993, p5.

31. During the war between Georgia and South Ossetia, V. Adamia (leader of the Georgian military), claimed that both his forces and South Ossetian units rented Russian heavy weapons and personnel for military operations.

32. *The Georgian Chronicle*, monthly bulletin, January-February 1993, p7.

33. Interview with UNOMIG commander Brigadier-General John Hvidegaard, Sukhum, June 1995.

Chapter 10

1. The Russian term *vozhd'* has a nuance difficult to capture in English; it is equivalent to German *Führer* or Italian *Duce*. — *(Editor)*

Chapter 11

1. In both this and the Lomtatidze/Klychev article an oversight resulted in the phonemes /ts, dz, ts'/ being omitted from the charts on pp 41 & 94 respectively.

2. Also often indicated for typographical reasons as 'y' or 'ı'.

3. Sometimes represented as 'ǰ' or 'ȝ', in which case the palato-alveolar affricate could be represented by either of these with a hachek '˘' above them.

4. Sometimes represented as 'c'.

5. Also representable as 'ch', or as 'c' with a hachek above it.

6. Also representable as 'sh', or as 's' with a hachek above it.

7. Also representable as 'zh', or as 'z' with a hachek above it.

8. Also representable as 'kh'.

9. Also representable as 'gh'.

10. Palatalisation is sometimes marked by placing an acute accent either above or immediately after the relevant consonant.

11. Some commentators place these last six fricatives with the uvular plosives; I normally call them 'back fricatives', as their articulation can shift between more velar and more uvular depending on the phonetic environment.

12. For typographical simplicity, 'h' is normally substituted.

13. Usually one symbol, either this raised '^{w}' or the degree-sign (°), is used for all varieties of labialisation.

14. One could represent this as 'ǰ^w', as generally in this volume.

15. Cf. also the root x^w- as cardinal '5'.

16. Cf. *jy-'ly-j-ta-Ø-jt*' 'he gave it/them to her."

17. Uslar went on to lay the foundations of North Caucasian philology by composing grammars of Chechen, Avar, Lak, Dargwa, Lezgian, Tabasaran.

18. Although the switch to Roman was apparently discussed even for Russian, the three traditional orthographies of Russian, Georgian and Armenian survived.

19. Though not all will necessarily agree with this view!

20. In 1865 I. Bartolomej had devised a 52-letter orthography.

21. The same could be said *mutatis mutandis* for non-Russian children across the Union.

22. Personal correspondance from Slava Chirikba, based on his personal recollections of schooling in Gagra.

23. Compare this with the derisory figure of a mere 25.5 per cent of 'Georgians' (i.e. Kartvelians) making such a claim.

24. Knowledge of Mingrelian in the north was rare, though Turkish was not uncommon there in earlier days.

Chapter 12

1. These are two or four-line folk verses, usually humorous and topical, sung in a lively fashion.

2. The post-war situation of Abkhazian literature has been described thus: "The work of Abkhazia's creative organisations diminished. For years the Writers' Union had no printing organ of its own (publication ceased during the war and was not renewed). Works of Abkhazian literature were published ever more rarely in the native language. The very terms 'Abkhazian literature' or 'Abkhazian writers' were not used; instead the artificial expressions 'Abkhazian group of Georgian writers', 'literature of western Georgia', 'autonomous part of Georgian literature', etc were introduced" (Inal-Ipa, 1978, p38). Note the parallel between (mis)describing Abkhazian literature as "literature of western Georgia" and the (mis)naming of the Abkhazian Kingdom as a "kingdom of western Georgia," noted elsewhere in this volume. — *(Editor)*

3. Contrast these facts with the ease with which nonsense about Abkhazia and its history can be published in the West: "The Abkhaz are a Caucasian people . . . inhabitants of the region for many centuries. Their numbers however are small. *So small in fact that in the Second World War Stalin exempted Abkhazians from serving in the USSR armed forces for fear that they might become totally extinct. According to Georgians, this exemption was an incentive for other people*

to declare themselves Abkhazs thus artificially swelling their numbers' (stresses added). This slur against every Abkhazian who fought, was wounded or gave up his life for his country appeared in the pamphlet *The birth of a Georgian State: giving Georgia a second chance*, produced for the London-based NGO Vertic in 1994 by Dennis Sammut, in charge of the organisation's activities in Georgia. — *(Editor)*

4. Carried off by Kartvelian forces at the time of their occupation of south-eastern Abkhazia in 1992-93 and never heard of again. — *(Editor)*

Chapter 13

1. The Abkhazian (and, more generally, Caucasian) scenes fashioned in the style of icons by this Russo-Tatar artist immediately catch one's eye. When the forces of the Abkhazian alliance recaptured Sukhum in September 1993, she was discovered to have been hanged. — *(Editor)*

2. I am grateful to my SOAS colleague, Sandy Morton, and to members of the British Museum's Department of Scientific Research for the suggestion that sees in the term 'crabs' probable reference to tripod supports used in the firing-process. — *(Editor)*

Chapter 14

1. This chapter focuses primarily on the religious practices of the Abkhazians in Abkhazia.

2. Inal-Ipa (1965, p374) and interview with Batal K'obakhia, Sukhum, March 1997.

3. Now generally known as Pitsunda.

4. Present day Sukhum. See also Chapter 4, above.

5. The second edition is forthcoming (Maikop, 1997).

6. A translation of St John's Gospel by Zaira Khiba, originally published anonymously in 1981 by the Swedish Institute for Bible Translation, has already been on sale in Abkhazia.

7. Information bulletin on Abkhazia, produced by the Ministry of Foreign Affairs of the Republic of Abkhazia (Gudauta, October 1993).

8. Jurij Voronov in an interview with the author in September 1995.

9. The Abkhazian word *'alamys*, a central element of *'apswara*, incorporates both a sense of individual conscience and also a more collective 'conscience of the people'.

Chapter 15

1. Note that we are not denying that the phenomenon of Abkhaz longevity exists.

2. The discussion of contemporary material by Hewitt (1993b, pp 275-77; 1995b, note 15) clearly supports the former. — *(Editor)*

3. A well known 1895 book that for statistical data relied mainly on the 1886 Family Lists gave the population of Abkhazia as 72,415, of which (it stated) 30,000 were often counted as Mingrelians; this fits well with reconstructed 1873 figures. See Erckert (1895).

4. We concentrate on the first category here, although the other two also merit attention. Tsarist statistics are notorious for over-representing the state church. Of all Samurzaq'anoans and Abkhaz in the *Okrug*, only seven per cent were listed as Sunni Muslims, 93 per cent as Orthodox Christians. See *Svod statisticheskikh dannykh o naselenii Zakavkazskago kraja, izvlechennykh iz posemejnykh spiskov 1886 goda*, Tbilisi, 1893.

5. In Sukhum town: 'Mingrelians and Laz'.

6. Georgians, Imeretians and Gurians are not neatly separated in all tables (Imeretian is the primary of the western Georgian dialects; Gurian is second in importance). In the village tables, 62 Georgians are listed, but neither Imeretians nor Gurians; overleaf, in a summary table, we read of 62 Imeretians (and no Georgians). For Sukhum, we find Imeretians and Gurians but no Georgians, and for Ochamchira, 515 Georgians but neither of the other groups. We assume that of all these 608 people, most were acually Imeretians, if not Mingrelians.

7. In Sukhum town: 'Kabardians and other Circassian tribes'.

8. One bibliographical rarity not mentioned in this article is Mach'avariani (1913). This

Mingrelian-born Kartvelian, raised in Samurzaq'an(o)/Abkhazia, had been arguing since the 1890s that Samurzaq'anoans were Abkhazians. In 1913 he calculated that Abkhazia's population was 140,000; of these he numbered the Abkhazians at 82,960 (including 33,639 Samurzaq'anoans who deemed themselves to be Abkhazians), making Abkhazians 60 per cent of Abkhazia's population (pp 7, 116, 139, 150, 179). — *(Editor)*

9. For a dissenting analysis, see Schuchardt (1897).

10. *Pervaja vseobshchaja perepis' naselenija Rossijskoj imperii*, St Petersburg 1899-1905 (89 vols).

11. Cross-tabulating language and religion, the source lumps together Abkhaz and the Circassian dialects (i.e. Circassian and Kabardian). Of all 58,715 speakers of Abkhaz (58,697) and Circassian + Kabardian (18) in *Sukhumskij Okrug*, 49,367 (84, 1 per cent) were registered as Orthodox Christians, 9,342 (15.9 per cent) as Muslims, with six others. However misleading, this is the last comprehensive account of Abkhaz nominal religious affiliation.

12. Note that the classification of Daghestani languages in this census was vastly different from later ones, making comparisons very difficult: Most languages in the Samurian subgroup (other than Lezgian proper, Aghul, Rutul, Tsakhur and Udi) were then included with non-Samurian Lak, as were two of the Dido languages (Hunzib and Bezhta); only Aghul, Rutul and Tsakhur were listed with Lezgian. The other three Dido tongues and the eight Andi languages were listed with Avar. Thus, of all categories, only internally divergent Darginian (including, as today, Kubachi and Kaitak) and Udi are equivalent to those employed today.

13. Whereas Imeretian is a Georgian dialect, Laz is not. Of 25,873 Kartvelian speakers, 14 were registered as Jews, 82 as Muslims; these latter would be Ajars and Laz, with perhaps a few Ingiloans or Meskh(et)ians.

14. One of these 136 was registered as an Orthodox Christian. According to religion, 162 Jews were registered.

15. *Kavkazskij kalendar' na 1914 god*, Tbilisi, 1913. I regret I have to quote the figures for 1916 from a rounded German version, as I cannot obtain the originals. See 'Die Bevölkerung Transkaukasiens', in *Der Neue Orient* (Berlin), 1918, p436. Note that the figures were not derived from a census.

16. Figures are from *Pouezdnye itogi Vserossijskoj sel'sko-khozjajstvennoj i pozemel'noj perepisi 1917 goda*. Moscow 1923, and from *Zakavkaz'e: statistiko-èkonomicheskij sbornik*, Tbilisi, 1925.

17. Both papers are quoted according to German intelligence reports as reported in Bihl (1992, pp 312f).

18. There were additionally small numbers of Abkhaz in other cities across Georgia: 225 in Batumi, 71 in Tiflis, four in Kutaisi, two in Poti, and one in Ljuksemburg (modern Bolnisi). The source is *Zakavkaz'e . . .* (op. cit.).

19. *Bol'shaja Sovetskaja Èntsiklopedija*, 1st ed., vol. 1, Moscow, 1926, entry 'Abkhazskaja SSR'.

20. *Vsesojuznaja perepis' naselenija 1926 goda*, Moscow, 1928-33 (56 vols).

21. The discrepancy between republic (67,494) and *uezd* results (67,491) is that of the source.

22. In the 'Dictionary of nationalities' (*Slovar' narodnostej*) that accompanied the census results (see e.g. vol. 14), the Samurzaq'anoans were (still) listed as a subgroup of the Abkhaz.

23. Consult 'Polveka molchanija (Vsesojuznaja perepis' naselenija 1937 g.)', in *Sociologicheskie issledovanija* (Moscow) 17 (1990), No. 7, pp 50-70, referring to 1932: p54.

24. *Vsesojuznaja perepis' naselenija 1937 g[oda]: kratkie itogi*, Moscow, 1991; and 'Vsesojuznaja perepis' naselenija 1937 goda: iz arkhivov Goskomstata SSSR', in *Vestnik Statistiki* (Moscow), 1990, pp 65-79.

25. *Vsesojuznaja perepis' naselenija 1939 goda: Osnovnye itogi*, Moscow, 1992. The Greek figure for 1939 may include some of the 10,802 foreign Greeks not included in the 1926 total. Note that 1939 figures generally seem high: 2,097,169 Kartvelians, including 88,230 Ajars were listed for 1937, but 2,249,636 (+7.3 per cent) for 1939.

26. *Itogi vsesojuznoj perepisi naselenija 1959 goda. SSSR. Svodnyj tom*, Moscow, 1962.

27. *Itogi vsesojuznoj perepisi naselenija 1970 goda. Tom IV. Natsional'nyj sostav*, Moscow, 1973; *Chislennost' i sostav naselenija SSSR. Po dannym vsesojuznoj perepisi 1979 goda*, Moscow,

1984; *Natsional'nyj sostav naselenija SSSR. Po dannym vsesojuznoj perepisi naselenija 1989 goda*, Moscow, 1991. The figure for Abkhaz in Ajaria in 1979 and 1989 (preliminary) are from the Tbilisi daily *Zarja Vostoka* (March 23th 1990, p2).

28. Diaspora figures are from *Vestnik Statistiki*, Moscow, 1990, nos. 10-12, and 1991, nos. 4-6.

Chapter 16

1. See Kopeshavidze (1989) for Abkhazian recipes. — *(Editor)*

2. Though this word basically means 'salt', it is widely used to refer to the potent brown mixture just described. For ordinary salt Abkhazians say *a'dzhyk'a xys*.

3. See Hewitt & Khiba (1997b) for more details. — *(Editor)*

4. The editor of this volume met an old man in the late 1970s carrying a pistol because of a quarrel between his and another family. — *(Editor)*

5. This factor should be borne in mind by those who advocate a mass repatriation of the Kartvelian refugees throughout Abkhazia despite the excesses committed by them or their relatives during the months when south-eastern Abkhazia was under Kartvelian military occupation — it is simply a recipe for greater bloodshed. When the International Helsinki Federation for Human Rights (IHF) and Caucasia in their joint report of February 1997 state: "The return of IDPs (internally displaced persons) has been thwarted because of arbitrary restrictions imposed by Abkhazian authorities and acquiesced to by the Georgian authorities and the UNHCR" (p10), they reveal how poorly they appreciate the situation on the ground. On the same page they speak of a mere 300 returnees before the suspension of the Quadripartite Agreement of 1994 — compare with the statement of 6th January 1997 from the Abkhazian Foreign Ministry in which we read: "At the same time, in view of the stabilising of the situation in the Gal District, a spontaneous return of refugees began there. The Abkhazian side took no measures to impede this process. On the contrary, we several times approached the UNHCR and Russian Foreign Ministry requesting a start to the registration of the returned refugees in order to confirm our assent to their return. However, even this initiative of ours found no support. We then undertook our own registration of the returned refugees. At the present time about 80 per cent of the refugees have returned to the Gal District," and the Gal District is the one where the bulk of the Mingrelians living in Abkhazia resided before the war. — *(Editor)*

6. Another area causing difficulty for outsiders are the rituals associated with death and burial, which can be lengthy and demanding, especially in those regions most susceptible to Mingrelian influence. Here the corpse might lie in state for up to a week in the family-home, attended by male relatives or friends and framed by females clad in black, periodically continuing the ululation that originally signalled the death. As mourners approach the yard/house, women start to keen; inside they are conducted by a master of ceremonies to the usually open coffin lying on a draped catafalque, where tears (real or mock) are shed and respects paid, followed by condolences to those closest to the deceased and finally to the line of attendant males. Visitors are provided with food. The whole process is repeated on the day of the funeral (there are no cremations), after which a huge meal is prepared, though no meat is consumed until some days after the funeral. Male relatives do not shave and women keep their black attire until the 40th day ceremony (though black may be worn for considerably longer by some); this involves a meal, lighting of candles, and visit to the grave, where offerings of food and drink will be left, as no doubt previously and thereafter. A similar commemoration may take place to mark the anniversary. — *(Editor)*

7. Westerners usually associate the extreme lengths to which the laws of hospitality are taken in the Caucasus exclusively with the Georgians. This is largely due to the fact that in Soviet times foreigners travelling to the Caucasus were usually allowed to visit Georgia alone, where it was primarily Georgians whom they met. Those of us who have had the privilege to meet other Caucasians know that this phenomenon is attested almost universally throughout the Caucasus — *(Editor)*

Index